The Final Film
of Laurel and Hardy

To Sylvette Baudrot

The Final Film of Laurel and Hardy

A Study of the Chaotic Making and Marketing of Atoll K

NORBERT APING

Foreword by GLENN MITCHELL

McFarland & Company, Inc., Publishers
Jefferson, North Carolina, and London

This book originally appeared, in German and in
somewhat different form, as *Laurel und Hardy auf dem Atoll*,
published in 2007 in Germany by Schüren Verlag GmbH.

LIBRARY OF CONGRESS CATALOGUING-IN-PUBLICATION DATA

Aping, Norbert, 1952–
[Laurel und Hardy auf dem Atoll. English]
The final film of Laurel and Hardy : a study of the chaotic making and
marketing of Atoll K / Norbert Aping ; foreword by Glenn Mitchell.
p.   cm.
Includes bibliographical references and index.

ISBN 978-0-7864-3302-5
softcover : 50# alkaline paper ∞

1. Atoll K.   2. Laurel, Stan.   3. Hardy, Oliver, 1892–1957.
I. Title.
PN1997.A849A65   2008   791.4302'80922 — dc22   2008022981

British Library cataloguing data are available

On the cover: 1958 German lobby card, *Dick und Doof erben eine Insel*
(author's collection); background ©2007 Shutterstock

Manufactured in the United States of America

McFarland & Company, Inc., Publishers
Box 611, Jefferson, North Carolina 28640
www.mcfarlandpub.com

Acknowledgments

"Who started all this?" asks policeman Tiny Sandford in Laurel and Hardy's delightful silent short *Big Business* (1929). But it wasn't Stan and Ollie themselves who set this book in motion. The culprit was, in fact, Alfred Hitchcock.

My friend Alain Kerzoncuf and I share a common interest in Mr. Hitchcock. In the course of conversation in February 2005, he delivered an electrifying message. Alain, who resides in Paris and whose expertise had often greatly contributed to my research, told me he had spoken with Sylvette Baudrot, who had served as script girl on Hitchcock's *To Catch a Thief* (1955). During his visit he discovered that she had also worked on Laurel and Hardy's last movie, *Atoll K*, at the beginning of her career. He also sent me a photo from Sylvette Baudrot's personal collection, which I seemed to know from Randy Skretvedt's Laurel and Hardy book. But Sylvette Baudrot's photo revealed many more individuals. So I contacted her, and she invited me to visit her. At her home she surprised me by bringing out the original trilingual shooting script, complete with countless inserts, annotations and changes, as well as candid photos of the shoot on the Côte d'Azur and at the Nice studios La Victorine. This incredible wealth of documents in my hands allowed me to revisit the shooting of *Atoll K*— 55 years after the fact! Sylvette Baudrot gave me these precious papers to study them unhurriedly at home. Moreover, she contacted Léo Joannon's assistant director Pierre Nivollet, who patiently answered my countless questions. Above all, she gave me her ongoing attention. More visits to Paris followed, as well as many telephone conversations. Sylvette Baudrot's kindness, helpfulness, professionalism and knowledge was overwhelming. Business took her away from home so frequently over the years that she considered 2001 her silver wedding celebration — when, in fact, it was her golden anniversary.

Of course, no research project on *Atoll K* would be complete without an interview with the film's leading lady, Suzy Delair. Surprisingly, during decades of Laurel and Hardy research, no one seems to have talked with her about her contribution to the men's final film. Fortunately, Suzy Delair felt up to sharing her recollections on *Atoll K*. During an exhaustive, as well as inspiring interview in which Sylvette Baudrot, Alain Kerzoncuf and Jacqueline Willemetz also took part, Delair proved to be every bit the energetic and quick-witted artist displayed in her film roles.

Considering the multinational production of *Atoll K*, my research naturally took on global proportions. Laurel and Hardy enthusiasts from the four corners of the world played an important role. Being true *Helpmates* they lent a hand wherever they could: Robert G. Dickson (Los Angeles, coauthor of *Cita en Hollywood*), Ray Faiola (Ellenville), Benedetto "Enciclopedia" Gemma (Bari, coauthor of *I Film Antologici di Stanlio & Ollio*), Mathias Günther (Landstuhl), Juan B. Heinink (Bilbao, coauthor of *Cita en Hollywood*), Harry Hoppe

(Düsseldorf, editor of the *Laurel und Hardy Journal*), Scott MacGillivray (Boston, author of *Laurel & Hardy: From the Forties Forward*), A. J. Marriott (Blackpool, author of *Laurel & Hardy: The British Tours* [available through http://members.aol.com/Lahbritishtours/index.html]), Peter Mikkelsen (Kopenhagen), Glenn Mitchell (London, author of *The Laurel & Hardy Encyclopedia*), Bram Reijnhoudt (Hilversum, editor of *Nieuwe Blotto*), Chris Seguin (Toronto), Bob Spiller (Liverpool), Randy Skretvedt (Hollywood, author of *Laurel and Hardy: The Magic Behind the Screen*) and Ali Stevenson (Manchester [USA], www.looserthanloose.com). To all of them a cordial "tip of the bowler."

Dr. Ulrich Rüdel was an unfailing critic throughout all phases of the project, including the English translation. Dr. Ulrich von Thüna dug deep into his movie library time and time again. My thanks go also to Julien Eger, Keith Johnston, François Justamand, Hans-Jürgen Kluh, Hooman Mehran, Michael Lippe, Klaus D. Oberdieck, Dr. Peter Pohl, Vittorio Martinelli, Steve Massa, Eberhard Spieß, and Olaf Strecker as well as the members of the Italian Laurel and Hardy Tent Oasis 165 "Noi Siamo le Colonne/*A Chump at Oxford*" (especially Andrea "Er Lupo" Ciaffaroni and Andrea "Drin Drin" Benfante).

I am especially thankful for Glenn Mitchell's and Dr. Ulrich Rüdel's assistance in the English translation, and most of all for Chris Seguin's outstanding and caring reworking of the entire manuscript into his native tongue.

My research also connected me with many institutions (mostly movie archives and libraries); their assistance consistently went above and beyond. My gratitude goes to Silvio Alovisio (Museo Nazionale del Cinema, Turin), Thomas Ballhausen (Filmarchiv Austria, Vienna), BFI (National Library, British Film Institute; London), Claudia Bozzone (Museo Nazionale del Cinema, Turin), Cecilia Cenciarelli (Cineteca di Bologna), Pierre Chaintreuil (Centre National de la Cinématographie, Paris), Ray Edmondson (National Film and Sound Archive, Canberra), Andrzej Kawecki (National Film Archive, Warsaw), Kate Guyonvarch (Association Chaplin, Paris), Ute Klawitter (Bundesarchiv — Filmarchiv, Berlin), Valdo Kneubühler (Bibliothéque du Film, Paris), Rüdiger Koschnitzki (Deutsches Filminstitut, Frankfurt am Main), Kristine Krueger (National Film Information Service, Los Angeles), Julika Kuschke (Bundesarchiv-Filmarchiv, Berlin), Yves Laberge (Université Laval, Québec), Charles W. Leary (New York University), Anne-Marie Lorenz-Tröstrum (Filmmuseum Berlin), Angel Martínez Juárez (Filmoteca de Unam, Mexico City), Duncan Moss (British Board of Film Classification, London), New York State Archives (New York), Fernando Ohem Ochoa (Filmoteca de Unam, Mexico City), Pier Luigi Raffaelli (Archivio Centrale di Stato, Rome), Eric Le Roy (Archives Françaises du Film, Bois d'Arcy), Christof Schöbel (Deutsches Filminstitut, Frankfurt am Main), Quentin Turnour (National Film and Sound Archive, Canberra), Erika Wottrich (CineGraph, Hamburg), Karel Zima (Národní filmový archiv, Prague) and Angelika Zimmermann (TaurusMedia Licence Service GmbH, Unterföhring).

I owe many thanks to my Ph.D. supervisor Dr. Knut Hickethier, University of Hamburg. He not only encouraged me, but gave this project his informed attention throughout its creation. My thanks go also to Dr. Harro Segeberg for his helpful suggestions and his supportive and scholarly second opinion.

Rainer Dick (author of *Laurel & Hardy: Die größten Komiker aller Zeiten*) and Nicoline Koeniger read and reread the manuscript thoroughly, as only friends can do — thus saving me from many a mistake.

Finally, my unending thanks go to my wife Gabriele and my sons Christoph and Marcus, who patiently endured my work on this book.

Table of Contents

Foreword by Glenn Mitchell

Every now and then, one of the many comedy historians takes the opportunity to list the final films made by each of the screen's greatest comedians. I shall not do the same here, since it makes discouraging reading and, besides, anyone with a sufficiently specialized interest to read a book about *Atoll K* will doubtless already be familiar with the titles in question. Titles actually outnumber the films themselves in this list, because they tend to have been either (a) troubled productions, (b) chaotic, internationally-produced affairs or (c) both, all of which frequently conspire to the acquisition of different names for a single project.

Atoll K—or *Utopia*—or *Robinson Crusoeland*—or, for that matter, any of the various titles this unfortunate film has gathered — is Laurel & Hardy's entry in this rogue's gallery. It has for many years been dismissed either as a tragic misfire, a brave experiment compromised by unfavorable conditions, or, based largely on Laurel's all-too-apparent illness during production, nothing less than a horror film, which many of the team's admirers refuse to watch even once.

The mythology surrounding *Atoll K* has been perpetuated further by a tendency to accept verbatim the testimony of Laurel's wife, Ida, concerning the problems that beset its production (in my 1995 book, *The Laurel & Hardy Encyclopedia*, I was one of the culprits). While her recollections are substantially correct, there are both minor discrepancies and areas where a fuller understanding of the background is required. In these respects, Norbert Aping has done much to fill in the missing history and, perhaps most importantly, to explain *why* the film turned out as it did, rather than merely state *how*. Equally valuable is his placing of Laurel & Hardy within their European context. It has long been established that, despite their considerable popularity within the United States, Laurel & Hardy's greatest following was overseas, and this may be perhaps the first account of *Atoll K* to integrate that aspect into the circumstances that inspired its creation.

Thanks in part to claims made on the packaging of some of the numerous video editions (the result of its seeming public-domain status, at least in the United States), *Atoll K* has frequently come to be thought of as Laurel & Hardy's final work, which is far from true. After Laurel's health was restored, he and Hardy were able to embark on two European theatrical tours and were caught on camera by both the newsreels and television. Their final engagement as a team was for a filmed insert in a 1955 BBC TV program (still extant) about the Grand Order of Water Rats, entitled *This Is Music Hall*. Norbert's book will, I hope, serve to position *Atoll K* more accurately in the chronology.

Although the present work is not an attempted rehabilitation of the film's reputation — there are, after all, some things that cannot successfully be defended — it may, perhaps, inspire some commentators to reassess its worth, savor its occasional strengths and at least recognize how good it *might* have been. Though current trends towards revisionism — in almost every area of history, not just that of film comedy — invariably make my blood boil, it has to be said that *Atoll K* presents a version of Laurel & Hardy that is relatively free of the out-of-character intrusions of their big-studio films of 1941–5, and has more in common with the reversion to their earlier selves that one sees in the newsreels covering their European visits. One might add that its intended satirical element echoes the spirit that guided some of the generic parodies within the team's best work, as well as some of the lampoons of specific films made by Laurel in his earlier years as a solo film comedian.

It should also be mentioned that the fragmented production and distribution history of *Atoll K* has resulted in there being no single version that is absolutely complete, which means that one can never truly claim to have seen the film without summoning the tenacity and patience to examine all of the available editions. Norbert Aping is among the few to have done so.

So, if anyone is willing to donate the required kitchen apron, I shall make up an impromptu Crusoeland flag and fly it, if not for *Atoll K* itself, then for Norbert Aping's valuable work in chronicling its history.

Introduction

For more than eight decades, generations of moviegoers all over the world have not only enjoyed tears of laughter, but also felt an unrivaled fondness for Stan Laurel and Oliver Hardy, the greatest comedy duo of all time. Few comedians of the silent and early sound era of the last century have experienced a similar popularity. It is all the more remarkable that the two comedians still hold a solid place in the popular consciousness of the 21st century, considering how the current younger generations have been socialized in an entirely different media environment compared to generations of the silent age or the post World War II years. Midway through the last century, the pop-culture media of pulp novels, cinema and radio were joined by the expanding market of two distinctly novel visual entertainment forms, comic books and television. This cultural environment is worlds away from today's endless sensory assaults via cable television, computer games, portable media devices, and the special-effects extravaganzas that popular movies have widely degenerated into, threatening even to eradicate the popularity of reading.

What then is the reason for the ongoing appeal of Laurel and Hardy? After all, their films were nearly all produced in black and white, something that will already reduce their attraction for many young, modern viewers. In numerous short subjects and features the two comedians explored their relationship in a daily world familiar to everyone. Granted, modern daily life is much different from that of 1920s and the 1930s, the two decades of Laurel and Hardy's biggest successes. However, the basics of the human condition and of social life remain unchanged from the way the two master comedians presented it, distilled through their comic art. All that have changed are fashion, technology and environment. The human condition with all its complexity, however, stays the same — and it is this truth that Laurel and Hardy have masterfully shaped into their comedy, creating a universally recognizable comic world.

This alone would not have been enough to keep the audience's affection alive over generations. What elevates them is Laurel's unique skill in discovering and exploiting the funny side of daily life, to turn ordinary into grotesque situations that carry things to extremes. Few examples in film history work so forcefully and consistently toward chaos as Laurel and Hardy's comedy. It is as if famous Swiss playwright Friedrich Dürrenmatt was thinking of the films of the two comedians when he wrote in his "21 principles" for his ambiguous comedy *Die Physiker* (*The Physicists*) from 1962: "If you begin with a story, you'll have to think it to the very end. A story is over once it has taken its worst possible turn. The worst possible turn is not predictable. It happens by coincidence." As disturbing as this may sound, this is the basic principle of many of Laurel and Hardy comedies: consider the catastrophic finales of Laurel and Hardy masterworks such as *Helpmates* (1932) and *Sons of the Desert* (1933).

Ultimately, it is the human warmth that accompanies the escalation of chaos in the comedians' works that transforms them into art. This in turn is rooted in the deep friendship between the fictional characters of Stan and Ollie. In addition to the mere grotesque, this is the very reason for the audience's affection for the team, for people like you and me. Thus came about a tremendous cinematic treasure well worthy of further exploration and study which from the early 1960s has inspired a rich body of literature on Laurel and Hardy's works.

Many a Laurel and Hardy aficionado will wonder: "A book on a single Laurel and Hardy film, let alone on their last feature, *Atoll K*?" Should not this film be dismissed as a sorry effort, or, as Laurel himself described it to his biographer John McCabe, an "abortion"?

Naturally, most Laurel and Hardy research has dealt with their whole body of work, including major efforts to close the last gaps in their filmography by locating the few missing films of the duo, as well as complete prints of those existing only in part.

Most urgent has been the desire to find the comedy *Hats Off!* (1927), which has apparently been missing since the early 1930s. After a 16mm copy of a film with the same title was offered in the catalogue of Library Films of Manhattan in 1947 (most likely a sound movie of the same title), and following persistent rumors that a 9.5mm copy was guarded by a private collector, a new claim emerged in October 2001, when a fake report from the equally fake Email address "rpsutcliffe@hotmail.com" of a certain Booby (yes, not Bobby) Sutcliffe claimed: "I have found a copy of *Hats Off!*"

The search for the missing phonetic versions of Laurel and Hardy films (those in which the duo spoke their lines in foreign languages, reading from phonetically spelled cue cards) was no less intense and revealed a number of substantial finds during the last three decades, resulting in the availability of about half of all these alternate versions. The latest rediscovery to hit the news was that most of the 1930 German variant *Spuk um Mitternacht* (combining *Berth Marks* and *The Laurel-Hardy Murder Case*) had been found in Moscow in 2004 and subsequently reconstructed by the Munich Filmmuseum. Of course, this inspired some people to claim that copies of *Glückliche Kindheit* (*Brats*, 1930) and *Hinter Schloss und Riegel* (*Pardon Us*, 1931) also had been recovered in Moscow, this time in complete copies in good condition. The last of these "reports," in 2005, proved to be an April's Fool joke.

Furthermore, searches continued for the missing fragments of the Charley Chase two-reeler *Now I'll Tell One* (1927), as well as lost elements from the Laurel and Hardy classic *The Battle of the Century* (1927). For years only a mere three and a half minutes of the latter were available, but the rediscovery of the first reel brought the running time up to approximately ten minutes of its original 18-minute length.

Much attention has also been devoted to *The Rogue Song* (1930), an operetta in which Laurel and Hardy provided comic relief. While the soundtrack discs still exist, the film remains incomplete, despite widespread searches on several continents. Only a few scenes (including some Laurel and Hardy bits) and a trailer still survive. Even though it seems to be nothing more than an acceptable American film version of the Franz Lehár operetta *Zigeunerliebe* (*Gypsy Love*), no one would even dream of giving up the search for the rest of *The Rogue Song*.

Compared to *The Rogue Song*, *Atoll K* is at least a true Laurel and Hardy feature. While the former restricts the two comedians to cameo appearances, *Atoll K* is, in fact, their final starring role on the silver screen. The poor reputation of *Atoll K* may be due to the fact that the film has rarely been seen as it was originally intended. Considering all the research that has been done in the past four decades on the works of Laurel and Hardy, it is astonishing that no one has tried to research the fate of the complete version of the most recent surviving film of the duo, shot in 1950–51.

In his essential study *Laurel and Hardy: The Magic Behind the Movies* (1987), Randy Skretvedt first presented research on the making of every known Laurel and Hardy film. While focusing on the Roach films, he also included background information on the preparation of *Atoll K* and its chaotic development. Scott MacGillivray's excellent book *Laurel & Hardy: From the Forties Forward* (1998) was the first to compare different versions of the film, exploring in particular the marketing of the mutilated American version *Utopia*. In my own *Dick und Doof Buch* (2004), I studied the German adaptation of the film as well as the box-office success it enjoyed in Germany. And for the November 2005 issue of the Laurel and Hardy magazine *Nieuwe Blotto*, Bram Reijnhoudt, Chris Seguin and I compiled a dossier on *Atoll K*.

So has everything worth knowing been said about *Atoll K*?

The answer is a clear no! The genesis of *Atoll K* as a French-Italian coproduction with English-speaking stars has never been explored, nor have the differences among the release versions in their respective languages. It is in fact still unknown how long the original version really was and in what kind of derivative versions the film premiered in different countries. Publications in the United States usually refer to a review in *Variety*, in which the November 1951 Paris premiere is reported to be 100 minutes long. However, this information is incorrect. And claims that the film was a complete flop need to be rectified.

Unfortunately, sources as accessible and conclusive as those on Laurel and Hardy's Hal Roach Studios output do not exist for the production of *Atoll K*. Consequently, research for the book became a jigsaw puzzle of outlines, treatments, scripts, versions, running times and film-print lengths. In the end, a picture emerged that filled in the kind of omissions, misunderstandings and missing data that affected previous books, including my own, as far as the original versions of *Atoll K* were concerned (corrected in the second edition of the German-language book). Finally, it was even possible to reconstruct the original shape of the film (at least on paper), as well as to supplement the previously sketchy information on the cast and the crew.

Reports have always focused on *Atoll K*'s chaotic production. Yet, until now it was unknown which script the shooting was based on, which treatments preceded it, what the basic idea of director Léo Joannon was, and which ideas were later added under Laurel's guidance. It is certain that numerous changes were made during the shooting. In the end, the version of *Atoll K* first submitted to an European board of film censors in spring 1951 was substantially different from the previous concepts, thus reflecting the development of the film had meanwhile gone through. And this was followed by numerous later changes and editing of *Atoll K*, including its mutilation into *Utopia*, the video staple found in many an American supermarket bargain bin.

Another hallmark of Laurel and Hardy research has been tracking down actors and other film artists who had contributed to the films of Laurel and Hardy. For that reason many a special guest was invited to the international Laurel and Hardy conventions staged by the Laurel and Hardy appreciation society known as Sons of the Desert and interviewed by the "usual suspects" of film historians and aficionados active in that group. But in this regard *Atoll K* was again ignored. Except for John McCabe's interviews with Laurel and Hardy and their wives Ida and Lucille, only Frederick Kohner (the coauthor of a preliminary version of the script) and the widow of Alfred Goulding (presumably the supervisor of the film) had been interviewed by Randy Skretvedt in the 1980s.

For instance, there never was any published interview with the European costars and other contributors to the film. These included Suzy Delair, the female lead and a much more high-profile costar than most other female leads in Laurel and Hardy films — excluding, of course, such fierce women as Mae Busch or Anita Garvin.

When the idea for this book developed, of all the artists who worked on *Atoll K*, Suzy Delair, Sylvette Baudrot (a script girl) and Pierre Nivollet (assistant director) were still available. Others were too old to be interviewed, could not be located or had already passed away. This is especially regrettable in the case of American director John Berry, who died in 1999. Berry certainly could have shared additional information on his work as director, especially in the Paris studio in Billancourt. Berry's input would have obviously brought further insight into how he shared work with the French director Léo Joannon, the only one to be credited for this function in the finished film. More knowledge could have been added by Isabelle Kloucowsky, who died in 1996. Not only did she interpret for Berry, but she also worked on the English and French version of *Atoll K* and contributed to the production of the movie in other ways. Rumor has it that she was interviewed about the film years ago, on the occasion of the fortieth anniversary of the shooting of *Atoll K* on the Côte d' Azur. Yet, such an interview could not be substantiated, let alone located, for this book.

However, the international research conducted for this study did result in a broader picture of the making of *Atoll K*. It is a rather complex story due to different handling in the various countries. Previously unknown original files from the production, the financing, as well as unknown photos of the filming and interviews with Sylvette Baudrot, Suzy Delair and Pierre Nivollet made this possible. And, at long last, the elusive British version *Robinson Crusoeland* has resurfaced.

The poor reputation of Laurel and Hardy's final film may be the reason that some Laurel and Hardy fans actually refuse to watch *Atoll K*, let alone embark on a quest for missing film material. But I am not alone in contending that *Atoll K* does not deserve this unconditional dismissal. Certainly the film is not Laurel and Hardy's masterpiece, but it is their final feature film, after all. In fact, it was the most elaborate production of all their films, with the largest budget of their career, as well as an international cast. Why has this film earned such critical disdain, and is it truly as bad as its reputation?

The negative opinion of the film is mostly based on reports of the chaotic shooting — most notably in every book John McCabe wrote on Laurel and Hardy — as well as Laurel's own disparaging remarks. Certainly the film is further plagued by the fact that Laurel and Hardy were obviously not in their best physical condition. Mr. Hardy seems heavier than he ever was in his screen appearances while, with a few exceptions, his partner Mr. Laurel spends much of the film looking ill and fatigued.

Advancing age and illness are problems in their own right for comedians such as Laurel and Hardy and their movie presence. In this case it was the final blow for *Atoll K* and its more commonly seen abridged version, *Utopia*. Though the English variant is the only one that featured Laurel and Hardy's pleasant original voices, this version was heavily edited and shorn of 18 minutes, making it hard to even follow the plot. Furthermore, the disastrous English-language dubbing of the other parts of the film turns it into an artistic catastrophe.

But there was one fundamental flaw. At the very beginning of the production, there were problems with the film's script which never could be finally resolved. Billy Wilder was right when he stated: "To produce a successful film you need three things: a good script, a good script, and a good script."

Regardless, the complete film *Atoll K* does benefit from a string of new, unknown Laurel and Hardy gags. The two comedians tried to make an up-to-date comedy, leaving behind the modus operandi of their notoriously weak 1940s Fox and M-G-M movies. Against all odds, they had not lost their meticulous comic timing. Neither should one fail to notice that, toward the end of their film career, Laurel and Hardy were courageous enough to try something new for them: a political satire. Also, a closer look at all the other artists who contributed to the making of *Atoll K* reveals that they were far from amateur, making it highly unfair to put the movie in a category with, say, Ed Wood's schlock films from the 1950s such as *Plan 9 from Outer Space*.

I invite the reader to join in the discovery of an ostensibly well known, but actually largely uncharted island in Laurel and Hardy's oeuvre; a production unlike any other Laurel and Hardy movie — not even the chaotic production *Babes in Toyland*, which seemed to spell the end of collaboration of Laurel and his producer Hal Roach in 1934.

It is the nature of a research project such as this — and the realities of the publishing business — that the story will never be 100 percent complete. An exhaustive, conclusive report could only have been given by a personal witness to every aspect of the making of *Atoll K*. Thus, omissions and errors are inevitable to some degree, and I invite the reader to contribute supplemental information or corrections by contacting me.

A final remark: in this book, "Laurel and Hardy" refers to the comedians, the private individuals and artists. "Stan and Ollie," however, are the film characters they play. Directorial information is given only for films other than those of the Laurel and Hardy team, with the obvious exception of *Atoll K*.

PART I

⸺•〰•⸺

The Production
of *Atoll K*

1

Preparations

In 1947 Laurel and Hardy embarked on a new chapter of their comedy career, which was to last until 1954, by launching the first of three successful British stage tours. The first began in March 1947, when they debarked from the *Queen Elizabeth* in Southampton in the company of their wives. The tour, in which they appeared in Laurel's *Driver's License Sketch*, was a phenomenal success in 20 English cities, so that eventually their stay extended to more than half a year. During that period, they paid visits to Belgium, Denmark, France and Sweden, finally returning to the United States in January 1948. Their French stopover was extensively covered in the local news. In November 1947, moviegoers in Germany got to see newsreel close-ups of the two comedians leaving the train in Paris.[1]

The European enthusiasm for the team was not a surprise. As far back as 1935 it had even led to the foundation of an international Laurel and Hardy Club by M-G-M. This club was based in Paris, but had chapters in Austria, Belgium, Italy, the Netherlands, Spain and Czechoslovakia. Its precise number of members is not known.

In April 1936, shortly before the official Austrian premiere of *Bonnie Scotland* (1935), the Vienna publication *Mein Film* ["My Film"] published an appeal to join the Stan-Laurel-und-Oliver-Hardy-Kinderclub ["Stan Laurel and Oliver Hardy Children's Club"]. The application form reads: "I recognize that no membership fee has to be paid. The only commitment that I am subject to is to obey the motto 'Always be cheerful' at any time!" Next to this are pictures showing Laurel and Hardy in Scottish uniforms holding the club's membership cards. The first 900 members were supposed to receive a free invitation to the screening of a new Stan Laurel and Oliver Hardy film.[2] The Stan-Laurel-und-Oliver-Hardy-Kinderclub's existence in Austria only ceased when the country was annexed by the Nazis on March 12, 1938.[3]

Similar membership cards with four different membership rules were issued in other European countries. And eventually, there indeed was an international club meeting held August 24 to 26, 1936. This was on the occasion of the European premiere of *The Bohemian Girl* (1936) in Paris. About 400 club members from Belgium, France, the Netherlands, Spain and Czechoslovakia attended.[4] No one, though, represented Germany, where the film was "verboten."[5]

In 1938 the Nazis in Germany had begun to ban American movies. Regardless, Adolf Hitler and Dr. Joseph Goebbels, the propaganda minister responsible for the movie industry, still enjoyed American films in their private screening rooms once in a while. The occupation of many European countries by the Nazi regime and the power of other European fascists in Italy and Spain had many horrible and well-documented consequences. But, in addition to all those, this also led to film censorship policies that spread like a wildfire and even affected Laurel and Hardy's completely apolitical comedies.

Before World War II, in fact practically since the beginning of their collaboration, Laurel and Hardy were the most popular comedians of all Europe. When the Nazi regime's reign and the most horrible war in world history were over, the European national film industries had essentially been destroyed. But movie audiences retained a tremendous appetite for their former favorites, who had been absent from the screens for years. So when the American organization Motion Picture Export Association Inc. [M.P.E.A.] united the eight largest U.S. distributors[6] in spring 1946, many Laurel and Hardy films finally returned to postwar Europe. The two comedians quickly recovered their status as audience favorites, and their films were especially successful, first in France and Italy, then in Austria and Germany.

In Italy, all the available features of the team were rereleased, followed by compilations of their short films. French audiences were also treated to both short film programs and selected feature premieres. In Austria, between April 1948 and May 1950, as many as thirteen mostly new [meaning previously unreleased in this country] Laurel and Hardy features premiered.

More exciting, though, in connection with Laurel and Hardy's European tour of 1947 and 1948, once again rumors surfaced that the duo planned to visit Vienna.

In response, Karl Hans Koiser wrote an open letter to the pair in the Austrian journal *Mein Film* in early 1948. Reminding the readers of the prewar Laurel and Hardy Club, he ensured the two comedians they were far from forgotten and welcomed the team as follows[7]:

Laurel and Hardy in Paris, 1947 publicity photograph (author's collection).

Wer will Mitglied des Stan-Laurel- und Oliver-Hardy-Klubs werden?

Stan Laurel und Oliver Hardy mit den ersten Mitgliedskarten ihres Klubs

Austrian Laurel and Hardy Club, 1936. Laurel and Hardy in *Bonnie Scotland* costumes with membership cards (courtesy Dr. Ulrich Rüdel).

Dear Stan, dear Ollie,

You are coming to Vienna to make the Viennese laugh. And this is good, because in these times Viennese have had not much reason to laugh anymore. Thus it will not be easy for you to move our weakened laughter muscles, but I have no doubt that you will succeed in doing so.

In Vienna many things have changed since your movies were last seen here. You cannot see our "Steffel"[8] in its full glory anymore, and the Laurel and Hardy Club does not exist any longer either. But what remains are memories of many amusing film nights in which you made us forget our sorrows. Films such as *The Bohemian Girl, Pack Up Your Troubles, Our Relations, Sons of the Desert, Bonnie Scotland* or *Way Out West* are still in our memory. Many moviegoers from back then remember with delight *Babes in Toyland*, one of the most charming fairy tale movies that we have ever seen.

I have always wished to be able to shake your hands and to thank you in person. The world is grateful to people who give laughter, since, as I said before, we live in times where we have forgotten to laugh...

In the end, Laurel and Hardy never came to Austria. So while Koiser did not get the opportunity to express his gratitude in person, his letter exemplified the sentiments of the movie audience. And, without doubt, other European moviegoers felt the same way.

Soon after the end of World War II, American businessman George H. Bookbinder realized that Laurel and Hardy still enjoyed star power in Europe which they had essentially lost in the United States. In New York Bookbinder operated the film distribution company Bookfilm International Corporation. At the end of the forties he renamed it All Star Pictures Sales Corporation [All Star] in order to enter the European market. He further founded a "Zentral-Vertriebsstelle für Europa" ["Central Distribution Point for Europe"] in Munich, which he led alongside a certain Fritz Kretschmer. Thus, from autumn 1949 onward, Bookbinder pretty much exclusively engineered the Laurel and Hardy renaissance in the German movie industry.[9] However, his ambitions included all of Europe. On January 1, 1954 the Motion Picture Association of America and M.P.E.A. began preparations to move their General European Office from Frankfurt to Paris.[10] For this reason Bookbinder decided to also relocate. By autumn 1954, he had moved his "Central Distribution for Europe" into a building on the Champs-Elysées in Paris. It was in fact the same place where Franco London Film S.A. [Franco London] resided, the future world distributor of Laurel and Hardy's final film *Atoll K*.[11]

During 1949, Bookbinder decided that what was really needed to fire up the revival of Laurel and Hardy's popularity was a new film by the two comedians. Bookbinder was also aware of the tremendous impact of World War II on the European film industry. It was hard to lure moviegoers to the theatres in times when they had little money. Real blockbusters were needed to accomplish this. So why not produce a new Laurel and Hardy film right in Europe, where Laurel and Hardy were still big stars? Also, the prospect of getting local funding of the films, granted through European governments in order to support their national film industries, provided additional appeal to the businessman.

Through Franco London head Henri [aka Henry] Deutschmeister,[12] Bookbinder contacted Salvo d'Angelo's Rome-based corporation Universalia, a "cultural catholic organization." D'Angelo had entered the movie business as a writer, but later moved toward film production, coproducing a couple of pictures together with Franco London. Thus he had pro-

All Star PRODUCTIONS CORPORATION

CABLE ADDRESS:
ALLSTAR NEWYORK

48 WEST 48th ST.
NEW YORK 19, N. Y.
PLAZA 7-0164-5

Letterhead, All Star Productions (author's collection).

George Bookbinder's signature (author's collection).

duced pictures such as *Germania Anno Zero* (*Germany Year Zero*; Roberto Rossellini, 1947/48) for the Italian company Tevere, *La Terra Trema* (*The Earth Trembles*; Luchino Visconti, 1948), and *Les Derniers Jours de Pompei* (*The Last Days of Pompei*; Marcel L'Herbier, 1949) for Universalia. Soon other productions such as *Prima Comunione* (*Father's Dilemma*; Alessandro Blasetti, 1950) and *Bellissima* (Luchino Visconti, 1951) followed. Further ensuring his success, his company Universalia was backed by money from the Vatican and the Banco di Sicilia; its antecessor Orbis had already been founded by the Roman Centro Cattolico Cinematografico.[13]

At this time international coproductions were as popular as they were artistically controversial. They promised higher revenues by pairing national stars with internationally famous actors. So Bookbinder not only considered Italian, but also French partners since, after all, Laurel and Hardy were especially popular in France. This made even more sense as d'Angelo's Universalia had previously joined forces with the French production É.G.É. for the French-Italian movie production *Prima Comunione*. É.G.É., in turn, had been founded by French producer Raymond Eger in 1949. Eger had been in the movie business since 1938 and was responsible for famous and successful films such as *Quai des orfèvres* (*Jenny Lamour*; Henri-Georges Clouzot, 1947) and *Patte Blanche* (Jean Grémillon, 1948).

By October 19, 1949, preparations were all set. On this day the French-Italian agreement on producing *Atoll K* between É.G.É., Universalia and three additional companies was finalized.[14] It was further decided what the particular objectives of those three companies were. In France and Italy, local companies were supposed to take care of the national distribution of the future Laurel and Hardy movie. These were the Paris-based Les Films Sirius [Sirius] for France and Rome-based Fortezza Film for Italy managed by Gastone Tomassini. Meanwhile, Deutschmeister's Franco London was to take care of international distribution. Thus Bookbinder's All Star company did not have to worry about any distribution aspect of the future film.

As the title credits of nearly all of the variant versions of the film *Atoll K* confirm, the basic idea plot of *Atoll K* was devised by its future director Léo Joannon. Only the Italian print is lacking this credit, most likely due to a mere defect of the copy at hand. Eger and Joannon had been collaborators for years. In 1938–39 Joannon had shot *Alert en mediterranee* (*Alerte in the Mediterranean*) with Pierre Fresnay and *L'Emigrante* (*The Emigrant*) with

Raymond Eger, 1960s (courtesy Julien Eger).

Edwige Feuillère for Eger. Further, he had written the script and directed the feature film *Le 84 prend des vacances* with Paulette Dubost.[15] This movie had been produced in 1949 on fifty-fifty terms by Sirius and Eger's newly founded company É.G.É.[16] The rest of Joannon's pre–1950 filmography also confirms that certainly he was not a comedy specialist, nor the type of American director who had directed Laurel and Hardy during the Hal Roach era. Rather Joannon was experienced in romantic subject matter, films that today we might even consider "corny."

The long-lost basic plot idea for *Atoll K* has now resurfaced in the research conducted for this book. In fact, research revealed as many as three distinct basic plot outlines for *Atoll K* in French, as well as a script draft and the resulting shooting script.[17] Finally, even the most important document was found to survive, the trilingual script itself, used during the location and studio shooting.[18]

The first of these documents is an undated, unsigned two-page outline under the title *Atoll K*. It was submitted to the French authorities in connection with the financing of the film. However, as will be discussed below, a later treatment based on this outline reveals Joannon as its author, leaving his authorship beyond any doubt. The outline presumably predates the contract from October 19, 1949, so that the occasionally quoted working title *Entente cordiale* must have been obsolete by this date.[19] It is also worth noting that this document contradicts the occasional claim that the working title was *Atoll*.[20]

The Outline

During a fleet maneuver of western navies in the Pacific, an atoll is discovered. It has just surfaced during a stormy night straight out of the ocean, and, best of all, it bears heavy deposits of uranium. Consequently, a race among the fleet federation commences to be the first to put a foot on the island. The Hague Convention, an international binding contract of the nations, regulates that a heretofore unknown piece of land will belong to the nation whose citizen is first to track this land.

The first to land on the island are the American units, so the question appears settled. But the American euphoria is quickly over once British units discover Stan, who apparently has arrived on the island earlier. As Stan turns out to be a stateless man, the UNO (United Nations) intervenes. They decide that a stateless man cannot take possession of an uncharted island. The atoll is to be the property of the country to whom Stan wishes to align himself. Consequently, all 65 nations united in the UNO begin to court Stan in hope of his favor.

Stan fancies Monaco, but the city state politely declines. Under pressure, Stan decides that he wants to be a citizen of the nation that succeeds in returning his old friend Ollie back to him. The two friends had been shipped over the oceans in a wooden crate and stranded on the atoll once it emerged from the ocean. Then, Ollie had embarked back onto the sea on a quest for matches, desperately needed to prepare warm meals. During this, Ollie had lost his memory, leaving him unable to find his way back.

Meanwhile Stan has allowed a freighter full of deportees to land on the atoll. This ship, however, had picked up Ollie and reunited him with Stan, without the help of any UNO state. And as life on the atoll is as close to paradise as you could imagine, Stan and Ollie decide that they are citizens of no country whatsoever, and rather prefer to be left alone.

But as money and power are serious business, the UNO imposes an ultimatum upon Stan. Within 48 hours, he has to decide which state to belong to. Quite unperturbed, Stan points out that his friend Ollie has put his foot on the island at the same time as he did. As his friend is a stateless man as well, consequently they both own the atoll. To move matters further ahead, each of the two friends decides for a different citizenship, and they suggest that

LES FILMS É.G.É

SOCIÉTÉ A RESPONSABILITÉ LIMITÉE CAPITAL 5.000.000 DE FRS
49 bis, AVENUE HOCHE - PARIS

AUT. MINISTÉRIELLE
303.4047
R. C. SEINE
349.409
RÉP. PROD.
... 86.76 ...
SEINE CAO
N° IMMATRICULAT.
CAISSE COOPÉRAT.
59.330633

TÉLÉPHONE
WAGRAM
03-76
ADRESSE
TÉLÉGRAP.
FILMÉGÉ
N° IMMATRICULAT.
ASSUR. SOCIALES
87 175.108 0272

FILM

" ATOLL K "

TECHNICIEN

Emploi .... SCRIPT - GIRL

Nom .... BAUDROT	Prénoms .... Sylvette ....
Adresse 39, rue Montmartre - Paris -	Téléphone : GUT.55.20
Né le 8/7/1928 à ALEXANDRIE	Nationalité française
(Egypte)	
Situation de famille .... célibataire	Nombre d'enfants .... néant
Carte Professionnelle N°	Carte de Travail N° ....
Immatriculation aux A.S. N°	Allocations Familiales N° ....
28.75.061776 - 7	

Paris, le .... 15 juillet 1950 ....

~~Monsieur~~ Mademoiselle,

Nous avons l'honneur de vous confirmer que, comme suite à nos récents pourparlers, nous sommes d'accord pour vous engager en qualité de : SCRIPT - GIRL

aux conditions définies ci-après.

Vous voudrez bien nous confirmer votre accord sur les termes et conditions du présent engagement en nous retournant, dans les plus courts délais, la présente lettre, dûment signée par vous, en faisant précéder votre signature de la mention manuscrite : « Lu et approuvé; Bon pour accord ». Vous voudrez bien également parapher chaque page.

Nous vous prions de bien vouloir agréer l'expression de nos sentiments distingués.

Pr la Société "Les Films E.G.É."
Le Gérant

Raymond Eger contracts Sylvette Baudrot for É.G.É on July 15, 1950 (courtesy Sylvette Baudrot).

ownership of the island rotate on a daily basis corresponding to the two citizenships of the friends. The UNO is not amused.

Thus, Stan and Ollie decide the atoll should be awarded as a prize in the horse race Mille Guinées ["the Great Award of Thousand Guinees"] which is to commence in England thirty days later. Until then, the UNO determines Stan and Ollie as the island's preliminary owners while they live there. Once they leave the atoll, though, rights will be divided between the three countries whose citizens were the first ones to land on the island right after them.

The three nations concerned do everything in their power to chase Stan and Ollie away from the island. Still, with the help of a mysterious nation, the two friends keep their grip on the atoll. During an attempt to starve them out, Stan and Ollie instead get to feast on caviar and zaghouski,[21] delicious cold and warm Russian appetizers. Even an invasion of mosquitos engineered by the three nations is successfully dealt with by use of a rather effective insecticide. Once these attacks have failed, the nations send the three most beautiful girls in the world to the atoll. They are to undermine Stan's and Ollie's morale and thus cause chaos, but the two friends fail to fall for the seductive trio's charms.

But time begins to run out for Stan and Ollie. The decision of the horse race Mille Guinées is imminent. In order to stay on the atoll forever, they invent the "great unknown," who had been on the island even before them.

The 65 nations are ready to pull more punches in the battle against the boys, when a massive thunderstorm approaches. As another earthquake rumbles, the uranium-rich atoll sinks back into the waters. Just in time, Stan and Ollie escape from the catastrophe by means of the very crate that had brought them to the atoll in the first place. After the storm has settled, and as if by a miracle, they strand on yet another atoll, freshly emerged from the depths of the Pacific. No better fortune could have happened to the boys, for now they have escaped the wrath of the 65 nations.

Fifty years later, Stan and Ollie appear dressed in rags and with long white beards reaching down to their knees. They carry a huge board which reads "Uranium, Gold, Platinum, Plutonium — all the valuable noble metals for whoever arrives on this land first." They have been trying for years to persuade passing ships to stop, but it is long known that Stan and Ollie's new atoll bears no precious resources at all.

So much for an outline[22] that has little resemblance to the later film *Atoll K*. The only ideas in common are those of an atoll loaded with uranium on which Stan and Ollie live, which will be awarded to the country whose citizen was the first one to enter the island, and which shall sink into the ocean again. Why the two friends navigated over the ocean in a crate only to be stranded on an atoll in an apparent emergency remains a mystery. And even in spite of the clever ideas regarding the citizenship issue, there is little to make this a typical Laurel and Hardy plot. In most films of the team, it was the kind of personal mishap and everyday misunderstanding that caused their problems, typically in a middle American town setting. Here, for whatever reason they are found in the South Seas, far away from any civilization, smalltown life and their typical troubles with the not-always-lovely women they sometimes encounter. Instead, they get entangled in diplomatic complications as Robinson-Crusoe–type hermits. The conflict between the 65 nations and the mystery nation is not elaborated upon in the outline. Nor, for that matter, is the unknown force which supplied Stan and Ollie with caviar and Russian appetizers to escape the famine engineered by Great Britain, France and the United States.[23] Yet there can be little doubt that this is the Soviet Union.

Furthermore, the idea to have the boys end up on yet another atoll emerging from the floods is not exactly an inventive finale. Apparently lots of work was left to do in order to develop the outline into a real Laurel-and-Hardy script ready for shooting.

The next step was an 18-page undated expansion of the outline in French. This so-called treatment was obviously based on and embellished from the scant premises of the outline. It bears a note attributing the plot to French script writers Alex Joffé, who cowrote the script for *Le 84 prend des vacances* with Joannon, and Jean Levitte in collaboration with the producer Eger and Joannon, based in turn on an idea by Joannon.[24]

The Treatment[25]

Stan has been carried away from his Florida home after a three-day cyclone on July 9, 1950 (a date presumably chosen to underline the timeliness of the story). Somehow finding himself in the Pacific, he discovers a useable life saver among the flotsam, only to slip out of it and sink from exhaustion soon afterwards. Once we fear that Stan has met a watery end, an atoll suddenly emerges from the depths of the ocean and lifts Stan back up to the air. On the atoll, Stan finds himself stranded in a shallow puddle. But his strenuous swimming and attempts to protect his eyes from the salt water prove that he still considers himself lost at sea. Soon the water has drained and Stan, exhausted from all the swimming, finally realizes he has been saved. After a sit-down he begins to explore the atoll.

Along with Stan, quite a bit of flotsam has been washed up on the atoll. Among the goods are some mostly disrupted crates, which hungry Stan searches for food. But the only things he finds are guns, machine guns, gas masks and hand grenades. In desperation, he throws some armed hand grenades into the sea. The resulting explosions raise pillars of water which, besides spraying heavily, launch a sperm whale up from the depths of the ocean and leave it floating, belly up, on the surface.

The flotsam also contains a crate that is still sealed. Lacking any suitable tools, Stan forces it open with yet another hand grenade. Inside is a grand piano, which Stan uses to regale us with a variation of the overture of *Fra Diavolo*. Slowly and mysteriously the lid of the piano opens, revealing, much to Stan's delight, his friend Ollie. Ollie greets Stan quite formally before engaging him for some four-hand playing on the piano. They congratulate each other for their performance and then start conversing: "Isn't it curious, sir; I think we have met somewhere, but only where?" Both are trying hard to remember: "Didn't we meet in the town where [Ollie] played the song *Come On, Darling*?" Stan shakes his head and starts to play a famous American jazz tune. But even that won't bring back their memory. Next, the British national anthem and the beginning of *The Battle at the Volga* are played. No luck, either, as apparently Ollie hasn't been in either place musically evoked. So the two involuntary islanders vigorously shake hands and introduce themselves.

At this moment the sperm whale unintentionally killed by Stan's hand grenade is washed to shore close by. Stan and Ollie escape into the instrument crate. Once they have confirmed the demise of the huge ocean mammal, they decide to use it as a preliminary food repository for the time being, planning to prepare it piece by piece. That still requires matches which they do not have. When their appetite becomes unbearable, the two cast lots to decide who is to go and to try to find matches. Ollie is the loser. He launches the instrument crate into the ocean to embark on his nautical quest for fire. Without any specific destination he navigates his nutshell using one of the many floating planks as a paddle.

As soon as Ollie has departed, Stan finds a box full of pocket lighters. He signals to Ollie, who is more than happy to return. But a current takes control of the makeshift vessel, and Ollie disappears behind the horizon. A tearful yet hungry Stan begins the work of turning the whale into a meal. But he does not get very far and, exhausted, he falls asleep on the spot.

Meanwhile, a French ship has appeared and discovers the uncharted atoll. A British ship is also approaching the freshly formed island. As instruments onboard the British and French ships indicate a heavy supply of uranium, both crews engage in a race full speed ahead. Each wants to ensure they are the first ones to put foot on the atoll, and once approaching the island they continue their race in rowboats. While the British and the French are busy with their rowing race, an American submarine surfaces. It, too, joins the fun and launches a speed boat toward the atoll. Yet the crew of the British ship has noticed the Americans just in time to shoot the Union Jack onto the island by means of a harpoon, just a few seconds before the Americans beach. Unimpressed, the U.S. sailors erect a flag pole for the star-spangled banner.

A conflict of international dimensions has now been guaranteed. The British claim the island as their flag was the first to fly on it. Meanwhile, the Americans insist that only the first one to put foot on the island can claim it. The French, in contrast, have to content themselves with a formal protest. At least, they were the first ones to spot the atoll with their binoculars. The international law, nevertheless, is clearly on the American side, and so they take possession of the atoll. The British, in the spirit of fair play, accept the American action, as do the fair-minded French. The Americans invite the disappointed British and French sailors to a pompous ceremony: first a minute's silence, drumroll and all, and then the island is christened Atoll Franklin Roosevelt. The Americans also thank the Lord for blessing their nation with such an atoll and all its uranium supplies, surely in order to secure their atomic hegemony and thus the ability to enforce world peace.

The solemn ceremony is interrupted by an enormous snoring, getting louder and louder. It is apparently emanating from the direction of the stranded whale. Emotions turn around, changing the confident Americans into meek sailors, while the British and French find it hard to hide their malicious joy. The snoring is Stan's, who wakes up in terror, waves his arms and abandons himself to all the sailors. Soon questioning commences to find out what his nationality is and when he arrived on the atoll. Ten hours ago, he replies, after checking his Omega brand pocket watch which apparently survived the immersion in the ocean without damage and still gives precise time. As further proof, he also presents the lifesaver.

Since Stan cannot name his nationality, the terrified sailors ask whether he is Russian. But soon the mystery is lifted. Stan is a stateless man! No one knows how to handle the situation. The Americans, who haul down their flag in disappointment, the British and the French all conclude that this is something their respective governments need to deal with. But Stan does not want to be left behind on the atoll. Immediately the ships' crews invite him to come aboard. As they still cannot agree who is to take Stan along, they decide to leave him behind with some provisions. However, without losing any time, they broadcast coded messages to their governments with the position of the previously unknown atoll (and its uranium) and the news of the stateless man who was first on the island.

Meanwhile, Ollie has been recovered by the ship *Salvator* which has stateless men from all over the world on board. Rather than being treated nicely as a guest, he has been knocked out with a rudder blade as a greeting. As a consequence, Ollie has lost his memory. But his amnesia seems to be contagious, and suddenly none of the stateless men on the Salvator can remember anything.

The American, British and French governments have quickly reacted to the radio messages from the atoll and sent three additional ships in its direction. Upon their arrival, Stan is informed that his problem has been submitted to the UNO. Furthermore, he has to stay on the island until a final decision has been reached. Stan is close to a breakdown and protests. But the representatives of the three powers do not give a damn. Stan's case is unique and has to be clarified under international law. And that, being quite a complex problem, might take time. As a comfort, the captains offer him a decent meal with all the comfort their ships can provide.

Soon the Americans, British and French are working against each other again. They are trying to outdo each other with "little presents" for Stan to make him give them little chunks of the atoll. The Americans woo Stan with a prefabricated house fully equipped, fridge and all. The British offer a decent supply of whiskey and the most exquisite clothing, while the French present a kitchen stove, champagne, selected wines and goose liver. Stan feels he is in seventh heaven and gratefully grants each and every nation a piece of territory.

At the UNO office in Washington, with 44 to 21 votes, it is decided that an island of this significance cannot be owned by a private person. Stan will have to decide in favor of one of the 65 UNO nations, and that in turn shall determine possession of the atoll. Until then, it shall be named Atoll K. Because of the enormous value of the atoll, a constant control commission is instated to report on a daily basis. To sanction the territorial claims that the Americans, British and French have obtained from Stan, the UNO decides without a single dissenting vote that Stan is allowed to give ten square meters of land to each of the 65 member countries for their own respective use. As an organization of its own, the UNO further demands additional land grants. Soon thereafter, an entire armada of ships, barges and boats of all kind are anchored near the atoll. They carry representatives of the 62 other nations who would also like to obtain territorial concessions from Stan. He accepts them all at once, and they make their submissions to him in chorus, putting all the riches of the world at his feet. Chomping on a big cigar, Stan relaxes, very pleased with himself, and one by one receives whatever is offered to him.

When the ship with the UNO control commission arrives, the atoll has changed quite a bit. At the center of the island is now a UNO base, a sort of Hollywood version of a *1001 Arabian Nights* palace. It is surrounded by 65 little villas, each protected by a huge fence and marked by the flag of the respective UNO membership state. Only one of the 65 territories looks slightly different. It is separated by an iron curtain and on its middle a huge eye seems to be painted, yet it blinks from time to time.

Through a narrow corridor, the members of the UNO control commission are forced to make their way single-file from the ocean to the fancy UNO palace. Petty jealousies and fights over status erupt among the representatives of the 65 nations on a daily basis. To worsen things, each delegation plays their national anthem at the same time as the others, producing an ear-splitting din. At last, the international cacophony comes to an end. In the central palace, a twelve-piece band, dressed in white and with plumed caps, plays a catchy tune signaling Stan's appearance to welcome the members of the control commission. Their chairman gives a little speech on the occasion and asks Stan to choose a nation whose citizenship he desires. When Stan favors Monaco, there is a whisper of disbelief all around. The representatives want to know why Stan votes for tiny Monaco, when the biggest and most powerful countries of the world have courted him. Stan has three crucial reasons: in Monaco there are no taxes and no compulsory military service, while they have the most polite and best-looking policemen in the world.

The UNO delegate has to submit himself to such convincing reasons. Meanwhile, the commission member lowest in rank, a little man representing the monarchy of Monaco, makes his way through the crowds to embrace Stan in friendship. In front of photographers who preserve the scene for posterity, he gives Stan a lifetime membership card for the Monte Carlo casino.

In the conference room of the Monegasque villa, located on the most picturesque rock on the atoll, the council of ministers of Monaco have assembled for an extraordinary conference. After intense deliberation they agree they feel tremendously honored by Stan's decision, especially since the rich uranium supplies turn Monaco into a world power. On the downside they recognize the risks which this decision entails. There would be lucrative offers from the most powerful countries of the world. The monarchy would likely become entangled in a maelstrom of jealousies and evil feelings emanating from states that lost the uranium race. In other words, this decision would cause Monaco to sacrifice its highest good: its neutrality. Thus, Stan's offer needs to be declined. Tearfully, Stan returns his lifetime membership card for the Monte Carlo casino to the Monegasque representative. The representatives of the other states do not even try to hide their delight. One of them strongly suggests to Stan that it is high time to quickly decide for another nation. Distressed, Stan declares that he will accept the nationality of that country which succeeds in returning his friend Ollie to him, whom he describes as one of the most gifted pianists ever. Soon everyone has embarked on a hectic search for Ollie.

Meanwhile, Ollie is still pent up among the homeless on the *Salvator* which approaches Atoll K in the hope for asylum, courtesy of the stateless Stan. Stan gladly receives the homeless and discovers among them Ollie, who, upon seeing Stan, suddenly regains his memory, hands over a box of matches and tearfully sinks into his arms.

Since it was stateless men who returned Ollie to stateless Stan, the question of the nationality of the atoll remains wide open. Consequently, it does not take very long until the next, not quite as friendly, invitation to decide on a nation reaches Stan. Stan and Ollie agree. They do not want to belong to any state, because this would subject them to the forces imposed on any citizen, while on the stateless atoll they can continue to enjoy abundance and freedom. If Monaco princedom does not want them, at least they can turn the atoll into a Monegasque-like paradise on earth.

The UNO responds with an ultimatum: within 48 hours Stan must make his final decision. Stan counters with the claim that Ollie, too, is a stateless man who even set foot on the atoll before him. And so he proposes to cast lots to decide on a nation for him and for his friend Ollie, taking daily turns. The UNO flatly rejects this.

Thus, Stan and Ollie decide to award ownership of the atoll in the Mille Guinées horse race which takes place in a month in England. This way they have gained one month's worth of time. The UNO grows more and more impatient, and denying Stan and Ollie any property rights for the atoll, demands they leave the island and splits the atoll between France, Great Britain and the United States, whose marines were the first to land there.

This is followed by relatively rude attempts by the American, British and French units to expel Stan and Ollie from the island. While in the original outline, a mysterious additional nation supported Stan and Ollie in their fight against hunger and mosquitos, here the picture is unambiguous. As suits a Cold War movie, it is, of course, the Russian delegation that has given food and drink to the friends. Three days into the food embargo Stan and Ollie are found snoring in front of a buffet stuffed with caviar, zaghouski, and barrels full of vodka. Sitting back to back, Stan and Ollie can even fight the mosquito swarms by using the Russian insecticide. Instead, the insects divert their attention to the American, British and French troops. No mention is made of the three voluptuous ladies who were to seduce Stan and Ollie and sway them into leaving the island. According to the authors of the treatment, the mission of womanhood was to fail, since the women argued among each other, leaving no time to seduce the boys.

Much like in the outline, the treatment also continues on the day of the Mille Guinées. Stan and Ollie have to come up with a new trick to remain on their desert island, mostly for the authors' sake, for an indefinite time. Therefore, they try to convince the UNO that an unknown person was already on the atoll even before they landed. As with the previous outline, the idea of the "great unknown" is not the desperately needed flash of genius the script requires. On this morning of the race, everything around on the atoll has changed. No ships are in sight, all villas are empty, and all iron curtains have been lifted, revealing the sight of scrub and barbed wire. Most of all, no traces are left of the daily caviar and vodka supply. Instead, the proverbial calm before the storm embraces the island before another earthquake rocks the atoll, while once again a hurricane sweeps over the coast of Florida. Head over heels, Stan and Ollie escape into the music box — their sail a patchwork of all the flags of the nations who had taken residence on the island. While the atoll slowly sinks into the ocean, the storm drives Stan and Ollie away in their music box at high speed.

The next day the sea is completely calm. Once again, all sorts of wreckage floats on the ocean. Stan and Ollie are completely exhausted, and water seeps into their slowly sinking box. Suddenly a new miracle: the box settles. They find themselves on yet another atoll just emerged from the ocean, uncannily resembling the formerly wooed Atoll K. All Stan and Ollie have to do is wait for the next onrush of nations and serve them the story of the "great unknown" who also arrived on this atoll before them, raising yet again the prospects of feudal Monegasque conditions.

The treatment ends much like the outline. For fifty years, Stan and Ollie have been sitting on an atoll which is anything but a paradise. Surrounded by piles of fishbones they try to land their lunch from the ocean with a mere line, lacking even hook and sinker. On the beach, they have raised a huge billboard to draw attention to the alleged treasures of the atoll's resources. Without exception all ships still pass by, as it is well known that nothing is to be gained here.

Where the outline was unsatisfactory, the treatment offers little progress. The authors have adhered to Joannon's outline, merely inflating the story somewhat. For a treatment of a Laurel-and-Hardy film it is beyond belief that Ollie does not even play any role for half of the plot. The barbecuing of the stranded sperm whale is far from a great idea to begin with. But the dead animal and the need for matches continues to serve as uninspired justification for Ollie's departure from the atoll. In contrast, it seems comparatively inspired when Ollie is found by a ship populated with stateless people. This, at least, is an idea that could meaningfully be integrated into the further plot. After all, Stan wants to accept the citizenship of the saviors of his friend which now cannot possibly work as they are stateless people as well. Finally, the authors of the treatment could not come up with any better closure than the forced landing on yet another newborn island.

However, it has to be conceded that some ideas are reasonably inspired. The presence of Stan and Ollie on the first atoll is explained more conclusively. The treatment is further improved by nice satirical sideswipes against national claims of power and the concurrent disdain for the individual citizen. Further improvements are the treatment's tribute to the Monegasque lifestyle and the well-caricatured characters of the apparently (but only temporarily so) philanthropic and supportive Russians.

Still, the treatment is far from a proper Laurel-and-Hardy script. In addition to all its problems, the plot is tailored around the international entanglements, rather than the two comedians, making them mere accessories.

Most likely this treatment was among the things the producers used to entice Laurel and Hardy for this project which promised their return to the screens after five years' absence. Surprisingly, it did not turn them away. The opportunity to restart their movie career with a current film was as appealing as the pay. Also, while in Paris, Laurel and Hardy were to be housed in the internationally renowned Hôtel Prince de Galles on Champs-Elysées, built in 1928 in the art-déco style.[26] Furthermore, Laurel was contractually assured the last word on the script,[27] a privilege he had last enjoyed in 1940 at the Hal Roach Studios. In France at that time, prime importance was attached to actors' artistic ambitions and contributions. Thus, the project appeared to suggest that Laurel would regain his long missed artistic freedom on the big screen. The shooting was scheduled to take only twelve weeks, an important reason for Laurel to agree to the project to begin with.[28]

The shooting budget was supposed to be the unusually high amount of $1.5 million U.S.[29] which means an equivalent of $18.2 million U.S. according to today's standards. The financing was based on a state credit. This was to be handled and controlled by the Centre National de la Cinématographie ["National Film Institute"], a board founded at the beginning of 1947 and responsible for the organization and all questions regarding the French movie industry.[30] This board received the treatment for approval by É.G.É. at the end of 1949 or the beginning of 1950. Then, the Commission d'Agrément et d'Étude des Scénarii ["Commission for the Approval of Movie Projects and Examination of Scripts"], a part of the Centre National de la Cinématographie, preliminarily gave the shooting of *Atoll K* the green light on January 24, 1950.[31]

This suggests that the first contact between Laurel and Hardy and the production companies must have taken place no later than early 1950 and most likely before October 19, 1949, when Eger's É.G.É. and d'Angelos Universalia had agreed to produce *Atoll K* together.[32] The outline as well as the treatment specifically mention Laurel and Hardy as characters. Also, the Centre National de la Cinématographie had preliminarily approved shooting at the end of January 1950 which would have been pointless unless contact with the comedians had been established by then. Along the same lines, the French-Italian contract between É.G.É. and Universalia would have made little sense without getting in touch with the duo. By no means would Laurel and Hardy have traveled to Europe with their wives, unless they had been formally contracted by the producers of *Atoll K*. As Laurel and his wife rented out their apartment in Santa Monica with a contract dating April 3, 1950, for the time of their stay in France and possibly left the United States for Paris only afterwards,[33] the European producers' contract with the two comedians must have been finalized by March 1950.[34] It is hard to imagine that this might have happened without any information on the contents of the movie.[35]

If Laurel and Hardy had been contracted in March 1950 after preliminary negotiations, the outline and the treatment must date at least a few months earlier.[36]

In contrast to statements by Laurel's daughter and her husband, the documents at hand confirm that the basic idea, a plot evolving around a big uranium find, was not Laurel's own idea. During their appearance in France in 1947, Laurel contemplated filming an extended version of their current *Driver's License Sketch*. When this did not work out, Laurel is reported to have said: "Hey, let's find uranium."[37] This casual remark may well be authentic, but does not allow any conclusions regarding a movie plot drafted by him. Rather it seems to be a mere coincidence that uranium was to play a role in the film *Atoll K*. Following the bombing of Hiroshima and Nagasaki and the atomic race of the Cold War, the idea of uranium was current, but certainly not inventive.[38]

The treatment allows further insight into the planning of *Atoll K*. To support Laurel and Hardy, the actors Rellys from France and Erminio Macario from Italy were considered. They were about the same age as Laurel and Hardy, and had gained experience in comedy in independent careers since the 1930s. Bourvil, Fernandel and Totò were also considered, while the Italian partners further suggested Walter Chiari and Carlo Croccolo as alternatives to Totò.[39]

At the beginning of April 1950, the Italian press reported on the imminent shooting of *Atoll K* in France with Laurel and Hardy as stars. According to this, Fernandel and Totò seemed to be replaced in the planning by Rellys and Macario.[40] In the middle of April 1950, the West German press reported that Laurel and Hardy were to shoot the film with Bourvil, commencing May 1950.[41] At the end of April 1950, Fernandel's name turned up again; Sirius had an intensive business connection with Fernandel and produced four comedies from 1949 to 1951 starring him.[42] The French press reported that Macario would represent Italy in the international coproduction, but it was still unclear whether Bourvil or Fernandel would be his French counterpart. Furthermore, this article claimed that shooting was to take place on the Mediaterrenean Île de Levant, a famous French nudist resort at that time.[43] In contrast, at the end of June 1950, the Italian press still named Fernandel and Walter Chiari as Laurel and Hardy's costars. Further Genoa (Italy) was reported as one of the locations for the *Atoll K* shooting.[44] Press reports did not indicate why neither Fernandel nor Totò, nor Bourvil, Chiari or Croccolo for that matter, were finally engaged. The Italian movie magazine *Hollywood* got even more explicit at the end of June 1950. By that time, Chiari was reportedly under contract by the Universalia for *Atoll K*, and the start of the shooting reportedly was planned the same month at the Côte d'Azur with Laurel, Hardy and Fernandel.[45]

However, Fernandel soon appeared in Marcel Pagnol's feature film *Topaze* in 1951, and Bourvil and Totò also had various movie engagements in France and Italy, respectively. Possibly, the three comedians were not even interested in *Atoll K*. Especially, Fernandel and Totò were accustomed to being starring comedians since about 1950, rather than second bananas for an aged American comedy team.[46]

Regardless, the Italian press release announced the collaboration of "four internationally renowned comedians" and briefly summarized the plot of the soon-to-be produced film. This roughly corresponded to what is found in the outline and was later expanded in the treatment.[47] Similar reports on the film were published soon thereafter in France.[48] Apparently the documents unearthed for this book were not merely used internally by the productions, but also as a basis for press releases.

At any rate, Laurel and Hardy did not have more than the treatment by Joffé, Levitte, Eger and Joannon at hand before Laurel and his wife embarked for Europe on their own. The idea was that Laurel would consult on the script in France. Hardy's travel to France was delayed since he was committed to appear in a cameo in Frank Capra's *Riding High* in 1950.[49] He was to follow soon, once the script for *Atoll K* was finished, and shooting could commence.[50]

After Laurel and his wife Ida had arrived in France, Hardy was interviewed on June 10, 1950 aboard the R.M.S. *Caronia* by host Jack Mangan for the show *Ship's Report* of the National Television Guild.[51] Hardy and his wife Lucille were departing for Paris that same day and Mangan, who had interviewed Laurel in his cabin when he set sail for France nearly two and a half months earlier, chatted with Hardy in front of a camera. A perplexed Hardy could be seen pulling his ticket out of his jacket and, in a conversation lasting approximately three and a half minutes, the two discussed Laurel and Hardy's teamwork and friendship of 23 years, his nickname "Babe," and the upcoming movie project[52]:

> MANGAN: This picture you're going to make in Paris is called *Atoll K*.
> HARDY: *Atoll K*.
> MANGAN: It sounds very atomic.
> HARDY: Well, we think it is, anyway, but we're mistaken in the end, of course, as usual.
> MANGAN: Well, it is about the atom bomb in a sense, then, isn't it?
> HARDY: Well, it's uranium, you know. We think we've discovered this island with uranium, and the different countries start bidding for our favor to get the island. Eventually we find out that it isn't uranium, so the country passes up and leaves us sitting on this island."

While sketchy on details about *Atoll K*, Hardy's comments are clearly in line with Joannon's outline and the treatment. The next treatment though was significantly different from anything else, as we shall see.

Even though its originator Joannon was not in charge of the treatment anymore, he was to be Laurel and Hardy's director on *Atoll K* and to work on the shooting script as well. Earlier, American Tim Whelan had been considered as director.[53] In fact, in the April 13, 1950, edition of her regular column, Hollywood gossip queen Louella Parsons specifically reported that Whelan was to leave for France on May 9, 1950, to direct *Atoll K* and an additional film for the Franco London company.[54] However, the government support of

"Ship's Report[er]" Jack Mangan interviews Hardy, June 10, 1950 (screen capture from the filmed interview).

the French film industry did not allow an American role in this production, with the obvious exception of the stars, Laurel and Hardy. The rejection of Whelan was not only unfortunate, but also short-sighted. Whelan was a very experienced filmmaker, among other things as codirector of the 1940 classic *The Thief of Bagdad* (Michael Powell, Ludwig Berger). More importantly he was very experienced in visual film comedy, having worked on the script of Harold Lloyd's 1924 and 1925 classics *Girl Shy*, *Hot Water* and *The Freshman*, all directed by Fred C. Newmeyer and Sam Taylor, as well as the Monty Banks comedy *Adam's Apple* (1928).[55] Even though this predated *Atoll K* by a quarter of a century, Laurel certainly would have had no objections to working with Whelan as a director. Indeed, when troubles occurred during later work on the treatment, Laurel personally approached Whelan to help draft a coherent and fluid, genuine Laurel-and-Hardy script.[56]

2

On the Way to the Script

Once the contracts with their European producers were signed, things looked rosy for Laurel and Hardy — for a while. Laurel's health seemed up to the challenge of the upcoming shoot; he had been aware of his diabetes since 1949, but seemed to have the condition under control medically, even though he had lost some weight, little by little. When Laurel and his wife Ida arrived at the Paris station Gare Saint-Lazare on April 13, 1950,[1] French Laurel-and-Hardy fans (wearing Hardy masks) enthusiastically greeted a healthy-looking Laurel who very much resembled the one they had seen during the comedians' last visit to France in 1947.[2] Optimistically it was stated that shooting of the "trilingual comedy *Atoll K*" was to commence on June 15, 1950,[3] already suggesting a delay of about six weeks compared to earlier reports. Meanwhile, in Germany, the distributor Prisma announced in May 1950 that they had secured the German distribution rights for this European "co-production of laughter."[4]

Yet reality was not so cheerful. The troubles that were to plague *Atoll K* had begun. Once everyone came to realize that Joffé, Levitte, Eger and Joannon had not created a usable treatment, Bookbinder intervened and tried to find suitable scriptwriters in the United States. Bookbinder contacted Paul Kohner, the famous Hollywood agent. Kohner had been lured from Czechoslovakia to Hollywood in the 1920s by Universal's Carl Laemmle. A clever agent, Kohner built an impressive list of clients over the years: Ingmar Bergman, Charles Bronson, Maurice Chevalier, Gert Fröbe, Greta Garbo, Rita Hayworth, John Huston, Curd Jürgens, Luis Trenker, Max Ophüls and Liv Ullmann, as well as writers such as Marcel Pagnol, Erich Maria Remarque and mysterious B. Traven. Through Paul Kohner's agency, Bookbinder got in touch with Kohner's brother Frederick. Frederick Kohner had established himself as one-half of a script-writing team with his colleague Albert Mannheimer.[5]

In his 1974 biography of Paul Kohner, Frederick Kohner recalls receiving the offer to work on *Atoll K* from his brother.[6] According to his report, he was on vacation in the snowy mountains of Idaho in March 1950, when he received a telegram from Paul which read: "What do you think of April in Paris? If agreed, please return call." Frederick Kohner indeed called right away and asked when the project was to start. Paul replied: "Whenever you want!" Paul Kohner informed his brother that the job was a Laurel-and-Hardy film, which needed a script based on a rough plot draft which he summarized to him as well. Frederick Kohner found all this very interesting, especially since he would be given artistic freedom — not only that, but Laurel and Hardy reportedly wanted to try something new after years of exile from Hollywood. According to Frederick Kohner, the comedians had been without income of any sort for quite some time. While Laurel had made provisions for such a case, Hardy was nearly bankrupt and was reduced to bit parts in Western films. Paul Kohner, however, was well aware that the duo was still tremendously popular in Europe, to the extent that people even kissed their hands on the streets. Frederick Kohner accepted.

Frederick Kohner's memories have to be taken with a grain of salt. Laurel and Hardy were not the fatigued, forgotten clowns that Frederick Kohner suggests, as their phenomenally successful 1947 tour of Great Britain attests. And Hardy was far from bankrupt or out of work. He certainly did not depend on cameos in Westerns; in fact he had only appeared in one such film, sharing the screen with his friend John Wayne in 1949's *The Fighting Kentuckian* (George Waggner).

Years later, Randy Skretvedt interviewed Kohner, who admitted his initial reservations about writing a Laurel-and-Hardy script without previous comedy experience. Nevertheless, Paul Kohner succeeded in selling the idea to Frederick. Not only was the subject matter appealing to the two brothers, so was the expected salary. Last but not least, Frederick Kohner was looking forward to working with Mannheimer again.[7] But when it turned out that Mannheimer was engaged elsewhere and could not join Kohner as coauthor, Hardy proposed his golf partner John Klorer as replacement. Klorer shared Kohner's concerns, but, like Kohner, preferred not to pass on the handsome salary either, which amounted to 35,000 old francs per week — equivalent to about ten percent of what a European middle-class car cost at the time, something very few could afford in the early postwar period.

Neither Klorer nor Kohner knew that in far-away Europe two additional scriptwriters were engaged for *Atoll K*: René Wheeler from France and the Italian Pierro Tellini.[8] They only

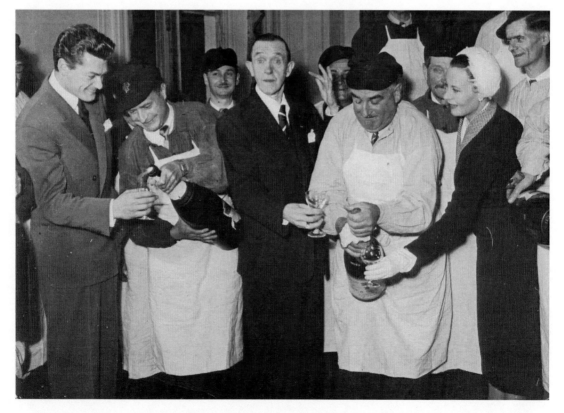

Cercle Interallié champagne tasting in Paris, May 10, 1950: Jean Marais [left], Laurel [center], Michèle Morgan [right] (courtesy Peter Mikkelsen).

learned about their existence when they got to Paris in April 1950. Even though each of the four authors was rich in experience and highly regarded in the industry, thanks to their previous work with famous first-class directors,[9] a smooth collaboration was far from guaranteed. In fact, as only Klorer and Kohner could communicate without any problems in English, confusion among the four script writers with three different languages was inevitable. The solution was to have each author write his own version in his own language; the four versions would then be condensed into a common script. Unsurprisingly, the result was a disaster. While Tellini desired a social-political take, Wheeler worked on a farce. Klorer and Kohner were between those two extremes. None, however, resembled a Laurel-and-Hardy movie.

Regardless, Eger was eager to make the life of his authors as pleasant as possible, regardless of the costs. Klorer and Kohner were allowed to go in conclave in the sunny Montfort near Paris. When they met Wheeler and Tellini in Paris later on, they had to admit that neither of them had a solid concept. The desire to launch a new Laurel-and-Hardy project could not overcome the writers' unfamiliarity with the art of the two great comedians.

By mid–April, Laurel and his wife had already been in Paris for some time. As intended, they stayed at the Hôtel Prince de Galles,[10] where the Hardys were to join them later. Laurel was displeased to learn from Eger that there was no progress with the script. It was obvious that the planned schedule was now hopelessly outdated. Laurel had no choice but to be patient and to bide his time. There was no shortage of public attention: for example, he joined famous film actors such as Jean Marais and Michèle Morgan for a champagne tasting on May 10,

Hardy's arrival at Paris train station Gare du Nord, June 17, 1950. He is welcomed by Laurel as well as Laurel-and-Hardy enthusiasts wearing Laurel masks (courtesy Peter Mikkelsen).

organized by the French society Cercle Interallié on the occasion of the shooting of a documentary film on the sparkling French beverage.

Meanwhile, Eger housed his four authors in a single hotel to expedite matters — to no avail. Even a luxurious hotel in the exclusive bathing resort Deauville in Basse-Normandie did not produce a breakthrough. Having an entire floor of their own meant lots of space, but not necessarily lots of accomplishment. In fact, Kohner's colleagues preferred to spend their high salary in the casino until the early morning hours. In the biography of his brother, Kohner further states that "the Frenchmen" hated the sunlight and consequently only worked at nighttime, while "the Italians" never even worked at all.[11] Thus the work of the four writers dragged on until the beginning of June 1950, when — according to Kohner — "several thousands [of] typewritten pages" of script had been generated.[12] Laurel signaled to his partner Hardy that it was time to join him in Paris. On June 10, 1950, the Hardys boarded the R.M.S. *Caronia* to France. Much like the Laurels before them in April, the Hardys were greeted by fans on June 17, 1950, this time at the Paris Gare du Nord train station.[13] On this occasion, the well-wishers wore Laurel masks. In fact, they were accompanied by the real Laurel, who would not miss the opportunity to personally welcome his friend and partner in the French capital. Furthermore, a huge banner with the greeting "La Grande Nuit de Paris[14] and Stan Laurel bid welcome to Oliver Hardy" was unrolled.

Now that both halves of the famous comedy duo resided in Paris, public attention grew all the more. On the day of Hardy's arrival, the two appeared in front of French television cameras. Laurel and Hardy performed a sketch on the popular Saturday afternoon magazine program *Le Jugement de Paris*, duly celebrated by an enthusiastic audience.[15]

As Paul Kohner had told his brother Frederick, the two comedians had even been recognized on the Champs-Elysées, and people revered them to the extent of kissing their hands.[16] All in all Laurel and Hardy enjoyed the pleasures of Paris. Hardy was especially fond of the Casino de Paris and the Folies Bergères, the metropolis's largest revue theaters, famous for their chorus girls.[17]

Shortly after Hardy's arrival, the time came to review the results of the four script writers' work. Laurel and Hardy met Klorer and Kohner in their Hôtel Prince de Galles between June 17 and 22.[18] The two writers were far from happy with the new treatment, which they had wrested from themselves and their colleagues Tellini and Wheeler,[19] and which in turn was the basis for a French version by Joannon, Levitte and Joffé. When discussion of the outcome of their work with Laurel began, Klorer and Kohner must have felt like unprepared students presenting their teacher a failed written test. Before reading the treatment, which amounted to a mere 21 pages (not the thousands Kohner seems to recall), a polite Laurel addressed their worries by stating that nothing is so good that it does not need improvement. Laurel agreed on meeting the writers the next day, giving him time to read their work.[20]

The treatment in Laurel's hand took the reader back into the Stone Age. Troglodytes Stan and Ollie approvingly listen to the sermon of another caveman, condemning mankind for greediness and evil. The motif of the sermon — and Stan and Ollie's approval — repeated throughout the course of history in ancient Rome, the Middle Ages, and modern-day Hyde Park in London, reminding us how throughout time humans have complained about their circumstances.

In the present day, Stan learns that his rich uncle has died. Ollie envisions how he and his friend will use Stan's inheritance for a carefree life from now on. Following the reading of the will, the devious notary, citing a bundle of excuses, demands all manner of reparations from poor Stan: inheritance and real estate taxes, registration fees, and enforcement costs, as well as legal and other expenses. As consolation Stan receives an island in the South Pacific, which the late rich relative also owned.

Stan and Ollie dream of their future, an idyllic life on the island, making it all the easier for the resourceful notary to sell them a ship to journey there. With all the attire needed for life in the South Seas (bast cloth, ukulele, sunshade and water skis), the two travel to Marseilles where their ship awaits at quay 32. At the same time, the most famous stowaway in Marseilles, Olivieri Coppini [an oddly chosen name designed to invite confusion between "Olivieri" and "Ollie"], tries to get on board the S.S. *All Will Be Good*. He is swiftly caught by customs officers and shooed away.

Meanwhile Stan and Ollie have brought their goods onto their nutshell. Apparently they have no idea how to get the ship moving, let alone steer it. Naturally, they get entangled in ropes and sailcloth. Suddenly they hear a hideous noise. High above them, the cargo crane of the S.S. *All Will Be Good* swings a monkey cage. The cage houses poor stateless Antoine, who has been traveling the oceans for years without being allowed to set foot on any country, since he does not own any passport. This time he has chosen a monkey cage for his escape — after all, monkeys do not need passports. But the customs officers show no mercy and Antoine has to return on board.

The captain of the *All Will Be Good* prefers to get rid of Antoine sooner than later, and once he sees Stan and Ollie's boat in the harbor, he knows what to do. Apparently the boys need help, and the captain convinces them that the unpopular stateless man is the most experienced sailor in the world. Antoine, in turn, is fooled into believing Stan and Ollie are eccentric millionaires on their way to the South Seas. After the relieved captain has hoisted Antoine onto Stan and Ollie's tub, the two tars activate various levers, switches and cranks to send their little cruiser on a wild, zigzag ride across the waves.

On the open sea, Ollie attends to the rudder, while Stan relaxes on a deck chair. Both are served milk and sandwiches by Antoine. The food mysteriously disappears. Olivieri Coppini has crept on board in Marseilles and is surreptitiously snatching the delicacies. Worse than that, the craft's engine expires in the middle of nowhere. Yet the so-called engineer seems to be incompetent in handling the tools the boys give him. Haphazardly, he uses pliers but only succeeds in clipping his fingernails. Finally he confesses that he has no clue.

Stan and Ollie try in their own way to disassemble the engine, a process that sees Stan plunging the engine parts into the ocean. In the end, they have no choice but to set the sails. When they unroll them, Olivieri tumbles out of his hiding spot within the sail's folds. He immediately and noisily complains about the poor tub he has found himself on. Yet Olivieri has about as many nautical skills as the boys and Antoine. When the sail is hoisted upon his command, it goes overboard; Ollie's ample trousers are recruited as a surrogate sail. After a month, the sea wind has gone and the four men have to row.

The four men revel in dreams of a better life on the South Sea island — without governmental intrusion and, most importantly without taxes. Along the way they make music and sing South Sea songs. But their supplies become exhausted and hunger rears its ugly head. Stan and Ollie, but also Antoine and Olivieri, ponder which crewmate to eat first to escape death from starvation. The boys find it hard to choose between Antoine and the Italian Olivieri. They choose: Antoine. After all, he is of French lineage, and French cuisine is the best.

A sudden thunderstorm arises and chases away the cannibalistic urges. Now all four are focused on fighting the forces of nature. Before they know it they are saved: the ship strands itself on an atoll that has just emerged from the ocean during the storm. At first sight it looks inhospitable, but a bounty of fish washed up on the beach promises a tasty bouillabaisse.

Under no circumstances do the four want to remain on the atoll, and so they concentrate on repairing their craft to escape the island as quickly as possible. Olivieri's proposal to build a cable car to pull the ship into the water is immediately dismissed due to the lack of materials. Stan and Ollie want to construct wooden wheels and set the ship on them. Antoine suggests that the four could shoulder the craft and carry it into the sea. Other fruitless ideas fly through their heads, such as refloating the ship by pulling it over round pebbles or digging a ditch to the sea. But this would require a lighter craft, and they give up in defeat.

Even though Stan has already cut some planks for further action, the four argue about what to do next. Ollie is the most furious. Sitting on a pile of débris from the empty boat, he is looking for something to destroy to vent his anger. He notices a book and starts tearing it, only to glance at the title: *Robinson Crusoe.* He begins to read the book to his comrades.

The four men give themselves new names. Ollie becomes Oliver Crusoe, Stan is rechristened Friday, Antoine is Saturday, and Olivieri is Sunday. Furthermore, they have a small dog called Thursday. Apparently they have lost hope of leaving the atoll any time soon. Under Olivieri's direction they build a house from whatever they can find. They even discover drinking water and construct a line directly to their house.

The castaways do not even have to worry about sufficient food — all they have to do is to pull it out of the ocean. For this, the modern Robinson Crusoes have built an automated fishing rod from a pole, a pulley and a stone as counterweight, connected to a flag. Once a fish bites, the line tightens, the stone falls, and the flag is hoisted.

Over time the foursome succeeds in reclaiming the land. Soon they have changed the atoll into a lush island with trees, fruits and vegetables of all kinds. Their house is finished and even has a patio. Life is good here. Stan and Ollie take care of the farming, Olivieri is working on building a wall, and Antoine is busy as a painter, with trowel and two paintbrushes, wearing a blouse as protection against paint splashes. He paints faster than Olivieri can build walls, grabbing individual stones and painting them before Olivieri can stack them. He paints with whatever paint is available, resulting in a wall that resembles a colorful quilt.

Meanwhile, unexplainable things seem to have happened on the beach. Stan and Ollie find huge impressions in the sand, which cannot possibly be of human origin. When they follow the trail to its end, it is revealed that the little dog Thursday had put on flippers and produced the strange footprints. The castaways decide to go fishing, but their first catch is nearly snatched away by a seal.

After dinner the men relax. Antoine smokes a piece of seaweed as a cigar, Stan plays with a radio, which has been out of order so far. But now instead of static it actually transmits newscasts. They are overwhelmed by what they hear: tax increases, strikes, unemployment, Mississippi floods, a heatwave in Melbourne, and other global unpleasantries. The four conclude that they are doing quite well on their island. So they do not care when a travel agency advertises a cheap holiday in the South Seas or when a famous female flying ace announces a flight around the world in a supersonic airplane.

In a new scene, a trade schooner is traveling in the South Seas. The captain is accompanied by a far-from friendly wife, a woman who makes Mae Busch at her worst look like an angel in comparison. While peering through her telescope she discovers an island, the perfect spot to abandon the woman she calls "the beast"—namely Colette Marly, whom the captain has taken on board. Colette enjoys life in a cabin on the ship, lounging in black lingerie that does little to hide her femininity. This is too much for the captain's wife. The two women engage in a constant exchange of pointed remarks. The captain's wife's concerns are understandable, though. Colette is a prostitute from Paris, who had been in Tahiti, and was later expelled from Pago Pago, the capital of American Samoa, by a crowd of women. Thus she now resides on the schooner. The jealous spouse wants to get rid of Colette as quickly as possible. Once she discovers the island she orders Colette onto the deck and into a tiny rowboat. Her husband protests, stating the island may be uninhabited. His objections are dismissed by his wife, who points out that this may well give the alleycat the opportunity to lead a decent life. Colette enters the dinghy but not without leaving an invitation to the captain: he is welcome to visit her once in a while.

The island, of course, is the one the four companions inhabit. Upon her landing, Colette blows a last kiss over to the schooner as its captain disappears on the horizon. She starts out in search of proper accommodations and soon finds the house of the comrades, who happen to be on the other side of the atoll at the time. There they are playing coconut baseball with the dog and a seal that has joined them. In what may seem the most baffling and pointless scene in all the *Atoll* drafts, the seal catches a fly which he hands over to the little dog, who releases it and catches his own fly, for reasons that even the script writers may not have fathomed.

When the men return to their lodging, they find Colette comfortably asleep on a couch in the hut. Her appearance triggers a reaction not unlike that of the Seven Dwarves on seeing Snow White. They treat the beguiling beauty like a fairy princess, going so far as to serve her breakfast in bed—certainly a novel experience for a lady from the demimonde. Once she learns that there is no money on the atoll she declares enthusiastically: "A wonderful destination for stranding!"

But the beauty soon creates unrest among the men. Colette decides to take a bath in a basin built next to the spring. As she begins to undress, the companions—gentlemen that they are—withdraw. Once Colette's seductive singing and cooing emanates from the basin, each begins plotting how to outrival the other. Soon their minds have cleared and the men promise each other never to let a woman between them. Colette, who has dressed again after finishing her bath, overhears this and assures the friends that she will never create disharmony and, particularly, not between fellows as nice as them. The seal applauds.

Yet, maintaining that mutual promise is easier said than done. In due time the feminine presence begins to leave its mark, even though Colette's attire has become relatively decent compared to that of her earlier life. Each man seeks her favor, picking flowers and decorating the hut they have built for her. Ollie even has Stan cut his hair which, according to the treatment, was to result in a "classic Laurel and Hardy scene." The struggle for Colette is particularly seething between Antoine and Olivieri. As a fight over Colette erupts on the beach, a control boat stuffed with measuring instruments lands on the atoll.

The boat carries surveyors on a mission to discern why the atoll has not been located earlier. Soon the troop discovers an enormous supply of uranium on the island, something Stan mistakes for a medical powder. The surveyors' supervisor quickly realizes that the island must be assigned to a nation. He inquires about the nationality of the comrades, and asks who among them was the first to put foot on the atoll, since the island will be property of that state whose citizen was the first to enter it. Stan suggests identifying stateless Antoine as the island's first inhabitant. This tremendously confuses the surveyors' supervisor, and he and his men leave the island to have the matter clarified by the United Nations. But even the high-ranking UNO officials cannot do anything but declare the status quo to assembled journalists from all over the world. Soon the media jump upon the news and report how a stateless man discovered virgin soil loaded with uranium.

Inevitably, all considered states' representatives plot to find a way to claim the valuable atoll. This forces the island's inhabitants to act, and they decide to form their own government with its own constitution which turns out to be a rather idealistic one: no laws, no taxes, no customs or border, no food rationing and no iron curtain either. That decided, the inhabitants of the atoll hoist their new national flag. But leisurely days for Colette and the four companions are over. First an airplane brings in a UNO delegate as well as a cluster of journalists, along with a gigantic radio antenna. All are thrilled by the idyllic conditions, vegetation, beauty, and the climate of the atoll. Reports spread around the world at lightning speed, and countless people are lured to try their luck on the island.

The first newcomers on the atoll are warmly greeted, but one lady among them is not quite happy when Colette hugs her husband, declaring that her hugs are not illegal on the island. Immediately, the woman wants to return home. Along with the newcomers, four postal bags also arrive on the island, carrying countless letters in which people express their delight over the tax-free status guaranteed in the atoll's constitution. They encourage Stan, Ollie, Antoine, Olivieri and Colette to not let themselves be annexed by any nation. However, the postal bags also contain a letter from the UNO announcing that they will send a delegation to the atoll to invite the fellows for a special session. This will decide the ownership and the sovereignty of the island, with the session held on board the UNO delegation's ship. Before Stan, Ollie, Antoine and Olivieri follow the invitation, they greet some more newcomers, who make themselves at home and take care of the atoll until the men return from the ship.

On the UNO ship, Stan, Ollie, Antoine and Olivieri create chaos. They rip down the UNO delegation's microphone, water decanters are spilled, chairs are toppled, and the translation device gets broken. The French delegate is treated to the German translation while the German delegate is baffled by the French translation. The group further mixes up the maps. Ollie swears to say nothing but the truth, while Stan's finger gets trapped in a stenographic machine. Antoine modulates his voice into sounding like the assembly's chairman, stating that the incompetent officials who denied him citizenship will be called to account. In all the turmoil the chairman of the UNO delegation declares that international law gives people on the atoll the right to decide their own fate in a referendum. Under thundering applause the island's sovereignty is thus acknowledged. During the congratulation of the UNO delegates, the U.S. delegate jokingly asks if the atoll would like to sign a non-aggression treaty with the United States. While enjoying a work meal with the delegates of France, Great Britain, Russia and the United States, the foursome cannot help but think that these delegates would love to change places with them. As the British delegate confirms: "We envy you!"

But, in their absence, things have changed on the island paradise that will leave Stan, Ollie and the others envied by nobody. The atoll has attracted virtually all of the underworld and is now ruled by a prime minister with his own police force. The friends and Colette are powerless; even their seal has been locked in a cage. Things have also changed around their cabin. Historical monuments have been surrounded by iron barriers, and when the companions try to climb over, they are swiftly arrested. Eventually they are released, but told not to return to their huts from now on. A single room will have to suffice for four people.

Then the police send the friends to the prime minister. He declares that the need for law and order necessitated the changes. During their absence, the men's affairs have been taken care of and a recompensation has been calculated. The fellows obtain a sum of money from the chamberlain, who immediately reclaims the same amount in much the same manner as the dubious notary at the beginning of the plot. They are charged with a fee for using the atoll, and furthermore a dog license fee is imposed on the little dog who will have to wear a tag from now on. Completely disillusioned, Stan, Ollie, Antoine and Olivieri leave the seat of the government to meet Colette near the exit. Her fate has been even worse than theirs. They sit down on the lawn of the government building. But there is a "Keep Off the Grass" -sign, and a policeman chases them away immediately. The five walk to the beach, where lively trade takes place. A man has obtained the fishing concessions and all the associated rights, so that fishing and using the coastal rocks now has to be paid for. Of course, the five do not have any money. No problem; the resourceful businessman readily offers them credit.

Finally they walk to the ship that brought Stan, Ollie, Antoine and Olivieri to the island. In memory of this historic event, the new government has restored it. The five friends hope to find at least a little bit of peace here. They find an edition of *Robinson Crusoe*, from which Ollie reads how Robinson escaped from his island on a boat. This is the solution! The next day the men launch their ship with Colette, the little dog, and the seal on board. They are ready to sail out onto the endless ocean — but poor Stan is unexpectedly pulled back to the shore by a rope leaving him separated from his friends.

In the end, Klorer, Kohner, Tellini and Wheeler's new treatment did approximate the structure of the later film *Atoll K*. With their forces united, they prevented the film from being loaded with excessive political ideas, as Tellini had proposed. None of the states that are striving to obtain the uranium-rich atoll is named, nor does the Soviet navy appear to confront the Western nations in the struggle for the possession of the island. The treatment shows other progress. Stan and Ollie's arrival on the atoll is now far more plausible. It is not left to the reader's imagination as it was in the outline, nor does it rely on a *Wizard of Oz* type of thunderstorm to bring the friends to an island thousands of kilometers away, much like Dorothy's whirlwind from Kansas to the magic land of Oz. But the connection between the authors' idea of greed throughout history, down to Stan and Ollie in the notary office where Stan has to struggle for his share of his inheritance, seems to be weak at best.[21]

The new treatment did establish three more main characters in addition to Stan and Ollie. Antoine has taken the role of the "great unknown" from the first treatment, grounding the concept in reality. The three new characters, Antoine, Olivieri and Colette, influence the plot and draw focus away from the two comedians. The five inhabitants of the atoll also have two pets, a little dog and a seal. At least the presence of the dog is justified by the dog fee imposed upon Stan and Ollie's return.

At first glance the idea of making stateless Antoine a key character seems original: a man who is not allowed to enter any country without a passport is to be the key figure in determining the political affiliation the atoll. Antoine's conflict suspiciously resembles the problems of B. Traven's main character Gerard Gale in the classic adventure novel *Das Totenschiff* (*The Death Ship*) from 1926. The book had been a huge success first in Germany and then, in translations, in many other territories including France, Italy and the United States until 1950. Consequently all four authors may have known Traven's novel.[22]

The newly constructed plot, however, had difficulty accommodating the character of Colette. While we learn about Colette's past as a prostitute, her dramatic function as a modern Snow White creating conflicts among the inhabitants is lost once the constitution of the island has been decided upon. Nor does the second treatment elaborate on her transformation from a whore into a fully responsible young maid. In the end, she merely sails away from the atoll with the others.

The implications of the political affiliation of the atoll have now been tightened. Yet they are somehow less funny than they were in the first treatment with its political potshots. An entirely new aspect is the invasion of soldiers of fortune. However, this notion only creates further confusion: Why are Stan, Ollie, Antoine and Olivieri, as founders of the island paradise, excluded from every political decision during their stay on the UNO delegation's ship, returning to find a new constitution, a new organization and a new police force? Obviously the temporary government already had a prime minister on hand just in case. The new situation has nothing to do with the original constitution of the island, which everyone envied. Consequently, the film ending is nothing more than a makeshift solution. Where do the friends go from here? Back into the "good old world"? And will Stan have to remain in the hellish society the atoll has become?

Comparing this treatment to any short from Laurel and Hardy's golden years reveals that the two comedians only need a minimum of plot in order to launch a myriad of gags. Viewing two-reelers such as *Angora Love* (1929), *Big Business* (1929), *Helpmates* (1932), and *Busy Bodies* (1933) would have not only been fun for the scriptwriters, but highly instructive as well.

When Eger presented the treatment to the Centre National de la Cinématographie on June 27, 1950, he promised that scenes with the navy had been omitted from this version and that the overall approach had been "enriched with gags by specialized authors."[23] These "gags by specialized authors," though, are the problem. Certainly there are some gags in the treatment — the cutthroat notary with his threadbare excuses for fees and taxes; the captain of the S.S. *All Will Be Good* setting up Stan and Ollie with Antoine; even Ollie's oversized pants turned into a sail. Where the treatment fails considerably is in tailoring the subject matter into a suitable Laurel-and-Hardy vehicle, leaving precious little room for the duo's brand of humor. It is symptomatic that the treatment only once suggests a "classic Laurel and Hardy scene," the scene where Stan is to cut Ollie's hair to impress Colette.

In the end, the new treatment missed the basis of a solid comedy and failed to grasp the type of humor unique to the duo. Klorer and Kohner might have been aware of the deficiency of this particular script, which ended up useless. It provided not only a sleepless night for Klorer and Kohner, but also for Laurel once he had finished reading it. According to Kohner's report, Laurel had bloodshot eyes after reading the treatment and made no effort to hide his disappointment and anger: "Is this what you did all these months, boys? Did you really expect us to accept this rubbish?"

In vain, Klorer and Kohner tried to convince the two comedians that they had something entirely new and special in their hands. As a result of this devastating situation Kohner finally bowed out from the project. The remaining writer, Klorer, again tried to convince Laurel of the treatment's sparkling ideas and stayed a few more days in Paris, but to no avail. Soon, he followed Kohner back to the United States as well.[24]

Now Pandora's box was open. Something radical had to happen to remedy this dilemma. In his memoirs, Kohner not only complained about what he viewed as an obsolete "Laurel and Hardy style," but further relates that countless sheets of paper full of good ideas were discarded, only to have "an old buddy of the clowns from Hollywood's silent era" sent to Paris to help create, "a mixture of all the old cliches overnight to make them feel at home," according to the motto "if it worked 99 times, why should it not the 100th time." This apparently referred to Monty Collins (more on him later). In his final estimation, Kohner could not resist claiming that, to his mind, *Atoll K*'s failure was entirely the fault of Laurel and Hardy.[25] This ignores that this second, anemic treatment tendered to Laurel would have spelled the end of the project. Was Kohner's statement from decades later nothing more than the bitter view of an insulted, rejected author?

Speaking of "an old buddy of the clowns from the silent era of Hollywood," Kohner not only alluded to Tim Whelan, who had been considered as director, but also to Monty Collins. Monty Collins's experience in American slapstick went back to the silent era. Either as supporting actor or as writer, Collins had contributed to more than hundred films. He played an extra in Laurel and Hardy's early silent short *45 Minutes from Hollywood* (1926), but also roles in later sound shorts of important comedians such as Charley Chase, Buster Keaton and Harry Langdon.[26] Collins and Whelan were indeed won over to work on the script and traveled to France to start their collaboration.

This change of events made one thing obvious: the script was nowhere near being ready for shooting, and commencing production in mid–June 1950 as originally planned was out of the question. Furthermore, there still was no cast for *Atoll K*. Much like Laurel on his arrival, both Laurel and Hardy found themselves with several weeks of time to kill until a script was ready to begin shooting. After witnessing Laurel and Hardy's enormous popularity in France, it was an obvious choice for the French-Italian production to send the duo on a goodwill tour through Italy, capitalizing on their popularity there to promote the yet-unfinished film.

Laurel and Hardy's Italian trip began on June 22, 1950, via Ventimiglia[27] with a first stopover in San Remo. On June 23, they attended a repremiere of the Italian-dubbed feature *Fra Diavolo* (1933), actually set in Italy, in Genoa, where their presence caused traffic chaos. The following day they stayed at Milan's Hotel Dei Cavalieri.[28] In that city, they gave a press conference before heading for yet another screening of *Fra Diavolo*. The film had a tremendous (and obvious) significance in Italy for the duo, resulting in their Italian nicknames Stanlio and Ollio.

After the Milan stopover, Laurel and Hardy continued to Rome on June 25, where they stayed in the Grand Hotel.[29] Cheering crowds greeted them at the Stazione Termini, the new train station of the Eternal City. In fact, Laurel was hoisted, and people begged the duo for autographs. Most importantly, it was there that they met their Italian *Atoll K* producer, Salvo d'Angelo, on June 26, during a private party of the Universalia at the Casina Valadier.[30] Laurel and Hardy were also guests on two radio programs.[31] The attention of the Italian public surpassed all expectations. At least this Eger and d'Angelo had anticipated correctly.

Even after their return to Paris at the end of June[32] Laurel and Hardy had no choice but to make the best out of the unsatisfying situation and at least have some fun in Paris. At the beginning of July they attended La Grande Nuit de Paris, an entertaining event whose organizers and participants had greeted Hardy upon his arrival at the Paris train station Gare du Nord. Here they enjoyed meeting the crowd who had assembled for an open-air event among the countless stands and stages between the Palais de Chaillot and the Eiffel Tower. All in all the event attracted 250,000 visitors who consumed ten thousands of liters of various beverages as well as tons of sweets and other food.[33]

But now, time was getting tight and shooting needed to start in the harbor of Marseilles, even though the script and casting still remained unfinished. On July 16, Laurel and Hardy

Laurel and Hardy's arrival at Rome's Stazione Termini, June 25, 1950. Walter Chiari, who was envisioned to contribute to *Atoll K*, appears between Hardy and his wife Lucille (author's collection).

traveled to the Côte d'Azur[34] to participate a script meeting with Collins and Whelan to move matters ahead. Afterward, they returned to Paris. As shooting was to begin soon, they left again on August 5 and traveled to Marseilles by train from Gare de Lyon,[35] to arrive in the morning of August 6, 1950 at the train station Gare Saint-Charles[36] to stay in the Hôtel Bristol in the local main street Canebière.[37] Then, in the middle of the month they continued to the Côte d'Azur again.

Laurel and Hardy's arrival in Marseilles was marred by a minor mishap: They had lost their luggage tickets. Within the day, and thanks to the help of identification papers and letters Hardy succeeded in recovering the luggage for himself, his partner and the wives. By that evening the misadventure was forgotten, and the two posed in front of the camera as chefs preparing spiny lobster.[38] In the hotel bar they were honored by the director of the Bristol, who handed over masks of caricatured likenesses of the duo.[39]

As in every other destination in France, Laurel and Hardy had numerous admirers in Marseilles. An eager press reported on the tremendous appreciation for the master comedians[40]:

Day and night hundreds of Laurel and Hardy enthusiasts beleaguer the surroundings of the Hôtel Bristol to obtain an autograph and a picture of Laurel and Hardy. Even in the morning the crowd intoned the comedians' theme song under the hotel windows and chanted: "Out on the balcony!," until Laurel and Hardy finally showed up, whether they were rested or torn out of sleep. Each time they left their hotel on foot or wanted to drive away in a car, fifteen policemen on bike or motor-

Laurel and Hardy meet their Italian producer Salvo d'Angelo during Universalia festivity at the Roman Casina Valadier, June 26, 1950 (courtesy Bram Reijnhoudt).

bike protected Laurel and Hardy against all-too-intrusive demonstrations of affection of the admirers. But the two comedians took also care themselves that souvenir hunters could not just snatch their wristwatches, writing pens, rings, jacket kerchiefs, glasses, and similar things in the turmoil, when they dared to go out in the streets to be pushed around by the people.

In one case Laurel and Hardy just made it into a taxicab. According to the relieved Hardy, "This crowd was dangerous."[41]

What remained was the people's enthusiasm, proving that the two artists were far from forgotten but still the great stars they had been in 1945 when they made their last movie. Why would this not be a good omen for Laurel and Hardy's *Atoll K* and feed the hope for a script suitable for a true Laurel and Hardy film?

3

On the Way to Shooting

While Bourvil, or Fernandel and Totò, or Rellys and Erminio Macario, respectively, were under consideration as Laurel and Hardy's partners, it was ultimately the French comedian Max Elloy who was hired for the part of stateless Antoine. Following his debut in 1942, Elloy had gained movie experience typically in supporting parts. However, for the role of Olivieri Coppini, Rellys was still discussed. While Rellys remained in contention it was reported that Chiari already had been hired.[1]

At least Tellini's and Wheeler's work on the script moved ahead following Klorer and Kohner's goodbye. In addition to Laurel and Hardy and their atoll confederates Antoine and Olivieri, they expanded the fifth part of Colette Marly into a female lead. Famous actress Simone Simon seemed to correspond perfectly to the character. However, producer Eger preferred Suzy Delair, at that time a popular chanson singer, dancer and actress in France. Her songs were favored as records as well as in the form of sheet music. She had already made the blockbuster *Quai des orfèvres* (*Jenny Lamour*; Henri-Georges Clouzot, 1947) in addition to *Patte Blanche* (Jean Grémillon, 1948). And, of course, her talents as chanson singer and dancer were very familiar, most recently from her film *Lady Paname* (Henri Jeanson, 1950).

1950 Suzy Delair publicity shot (author's collection).

In the end, the script was even tailored toward the actress,[2] resulting in the part of Chérie Lamour, a woman notably different from the original Colette. Whether Cherie's surname was inspired by Suzy Delair's successful part of Jenny Lamour in *Quai des orfèvres* must remain speculation.

When Eger approached her and disclosed to her that Laurel and Hardy were to be the stars of *Atoll K*, she was less than enthusiastic: "I was not too thrilled with the planned plot and wondered what I could contribute to a Laurel and Hardy film.

1950 French poster art for *Lady Paname* (author's collection).

Consequently, for the time being I declined Eger's offer." But Eger did not give up. Both he as well as director Joannon had their minds set on Suzy Delair for the main part. Joannon told her: "If not you then nobody can play a role like this!"[3] At this time Suzy Delair was friends with film journalism expert Georges Cravenne, the initiator of the French movie award *César* (comparable to the American Oscar). So Eger approached Cravenne in order to win Suzy Delair for the project *Atoll K*. And indeed, Cravenne finally succeeded in convincing her that it would be very advantageous for her to appear with two representatives of the American cinema as famous as Laurel and Hardy. In addition to that, Eger did offer Suzy Delair a salary in line with her expectations. She agreed and signed the contract with Eger who further hired Cravenne for the marketing of *Atoll K*.[4]

Suzy Delair's commitment, though, was under the condition of being able to influence part of the production. This demand was met to large extent. Suzy Delair requested Jacques Fath to design her wardrobe as well her hats. Fath was a famous French couturier who had been in business since 1947. Together with Pierre Balmain and Christian Dior, Fath was a member of the fashion triumvirate Chambre Syndicale de la Haute Couture. In his Paris salon, later notables such as Hubert Givenchy and Guy Laroche received finishing touches. Fath was also familiar with the movie business and had already worked with Suzy Delair on the film *Quai des orfèvres*. She particularly liked his creation of extravagant large hats, one of which is prominently on display in *Atoll K*.

Furthermore, she demanded her own hairdresser as well as a make-up artist at her dis-

Laurel and Hardy with Suzy Delair at the Paris restaurant La Tour D'Argent, July 1950 (author's collection).

posal. However, Suzy Delair's influence extended beyond taking care of her own visual appearance in the film. It is to her credit that *Atoll K* received an excellent musical setting, because it was her, who campaigned for a composer and lyricist who were familiar with her and had musically supported her in a few films until the beginning of the 1950s: "Since chansons mean a lot to me I desired to sing in *Atoll K* as well. As composer I suggested Paul Misraki, whom I personally appreciated very much. As author of the lyrics I could well imagine André Hornez who had already written texts for my successful chansons in *Quai des orfèvres, Avec son tra la la* and *Danse avec moi. Quai des orfèvres* had been produced by Eger together with Van Loo."

It was an excellent choice. Misraki's artistic career spanned from 1931 to 1993, and his work included musical scores for *Le Doulos* (*The Finger Man*; Jean-Pierre Melville, 1962) and *Alphaville, une étrange aventure de Lemmy Caution* (*A Strange Case of Lemmy Caution*; Jean-Luc Godard, 1965). The chansons *Laissez-moi faire* and *Tu n' peux pas t'figurer*, which Misraki and Hornez wrote for Suzy Delair to perform in *Atoll K,* turned into international successes far beyond the film, and even sheet music for them was available in 1951.

Top: 1947 record with Suzy Delair's songs *Avec son tra la la* and *Danse avec Moi* from the movie *Quai des orfèvres* (author's collection). *Bottom*: Max Elloy, Suzy Delair, Laurel and Hardy, and director Léo Joannon in Paris, July 1950 (author's collection).

Last but not least, Suzy Delair asked that her friend Isabelle Kloucowsky be hired as an on-set interpreter to facilitate communicate with Laurel and Hardy. Isabelle Kloucowsky, who was able to speak English, had experience in writing dubbing dialogue, translating foreign film dialogue into French. In this function she was well known in Europe, as well in the United States. Furthermore, she successfully ran an actors' agency in Paris. In the end, Isabelle Kloucowsky wrote the French dialogue, together with Eger's brother Jean-Claude, and participated in writing the English dialogue. She also provided artistic and technical advice to the production.

It is also worth mentioning that Suzy Delair was especially fond of the Cap Roux on which an essential part of the shooting was to take place. At that time it was for sale at one million old Francs [which today corresponds to about $106,000 U.S.], but she decided not to acquire it.[5]

Thus, the casting of the expanded female lead was all set, when Suzy Delair, Elloy and Laurel and Hardy staged a scene at the Paris train station Gare de Lyon for press photographers on August 5, 1950—Delair, Elloy and Laurel labored to push heavyset Hardy into the train, before heading down south.[6] At this time, it was still undecided who the Italian actor with Laurel and Hardy would be (in place of Totò or others). This was still officially a secret a few days after their arrival in Marseilles.[7] However, the veil was lifted on August 10.

On this day, the newspapers *Le Provençal* and *Le Soir* arranged for the semifinal of an accordion contest in the Marseilles Théâtre Silvain. Two days prior, Laurel and Hardy had agreed to appear as honorary guests of this musical event.[8] When the team greeted the audience, Hardy by saying "Bonsoir" and Laurel with "Ici Laurel," they were in the company of their future *Atoll K* co-stars Max Elloy and Adriano Rimoldi.[9] In other words, just in time for the first week of shooting[10] an actor for the part of Olivieri Coppini, now renamed Giovanni Coppini, had been found. The production contracted Rimoldi, as a comedian was no longer sought to play this role. Thus, for example, Croccolo was rejected, though the future Italian distributor of the movie wanted him.[11] Rimoldi had contributed to more than 40 theatrical feature films from the 1930s on, in Italy and Spain, and thus had established himself in the Italian film market. This completed the multinational team of Suzy Delair, Max Elloy and Adriano Rimoldi as supporting actors of Laurel and Hardy.

It is not known when the other actors had been engaged. However, it seems reasonable to assume that this happened one by one while the final script was finished and it was clear which roles were needed to be cast. And the final script had only just been finished right after Laurel and Hardy's arrival in Marseilles, but had yet to be approved by the French Film Office.

While the production evidenced its desire for quality by choosing Laurel and Hardy as well as Suzy Delair, the technical crew of *Atoll K* was also noteworthy and had been hired one by one following Laurel and Hardy's departure towards Marseilles. It consisted of numerous experts who had been in business for a while and were to have a hand in successful films for a long time to come.

For example, production manager Maurice Hartwig was in charge for the blockbuster *Fanfan le tulipe* (*Fan-fan the Tulip* aka *Soldier of Love*; Christian-Jaque, 1952). The design of the film and the pyrotechnics were the responsibility of René Albouze who evidenced his talents 30 years later in the James Bond movie *Moonraker* (Lewis Gilbert, 1978). He was assisted by Raymond Gabutti and Paul Moreau, whose talents were displayed in the atmospheric *Razzia sur la Chnouf* (*Razzia* aka *Chnouf*; Henri Decoin, 1954–55) and *Le Trou* (*The Hole* aka *Nightwatch*; Jacques Becker, 1960), respectively. In addition to couturier Fath, Jean Zay was the wardrobe supervisor. He later worked on Fred Zinnemann's 1972 *The Day of the Jackal*, as well as on the two lavishly mounted musketeer movies made by Richard Lester from 1973–1974, and the aforementioned *Moonraker*.

Much like Laurel and Hardy, director of photography Armand Thirard had been active in the movie business since 1926 and had just finished a film project prior to *Atoll K*.[12] His exquisite camera work, assisted by his team of cameraman Louis Née, operative cameraman Jean Dicop and second cameraman Robert Florent, is notable in the unforgettable Henri-Georges Clouzot masterpieces *Le Salaire de la Peur* (*The Wages of Fear*, 1953) and *Les*

Max Elloy, Laurel and Suzy Delair pushing Hardy into the train to Marseilles at the Paris train station Gare de Lyon, August 5, 1950 (author's collection).

STAN LAUREL
ET
OLIVER HARDY
SERONT
JEUDI 10 AOUT
AU
THEATRE SILVAIN
pour la demi-finale
DE NOTRE
GRAND CONCOURS D'ACCORDEON
AVEC
RENEE LEBAS

Announcement of Laurel and Hardy's appearance at the Marseilles Théâtre Silvain on August 10, 1950 (author's collection).

Diaboliques (*Diabolique* aka *The Fiends*, 1956). Furthermore, Thirard also directed the photography of Clouzot's *Miquette et sa mère* in 1950. Speaking of photography, the stills of *Atoll K* were taken care of by the respected photographer Henri Moiroud, who was often to be found in Marel Pagnol's Marseilles studio.

Equally experienced in his field was recording director Pierre Calvet, who had worked with famous directors such as Jean Cocteau in *Orphée* (*Orpheus*, 1950), Jacques Becker 1954 in *Ali Baba et les quarante voleurs* (*Ali Baba and the Forty Thieves*), and Alain Resnais in *Hiroshima, mon amour* (*Hiroshima, My Love*, 1959). Editing was taken care of by Raymond Isnardon who much later worked on films such as Louis de Funès' *L'aile ou la cuisse* (*The Wing and the Thigh*; Claude Zidi, 1976). He was assisted by his wife Monique who was to edit films

Director of photography Armand Thirard [with cap, right] and clapper boy on Cap Roux in front of the booth in which Chérie mistakenly knocks down her friends, September 1950 (courtesy Sylvette Baudrot).

such as the animated *Asterix* features of the 1980s and blockbusters like *La cage aux folles II* (Edouard Molinario, 1980).

As production secretary or script girl, the experienced Madeleine Longue was hired, whose task was to control the course of the production, particularly the consistency of set and decor details. This is one of the most important functions of the shooting of a film. To this day it is very uncommon for a film to be shot chronologically as per the script. Rather the scenes are shot by locations, out of sequence. This results in the most economic way of producing, while the film is later assembled to sequence at the editing stage.

Another script girl was contracted as member of the second unit. She was responsible for outdoor shooting as well as special effect and stunt scenes, shot in parallel, since they did not necessitate the presence of the highly paid main stars. The script girl of the second unit

Script girls Madeleine Longue [left] and Sylvette Baudrot on board the freighter *Medex,* harbor of Marseilles, August 9, 1950 (courtesy Sylvette Baudrot).

1951 Laurel and Hardy autograph to Sylvette Baudrot (courtesy Sylvette Baudrot).

was young Sylvette Baudrot, who had signed a contract with producer Eger on July 15, 1950, for an anticipated shooting time of eleven weeks.[13] Following her training she had contributed to four French films as a volunteer (script girl and editing) in 1949, including Cocteau's *Orphée*. In 1950 she first worked as a freelance script girl in the second unit of German director's Ludwig Berger's film *Ballerina*. All this (and *Atoll K*, of course) was only the start of an unparalleled career in the movie business. Most importantly, Sylvette Baudrot contributed to three of the undisputed masterworks of twentieth-century film comedy, features by author-director-actor Jacques Tati, who is often mentioned in the same breath as Chaplin, Keaton, Lloyd, and Laurel and Hardy. The films were *Les vacances de Monsieur Hulot* (*Mr. Hulot's Holiday*; 1953), *Mon oncle* (*My Uncle, Mr. Hulot*; 1958) and *Play Time* (1967).[14] Furthermore, she worked on countless prominent productions by many different directors of world fame, a list that reads like a who's who of the movies: Constantin Costa Gavras, Stanley Donen, Richard Fleischer, William Friedkin, Alfred Hitchcock, Gene Kelly, Henry Koster, Mitchell Leisen, Louis Malle, Vincente Minelli, Edouard Molinario, Jean Negulescu, Gérard Oury, Roman Polanski, Alain Resnais, Alain Robbe-Grillet, George Stevens, Preston Sturges and Richard Thorpe. She was on Costa Gavras's team for most of his political thrillers and script girl for all of Polanski's movies starting with *Le locataire* (*The Tenant*, 1976), as well as a crew member of Alfred Hitchcock's classic *To Catch a Thief* (1954). Due to her wealth of experience, it was only a logical step for her to publish her 1989 reference work *La Script-Girl*. This guide to her profession, an exercise book for students, has seen several updated editions so far.

4

At Last a Script!

Laurel was unquestionably unhappy with the structure of the second treatment. But options were running out and, for that matter, so was time. Meanwhile, Tellini and Wheeler kept working on the script from mid–July 1950, together with Collins, Laurel and Whelan. To save time, further assistance was provided by Joannon, Joffé and Levitte. On August 7, the French trade press reported that after ten weeks of work, Tellini and Wheeler had finished the script with Laurel's assistance.[1]

Contributions to the script by American director John Berry — an alumnus of Orson Welles's famous Mercury Theatre — cannot be substantiated.[2] The political subject matter of *Atoll K* is not necessarily proof of Berry's input. In fact, such overtones were already part of Joannon's two-page *Atoll K* outline. Thus, this claim seems solely based on Berry's critical attitude toward current political conditions in the United States. At the beginning of the 1950s, Berry was considered to be a believer in, and supporter of, communism. This made him a victim of the witch hunt lead by the infamous Senator Joseph McCarthy, which focused on anyone believed to be a communist or even a mere sympathizer. Berry, who had already directed the U.S. productions *Miss Suzie Slagel's* (1946) and *Casbah* (1948), was convinced he had no future in the United States. He fled to France, where he lived and worked for most of the remainder of his life.

Joannon's, Joffé's and Levitte's efforts resulted in a script, bearing their names, running 199 pages and with 697 shots.[3] Yet this was not to be the final version. Following Laurel's rejection, further changes and abridgements were made at lightning speed. The resulting version was called "scénario définitif" ("final script"), consisting of just 186 pages and 691 shots. It was eventually submitted to the Commission d'Agrément et d'Étude des Scénarii of the Centre National de la Cinématographie on August 11, 1950.[4] This brought back people's faith in the production to some degree.

Without actually reporting on the production's challenges, the promotion and news reports on *Atoll K* did reflect the undercurrent of turmoil. Georges Cravenne and Michael Ferry launched the promotion of the film in France. Media presence, from Laurel's arrival in Paris[5] until autumn 1951, was remarkable and unrivalled by any other French movie of the era. Even through lean periods, this succeeded in keeping interest in the production alive. Daily newspapers did not reflect this, however.

In mid–June 1950, coproducer Sirius published its 1950-51 program, including *Atoll K*, singling out Laurel and Hardy's contribution.[6] About one month later, a promotional illustration appeared, depicting a wooden plank and citing Joannon as director.[7] At the end of July, trade paper *La Cinématographie Française*, which represented the interests of the French movie industry, began to beat the drum for the upcoming project on a grand scale. Laurel

First *Atoll K* cover of the trade paper *La Cinématographie Française* no. 1,368, June 17, 1950 (author's collection).

and Hardy appeared on the front cover in much the same manner as Hardy's arrival in Paris, in fashionable, off-camera garb — but with swapped hats. It was further reported that the team had just arrived in the French capital for the shooting of *Atoll K*.[8] In fact, Hardy had arrived about five weeks before, while Laurel had been in France for nearly four months. Readers who kept the April issue as reference might have noticed the latter discrepancy.

Just as Laurel and Hardy were doubled in the Hal Roach era by Ham Kinsey and Cy Slocum, doubles were also needed for the shooting of *Atoll K*. At the end of July 1950, the movie magazine *Cinémonde* showed a photograph of Laurel and Hardy with two powerfully built gentlemen, one of them with Laurel in his arms.[9] The man was Victor Decottignies, a worker from Les Halles, the Paris market, who was chosen to be Hardy's stand-in. Age alone was sufficient reason to hire a double for Laurel in the more physically demanding scenes. This was French actor Julien Maffre from Marseilles.[10]

Hardy's stand-in Victor Decottignies carrying Laurel, July-August 1950 (author's collection).

On August 5, 1950, the trade papers finally reported that shooting of *Atoll K* was to commence on August 7, on the Côte d'Azur in the Anthéor Bay near Cap Roux, just a few miles southwest of Cannes. Suzy Delair's contribution to the upcoming project was also announced. One week later, photos of her and Laurel and Hardy alongside Max Elloy and Joannon were shown, promising the "atomic and funniest film of the century."[11]

But there was an error in these reports: as mentioned before, Laurel and Hardy first went to Marseilles to shoot *Atoll K*'s initial scenes in the local harbor — not the Côte d'Azur as claimed.[12] Indeed, shooting began as announced on August 7, 1950, in the Marseilles harbor.[13]

The final approval to commence shooting, however, was not granted by the Commission d'Agrément et d'Étude des Scénarii for the French Centre National de la Cinématographie, until August 17. Apparently the authority did not receive the script until August 11, and the script was needed to ensure that there was a sufficient working base for *Atoll K*. At the beginning of September 1950, the Comité des Avances a l'Industrie Cinématographique (Committee for Approval of Advance Payments of Movie Production) of the office accorded a total advance of 5.5 million old francs to É.G.É. as well as to Sirius, the distributor. This was approximately half of the loan of nine million old francs which the French state had promised for the production, and which by this time was fully paid out. By today's standards, the nine million old francs in credit would be the equivalent of a bit more than $952,000 U.S. This advance was a reinvestment of the revenue of the 1950 feature *Le 84 prend des vacances*. As previously mentioned, this film was produced by Eger and directed by Joannon, who had coscripted the film with Joffé.[14]

By the time shooting began, additional actors joined the aforementioned cast for scenes in the Marseilles harbor. Olivier Hussenot portrayed Bonnet, captain of the aging Panamanian freighter *Medex*, which Antoine is desperate to leave. Lucien Callamand plays the harbor official who divests Stan and Ollie of the remnants of the inheritance, as fees and taxes for the yacht.[15] Two further actors were contracted as policemen who thwart Antoine and Giovanni in Marseilles. Additional harbor workers from Marseilles were hired to ensure a realistic atmosphere.

At Pier 103, the old freighter *Medex* was already anchored, bearing its actual name in the film.[16] On August 9, 1950, Stan's inherited yacht, the *Momus*, was to arrive in the harbor. The craft's name was taken from the old Greek god of blame, mockery, and criticism,[17] and, according to the earlier treatments and the *scénario définitif*, it was to play a major role in the film. Once shooting in Marseilles was completed, the ship was to be completely disassembled, transported to the Côte d'Azur, and reassembled near Cap Roux.[18] For the four shipmates' misadventures at sea on the *Momus*, a surrogate was built in the Nice studio La Victorine.[19] The indoor studio shots aboard Stan's craft ensured the actors that they would not be exposed to weather conditions and the risks of a storm which would complicate location shooting.

The "final" script differs only slightly from the earlier 199-page version. The authors' plan to introduce the characters by having commentary over suitable caricatures was abandoned. Essentially, only a few bits of dialogue and an extended chase sequence at the end of the film were tightened. These changes will be discussed later.

The 186-page "final" script begins by introducing its main characters, the five future inhabitants of the atoll. First is Chérie Lamour, whose well-proportioned body is especially emphasized by the camera when we first see her. Originally from Paris, Chérie now works as a singer and dancer at the South Seas Nightclub in Tahiti. She flirts with the men in the audience without hesitation. Consequently, an elderly gentlemen's wife furiously chases her

3 - LONG SHOT - PAN & TRAV.
ANOTHER ANGLE - CHERI

We can see more of the
night club. It is Hawaian
style, and the audience
is select. All these types
we pick up as CAMERA PANS
CHERI around the room.

4 - LONG SHOT -

She's singing and pausing
here and there.

5 - DURING CHERI'S SONG CUT TO :
ANGLE RING SIDE TABLE.

An old wolf leers at Cheri's
who's flirting with him. A
hatchel wife comes into shot,
grabs her husband by the arm
and leads him away. CUT BACK TO

6 - CHERI SINGING - TRAVELLING.

During her number Cheri starts
to her table. On the way she
passes the table of Capt. Mike
Dolan, Merchant Marine. She ducks
him under the chin. Dolan smiles.

7 - CLOSE SHOT -

Cheri goes to the next table where
Lt. Jack Fraser sits alone. He doesn't
like Cheri's familiarity with Dolan.

He wears a kind of white marine uni-
form without badges.

Cheri's song will stop right when
she speaks

Shooting script page 2 (English version): deleted start of the film, Chérie flirting in the night club with an elderly gentleman and Captain Dolan in the presence of jealous Lieutenant Jack Frazer (courtesy Sylvette Baudrot).

husband out of the nightclub — shades of the saloon scene at the beginning of *Way Out West* (1937). Not the type to naturally restrain her charms, Chérie moves on to tickle the chin of Captain Mike Dolan, much to the disapproval of his neighbor, Lieutenant Jack Frazer, who has eyes of his own on Chérie. This sends Frazer into a jealous rage, prompting Chérie to ask Dolan when he will set sail. "Friday," he replies.

Cut to the stateless Antoine. For more than seven years, in nearly all the harbors of the world, he has tried to disembark from Captain Bonnet's freighter *Medex*. Unfortunately, this proves impossible: government offices only allow those with passports to enter their countries, not stateless persons without such papers. Antoine joins a bearded passenger who is to declare him his twin brother. Antoine's false beard fails to fool the control officers and quickly falls off. All Antoine can do is hope for success in the next harbor, which happens to be Marseilles.

Next we see Giovanni Coppini, hard at work. He is said to be the best bricklayer in Italy and is just putting the finishing touches on a wonderful wall he is erecting for a wealthy customer. The latter drives up in a big car and, in luxurious attire, announces to Giovanni that he has changed his mind: he prefers a wooden fence, so Giovanni will have to tear down his freshly built wall. Furious, Giovanni packs his things and heads off to try his luck in the big wide world, just like his father and grandfather before him.

Fade in on the Bond Street office of London lawyer Phineas Bramwell. Together with his two partners, attorney Yves Bonnefoy (French for "sincerity") and Pierre Poltroni (Italian for "lazy bones"), he awaits Stan, who has inherited a rich uncle's estate and is ready to accept it in the company of his friend Ollie.

Following handshakes and introductions, Stan helps himself to a slice of toast — and inadvertently butters Ollie's hand. This gag is a variation on a similar scene from Laurel and Hardy's short subject *Twice Two* (1932). In the short, Laurel accidentally butters his own hand instead of a slice of bread, under the acerbic gaze of his wife (who happens to be Ollie's sister). Stan overcomes his error by breaking off some bread and licking butter from his hand. In the *Atoll K* lawyer's office, Stan's embarrassment on realizing his faux pas quickly evaporates. Plucking the pocket square from Bonnefoy's jacket, he wipes off Ollie's hand and then returns the cloth to its proper place.

The two friends want to get down to business. Stan reacts to the three huge piles of money in front of them, saying "It never rains, but it pours." Just so, as they leave the office, the three legal representatives come up with a torrent of excuses to reduce the mountain of money to a molehill. As alleged taxes and fees diminish the inheritance, Stan and Ollie are all the more pleased to learn that Stan's uncle has also left them an island in the South Seas, which happens to be tax-free and comes with a yacht anchored in Marseilles. The boys' eagerness to leave results in a nasty encounter between Ollie's umbrella and the shocked attorneys' tea service.

As scripted, this was a worthy start for a Laurel and Hardy film, reminiscent of the reading of Angus MacLaurel's last will in *Bonnie Scotland* (1935), where hopeful would-be millionaires Stan and Ollie receive a bagpipe and a snuff box.

Meanwhile, Stan and Ollie arrive in Marseilles pushing a cart full of food and supplies for their forthcoming trip to Stan's island. However, the *Momus* turns out not to be the magnificent yacht they have come to expect, but a shabby little dinghy, not unlike the former *Queen of the Seven Seas* Stan and Ollie found themselves aboard in *Saps at Sea* (1940). To make matters worse, harbor fees and taxes on the *Momus* leave the boys bankrupt. An elegant young man in casual sailing attire witnesses Stan and Ollie's efforts to maneuver their heavy cart aboard via a narrow plank. He declines to help, saying that he must lead a sailing regatta that day; making a snappy U-turn he plummets straight into the harbor.

Stan and Ollie decide to conduct a thorough inspection of the *Momus*, unhampered by any actual knowledge of ships. Noticing the fuel gauge, a satisfied Ollie confirms "full tank." Stan startles his friend by involuntarily sounding the foghorn. Below deck, Stan is terrifically frightened by a family of cats who have made the bed frame their home.[20] Ollie inspects the galley and drenches himself in the process. The pair also find an inflatable lifeboat, designed to accommodate four persons. Stan glances at Ollie's heft and voices concern over whether there would be space for him. Ollie is deeply hurt and Stan apologizes profoundly.

Anchored alongside the *Momus* and the *Medex* is a third ship, the S.S. *Albatross*. Two harbor policemen have caught Giovanni in this third attempt of the day to stow away aboard the ship. The harbor workers suggest to the officers that they would be better off nailing Giovanni's shoes to the quay wall.

Back on the deck of the *Momus*, Ollie is using a sextant, explaining to Stan that the instrument charts their current position. Stan looks at a harbor building labeled "32" and declares, "Oh, I can tell you that. We're on pier No. 32." Ollie is immediately insulted: "So you want to show me how to navigate."

Shortly thereafter, Antoine is unloaded from the *Medex* in a monkey cage (a scene suggested as early as the second treatment). The alert harbor patrol puts a stop to his latest attempt. Everywhere he goes — Petrokovak (the former Petrograd?), Nagasaki, Caracas, Sydney, Brooklyn, Thessaloniki — the result is the same: no passport, no boarding; no citizenship, no passport. The policemen shrug their shoulders over the absurdity of Giovanni's and Antoine's situation ... but it is beyond their power.

As in the second treatment, the *Medex* captain (now named Bonnet) decides to foist the stateless Antoine on landlubbers Stan and Ollie as an excellent machinist. The boys are delighted to have a knowledgeable seaman aboard. As Antoine is dropped onto the *Momus*, he hits the ignition switch and sends the tiny ship off on a wild ride into the ocean.

It is not until they hit the high seas that Stan and Ollie realize that Antoine's seafaring skills are the equivalent of their own: nonexistent. As they discuss the ship's course, Antoine announces it is time for lunch. He may not be a sailor, but at least he can cook.

A few days have passed since the departure from Marseilles, and strange things are happening. According to the second treatment, a mysterious hand swiftly and silently pinches food from Stan's plate and even empties his wine glass. Stan filches food from Ollie's plate, believing it was Ollie who pilfered his meal. The accusations soon fly, and during their bickering they realize that the engine has stopped. They take it apart piece by piece; soon the cogs and pipes have plunged to the ocean floor. That is when they realize the fuel tank is empty. They decide to set the sails, and in hoisting the canvas Giovanni falls onto the deck. He has snuck aboard the *Momus* as a stowaway, and is clearly unhappy about being discovered. Stan denies his right to be onboard, but Giovanni energetically replies that even a stowaway has some rights. Learning that Stan and Ollie have dropped the entire engine in the ocean, he complains that of all the ships in the world, he had to pick the one with two such chumps. Stan is rightly insulted. But Giovanni's tirade continues, revealing himself to be the mysterious food thief and complaining about Antoine's boring cuisine, with which he is now all too familiar. Giovanni just cannot understand why Antoine prepares fish without garlic, and has

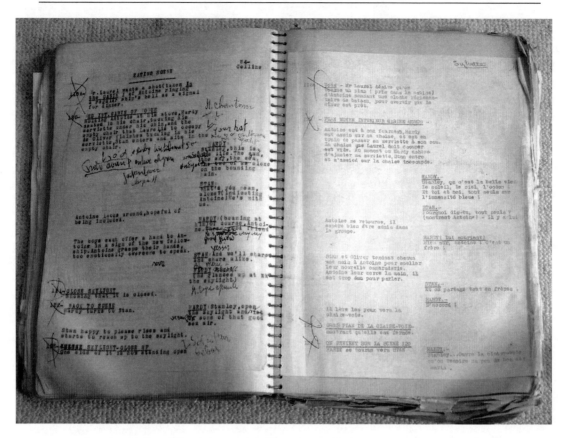

Shooting script of the eating scene (English version) (courtesy Sylvette Baudrot).

not served spaghetti in nine days. So Stan asks Antoine to prepare spaghetti for Giovanni. "But with Bolognese sauce, please!" Giovanni adds emphatically.

After introductions all around, the sails are lifted to set the *Momus* back on course. Unfortunately, the sails go overboard ... and so do Stan and Ollie. This was not the first time a raised sail led to disaster for the boys, if you recall *Towed in a Hole* (1932).

Once the boys are fished out, Giovanni's hotly demanded spaghetti is served and he devours a double portion. Ollie, dressed in pajamas and his admiral's hat, comes on deck seeking his trousers. It turns out that they have been transformed into a sail and, assisted by an umbrella, serve to propel the good ship *Momus* forward.

After the meal, Antoine and Giovanni play a tune on harmonica and ukulele while Stan and Ollie doze on the deck. Eventually the question surfaces: why has Giovanni left Italy? He tells them that he wants to make a fortune far from home, to return to Italy as a rich man, and then build a beautiful house where he can sleep all day, drink wine, and be lazy. Meanwhile, Stan cleans the foghorn, which makes strange noises, honks loudly, and sprays Ollie with water. When the foursome compare their current situation to playing truant, Ollie objects: Stan has never attended school! Ollie dreams of a wonderful life on the inherited island, and the men croon "O Sole Mio." Giovanni accompanies them on his ukulele, then plays a Dixieland version of the same tune.

Eventually, the four realize they need to get their ship going again. Paddling seems to be the only option. Stan and Ollie study their nautical charts. The only instructions they can

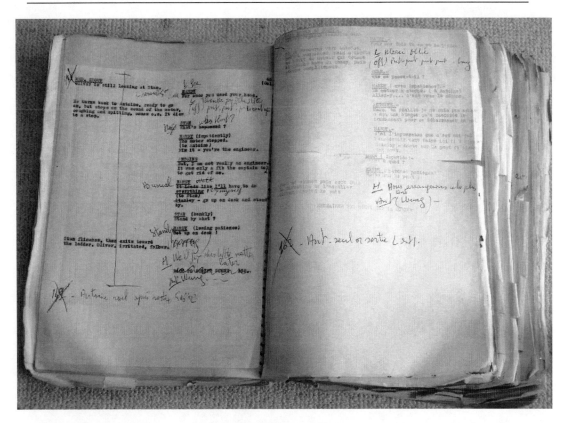

Shooting script of the motor running out of gas during the meal (English version) (courtesy Sylvette Baudrot).

make out are "Up and Down," "Pull" and "Row for Your Life." None of this brings the crew closer to their destination. Ollie states, "It is a mere 1,280 miles more," but Stan replies, "We've been here before."

Food supplies have dwindled to nothing, and the four men are obsessed with food. Ollie hallucinates about endless piles of French fries. Worse, the solidarity among the crew is weakening. The men isolate themselves. Stan and Ollie fret over their hunger, while Antoine and Giovanni's macabre conversation (in French) is more pragmatic. Cannibalism seems like a good idea: Stan points out that Ollie's arm alone would make a full meal. Antoine and Giovanni, in comparison, want to devour all of Mr. Hardy, well aware that he has more to offer than his meager friend. On the other hand, Stan and Ollie agree that the bricklayer Giovanni is too tough, and that Antoine is just too friendly to be eaten. But growing hunger invites reconsideration: "Just imagine Antoine in spicy sauce — could be delicious," Ollie muses.

The four continue to paddle and smile, while still fantasizing over the tastiness of their companions. They break into a song, but a thunderstorm soon squelches their cheerful melody. The *Momus* is rocked back and forth, and darkness overcomes them. An alarmed Stan fetches the inflatable lifeboat from the cabin, but Antoine takes over the job. Not that he is any better — the rubber lifeboat automatically inflates, sweeping all four off the deck.

Fate soon intervenes. The threat of death at sea vanishes as an atoll emerges from the turbulent waters, elevating the ship and wrecking it at the same time. Soon the ocean calms and the sun reappears, shining down on the four sailors who find themselves beached among

~ 62 ~

ANTOINE
Maybe you're right. Be careful they're looking at us

214 - MED SHOT - LAUREL AND HARDY -
NAT. LOC. or TWILIGHT LOC.

(taken towards bow)
As they lean on their ears
sudying the other two.

HARDY (whispers)
I wonder what they'd say if
they knew we are talking
about.

LAUREL
Have you picked out which
one, Ollie.

HARDY (giving it thought)
I'm afraid Giovanni would
be too tough — you know how
bricklayers are.

LAUREL
I never ate a bricklayer
before.

HARDY
It'll be better if we
chose Antoine.

LAUREL (sympathetically)
Oh — and he's such a nice
fellow. I've gotten to like
him a lot.

HARDY
You'll get to like him bet-
te r if he was covered with
gravy ... and smothered with
onions.

Laurel comes up with a blank
grin.

215 - CLOSE SHOT - NAT. LOC. or
TWILIGHT -(taken towards the
stern)
Laurel and Hardy smile affably
and they bow to the other two
accross the boat.

Shooting script page 62 (English version): Stan and Ollie's deleted cannibalistic thoughts (courtesy Sylvette Baudrot).

fresh fish, lobsters and squid — the ingredients for a fine bouillabaisse. Antoine savors the moment: "The first time on land in seven years. I'll never leave again." Giovanni, however, does not want to be a stowaway anymore. Certainly not on a wreck beneath his dignity.

Joining forces (and wood and paper), Stan, Ollie and Giovanni light a fire while Antoine begins cooking. The delicious meal satisfies everyone, and Ollie begins to read aloud from the famous novel, *Robinson Crusoe*. A title card explains: "Thus, Oliver Crusoe found his fellows Friday, Saturday and Sunday. All engage in organizing the new life on the atoll." Work is hard, and soon their clothes are tattered and their footwear mere rags.

Farming the atoll is not made any easier by the thieving seagulls that steal their seeds. Stan and Ollie make advances in an irrigation system, though; a makeshift waterwheel that Ollie has engineered from needles and thread transports water into a canal dug by Stan. Ollie has also invented (and extensively self-tested) a back-scratching device. Construction has also progressed, albeit with little help from Ollie. When Stan and Antoine load stones onto a platform, they wake Ollie from a nap. He climbs onto the platform to help, which promptly topples. Antoine goes back to what he does best — catching fish and grilling them on a driftwood fire.

After years of hard work, two buildings, a house, and the Café Crusoe grace the atoll, next to the wreck of the *Momus*. The ship's oven has been salvaged, and Antoine's café is the heart of the all-male island community. When Giovanni wants to shave, Antoine chops herbs with the razorblade, telling Giovanni to wait until after they have eaten. Stan and Ollie are surrounded by their usual chaos: when Stan tries to mend Ollie's tattered trousers with Ollie still in them (sparing him the embarrassment of disrobing, similar to a gag photograph from the period they shot *Hollywood Party* [1934]), Ollie's derrière gets pinched.

Following a meal at Café Crusoe, Ollie uses his fork and knife to fix their broken radio. Stan has doubts about Ollie's success. After all, Ollie has made several attempts over the past years with the same result: failure. "Rome wasn't built in a day," counters Ollie. Antoine, enjoying a coffee break, muses about how much he would miss the atoll if they were ever rescued. Everyone agrees that life without money is better, a belief that is quickly reinforced. Ollie throws the radio onto a table in frustration; the jolt is just the fix it needs. News of the world floods in over the airwaves. In their nine years on the atoll, the civilized world has gone to hell. News is heard of a heatwave in Madrid, ten casualties due to a blizzard in Boston, income-tax increases in London, 570 stateless men interned in New York, homeless people sheltered in Parisian subways, and a 10 percent increase in food prices worldwide. "And this is the world we've left behind," the men declare, concluding, "World — stay away from our door!"

Once again merciless fate works against the island dwellers. A ship drifts nearby, and the shrewish wife of Captain Mike Dolan is agitatedly pacing the deck of her husband's freighter, scanning the horizon through binoculars. The cause of her agitation is Chérie Lamour, whom Dolan took on board in Tahiti. Chérie lounges in lingerie in her cabin below deck, leisurely perusing a journal and occasionally sipping on a highball. According to the script, Chérie had entered Tahiti with her band and turned out to be a "luscious dish of cherries." The script compares Chérie to the morally questionable barmaid Miss Sadie Thompson, made famous by William Somerset Maugham in his short story of the same name, who ends up entertaining the soldiers of a South Seas marine camp. Mrs. Dolan, whom the script expressively characterizes as "unfeminine," drives Chérie out of her cabin with a plan to abandon her on an island she has spotted through her binoculars. While dressing, Chérie provocatively drapes her stockings over the barrel of Mrs. Dolan's rifle. Obviously, Mrs. Dolan is cut from the same cloth as the many shotgun-toting women Laurel and Hardy have encountered before in films such as *Blotto* (1930), *Be Big* (1931) and *Sons of the Desert* (1933). The brusque Mrs. Dolan dismisses the protests of her husband, since she has observed buildings on the island. She also dismisses her husband's objections that Lieutenant Frazer might resort to murder if he ever finds out what happened to Chérie. At least Captain Dolan will ferry the girl to the island — a suggestion that Mrs. Dolan rejects.

Naturally, Chérie lands on the very same atoll that is home to Ollie, Stan, Antoine and Giovanni (aka Oliver Crusoe, Friday, Saturday and Sunday). As they introduce themselves, Stan points out that they have been on the atoll for three years, four months, seven days and three hours (contradicting the nine years mentioned when the radio was repaired).

With dinner done, Chérie retires to the Café Crusoe while the men stay back in Stan and Ollie's bungalow. Together they vow never to allow a woman to come between them. Then Giovanni is assigned to build a new home for Chérie as quickly as possible, so that the four men will not be forced to share Stan and Ollie's double bed. Once Stan has extinguished the candle, the bed collapses under the weight of the four men and Stan's pet lobster Oscar (whom the script mentions for the first time in this scene).

The next morning, the men dress up to impress Chérie. Antoine shaves, while Giovanni presses his trousers between hot stones. Meanwhile, Ollie allows Stan to give him a haircut using a pot that fits neatly over his head. Slowly realizing why his friends are primping themselves, Stan asks for a haircut like Ollie's. Antoine informs them that Chérie has invited them for breakfast. Hoping that Chérie will serve something other than bouillabaisse (their mainstay for years), they find the lady waiting for them with fresh buns to accompany her freshly prepared bouillabaisse. The men have no option but to feign enthusiasm: "We love that soup!" One of its ingredients is lobster; whether Oscar found his way into the broth is unclear.

Later, when the five inhabitants do their laundry, a photo of jealous Jack Frazer from the South Seas Nightclub falls out of Chérie's blouse. The men cannot help but notice. Chérie demonstrates her gratitude for the men's hospitality by crafting them simple wicker hats. When Antoine and Giovanni insist on returning to their home in the Café Crusoe, Chérie understands — after all, she knows from experience what it means to be thrown out.

Giovanni has finally put the finishing touches on Chérie's new home, and everyone gathers to see it. The four men had tried to fool Chérie into thinking that Giovanni had built a new warehouse, but Chérie had already seen through their ruse and begun to sew a new set of curtains. During the housewarming, Chérie begins to sing *The Best Things in Life Are Free*, accompanied by Giovanni on harmonica while the men sing the chorus. Grateful once again, Chérie gives each man a peck on the cheek.

Suddenly, if not quite believably, Frazer enters their idyll, inquiring whether they are playing Snow White and the Seven Dwarves. Chérie introduces her comrades as Oliver Crusoe, Friday, Saturday and Sunday — and herself as Monday. Stan misunderstands, thinking Chérie is telling Frazer she landed on a Monday, when it was actually on a Wednesday. Chérie corrects him: it was Thursday. The focus now turns to Chérie and Frazer, who dismisses Chérie's accusation that he followed her to the island. He is here on a mission: to explore uncharted islands (this means Frazer has now taken the role of the second treatment's nameless surveyor). He tells Chérie to pack her things and come with him, but she refuses. One of Frazer's men bounds into the room, excitedly reporting on an enormous find of uranium revealed by the Geiger counter. The remainder of the scene corresponds to the second treatment, with Antoine being pushed forward as the first one to set foot on the atoll, meaning

Frazer will have to leave the decision to a higher authority. Stan mistakes Frazer's reference to the Hague Convention, confusing it with a scotch called "Haig." Giovanni asks if the atoll will inherit any economic crisis suffered by the mother country. Frazer confirms.

The news of the uranium discovery creates turmoil in the Washington ministerial office that must decide on the future nationality of the atoll. An important official hands over a folder labeled "International Commission for Geodetic Research, Matter 2860, Atoll K" to the journalists who have assembled for a press conference. Soon, reports are broadcast in every language around the world with the latest updates on the search for the island's nationality. The newscasts are also received by the inhabitants of the atoll, and Chérie suggests they form a government of their own. After clarifying what the citizens would *not* want, Ollie drafts a constitution on the pages of the book *Robinson Crusoe*. The new state of Crusoeland will abolish all things the islanders abhor: passports, prisons, taxes, laws and money. Ollie proposes himself as president, and is promptly elected. Antoine, Chérie and Giovanni are the new ministers, while Stan will be the people of Crusoeland. As "the people," Stan signs the new constitution with a "P," a gag similar to his signing on the registration form at the Mexican hotel in *The Bullfighters* (1945).[21] Moreover, Ollie asks his comrades to swear to do all he orders. Finally, a national flag has to be created. Chérie takes off her knee-length skirt adorned with a ship's pattern. The flag is raised, accompanied by a ceremonial speech by Ollie.

A delegation of high-ranking international officials soon arrive on Crusoeland, along with a pack of journalists. The officials declare that Crusoeland is now recognized as a new, sovereign state, although the chairman of the delegation informs Ollie that it was difficult for the commission to approve such an unusual constitution. Ollie grants a radio interview touting the advantages of the new "utopia," triggering mass immigration to the newfound nation.

In no time ships set sail from Marseilles, a plane takes off from Nice, and a train hurtles toward the utopian destination. Camel drivers, cowboys, skiers from the Swiss Alps, a tandem bike from Naples, a Chinese rickshaw, and a gondola from Venice all leave their homes for Crusoeland. Stan and Ollie are tidying up their bedroom when a piper, an Eskimo, an Indian and then a bicyclist wearing a striped tricot all pass their bungalow. Stan, Ollie, Antoine, Giovannie and Chérie helplessly watch people flood the atoll, while settlements sprout like mushrooms, all boasting such Western necessities as Coca-Cola and hot dogs. The original five inhabitants decide to transform Café Crusoe into a big saloon.

Upon the café's reopening, Ollie pronounces himself the father of all the happy people now living on Crusoeland. Stan is confused: "My father, too? And what about Mother?" Unfortunately, Ollie's moment in the sun does not last long. A young man asks for a drink and is granted a free bottle of whiskey by Stan and Ollie. This is too much for Rub Out Raymond, a thug who has come to Crusoeland to sell liquor. The fact that this activity is against the constitution does not concern him — he just wants his money. At that moment, another new arrival enters the saloon: Alecto the Cossack. He demands that Stan hand over another bottle of whiskey, taking his pick by shooting all the other bottles on the shelf. When Ollie informs him that he will have to pay the gangster for the whiskey, Alecto stares daggers at Rub Out. Rub Out is already aware of Alecto's vicious reputation, and slinks out of the saloon while remarking that the customer is always right.

But Alecto is not the type to be satisfied with liquor and dispatching undesirables. With one vigorous thump, he knocks Stan onto the ground, and has to be restrained by Antoine and Giovanni. He also decides to claim Chérie for himself. He counters her rejection, "That's not possible!" with a nonchalant, "Why not? This is a free country!" This earns him a slap in the face from Chérie, and Ollie smashes a tray over Alecto's head with such force that it forms a collar around his neck. Stan, Ollie, Antoine and Giovanni drag Alecto outside the Café Crusoe, where Stan gives the rabble-rouser such a strong push that he spins away like a top.

However, Alecto's presence has made an impact. Suddenly, a bunch of Lilliputians enter Café Crusoe to snatch all the furniture for their own home. The government of Crusoeland tries to prevent this, but the atoll's constitution provides for neither laws nor punishment. Even worse, two Greeks show up in bulldozers to steal the café's inventory to stock their own saloon. Stan, Ollie, Antoine, Giovanni and Chérie quickly realize the faith in humankind on which their constitution was built may have been a mistake. After a cabinet meeting, it is decided that law and order will come to Crusoeland. What is more, people will now have to pay taxes. As Ollie posts this proclamation in the middle of the settlement, he puts the tacks in his mouth to free his hands. Anyone familiar with earlier Laurel-and-Hardy classics, particularly *The Finishing Touch* (1928), will foresee the results — he swallows the tacks the moment Stan gives him an appreciative pat on the back.

The plot now takes a turn reminiscent of the British Ealing comedy *Passport to Pimlico* (Henry Cornelius, 1949) which opened in April 1949 in the United Kingdom, and in France on October 26, 1949 under the title *Passeport pour Pimlico*. Between the time that production of *Atoll K* was announced and the first draft was finished, Joannon and the other authors had several months to see the British film.[22] In *Passport to Pimlico*, a World War II dud is found in the tiny London suburb. During efforts to defuse it, some children accidentally trigger the bomb. The resultant explosion reveals papers that suggest the inhabitants of Pimlico are not British, but rather belong to the Duchy of Burgundy. Consequently, they declare their independence from Great Britain. As taxes are outlawed in Pimlico, the place is soon overrun by black marketeers. Eventually, the United Kingdom imposes a total blockade on the suburb; that tactic is undermined by sympathetic Londoners. In the end, Pimlico rejoins the United Kingdom, and its denizens regain their British citizenship, along with the terrible British weather.

Back on Crusoeland, Stan and Ollie survey the seemingly quiet crowd, satisfied that they have regained control. Ollie firmly believes that his firm presidential stance is responsible for the quietude. He puts on his admiral's outfit to walk among the people. He's quickly proven wrong, as Alecto has rallied the crowds against the government. He tears down the proclamation, clobbers Ollie with it, and arrests him. Alecto determines that Stan, Antoine and Giovanni will be hung as soon as possible, after a very short but "fair" trial. Ollie will be executed later. As Alecto's future first lady, Chérie's fate is secure, although she is seen as a traitor by her friends.

Alecto, with malicious delight, tells the doomed men that he prefers his victims to construct their own gallows. But they have been beaten to it, and the trio soon feel the hangman's noose around their necks. While Alecto nails the announcement of the execution onto the scaffold with the butt of his revolver, Chérie surreptitiously spirits away his knife and cuts the bonds of her friends. Alecto checks the gallows, and Chérie "accidentally" releases the scaffold's trap door. Alecto lands with a thud at the feet of Stan, Antoine and Giovanni, who politely help him to his feet and pat the dust from his clothes before returning to their place below the gallows. Chérie distracts Alecto long enough for the threesome to escape, sneaking away to Ollie's bungalow in order to free him. They find Ollie fearing for his life. Antoine jumps onto the Greek guard's foot, and the other guards pursue him. Antoine evades them by zigging and zagging, entering into a relay with Stan until both guards fall exhausted to the ground. Now it is Stan's turn to chase after the Greek, who gives up in no time.

When Stan, Antoine and Giovanni enter the bungalow to free Ollie, he mistakes them for Alecto's henchmen and knocks them out with a hammer. Realizing his mistake, he covers his unconscious friends with a blanket to hide them from Alecto. The Cossack enters, informing Ollie that his time has come. There will be no last meal, as Alecto makes it clear that it would be unnecessary. Ollie is presented with a blindfold; it has peepholes so that Ollie will be forced to face his gleeful executioner.

In the meantime, Chérie has snuck into a radio operator's tent in an effort to contact Frazer. She seductively comments on the man's intelligence. He matter-of-factly responds, "Smart enough not to flirt with Alecto's girlfriend!" She tries another approach: would the operator like to attend the execution? That does the trick, but he goes alone so that Alecto will not spot him and Chérie together. With the operator gone, Chérie reaches Frazer. Still consumed with jealousy, Frazer wastes no time reminding "Snow White" that she does not need him — why does she not ask Dolan for help? Chérie blurts out that she loves him, not Dolan. If he loves her too, he'll have to hurry to help. Unexpectedly, the radio operator returns, convinced that Chérie lured him away to flirt with another man. He scornfully pushes her away from the radio.

The agitated mob is now waiting in front of Ollie's bungalow. Stan, Ollie, Antoine and Giovanni successfully overpower Alecto, and dress him in Ollie's presidential attire, stuffing the outfit with pillows to approximate Ollie's heft. With Ollie in the Cossack's clothes, Alecto-as-Ollie is led to the gallows. Chérie, unaware of the switch, pushes forward to plead mercy for Ollie, promising he will not alter any laws in the future. The mob does not trust Ollie, demanding to see his fearful face. The bogus exchange is revealed, and Alecto regains his place of power, thanking Chérie for her loyal help. He orders the mob to put Stan, Ollie, Antoine and Giovanni on the scaffold, but the friends have managed to escape again, with the angry mob in hot pursuit. Before the mob can catch them they slip into a tent, which they rig to collapse around their pursuers. The foursome tie the mob up in a tidy package, dragging them away with a tractor in a scene similar to *Pack Up Your Troubles* (1932), where World War I soldiers Stan and Ollie capture a German battalion by entangling them in barbed wire.

Chérie returns to the radio operator's tent and begins twisting and turning knobs in a frantic attempt to save her friends. The escapees have snuck into a Mexican shop, and disguised themselves with sombreros and serapes. They are spotted, and seek shelter in a mining depot loaded with explosives. They roll a barrel of explosives downhill toward their pursuers. The barrel leaves a trail of powder that they ignite. Unfortunately, the fire takes a zigzagging course straight back to Stan, Ollie and the other two. They narrowly avoid being blown to bits.

Stan, Ollie, Antoine and Giovanni keep running, using a wooden water conduit as a slide. At the bottom they find more barrels that they roll downhill toward Alecto's henchmen. Finally they enter a brickworks and start hurling bricks at the mob. Antoine ingeniously builds a catapult to fire a huge quantity of bricks in a single blow.

Chérie continues to feign allegiance with Alecto, while doing everything she can to protect her real friends. She wraps up a brick in her scarf and knocks out one of Alecto's thugs; as soon as Alecto turns around she tends to the unconscious man like a nurse.

The friends keep fighting for their lives. They resort to freshly made cement as a weapon;

when Stan comes face to face with Alecto he smashes a handful of concrete into the thug's mug, topping it off with a brick. As Alecto tries to free himself, Ollie, Antoine and Giovanni throw more and more cement at their attackers. Chérie joins her friends but slips on the concrete, leaving an impression of her derrière in the fresh cement, similar to Anita Garvin's pratfall into a pie in *The Battle of the Century* (1927). According to the script there was to be a closeup shot of the impression.

The supply of bricks and cement runs out, so Chérie and her friends have to flee again. They take refuge in a house built near a steep slope. Alecto and his men try to break the door down; when Chérie suddenly opens the door, the surprised mobsters tumble in. The house shifts nearer the slope, and Chérie and her friends take the opportunity to slip out of the house and lock the henchmen inside. Alecto is forced to raise a white flag to avoid plummeting to his death. Alecto pleads to negotiate with president Ollie, but Ollie demands unconditional surrender. Chérie joyfully joins her friends shouting, "Vive la Crusoe!"

The friends celebrate their victory as the defeated Alecto bows to his victor. But Alecto's loyal henchmen seize the opportunity to knock out the friends with bricks. Sinking to the ground, Stan pauses to complain about the unfair attack. Now it is Alecto's turn to parade the men to the scaffold yet again, while Chérie is given the role of reluctant hangman. When Stan asks to be first to walk the last mile, Ollie pushes him aside in typical Hardy fashion: "Wait a minute! The president comes first!" Alecto replaces a sign reading "reserved for one person" with a new one inscribed "reserved for four." The trap door is tested, and the mob anxiously awaits the execution.

At the moment Ollie is about to be hanged, a fierce thunderstorm breaks out, followed by an earthquake. When a tsunami sends the mob shrieking, Antoine remarks that this is the very same sound they heard when the atoll emerged from the ocean years ago. The storm is so forceful that the atoll floods and sinks. Cherie and her friends manage to grab hold of the scaffold and are washed out onto the open sea.

Apparently Chérie's declaration of love has convinced Frazer to come to the rescue. But he becomes desperate when he sees nothing but ocean where the atoll once rose. At last he spots the scaffold bearing the flag of Crusoeland. As Frazer's ship approaches the makeshift lifeboat, Ollie turns to Stan and blurts the expected, "Well, here's another fine mess you've got us into" (with a slightly different phrasing from before, using "fine" instead of "nice" and "got" instead of "gotten"). Nevertheless, we have an apparently happy ending, with Chérie sighing, "At last, the Lieutenant has found us!"

The happy ending does not last long. Frazer and Chérie return to Tahiti to get married, but start arguing in the midst of the ceremony. Back in Italy, Giovanni is resigned to his fate, tearing down the stone wall to build a wooden fence. In yet another port, Antoine once again meets a bearded man and asks him if he has a twin brother, pulling a huge pair of scissors out of his bag. Stan and Ollie, however, stand in line at the tax office to pay "penalty loadings on income tax." Ollie scolds his friend: "You and your heritage!" When the boys are called in, Stan's final words are, "Yes, it has been a terrible night."

Laurel's intense rejection of the second treatment seems to have motivated the writers. Under his supervision the script has been fleshed out with comic moments that allow the team to do what they do best, particularly the scenes at the notary's office, in the harbor, during the meal scenes on the *Momus* and on the atoll. Most important, the new structure allowed Laurel and Hardy to ad lib without being tied to each word and action in the script. The script rejected the unsatisfactory second treatment's finale where Stan, Ollie, Antoine and

Giovanni return from the UNO delegation's ship. It now returned to the ending plotted in Joannon's outline and the first treatment, where the doomed atoll sinks back into the sea.

But the script has grown too complex, threatening to overwhelm both Laurel and Hardy's perfectly timed comedy and the audience's patience. The authors apparently found endless comedy in having Ollie mistaken for Alecto and vice-versa, and countless rescues and escapes. It made for a wild pursuit but, although there are definitely funny moments, the chase consumed far too much time. Even in its slightly shortened version it runs no fewer than 25 pages — one-seventh of the entire revised script.

In comparison, Stan and Ollie's adventures on the inherited and seemingly tax-free island are much too short. Even though the promise of paradise was the reason for the boys' odyssey, the script does nothing with it, missing the comic opportunities the end of the story could have provided. In fact, the scriptwriters take only superficial jabs at the governmental robbery and greedy lawyers who bamboozled Stan and Ollie.

Although the role of Chérie Lamour was better suited to Suzy Delair than that of Colette Marly, the character remains ambiguous. Chérie does not burst into the movie as Colette did, and her character's motivations at the beginning of the film are vague. The viewer may wonder about her morals, thanks to her flirtatious behavior during her nightclub performance, but tickling Dolan during her song may just have been a well-rehearsed part of her act. The reason behind Chérie's complicated mind games with Frazer, asking Dolan to take her onto his ship ruled by the ruthless Mrs. Dolan, does not make total sense. In fact, her relationship with Frazer is unclear for a large part of the film. Only minor hints as the story progresses suggest that Frazer and Chérie will meet a happy ending by the end of the third act. There is a long gap in time between Chérie's introductory performance and her reappearance on Dolan's freighter. And the script still seems to present her as a floozy of dubious moral conduct. Obviously the authors were undecided whether to present her as a vibrant young woman or something worse. Comparing her to Miss Sadie Thompson, as the second treatment did, still paints her as a prostitute.

These insights show how difficult it was to develop the overly complicated plot of the previous efforts. More work was still ahead once the cameras started rolling. Several changes were made, some scenes were never shot, and others that were filmed ended up on the cutting room floor. New scenes were also developed, which altered the plot considerably. Even in the final days of shooting, strenuous efforts were made to improve the consistency of the plot and emphasize the comedy.

5

Shooting Begins in Marseilles

Finally, the actors had a final script in hand, even though the script was not approved by the Commission d'Agrément et d'Étude des Scénarii of the Centre National de la Cinématographie until the first week of shooting in Marseilles was completed. Three versions of the script were prepared: an English script for Laurel and Hardy, French for the French actors, and Italian for the five Italian actors hired, so that *Atoll K* could be designated a French-Italian coproduction. Vittorio Caprioli was cast as greedy lawyer Poltroni, Adriano Rimoldi portrayed Giovanni Coppini, Guglielmo Barnabò was Giovanni's employer who rejected the recently erected stone wall, and Luigi Tosi played Chérie's combative fiancé Lieutenant Jack Frazer. Finally there was an unknown Italian radio speaker who, like Barnabò, spoke just a few words. Scanning the names of the Italian actors and their filmographies, it is obvious that Universalia and Fortezza had not sought out the most prolific or best-known Italian performers. Certainly none could be called stars. Later, a scathing Italian critique of *Atoll K* would state: "The movie is called a Italian one, but there are no more than two Italian extras."[1] Thus French actress Suzy Delair remained the only international star alongside Laurel and Hardy.

Throughout production the cast and crew worked from the English and French scripts. Since the Italian actors spoke their lines in French, the Italian script was used solely as support.[2] With the exception of Laurel and Hardy and the non–French-speaking radio announcers, all other dialogue was recorded in French. Therefore, Fortezza had to dub the movie into Italian for its Italian release. For the English-language version, Bookbinder had to dub the complete film into English — except, of course, for the English speaking radio announcers and the film's stars, Laurel and Hardy.

Strangely, any assumption that the production hired professional interpreters for its trilingual project would be wrong. Why this well-funded international coproduction decided to save money at this crucial point is anybody's guess. Only Suzy Delair demanded she have her friend Isabelle Kloucowsky on the set as her personal interpreter. At least the young French script girl Sylvette Baudrot was also fluent in English and Italian. In the end, she served as proxy interpreter, as well as performing her other tasks — therefore identifying her as the unnamed script girl mentioned in Skretvedt's 1987 book.[3]

Laurel and Hardy were left with their own communication challenges. With the exception of Sylvette Baudrot and Isabelle Kloucowsky, nobody spoke English on the set. Even director Joannon barely understood the language. The two comedians spoke only in their native tongue. Some twenty years earlier while filming phonetic versions of their early talkies, Laurel and Hardy read their foreign language dialogue — including French — from blackboards. Laurel had considerably less feeling for foreign tongues than Hardy, who delivered his lines with enthusiasm and flair. However, Hardy did not learn any more French than his partner during their current stay in France. His French repertoire was limited to just two sentences reflecting his favorite pastimes: good meals and lovely ladies. The first sentence was: "Allons à la jaf" ("Let's have a meal!"), the other one: "Allons à les petites dames" ("Let's go to see the pretty girls!").[4] The latter phrase referred to the famous Parisian nightclubs Casino de Paris and Folies Bergères, which Hardy appreciated for their permissive chorus girls. Sadly for Mr. Hardy, no such shows were found on Cap Roux.

The French crew and actors spoke only French, with the exception of multilingual Sylvette Baudrot. As the Italian actors spoke remarkably good French, often without an accent, they provided fewer complications. Therefore, the few contemporary reports on the chaos created by the polyglot production needs to be reexamined somewhat. Nevertheless, the Italian actors were unable to speak English.

The Italian actors' knowledge of French was of little comfort to Laurel and Hardy. In a letter to her mother written in late August 1950, Hardy's wife Lucille pointed out the difficulties the team confronted. These circumstances made it nearly impossible to come up with fresh ideas during the shoot. The comedians were forced to explain their ideas in detail, at which point they would be translated and discussed in the various languages before any decision was made.[5] Laurel and Hardy also demonstrated to their costars and crew how to complete their scenes in a minimum of takes. According to Lucille Hardy, everyone involved — with the exception of the two stars — thought it impossible to shoot scenes without rehearsal. They simply could not understand that Laurel and Hardy, with nearly 25 years experience together in front of the camera, were accustomed to shooting their scenes in a single take. To everyone's surprise, they succeeded again in *Atoll K*.[6]

According to Sylvette Baudrot, the team's efficient professionalism did not come across as demanding or arrogant. Suzy Delair, too, knew the value of the artists' craft. She fondly remembers the team: "Laurel and Hardy were true gentlemen, very charming. At work they were true professionals in the best sense. I enjoyed having met them and working together with them in *Atoll K*."[7]

From the beginning, director of photography Thirard and his cameramen shot *Atoll K* in black and white, as was common at the time. The use of black and white would not hamper the successful marketing of a film, as proven by the many black-and-white box-office successes of the time, including classics by famed French directors Henri-Georges Clouzot and Christian-Jaque as well as the *Don Camillo and Peppone* series featuring Fernandel.[8]

In Marseilles, Cap Roux and the surrounding area, the script was filmed largely on location. Most of the indoor scenes would be shot later in the Parisian studio, the exception being the scenes onboard the *Momus* which were filmed in the Nice studio La Victorine.

Antoine's scenes in the harbor of Marseilles were shot as scripted, including his conversation with the captain and his attempt to get ashore by posing as the twin brother of a bearded man (he will meet him again at the end of the plot, shaving off the man's beard to disguise himself with it). But Laurel was still unhappy with this version of the script. The basic lack of gags meant that ongoing work on the script was essential. Laurel called in Collins and Whelan, resulting in a continuing series of substantial alterations to the script throughout the shooting. The first scene shot in the harbor shows Antoine being lifted secretly ashore in a monkey cage. But now there was also a new scene with a macabre edge, saved for the end of the movie. Once again Antoine attempts to escape in an animal's cage — this time, however, it is a lion's cage, where Antoine's chewed-up shoes and suspenders indicate his fate. Laurel's dark sense of humor was justified years later when critic and Laurel and Hardy

- 5 -

ANTOINE
We're identical twins,
We only use one passport.

SHIP & WHARF
SHOT & COUNTRY SHOT

13 - CLOSER SHOT

The guard scratches
his head

14 - CLOSE SHOT

Antoine reaches for
his suitcase and the
beard falls off

15 - MEDIUM SHOT

The guard propels

GUARD
Identical twins! Get
back on that boat.

The guard propels
Antoine back up the
gangplank.

16 - CLOSE SHOT

Where the captain
leans on the railing
watching.

17 - CLOSE SHOT - CAPTAIN
& ANTOINE

ANTOINE: What's the next
port, Captain?

CAPTAIN: Marseille.

Shooting script page 5 (English version): Antoine as pseudo-bearded twin [deleted scene] (courtesy Sylvette Baudrot).

aficionado William K. Everson praised this particular scene in his 1967 book *The Films of Laurel and Hardy*.[9] Everson's enthusiasm came at a time when *Atoll K* was widely ignored and nobody thought to examine scenes such as this in detail.

Among the other scenes filmed: Antoine's complaints to the harbor policemen that animals are permitted to go ashore without a passport but not human beings; Giovanni's aborted attempts to board a ship; and the policemen discussing the situation. The scene of the captain of the *Medex* foisting stateless man Antoine on Stan and Ollie, resulting in their wild ride out of the Marseilles harbor, was also shot.

Laurel and Hardy's scenes in Marseilles are among *Atoll K*'s best moments. Their stand-ins Maffre and Decottignies were present for these scenes, although their duties would not really begin in earnest until shooting started on the Côte d'Azur. In their first scene Stan and Ollie are dragging their belongings on a pushcart. Stan already wears his transparent plastic raincoat, disparagingly called a "snakeskin" by Ollie. The pair are eager to set out for the South Sea island onboard the rundown *Momus*— the final vestige of Stan's once-vast inheritance. Special stress was put on Laurel and Hardy's comic presence in this early scene. Having collected the necessary harbor fees and taxes, the harbor official has nearly departed before he overhears Stan's offhand remark, "We are lucky that he did not request taxes on the fee." He returns to collect the money; Ollie generously tips him with their last remaining coin.

They next explore the *Momus*, moored at pier 103 next to the freighter *Medex*. Stan accidentally pushes the starter, enveloping Ollie — who has been examining the engine — in a cloud of exhaust. Stan also gets his foot stuck in a bucket, requiring Ollie to free him, just

Laurel and Hardy at the harbor of Marseilles with their stand-ins Maffre and Decottignies and their wives, August 1950 (author's collection).

as he did so long ago in *Helpmates* (1932). Scenes scripted but not shot included their encounter with the less-than-helpful yachtsman, their attempts to jockey the pushcart across the gangplank, and Ollie's self-assured use of navigation tools.

Replacing the unfilmed scenes were new, simplified gags focused on the pure comic camaraderie of Laurel and Hardy. Ollie instructs Stan to toss the supplies to him on the deck of the boat, using a whistle as a signal (the whistle was to play a prominent role throughout the movie). In typical Laurel-and-Hardy fashion, Stan confuses Ollie's commands. Ollie falls fanny first onto a huge watermelon and Stan, caught up in the rhythm of unloading the supplies, tosses a crate directly onto Ollie's head. Realizing what he has done, Stan boards the *Momus* and brushes off Ollie's behind with a bouquet of vegetable leaves. Ollie is not amused.

Laurel and Hardy's intuitive comic ability definitely benefited the movie. As in their heyday, they ad-libbed impromptu comic ideas not found in the script, but befitting the story's situation. In the end, scene after scene in *Atoll K* proves that Laurel and Hardy had not lost their comedic skills, the ultimate advantage of the entire production.

The further events in the harbor were shot according to script. While in Marseilles, the opportunity was taken to film a ship loaded with emigrants to Crusoeland departing the Marseilles harbor. At the same time a couple of stills of Stan and Ollie inside the *Momus* were

```
54 - ... towards the wharf.

      ... the end of the gangplank
      laying on the wharf.
      Laurel, on land is blown up.

55 - The cart falls down on deck
      and with it all the parapher-
      nalia.

56 - (SAME SHOT THAN N° 50)

      A very elegant man (yacht
      man's cap blue jacquet, white
      pants and white shoes) is
      standing right at the back
      of the ship where the gang-
      plank stood. He is back to the
      wharf, speaking towards inside
      the ship.
```

                                                THE ELEGANT MAN
                                                Of course, of course, but
                                                I can't manage it to day
                                                because I preside over
                                                a yacht race.

```
      In a quick movement he turns
      over and instead of the
      gangplank he falls in the
      water.
```

Shooting script page 17 (English version): an elegant gentleman offers to help Stan and Ollie [deleted scene] (courtesy Sylvette Baudrot).

taken. At least one of these stills shows the boys wearing bowler hats, with Stan in his "snake-skin" and Ollie wearing his opera cape. The striking thing about this still is Stan's physical appearance — he seems to be remarkably healthy, and one wishes that he remained this hale looking throughout the film. If he had, *Atoll K* would likely have avoided the bad reputation it has had to endure.

In Marseilles Laurel's physical condition remained strong. He seemed to have his diabetes under control, and still resembled the familiar — if somewhat older — Stanley. However, ill health would soon take its toll to the point that Laurel became almost unrecognizable. This is evident in the Marseilles scenes onboard the *Momus*. Stan and Ollie descend the deck into the cabin; the scenes below deck were shot months later in the studio. He seems to have aged drastically within a matter of seconds. Reemerging on the deck later, the fresh air seems to rejuvenate him and we suddenly see a much healthier Stanley.

This was the result of shooting *Atoll K* out of sequence, a process Laurel and Hardy avoided when filming their 1930s classics. Years later, Laurel would complain that this process virtually handcuffed him and his partner, severely limiting their comic spontaneity. Laurel cited the shipwreck on Cap Roux as an example. The wreck was shot before the thunderstorm that ultimately landed the ship on the atoll. In Laurel's opinion, this illogical way of working prevented him from getting a feel for what would occur before the already-filmed catastrophe.[10] However, shooting out of sequence had long been the norm even before 1950,

Ollie and a well-looking Stan below the deck of the *Momus*, August 1950 (author's collection).

and Laurel and Hardy's working methods at Roach were the exception to the rule. Shooting all necessary scenes at one location before moving on to the next is obviously a much more economical practice, and the typical moviegoer would never see the process in action. Unfortunately, Laurel's physical deterioration unwittingly reveals this cost-cutting technique.

Upon completion of shooting in Marseilles in mid–August 1950, the cast and crew moved to St. Raphaël, a French resort at the Cote d'Azur, approximately 30 kilometers southwest of Cannes and 130 kilometers northeast of Marseilles. Along the shore, the massive Corniche d'Esterel winds through the bays and rocky outposts of the Liguric Sea toward Cannes. Located between St. Raphaël and Cannes are the coastal site of Agay and the bay of Anthéor, where *Atoll K*'s seaside scenes were to be shot. The atoll itself was to be the tiny red-rock peninsula Cap Roux, connected to the mainland and nearby Cannes by an isthmus. Cap Roux had been leased by the producers for a handsome amount. The hefty fee gave the production access to water, electricity and telephone.[11] The crew built bamboo storage huts on the peninsula, and army tents were pitched to protect cameras and equipment from the summer heat.[12] The stranded wreck of the *Momus* was also erected here. To help disguise Cap Roux as a South Sea island, the area's naturally sparse smattering of palm trees was augmented by artificial trees made of plaster.[13] There was one other location in the surrounding area: Chérie's bungalow on the atoll was actually situated in Valescure, in the northern district of St. Raphaël.

An emaciated Stan during the shooting of the same scene at Billancourt, January–March 1951 (screen capture from *Utopia*).

Cap Roux, August/September 1950 (courtesy Sylvette Baudrot).

While the crew was relegated to the more economic lodgings in St. Raphaël, Laurel and Hardy and their wives stayed in the luxurious Hôtel Excelsior,[14] situated next to the beach with a stunning view of the Mediterranean Sea. Hardy, in particular, was fond of the Excelsior. Being a connoisseur of French white wine, he stocked several crates on the balcony of his suite in the event of a grape shortage.[15]

Location shooting in the area surrounding St. Raphaël and the subsequent work at La Victorine (approximately 30 kilometers northeast from Cannes) was originally scheduled for six weeks, including three days at the studio in Nice.[16] As the total shooting schedule was planned for twelve weeks, with the first week's shooting in Marseilles already completed, work

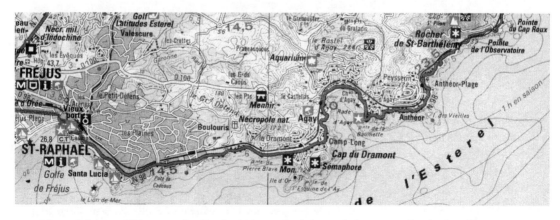

Map of the area Valescure, St. Raphaël, Agay, Anthéor and Cap Roux (author's collection).

at the Paris Studio Cinéma in Billancourt was scheduled for another five weeks commencing October 1950.[17]

Although a roster of supporting actors would be needed throughout the production, only a handful were needed on the Côte d'Azur. Among them were Guglielmo Barnabò as the employer who causes Giovanni to leave Italy, Charles Lemontier as the high U.N. official who approves the sovereignty of Crusoeland, Robert Murzeau as Captain Dolan and Suzet Maïs as his aggressive wife. Other actors were requested for the shooting in Paris: André Randall, Robert Vattier and Vittorio Caprioli as the three avaricious lawyers, Felix Oudart as the registrar of Papeete and Nicolas Amato as the profiteering gangster Rub-Out Raymond. The production hired established character actors throughout who, like all other artists and technicians who contributed to *Atoll K*, were experienced professionals.

One particularly noteworthy addition was Michel (aka Michael) Dalmatoff as the vicious Cossack Aletco, who overthrows Ollie's government and wants to lynch all its members — minus Chérie, of course. Dalmatoff made his debut in Paris with a more significant role as a singer in the famous Johann Strauss operetta *Die Fledermaus* ("The Bat").[18] He also contributed to such Hollywood productions as *For Whom the Bell Tolls* (Sam Wood, 1943), alongside Ingrid Bergmann, and *Shanghai Gesture* (Josef von Sternberg, 1941), starring Gene Tierney. Back in

France he appeared in two American feature films which were partly shot in Paris: *My Daughter Joy* (Gregory Ratoff, 1950), starring Edward G. Robinson, and *Gunmen in the Streets* (Frank Tuttle, Boris Lewin, 1950), featuring Dane Clark and Simone Signoret.[19]

Leading lady Suzy Delair was required only sporadically during the location shoot. As she had no scenes in Marseilles, she didn't start work on the Côte d'Azur until the beginning of September 1950, lodging at the Hôtel du Golfe de St. Raphaël.[20] Shortly after her initial arrival on the set of *Atoll K*, a promotional photo of Suzy Delair, with a considerably shorter hairstyle than she wears in the film, framed by caricatures of Laurel and Hardy was used on the cover of the French trade paper *La Cinématographie Française*.[21]

Despite three different languages being spoken on the

Hardy enjoys a bottle of wine on Cap Roux, September 1950 (author's collection).

set, there was still hope for a smooth production. Although Laurel's unstable health had yet to affect the shoot, the production still faced serious concerns. Chief among them was Laurel and Hardy's disapproval of the crew's raucous partying each night, as reported by Lucille Hardy.[22]

As early as the first week of filming the papers were reporting that director Joannon was facing challenges shooting in the harbor, taking three days to shoot the Laurel-and-Hardy scenes and relying on their stand-ins.[23] Commencing with John McCabe's 1961 Laurel-and-Hardy biography, *Mr. Laurel and Mr. Hardy*, it is almost impossible to find a positive word about Joannon's work on *Atoll K*. Laurel, his wife Ida, and Hardy's widow Lucille criticized Joannon vociferously, claiming he had "zero knowledge of directing and film comedy." Joannon was portrayed as a comic cliché, stomping around the set in pith helmet and puttees, spitting out instructions through a series of megaphones like a would-be Cecil B. de Mille. Laurel was particularly amused by Joannon's use of various-sized megaphones: "Joannon is funnier than the picture — although *that's* not saying a hell of a lot."[24] Furthermore, Joannon preferred to distract himself with activities that did not contribute to the production. For example, he decided to shoot a lake for three days, simply because he found it photogenic. At first Joannon seemed unable to make up his mind whether Cap Roux should be the center of location shooting. During the stay on the Côte d'Azur, the surrounding area of the originally selected Île de Levant was inspected during trips to the seaside venue Le Lavandou — 50 kilometers southwest of St. Raphaël — and the offshore Ligurian isle of Port Cros.[25]

Laurel and Hardy partying with Suzy Delair and Adriano Rimoldi at St. Raphaël, approximately September 1950 (author's collection).

Cover of *La Cinématographie Française* no. 1,380, September 9, 1950: Suzy Delair framed by Laurel and Hardy caricatures; note the spelling of Adriano Rimoldi's last name: "Remoldi" (author's collection).

Laurel and Hardy and director Joannon during the shooting at Marseilles, August 1950 (author's collection).

Simply put, Joannon was an extraordinarily slow-working director. While most directors might average fifteen set-ups per day, Joannon generally completed three or four. On one occasion, when Joannon completed ten, the crew considered it a miracle. Furthermore, Laurel complained that props as simple as a pencil sharpener were not available at the Côte d'Azur, meaning they had to be obtained from Paris, a considerably time-consuming process.[26]

It has been frequently said that U.S. director John Berry, who was once slated as one of *Atoll K*'s screenwriters, codirected the film. Suzy Delair has confirmed this: "John Berry was a highly talented director. He directed an important part of *Atoll K*." Though Berry himself did not refer to *Atoll K* during two exhaustive interviews on his career, and excluded the film from his own filmography,[27] his contribution to *Atoll K* fits the arc of his career after fleeing to France in the early 1950s. He met both Suzy Delair and Isabelle Kloucowsky early in his stay in France, when his grasp of the French language was still uncertain and he could happily rely on Isabelle Kloucowsky as an interpreter.

It is impossible to determine precisely which scenes Berry directed, since daily reports of the production no longer survive. Suzy Delair could not commit to specifics. Sylvette Baudrot did not remember meeting Berry on the set at all. Joannon's second assistant director, Pierre Nivollet, could not remember Berry's name but recalled the following incident: "After Laurel had fallen ill and had to be submitted to the hospital, an American director hired by the American producer of *Atoll K* was to direct the Hardy scenes in the studio. The Italian producer had brought in an Italian director to direct Rimoldi, while Léo Joannon [tried] to work [from] the French script to some degree." Even though Pierre Nivollet refers to an up-to-now unknown Italian director, this confirms how Berry and Joannon shared directorial duties, and is in line with Suzy Delair's recollections. As Sylvette Baudrot worked mainly on location and on non–Laurel-and-Hardy scenes, and most of Suzy Delair's scenes were shot in the studio, it makes sense that Berry's activities were largely focused on the shooting in Billancourt, and perhaps in the editing room. If Berry, according to Pierre Nivollet, worked on scenes with Laurel and Hardy, this represented a pivotal moment in production. Most likely Berry directed the Laurel and Hardy scenes shot in Paris, while Joannon worked on the other scenes. As already mentioned in the introduction, neither John Berry nor Isabelle Kloucowsky could be interviewed for this book. Script girl Madeleine Longue, who was also responsible for shooting

Director Joannon with one of his notorious megaphones; Madeleine Longue on the left. At sea offshore Cap Roux, September 1950 (author's collection).

Joannon [left; at his right: Madeleine Longue] shoots a "lovely" lake, September 1950 (courtesy Sylvette Baudrot).

in the Paris studio, has also passed away. Any documents she may have had seem to have vanished. Therefore, it seems impossible to shed more light on Berry's contribution. However, Nivollet's quote suggests that American producer Bookbinder did indeed hire his countryman Berry for the project.

It also makes sense that Berry's name is nowhere to be found in the credits of any version of *Atoll K*. Bookbinder had always intended an American release of the film; at the time, the political situation in the United States bordered on anticommunist hysteria. To give screen credit to someone like Berry, who had fled the country for France, would have meant instant box-office disaster for *Atoll K*.

Although Pierre Nivollet could not remember the name of the Italian producer, it was not Salvo d'Angelo acting for Universalia, but Gastone Tomassini for Fortezza. Universalia had already ceased production in 1950 for economic reasons; in 1951 the only movies that were sold were those that had already been finished.[28] In fact, according to the 1951 information of the Italian distributing organization Unitalia, Fortezza was named as the producer of *Atoll K* without any mention of Universalia.[29] Consequently, Universalia is neither mentioned in the 1951 Italian distribution documents nor in the credits of most versions of the film. Universalia is only mentioned in the 1952 British distribution information relating to *Robinson Crusoeland*; this refers to the original contract of coproduction without taking into account the changing nature of the Italian production companies.

Joannon's laissez-faire direction, the constant changes to the script, and the multilingual mix-ups on the set were not the only challenges. Both Laurel's and Hardy's health became major issues. Before shooting, Laurel's weight loss brought on by his diabetes, wasn't a cause for concern prior to shooting. However, during shooting at the Côte d'Azur, Laurel suffered debilitating pain and was unable to urinate. His condition deteriorated further as a heatwave engulfed the area of Anthéor, Cap Roux and Valescure.

The unprecedented temperatures not only put the technical equipment at risk, it added undue stress for everyone involved in the filming. While the behind-the-scenes crew could dress for the extreme weather, the actors before the camera were forced to wear costumes better suited for a gentle tropical breeze. When journalist Lise Claris visited the shooting on the Cap Roux set in late August/early September 1950, she reported[30]:

> The camera groans under a black sunshade. One is only waiting for its collapse. The technicians are trying everything to keep their heads protected against the heat using silk scarves, handkerchiefs, police and legionnaire caps. They are wearing shorts, and they are sunburnt like a beach Adonis.
>
> The actors are less lucky having to do their parts in full dress with hat, jacket, striped trousers and bow tie, and without the chance to sit down. The ground is red-hot without the slightest bit of shade. When Oliver Hardy tries to get some protection beneath a meager plaster palm tree, not even his back is covered."

Joannon directs Laurel and Hardy at sea during the scorching heat wave, off Cap Roux, September 1950 (author's collection).

On-location photos document the heat. One shot of particular interest, dated September 3, 1950, shows most of the crew assembled for a group photograph in Valescure, including Laurel and Hardy, their wives, Suzy Delair, Max Elloy, Adriano Rimoldi and Luigi Tosi. It is published here for the first time in its entirety.[31]

Laurel's declining health made the need for a doctor inevitable. According to his widow, Laurel met a doctor as inept as Joannon was as a director. On top of this, Laurel was so alarmed by the disharmony and inconsistencies on the set that he asked his friend and lawyer Ben Shipman to come to France.[32] Either Shipman, witnessing the havoc with his own eyes, decided to call in UK–based director Alfred Goulding to take the reins, or Laurel himself contacted Goulding to accompany Shipman to the Côte d'Azur.[33] Goulding's relationship with Laurel dated back to 1918: it was Goulding who spotted Laurel in vaudeville and recommended him to the Hal Roach Studios. He also directed Laurel and Hardy's successful Roach production *A Chump at Oxford* (1940), and Laurel continued to keep in touch with him over the years. Goulding's longstanding industry expertise made him the perfect candidate to supervise the shooting of *Atoll K,* outlining directorial tasks to Joannon, and his presence brought an extra comfort level to Laurel, in that the two could communicate in English.[34]

As with Berry, Goulding's influence is open to debate. According to the recollections of his widow Betty, her husband had been assigned by Laurel to supervise production. However, with the exception of Laurel and Hardy, Goulding was met with profound resistance from all involved. Joannon, particularly, felt that his authority was being jeopardized by Goulding's presence. It has been said that Goulding's undoing may have been the French labor union which zealously insisted that a French director be employed for a French production.[35] (Berry may have been an exception since he had sought political asylum in France.) This view contradicts other reports that Goulding directed most of the Laurel and Hardy's scenes with Joannon's approval — which, of course, would have been the smartest solution.[36] But it is interesting to note that neither Sylvette Baudrot, Suzy Delair nor Pierre Nivollet could recall seeing Goulding on the set.

Despite Goulding's presence, Laurel's progressive illness caused a devastating delay in the shooting schedule. To keep production at the Côte d'Azur going whenever the weather was agreeable, Laurel decided to step in front of the cameras for as long as his strength held out. A makeshift hospital tent was erected in case he needed medical attention, which happened often. Laurel was unable to perform for more than 20 or 30 minutes at a time, after which he required a lengthy rest. Suzy Delair remembers this problem especially well: "Laurel's illness completely obstructed the smooth work flow. For quite a long time he was not at the Côte d'Azur at all, and when he was on the set he was only able to work for a very short lapse of time. In such a case I sometimes received a call out of the blue to appear on the set as soon as possible."

The delays in shooting did not elude the French movie experts. They were waiting for *Atoll K* and the anticipated box-office results. Therefore, the press had to be continually informed that there was progress on the production; for example, using "a helicopter for spectular effects."[37] Ultimately, the helicopter did not add much to the finished film, but it did bring much needed publicity. One photo presents Suzy Delair operating the pilot's throttle, while Laurel and Hardy posed with airport signals for another promotional still.[38]

To make matters worse, Hardy had health problems of his own. Over the last few years his girth had expanded to a dangerous level. He now weighed approximately 330 pounds, putting enormous stress on his heart and affecting his circulation. Consequently, Hardy

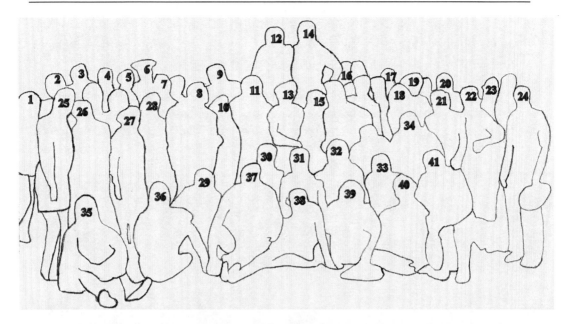

1. Suzet Maïs (Mrs. Dolan); 2. Adriano Rimoldi (Giovanni Coppini); 3. Armand Thirard (director of photography); 4. Guglielmo Barnabò (Giovanni's employer); 5. Louis Née (cameraman); 6. Max Elloy (Antoine); 7. René Daudin (hairdresser); 8. Luigi Tosi (Lieutenant Jack Frazer); 9. Roland Quignon (set designer); 10. Carmen Bresle (make-up); 11. Oliver Hardy (Ollie); 12. Robert Florent (second cameraman); 13. Suzy Delair (Chérie Lamour); 14. Jean Dicop (operative cameraman); 15. ? (wardrobe mistress); 16. Maurice Hartwig (production manager); 17. Paul Joly (executive producer); 18. Sylvette Baudrot (script girl, second unit); 19. Paulette Boréal (set secretary); 20. ? (senior set worker); 21. Lucille Hardy; 22. Ida Laurel; 23. Julien Maffre (Laurel's stand-in); 24. Stan Laurel (Stan); 25. Jean Zay (wardrobe supervisor); 26. ? (garderobiere); 27. ? (make-up); 28. Suzanne Pinoteau (wardrobe mistress); 29. ? (set worker); 30. ? (set worker); 31. ? (set worker); 32. René Touillaud (chief electrician); 33. Maurice Dagonneau (boom operator); 34. Pierre Franchi (first assistant director); 35. Pierre Nivollet (second assistant director); 36. ? (set worker); 37. ? (clapper boy); 38. ? (set worker); 39. Dedé Cretel (transports Tructo S.T.A.B.); 40. Madeleine Longue (script girl); 41. Léo Joannon (director). Not in the photograph: René Albouze (props and pyrotechnical effects), Michael [aka Michel] Dalmatoff (Alecto), Victor Decottignies (Hardy's stand-in), Robert Murzeau (Captain Dolan).

suffered terribly under the heat, contracting cardiac fibrillation which caused a further delay in shooting.

The health of the stars was not the only thing hampering production. Soon after shooting started on Cap Roux, toward the end of August 1950, Adriano Rimoldi suffered an accident that kept him from working for a month. He fell from the wreck of the *Momus*. In a letter dated September 18, 1950, he reported[39]: "At last I am doing better after my accident I suffered approximately a month ago. When we were shooting a scene on the ship on which a great deal of the movie takes place the area I was standing on knuckled down, and I was cast away some three meters. Unfortunately, the ship was not on the water like a good solid vessel, but stood on the rocky shore of the atoll. Fortunately, during the downfall my legs only hit against the ship's side."

Opposite: Actors, crew and guests in Valescure, September 3, 1950. This full photograph is published here for the first time (courtesy Sylvette Baudrot).

The mishaps continued. In preparing a special effect, pyrotechnician René Albouze prematurely ignited a blasting compound aboard the ship *St. Louis*, which in the movie is commanded by Lieutenant Frazer. The vessel was heavily damaged and had to be refurbished.[40]

This series of unfortunate events ultimately threw the schedule into a spiral. The producers attempted to make the best of the delay. According to Suzy Delair, editing started in a Parisian studio while shooting on the Côte d'Azur continued, as there was no cutting room near St. Raphaël.

Suzy Delair in the helicopter on Cap Roux, September 1950 (courtesy Suzy Delair).

Lucille Hardy, Hardy and Sylvette Baudrot on Cap Roux, September 1950 (courtesy Sylvette Baudrot).

Lucille Hardy, Hardy and hairdresser René Daudin during scorching heat on Cap Roux, September 1950 (courtesy Sylvette Baudrot).

Summoning up what little strength he had, Laurel stuck through the shooting on the Côte d'Azur and at the Nice studio La Victorine. By mid–October 1950 it was obvious that the filming scheduled for the Paris studio could not be continued as planned. Though Laurel's condition seemed to have improved slightly, he now contracted a severe colitis and he could not stomach certain regional food.[41] Laurel's weight plummeted from 165 pounds to a mere 114,[42] a dramatic drop which is all too evident in the finished film. In his letter dated December 1, 1950, mailed from Paris to Fred Karno Jr., the son of his former British impresario, Laurel wrote: "I started to get O.K. then developed a bad case of dysentry [sic] which they have been unable to check. Lost a lot of weight [and was] awfully weak."

Finally Laurel had no choice but to commit himself to the American Hospital of Paris for further treatment. Therefore, on October 10, 1950, work on *Atoll K* was discontinued.[43] In the American Hospital, Laurel was examined by several doctors who, according to his widow, were not able to diagnose anything for certain. Due to Laurel's diabetes they were afraid to risk surgery. After that, a recognized doctor, whose name could not be verified, also examined Laurel. He called for immediate surgery, leading to the discovery of a prostate ulcer that had to be removed. According to Ida Laurel's recollection, Laurel also suffered from language problems in the Hospital. She remained at her husband's side throughout his stay, bridging the communication gap between Laurel and the hospital staff night and day. Unlike her husband, Ida Laurel spoke French. Sometimes she also changed his bandages.[44]

American Hospital of Paris, November 2005 (author's photograph).

At the beginning of November 1950, the French movie magazine *Cinémonde* sent Laurel best wishes for a speedy recovery, reporting at the same time: "The crew returns into the studios of Paris."[45] However, studio shooting would not begin until January 12, 1951, when it was scheduled for another six weeks.[46] On paper that meant another delay of two weeks.[47] The production was not quite so lucky.

At the end of November 1950, approximately six weeks after entering the hospital, Laurel was released and greeted by Mr. Hardy.[48] Laurel and his wife moved into the Parisian Hôtel D'Iena at the Avenue D'Iena, where he continued to receive medical treatment. He hoped to regain sufficient strength to resume work in January 1951. In his previously mentioned letter to Fred Karno Jr. dated December 1, 1950, Laurel explained[49]: "Was in Hospital about six weeks, got back to hotel about a week ago. Still under doctor's care."

Of course, Laurel still had a tremendous amount of weight to recover. When the trade paper *La Cinématographie Française* reported in mid–January 1951 that Laurel would have to regain three or four kilos,[50] he was still miles away from his original weight. He would not recover his former strength until well after shooting was wrapped.

The discontinuation of shooting had financial consequences, too. As Suzy Delair had to be engaged for *Atoll K* longer than contractually agreed, she had to decline other offers for film and theater work. Therefore, Eger and Suzy Delair signed an additional contract, renegotiating her salary.[51] It is said that the production costs soared to $2 or even $3 million U.S.[52]—approximately $27.5 to $41.25 million U.S. by today's standards.

The delay resulted in tremendous financial difficulties for É.G.É. On November 17, 1950, the É.G.É. was forced to apply for a state-run credit of twelve million old francs. To enforce the applications, Eger's partners Sirius and Franco London wrote the same day to the Comité des Avances a l'Industrie Cinématographique of the Centre National de la Cinématographie, pointing out that the release of *Atoll K*, originally scheduled for November 24, 1950, had to be postponed until December 1950 in Paris — a highly optimistic opening date designed to convince officials that production was not completely off track. Furthermore, Sirius projected France box-office receipts totaling 180 million old francs (today's value approximately $25.8 million U.S.) during the first two years of the movie's release, accounting 2.5 million old francs (approximately $264,000 U.S.) to future screenings in North Africa, including Algeria, Morocco and Tunisia.[53] Franco London who was to organize the worldwide marketing outside France, presented a list of countries where distributing contracts for *Atoll K* already had been signed. Thereupon an advance payment of eight million old francs from É.G.É.'s receipts from the feature film *Sa majesté Monsieur Dupont* was granted at the end of December 1950.[54]

Within a few days, when it became clear that *Atoll K* could never be released before the end of 1950, the payment was increased by another 3.6 million old francs. This time the advance payment was refinanced by the receipts of Joannon's movie *Le 84 prend des vacances*, which had been released at the beginning of September 1950.[55] Still, this was not enough to cover the production's financial needs. In January 1951 Sirius applied in two steps for another advance payment of nine million old francs which was granted with an additional seven million old francs. In turn, this had to be refinanced by the receipts of the 1950 feature films *Amour et compagnie* and *L'homme de joie* directed by Gilles Grangier.[56]

Therefore, the state-run funding of *Atoll K* eventually totaled at least 27.6 million old francs, including the credit of nine million old francs. That means a total of roughly $3 million U.S. in today's economy.

6

Shooting on the Côte d'Azur and in the Studio La Victorine

Once shooting in Marseilles was completed in mid–August 1950, the cast and crew moved to the Côte d'Azur, where all location scenes were filmed. Laurel and Hardy resumed shooting on August 16, 1950. In a letter dated August 22, 1950, Laurel wrote[1]: "We started on the film last Wednesday. I think getting back in harness again is doing me a lot of good. I was getting very tired sitting around doing nothing. I used to go shopping in Market St. [Raphaël] with Grandma Metcalfe—That was a big event for me! She used to buy me Beer's Treacle Toffee—it sure was good."

With a few exceptions, the voyage of the *Momus* on the calm sea, until the final shipwreck, was shot within the walls of La Victorine studio in Nice. The thrilling thunderstorm scenes and Ollie's subsequent salvation after his valiant attempt to hoist the sail were filmed later in Nice. All other location scenes were shot in the surrounding area of Cap Roux, Anthéor, Agay, St. Raphaël and Valescure.

Giovanni's conflict with the wealthy homeowner was filmed in front of an estate surrounded by a stone wall, in an unknown location somewhere in this region. According to the Italian distribution documents, the homeowner was actually the mayor ("sindaco"). During the argument over the wall, Giovanni gesticulates madly when he decides to leave his home country in search of global fame as a master stonemason. The closing scene depicting Giovanni's fate, resigned to tearing down the wall and nailing up a fence, was also shot here.

The scenes following the storm were also filmed on location on Cap Roux. Stranded on the atoll, Stan and Ollie share a piece of dialogue that seems like a metaphor for Laurel's real-life physical state. Ollie calls out, "We're on an island, take a peep! Take a peep!" Stan answers: "I'm too pooped to peep."

Spotting fish, lobsters and squid beached on the atoll, Antoine calls upon his comrades to bring a cooking pot and search for firewood, so that he can prepare his bouillabaisse. But his euphoric exclamation—"Land! For the first time in seven years! I will never leave this place!"—was deleted from the script, as was Giovanni's remark that he will no longer stay on the wreck as a stowaway.

As in Laurel and Hardy's early sound short *Berth Marks* (1929), Stan and Ollie's debarking from the *Momus* was milked for maximum comic effect. In the earlier film, they ineptly (and laboriously) entangle themselves in each other's clothes as they climb into a sleeping compartment. In *Atoll K*, Stan's leg gets caught in Ollie's jacket to similar fashion. This leads to a coat-ripping scene, again similar to the one in *Berth Marks*. The scene continues with a series of undistilled Laurel and Hardy gags: Stan comments on the shipshape condition of the

Laurel, Hardy, Max Elloy and Sylvette Baudrot [extreme right] with the wreck of the *Momus* on Cap Roux, August/September 1950 (courtesy Sylvette Baudrot).

Momus, moments before the ship's entire contents avalanche on top of Ollie. A wrapped fender (a buffer used to prevent small collisions between the ship and quay) then tumbles onto Ollie's head. Finally, Stan drops an armload of books on his prone partner. The sight of props crashing onto Ollie's head is familiar stuff, revisited from earlier shorts such as *Hog Wild* (1930), *Laughing Gravy* (1931) and *Dirty Work* (1933).

The script, which varies slightly from the finished film, goes on to have Stan and Ollie light a fire so the foursome can enjoy a hot meal. As they finish dining, Ollie reads from Daniel Defoe's *Robinson Crusoe*. Following the novel's example, the men are renamed and begin exploring the atoll. Stan and Ollie bicker over space under an umbrella to shelter themselves from the blazing sun. But creating a home on the island paradise requires hard work. This was illustrated by a scene showing the castaways tilling the land, their efforts made futile by greedy seagulls who devour the seeds. Giovanni busily builds a house, using Antoine's cooking pot to mix concrete. Later on, Antoine delicately cuts herbs from his spice garden with a razor, and avails himself to a barbecue grill of Giovanni's construction. There are less productive moments, however, evidenced by Ollie's strangely assembled waterwheel and a slapstick-sabotaged transportation of stones. The hard work shows in the men's tattered clothing: their shoes are so worn they are now replaced with rags wrapped around their feet.

Another scene deleted from the script showed Antoine catching fish with a self-made fishing rod, then tossing them directly onto the grill.

On Cap Roux, two entirely new scenes with Stan were added. He has formed a friendship with a lobster named Oscar, building a crustacean kennel next door to the bungalow he shares with Ollie. On the roof of the kennel is a French inscription reading "Chien méchant"

Hardy and his wife with technical crew in Valescure, September 1950 (courtesy Sylvette Baudrot).

("Biting Dog"). The front is labeled "Beware Ferocious." Later on in the film, when the four are imprisoned in Stan and Ollie's bungalow, yet another inscription is seen on the left exterior wall, this time in Italian: "Attenti al cane" ("Beware the Dog").

Stan kindly places a frying pan filled with water in front of the kennel. Luring his pet out, he pulls a thick, long, iron chain with Oscar tied to the end[2]; this is reminiscent of early Laurel solo and Laurel-and-Hardy gag photos, in which small dogs are walked with the help of an especially long or thick rope instead of a leash. The playful lobster splashes happily in the frying pan, which Stan then uses as a tennis racket to skim stones out to sea. The skipping stones lead us miles away to Tahiti, where a new chapter of the plot begins. It is here that we finally meet Chérie Lamour. By this time the filmmakers had decided not to introduce Chérie at the beginning of the film, in the rather dubious nightclub scene, but much later when the plot had first established the creation of the atoll.

In the last chapter there was an example of a press photo indicating that certain stills were photographed before the actual shooting of the scene. The same is true of a still from the shooting on Cap Roux, depicting a rather healthy-looking Stan kneeling down in front of Oscar's kennel. In the finished film, however, Stan looks thin and tired.

1966 German *Superschau des Lachens* lobby card: a well-looking Stan in front of Oscar's kennel on Cap Roux, beginning of September 1950 (author's collection).

Cap Roux, later in September 1950: in the movie Stan appears in inferior physical condition (screen capture from *Utopia*).

The scenes on Dolan's freighter, where Cherie is confronted by the jealous captain's wife and eventually sets off in a rowboat, were shot offshore from St. Raphaël and Cap Roux. This is practically the same location where Frazer's ship is seen at sea, for example, when he rushes to rescue Stan, Ollie, Antoine, Giovanni and Chérie on their gallows raft. Due to the size of the two ships, it was impossible to shoot this part at La Victorine studio.

In fact, only a very few shots with all the main characters (Stan, Ollie, Antoine and Giovanni, as well as Chérie in one scene) were filmed on location in Valescure, Anthéor and on Cap Roux. Most of the action occurs in the bungalows, and was shot later at Billancourt.

In a new scene prior to Chérie's arrival on the atoll, Ollie tells Antoine and Giovanni that he heard a ship pass by. Stan confirms this as fact. He did not tell his friends about the ship, since he waved and nobody waved back. Appalled, Giovanni suggests that Stan is dumber than most people. Antoine agrees, remarking that no single person can be that dimwitted.

Chérie arrives at the foursome's bungalow on Cap Roux. The castaways tell her how long they have been living on the atoll, and ask her how she has come upon the island. Chérie replies, "Well, I guess you might say I was dropped by a witch." Stan needs clarification: "Like the one that rides on a broom?" Chérie is more specific: "No, this one used a shotgun!"

In the first location shot featuring all five lead characters, the men escort Chérie to her bungalow. Immediately, Ollie begins to elaborate how he heroically rescued his friends on

From left to right: script girls Sylvette Baudrot and Madeleine Longue, executive producer Paul Joly and actor Guy Henry [Alecto's henchman]; Cap Roux, September 1950 (courtesy Sylvette Baudrot).

that fateful, stormy night. In another scene, the scrubbed and shaven men are on their way to breakfast prepared by Chérie. For the first time we see them wearing rags instead of shoes. Furthermore, the walk over Cap Roux to Chérie's newly constructed hut in Valescure was shot in open air. The men now wear straw hats woven by Chérie. In a minor alteration from the script, Chérie's show of gratitude was relocated outside her bungalow, where she kisses the men one by one. Finding the kiss singularly pleasant, Stan queues up again for another peck.

The much publicized arrival of the helicopter to the shooting location did not translate into the breathtaking scenes the production had hoped for. Still, it supplied the movie with a couple of aerial shots. There is a long shot of the arrival of Frazer and his men on the atoll, surveying the bay of Anthéor. In another aerial shot, Frazer's boat heads for Chérie's bungalow across a lake. During the shooting the helicopter was also sent flying over the islanders, waving at them with the rotor blades.

The bay of Anthéor also served as the location for the uranium find, and for Frazer's discussion with the islanders over the atoll's fate. With his little whistle (a remnant from the early scenes in Marseilles), Ollie calls a meeting to decide who will be presented as the first man to put foot on the island. Stan's line about the Hague Convention, which he innocently believes to be Scotch, had been rejected and was not recorded. Also deleted was Giovanni's concerned question as to whether the atoll would experience any depression suffered by its adoptive country. The hoisting of the national flag of Crusoeland was shot, but without Ollie's speech for this solemn occasion.

The same location saw the recognition of Crusoeland by the international commission, filmed during blistering heat. After close examination, the chairman hands the *Robinson Crusoe* book containing the constitution over to Ollie, thus approving Crusoeland's sovereignty. Yet their confidential discussion about the problems the commission faced in acknowledging the constitution was deleted. Therefore Ollie, now in full presidential regalia of admiral's hat, cloak and sword, immediately points out Crusoeland's uniqueness to an eagerly waiting reporter.

The travel agency inviting countless lineups of people to Crusoeland in four languages (English, French, Spanish and Italian) was also located on Cap Roux.[3] The horde of people traveling by air, sea and rail toward a better future on the island paradise was presented in a lavish montage using local extras in the bay of Anthéor, as well as the area surrounding Chérie's bungalow in Valescure. A liner setting to sea and an airplane leaving a runway were shot in Marseilles and near Nice, respectively, using a multilingual sign bearing departure information at the airport.[4] There was also a quick succession of scenes depicting the rapid growth of the new settlement brought on by the innumerable newcomers, including the remarkable moment in which a mother wipes the faces of her children with the national flag. Afterwards the throngs head for the newly reopened Café Crusoe, which welcomes patrons with a quadrilingual sign in English, French, Italian and Spanish.

Still of the main characters in front of Chérie's new bungalow in Valescure, September 1950. From left to right: Max Elloy, Adriano Rimoldi, Laurel, Suzy Delair and Hardy (courtesy Suzy Delair).

Ollie's interview after the declaration of Crusoeland's sovereignty. Sylvette Baudrot [second from left], reporter [on Laurel's left side] (courtesy Sylvette Baudrot).

At first the scriptwriters planned to make fun of villainous Alecto after the initial uproar at the Café Crusoe by transforming him into a human spinning top. This, however, was deleted. An indispensable shot was the posting of Ollie's proclamation to the wreck of the *Momus*, pronouncing the return of law and order to Crusoeland — after all, this was the catalyst for the revolution against Ollie's government launched by Alecto. The proclamation was prepared in English, French and Italian for each of the three originally planned versions of *Atoll K*. This meant the posting had to be shot three times, for each separate language. But only the Italian version actually shows Ollie fixing the sign with tacks. This was originally followed by Ollie swallowing the tacks after Stan gives him a congratulatory pat on the back. In the end there are slight differences between the three varying shots. Either there is minor bickering between a couple of islanders next to the proclamation, or we see a few laborers at work.

Further scenes shot on Cap Roux showed an enraged Alecto tearing down the proclamation, sparking the coup among the disgruntled people of Crusoeland. Among the rabble-rousers is a Greek in national costume. According to the script he was one of the malcontents to attack Café Crusoe with a bulldozer, looting it to open a Greek restaurant of their own. There was also a long shot of the gallows and the filming of most of the endless climactic chase, including the use of explosives and the battle with cement during which Stan presses a brick into Alecto's concrete encased face. A magazine reported on a further scene in which Stan, Ollie, Antoine and Giovanni disguise themselves as Mexicans with sombreros and serapes.[5] However, the planned glissade through a wooden water conduit as well as the barrels rolled down onto the pursuers by the comrades were dismissed.

It must have been during shooting on Cap Roux that severe concerns were raised over presenting such an overlong chase to the public, since at this point an entirely new — and much shorter — chase was developed. First there is a severely truncated version of the flight. The comrades run along the skeleton of a building to a lorry track, and drive away in the

Ollie's interview after the declaration of Crusoeland's sovereignty. From left to right: Laurel's stand-in Julien Maffre, Hardy's stand-in Victor Decottingnies, reporter, director Joannon, Sylvette Baudrot (courtesy Sylvette Baudrot).

Boats in the bay of Anthéor, September 1950. Jean Dicop [operative cameraman, behind the camera], Armand Thirard [director of photography, at his right side] (courtesy Sylvette Baudrot).

lorry. Ollie's jacket gets tangled in an operating lever, dumping his friends to the ground where they're seen by their wildly shouting pursuers.

When Chérie, hiding in the radio operator's tent, hears Alecto announce that the scaffold will soon be finished and the execution will take place in an hour, she hurries to free her friends. The authors originally wanted her to knock down one of Alecto's henchmen with a wrapped brick during her escape attempt, but this gag was expanded on the set into an extended scene lifting elements from Laurel and Hardy's early silent short *Why Girls Love Sailors* (1927). In this short, Stan dresses as a woman, lures disagreeable thugs and knocks them out. In this updated version, Chérie fills her tiny handbag with a rock. She also takes a pepper shaker and a flower from one of the tables at Café Crusoe. She peppers the flower and approaches the armed guard watching over Stan and Ollie's bungalow. Chérie lifts her skirt to expose a shapely leg and seductively waves the flower under the guard's nose. The pepper brings about an enormous sneeze, and Chérie immediately sends the guard to dreamland with a little help from her loaded handbag. Repeating the action on the second guard, she manages to free her friends. She throws Alecto and his men off the scent by claiming that the prisoners knocked out the guards and bound and gagged her.

Chérie continues to put her frilly weapon to good use. She has hidden herself behind the bar of a shack, and pops up every now and then to knock out more of Alecto's henchmen as they pass by. The four escapees hide in the shack too, and are separated from Chérie by a curtain. As they press themselves against the curtain, Chérie assumes them to be more of Alecto's thugs and knocks them out one by one. As each falls, Stan is bewildered — until Chérie's bag hits him first in the seat and then on the head. He manages to happily blurt out "It's

Chérie!" before the blow takes its effect. Stan falls to the ground, grinning broadly, as Alecto enters the scene. Wrongly interpreting the situation, he is convinced of Chérie's loyalty and praises her cleverness.

After the failed execution, the frantic mob of people who came to Crusoeland for its freedom now panic for their lives as the atoll sinks back into the sea. This was shot on Cap Roux as planned.

Having finished work on the Côte d'Azur, the cast and crew moved to the Nice studio La Victorine. Due to Laurel's illness the shooting apparently lasted longer than the initially scheduled three days.[6] Laurel's presence was absolutely necessary for the scenes shot in the studio. Here, he and Hardy would film the exterior scenes aboard the *Momus*. Unfortunately, the toll that Laurel's health was taking on his physical appearance, which was already all too apparent on the Côte d'Azur, could not be hidden any longer.

Several exterior scenes on the deck of the *Momus* were shot in the studio pool at La Vic-

Suzy Delair and Laurel: the 44th day of shooting on Cap Roux, September 1950 (author's collection).

torine. This includes the sequence where the motor of the broken-down yacht runs out of fuel, and Stan and Ollie attempt to fix it. Here the script relied on Laurel and Hardy's comedic skills, a wise decision on the screenwriters' part. For ten shots the comedians ad lib some of the finer moments in *Atoll K*, as Ollie disassembles the motor piece by piece and Stan places the parts a little too close to the edge of the deck. As expected, each piece falls into the ocean, its fate confirmed by Stan with an onomatopoeic (and fatalistic) "bloop." To top it off, Stan blows into a twisted pipe, alarming Ollie with its shrill whistle.

Stowaway Giovanni's tumbling out of the sails and volubly complaining about Stan and Ollie's ineptitude as sailors was also shot in the studio pool. When Stan denies Giovanni his right to be on board, the latter vigorously states that he has certain rights as a stowaway, new dialogue that Laurel created spontaneously on the set. According to the script, Stan, Ollie and Antoine introduce themselves to Giovanni, as Stan falls through the open door of the galley.

One deleted scene had Giovanni pointedly complaining about the monotonous meals served on board and Stan requesting that Antoine prepare Giovanni's beloved spaghetti. In the finished film we see just a few seconds of the group wiping their plates when Ollie reemerges from below deck having changed his wet clothing for pajamas.

Ollie's plunge into the Mediterranean during the unsuccessful hoisting of the sail was filmed offshore Cap Roux in a long shot, using Hardy's stand-in Decottignies. The close-ups of an irritated Ollie treading water were shot weeks later in the basin at La Victorine. The scene was sweetened by a gag not in the script, but from Laurel and Hardy's past. As in 1931's *Come Clean*, Stan throws the life preserver of the *Momus* to Ollie — this time, however, it sinks to the ocean's floor before Ollie can get hold of it.

The fact that it is Ollie alone who falls into the ocean seems like an obvious result of Laurel's poor health. Of course, Laurel's stand-in Maffre could have jumped into the

Hardy kisses Suzy Delair on Cap Roux, September 1950 (courtesy Suzy Delair).

sea off Cap Roux, but both comedians would have to be shown in the close-ups shot later in the studio. According to Suzy Delair, Laurel could not even withstand a single splash of water, let alone a full drenching. Seeing a soaking wet bag of bones simply would not capture the humor of the team's glory days.

A couple of scripted scenes originally scheduled for La Victorine were not shot. One was the music session on board, accompanied by Ollie's "O Sole Mio." Obviously the deletion was not due to Hardy's singing skills, which had been impressively displayed throughout his career.[7] The plot simply needed tightening, getting to the conversation comparing seafaring to playing hooky much sooner. This still results in a rather lengthy conversation.

Among the scenes that were never filmed was the one of the men fighting the doldrums and their thoughts of cannibalism. During the thunderstorm it was originally up to Antoine to fetch the lifeboat to the deck, which immediately inflates and sweeps the crew overboard. Fortunately the finished film delegates this task to Stan, whose battle with the lifeboat was now placed below deck and staged at Billancourt.

During the nocturnal storm sequence, Antoine and Giovanni both grab Stan's "snake-skin" and try to put it on at the same time, tearing it in half. These nighttime scenes were actually shot during the day at La Victorine, using filters to transform day into night. The special effects employed during the atoll's emergence from the sea, as well as its sinking at the film's climax, were staged by pyrotechnician Albouze using dry ice that not only dissolved into gusts of smoke and steam, but also created a volatile roiling of the water.

The shooting of the thunderstorm which leads to the sinking of the atoll: Cap Roux, September 1950 (courtesy Sylvette Baudrot).

Scene before Ollie plunges into the sea. Hardy at the water basin of the Nice studio La Victorine, September/October 1950 (courtesy Sylvette Baudrot).

Scene of Ollie's plunge into the sea. Hardy in the water basin of the Nice studio La Victorine, September/October 1950. Note the background of clouds for the daylight scenes on deck of the *Momus* (courtesy Sylvette Baudrot).

On the subject of the sinking of the atoll, the Scottish Laurel-and-Hardy magazine *Bowler Dessert* published a letter in 2005 claiming that *Atoll K* contained the following scene when shown in 1952 at the Nottingham cinema The Boulevard[8]:

> It was during the flood scenes, water swirling around the rooftops of houses, and people, including Stan and Ollie, clinging on desperately to avoid being swept away. Suddenly a mother and her children appeared, struggling in vain to reach the comparitive safety of the rooftop. Before they could get a grip, they were all swept away, the mother crying out in horror while attempting to cling on to her children. Stan did his crying act, Ollie wrung his hands and it was all over.

If such an improbable scene ever existed it would have been shot in the basin at La Victorine. But no surviving documents show any evidence of any such footage being shot. And it seems highly unlikely that a scene in which a desperate mother and her children are swept away and drowned would be incorporated into a Laurel and Hardy *comedy*. The 82-minute British version *Robinson Crusoeland* certainly does not contain such a scene.

Finally, the floating scaffold from which Stan, Ollie, Antoine, Giovanni and Chérie are rescued was shot at La Victorine. This is where Ollie was originally to chastise Stan with a slight variation of his well-known catchphrase ("Well, there's another fine [instead of "nice"] mess you've got *us* into!"), while Chérie adamantly declares her refusal to be saved by Frazer, because he didn't arrive quickly enough.

It took nearly two months to shoot on location in the area surrounding St. Raphaël–Cap Roux and the studio in Nice. In spite of all obstacles, the filmmakers managed to complete this portion of shooting before Laurel was finally confined to the hospital on October 10, 1950, causing the temporary shutdown of the production.

In order to keep this important production in the public eye, *Atoll K*'s publicity machine went into overdrive. The trade paper *La Cinématographie Française* published a "photo of the week" showing Chérie on the set and Alecto giving her a kiss on the hand.[9] Even though the completion of *Atoll K* was a distant proposition at the start of December 1950, the French coproducer Franco–London placed a two-page advertisement for the movie[10] announcing that it was due to be released soon, just as É.G.É. had told the Centre National de la Cinématographie.

But Laurel's hospitalization — and the resultant production delay — could not be kept secret forever. As mentioned earlier, the movie magazine *Cinémonde* wished Laurel a speedy recovery in early November 1950. The cover of this particular issue presented Suzy Delair as the captain of a motorboat under sunny skies.[11] This brought a touch of glamour to *Atoll K*, reassuring the public that production was still continuing. In reality there was absolutely no progress, and in mid–December 1950 the producers had to finally admit that production had stalled due to Laurel's illness. Any discussion of a precise date for shooting to resume was conspicuously avoided.[12]

The gloom cleared for Suzy Delair's birthday on December 31, 1950, which she celebrated at the renowned Parisian restaurant La Tour d'Argent, known as "the world's most

Laurel and Hardy and their stand-ins Victor Decottignies and Julien Maffre on Cap Roux, August 29, 1950 (courtesy Peter Mikkelsen).

Hardy congratulates Suzy Delair on her 33rd birthday at the Paris restaurant La Tour d'Argent, December 31, 1950 (courtesy Bram Reijnhoudt).

celebrated restaurant." She had invited members of the cast and crew, but whether or not Laurel was able to accept the invitation remains unknown. What is known is that Hardy celebrated with gusto. Being a connoisseur of wines, he did not hesitate to partake in some fine champagne. And despite his increased weight, Hardy remained a nimble dancer who was frequently found sharing the dance floor with Suzy Delair, among others. After midnight he put on a funny hat and greeted the New Year of 1951 with the other guests. He certainly hoped for a better year for Laurel and himself.

7

In the Paris Studio

At the beginning of December 1950, Laurel, recently released from the hospital, wrote: "Expect to start again in January — that is if I am strong enough."[1] His hopes were fulfilled. The stretch of inactivity came to an end with the announcement that studio shooting would commence on January 12, 1951. However, the schedule of approximately six weeks reported at that time proved inadequate.[2]

The ultimately prolonged shooting schedule was not due to the lavish set designed by Roland Quignon for Suzy Delair's nightclub performances in the finished film, although the setting and performances were not in the original script. The main reason that the schedule was exceeded was the health problems that would continue to plague the production. Though Laurel had recovered from surgery, he still suffered from being terrifically underweight. He was unable to regain his former weight until months later, after his return to the United States. But throughout his stay in France his physical condition remained unstable. Laurel could only work in short spurts, and production slowed to a crawl. By February 8, 1951, Laurel had exhausted himself from overwork. He was forced to rest until February 12, when he went back to work. Regarding his condition and the upcoming "rough stuff scenes" demanding his involvement, Laurel estimated another five or six weeks ahead.[3] The delays were simply a fact of life by this point. The material that had already been shot could not begin to be spliced together to create a coherent movie — the producers had to be satisfied with shooting Laurel whenever they could, in his current condition. The fact that Laurel stuck it out to the very end of the production is a testament to his professionalism.

Once again delays forced the producers to supply the media and film industry with reports that avoided any impression that *Atoll K* might never been finished. Such reports were released from February through April 1951.[4] At the beginning of March, Belgian movie magazine *Ciné Revue* prematurely reported that shooting had been completed.[5] In the same month the media was informed that American movie star John Wayne had visited the *Atoll K* set at Billancourt, publishing a photo of Wayne and Republic Studio head Herbert Yates posing with the film's leading actors.[6] Of course, Wayne did not come to Paris by chance. He had come abroad with another western actor, Forrest Tucker, to promote his latest feature film. Wayne had already shot several westerns for Yate's Republic Studios, including *The Fighting Kentuckian* (George Waggner, 1949), with Oliver Hardy costarring as his comic sidekick, and *Rio Grande* (1950), directed by John Ford.[7]

Just as shooting with Laurel and Hardy was to begin at the Paris Studios Cinéma, Hardy suddenly fell ill. Having gotten the heart and circulation problems he suffered on the Côte d'Azur under control, he now contracted the flu that was gripping Paris at the time. The string of unfortunate incidents seemed unending. In January 1951, Adriano Rimoldi wrote to his

Paris Studios Cinéma in Billancourt, 1960s (author's collection).

John Wayne visits the set at the Paris Studios Cinéma, March 1951. From left to right: Michael [aka Michel] Dalmatoff, Republic head Herbert Yates, Adriano Rimoldi, Hardy, John Wayne, Suzy Delair, Laurel, Max Elloy (author's collection).

brother with a trace of grim humor: "I would say the illnesses that are infecting this movie are a comedy of their own."[8] It went beyond comedy. Actor Titys, who played the registrar's deputy, passed away on March 13, 1951, during shooting at Billancourt.[9]

Fortunately, Hardy's recovery was swifter than expected. He was soon able to return to work, and to celebrate his birthday on January 18, 1951. Like Suzy Delair just three weeks earlier, Hardy hired the Paris restaurant La Tour d'Argent to host the celebration. Suzy Delair was among the guests, as was Laurel who, along with Hardy, appeared in their familiar costumes. A series of publicity photographs were taken at the party, with some candid shots published internationally.[10]

Health concerns were not the only problem. The ongoing reworking of the script had still not come to an end. If Laurel, Collins and Whelan had thrown in the towel, *Atoll K* would have turned into a complete fiasco — or gone unfinished or unreleased. Instead, the threesome called upon their considerable comic experience, giving traditional Laurel and Hardy material new and varied twists. These new gags helped give *Atoll K* a surprising amount of comic heft, resulting in a film that contradicts its reputation as a tired, laboriously paced comedy.

The strain took its toll on the crew and the working environment. The nerves of the producers were on edge as the schedule went out the window. Nothing seemed to put an end to the streak of bad luck. Tempers between the American, French and Italian

Suzy Delair attends Hardy's 59th birthday at the Paris restaurant La Tour d'Argent on January 18, 1951 (courtesy Peter Mikkelsen).

STAN LAUREL · OLIVER HARDY IN

RONDA DI MEZZANOTTE

REGIA: LLOYD FRENCH   PRODUZIONE: NAL ROACH

Laurel attends Hardy's 59th birthday at the Paris restaurant La Tour d'Argent on January 18, 1951. This is a lobby card for the Italian compilation *Ronda di Mezzanotte* (1978), combining the birthday party candid shot with a scene from *Pardon Us* (1931). Note the misspelling "Nal" Roach (author's collection).

producers constantly flared, often over which director would shoot the Laurel-and-Hardy scenes and which would shoot the scenes without them. Pierre Nivollet remembers the impossible situation:

> Laurel and Hardy's poor health terribly hampered the shooting. Therefore the three producers — the American, the French and the Italian — were upset [over] how to finish the movie without Laurel or even without Laurel and Hardy. So the script had to be rewritten. The precious Laurel shots they fortunately had in the can were to be combined somehow with scenes without him. Unfortunately, each of the three producers had made up his own mind how to manage it, and none of the solutions was compatible [with] the others. When Joannon also was not any longer the only director to helm the shooting the working climate deteriorated increasingly. That way much time was spent in vain. I was glad when I could say goodbye to the damned movie and to work elsewhere on another film, far away from Billancourt.

Fortunately, Laurel's positive influence on the script continued at Billancourt. With Berry now presumably the key director working with Laurel and Hardy, he was probably responsible for the upward trend in production. Against all expectation, the shooting at the Paris Studios Cinéma even resulted in an artistic breakthrough. Miraculously, many things that seemed impossible now seemed possible. In the end, the filmmakers made the best of a bad situation — although it was not enough to shape *Atoll K* into the movie everyone had hoped for.

To the film's benefit, Laurel and Berry could discuss plans and ideas without language barriers. In all likelihood their collaboration worked in much the same way that proved successful for Laurel during the Roach era. Though Laurel was never given official credit as director of the Laurel-and-Hardy films, he was much more: the director's director.

Prior to the restart of shooting, Suzy Delair recorded her two songs featured in *Atoll K*. On January 11, 1951, both *Laissez-moi faire* and *Tu n' peux pas t' figurer*, arranged by Wal Berg and accompanied by Paul Misraki's orchestra, were recorded in Raymond Ventura's Paris music studio.[11] Suzy Delair would later lip-synch to her recorded playback in front of the cameras, allowing her to concentrate on her performance during the shooting of these scenes.

Finally shooting began as announced at the Paris Studios Cinéma, working from the shooting script — or what was left of it after the many changes. As originally planned for the beginning of *Atoll K*, Chérie, Dolan and Frazer were introduced in the South Seas Nightclub which was rechristened Cacatoe-Club (English), Cabaret Cacatoès (French) and Cacatoa Club (Italian), named after the cockatoos dwelling within the cabaret. After a few stock shots of London and its Big Ben, a commentary accompanies the introduction. It tells about teatime in the British capital, before the camera moves on for a close shot of the notary's plate. Eventually there would be three different versions of the nameplate.

Stan and Ollie's scenes with the three lawyers largely follows the script, as the two comedians are in the spotlight. The flustered secretary announces the arrival of the heir from

From left to right: composer Paul Misraki, Suzy Delair, Max Elloy, Hardy, Adriano Rimoldi and Laurel; Paris music studio Ventura, January 11, 1951 (author's collection).

America. Stan appears in the door, but is pulled aside by Ollie's umbrella. As usual, Stan defers to Ollie, in a typical and very funny entrance for the two comedians.

Naturally there were some changes to the dialogue. After Stan's question "Is there any tax on the taxes?" his line "After taxes there isn't much" was replaced with "I wish uncle had left us the taxes." This alteration fits smoothly into Laurel and Hardy logic, and elevates this delightful opening scene for *Atoll K*. After introductions are made, Stan mistakes Ollie's hand for a sandwich. In a fine demonstration of slow burn, Ollie placidly lets his hand be smeared with marmalade before Stan notices his error, narrowly avoiding biting into his friend's hand.

Stan and Ollie are swiftly swindled by the greedy lawyers, who expertly provide their baffling legal rationale: "The taxes. To save you time, we had them all figured out," Bramwell states matter-of-factly while his jovial colleague Bonnefoy adds: "Including, naturally, a slight fee for our services." Poltroni chimes in: "The deductions represent income taxes, estate taxes, inheritance taxes, living taxes." Finally Bramwell reassures Stan and Ollie: "And a few other plain taxes." This financial pillaging of the two innocents fits perfectly into the Laurel-and-Hardy universe. On their way out, Ollie drags the tea tray onto the floor, blaming Stan for the mishap. The perfect ending for the film's first scene.

Furthermore, all scenes below the deck of the *Momus* were filmed in the studio. In Marseilles, Stan and Ollie went inside the nutshell. Now, months later in the Paris studio, the boys encounter a family of cats who've made their home below the bunk. When Stan sits down on the bed, the startled animals run away. But Ollie, too, causes some flurry in the hull. By mistake he sprays himself in the galley while he tries to fill a cup with water using the tap. Concerned Stan asks him: "What happened?" An irritated Ollie answers: "Mind your own business!"

Ollie spots an admiral's hat, an ornamental saber and a pair of plaid trousers (an element not in the original script), donning the hat and eventually wearing all these garments as president of Crusoeland. Stan opens a cupboard and out tumbles an inflatable lifeboat, leading to a disagreement between Stan and Ollie. The lifeboat is designed for four persons. Stan, however, doubts whether there will be space for him with Ollie aboard. Stan quickly regrets his comment, and finds it difficult to soothe the mortally offended Ollie.

The next scene to take place below the deck was heavily altered by Monty Collins under Laurel's supervision.[12] Collins's reworking was a huge improvement over the script and gave the boys a first-rate gag sequence. The dinner scene in the galley now focused on efficient sight gags and concise dialogue between Stan and Ollie. A mysterious hand is stealthily stealing Stan's food and drink through an open skylight. Of course, Stan thinks that Ollie is the culprit and tries to recoup his dinner. He fails and Ollie's reaction causes Stan to doubt his own senses. An excellent dialogue exchange — one of many in the movie — has Ollie state, "A man that would steal food from a friend is the smallest thing in the world," to which Stan replies, "Oh, I don't know." Also worth mentioning is the dialogue surrounding Stan's "good idea." He's tied the wheel on its course so that he will not have to navigate during the meal. Instead, the *Momus* drifts around in circles until it runs out of gas. Ollie, unaware of the consequences of Stan's idea, congratulates his friend: "Well, for once you have used your head!" Stan's answer seems alarming in retrospect: "Thank you, Ollie, I'll try to do that more often." When Ollie asks for Stan's help in fixing the engine ("Now give me a hand"), Stan takes him literally by putting forth his hand.

Other minor changes and deletions are less significant. Commodore Ollie has now been promoted to Admiral Ollie. In a deleted scene, one nobody would miss, Antoine serves sausages with mustard, leading Stan to mix up the term "pommes de tar" (tar apples) with "pommes des terres" (potatoes). This would have been another example of Stan's ongoing unfamiliarity with common phrases. In *Any Old Port* (1932), for example, Stan stumbles through a malapropism in grumpy Mugsy Long's motel, requesting a room not with a "southern exposure" but a "southern explosion."

It probably was not the best decision on the scriptwriters' part to have Antoine prepare the lifeboat during the storm at sea. Struggling with inanimate objects was a Laurel specialty, so this scene was wisely transferred from Antoine to Stan. As a result, the scene provided further evidence of Laurel's instinctive comic timing and skill, delivered masterfully despite his illness. When he descends into the cabin his hat falls to the floor, as he bends down to retrieve it the cabin table slides over him, completely unnoticed. Another wave sends the table back to its original position, just as Stan stands up. These shots were played back at slightly higher speed to boost their comic effect.

Laurel and gagman Monty Collins during the shooting of the first scene in the cabin of the *Momus* at the Paris Studios Cinéma, January–March 1951 (courtesy Dr. Ulrich Rüdel).

Sitting on the bed, a porthole opens and Stan is drenched by not one, but two waves. The soaked-to-the-skin Stan looks particularly gaunt and sickly. As Laurel could not bear soakings due to his ill health, the scene had to be separated into various setups to avoid exposing him to dampness at any great length.

Regardless, the comic sequence below deck builds effectively. After his involuntary shower beneath the porthole, Stan ponders how to calm the stormy waters. He remembers an old adage that he takes literally — and reaches for a small oilcan and squirts a few drops onto the raging sea. Suddenly the ocean seems to calm down, only to break out again a few moments later. Stan fetches the lifeboat which suddenly inflates itself, engulfing him. While the mast of the *Momus* collapses on deck, Stan hysterically cries for help down below. He manages to free himself from the lifeboat's grip, but the inflatable raft now looms over him menacingly. He wields a long fork like a trained swordsman and, at the moment he lunges, a bag of flour falls out of a supply cabinet. The lifeboat bursts into shreds and covers Stan in flour and dust, in much the same way Ollie was coated in flour in *Helpmates* (1932).

A later scene with Ollie's jerry-rigged backscratcher lacked the same comic impact, and was deleted. Unfortunately, another cut sequence had a great deal more promise: Stan's attempts to mend Ollie's trouser seat while he is still in them. This feels like the perfect opportunity for Laurel and Hardy to indulge in some typical ad-libbing.

Ollie's successful repair of the radio was filmed, but eventually cut; he gets the radio

Candid shot of Stan's fight against the life boat; Paris Studios Cinéma, January–March 1951 (author's collection).

working again by simply throwing it to the ground. The transmission of bad news from around the world convinces the men that life on the atoll isn't bad at all.

At the beginning of February 1951, the press reported that lavish scenes of Suzy Delair's musical performances had been shot at the end of January.[13] These were the two extended nightclub scenes that were not part of the original script or later variations. Roland Quignon's first-rate set design compared favorably to the opulent Pirate Club from Laurel and Hardy's 1936 feature *Our Relations*. For these scenes Suzy Delair's recordings from January 11, 1951, at the studio Ventura were used. This also proved a good time for a little public relations. Around this time the Belgian movie magazine *Ciné Revue* published a fashion spread featuring Suzy Delair; in one of these photos she appears in the dress worn during her nightclub scenes.[14]

The first of Suzy Delair's two numbers introduces Chérie with a tracking shot scanning her well-proportioned figure, finally settling on her foot which taps to the rhythm of the music. Around noon Chérie is ready to audition for the manager of the Cacatoe-Club. At first the busy manager is disinterested, but he is eventually charmed as Chérie sings *Laissez-moi faire* accompanied by the club's orchestra. She is signed to a contract right on the spot. This is a radical change from the original script, where Chérie was a dubious character who turned men's heads at the South Seas Nightclub. Once the cameras turned, she became an equally attractive as well as gay, sincere and optimistic young Parisian woman with artistic ambitions.

This seismic shift in Chérie's character made it impossible to stick to the events in the original script. New scenes had to be shot to define Frazer's and Chérie's relationship. She is now not merely a flirt, she is Frazer's fiancée. Frazer awaits her at the civil registry office at Papeete, joined by Captain Dolan as his best man. He paces impatiently, demanding to know the time, since his bride is nowhere to be found. When Chérie finally arrives 45 minutes late, Dolan chivalrously hands her a bridal bouquet while Frazer impatiently drags her to the chair next to him. As the registrar begins the ceremony, Chérie jumps for joy and whispers the good news of her contract to Frazer. This is far from good news for the hot-headed groom, who makes it clear to her that after the marriage he expects her to devote herself strictly to him, not to "work as a come-on in a clip joint." That is too much for Chérie. She does not want to be regarded as a "bum," but as a serious artist — the "female Caruso." She calls off the wedding. As Frazer storms off, Chérie asks Dolan to have Frazer come to the club the next evening, to judge her singing for himself. Otherwise, he will never see her again. Dolan agrees to share her request, but doubts that Frazer will accept her invitation.

Originally there was only one nightclub performance at the very beginning of the film. With the restructuring of the plot, a new scene had to be shot to explain Chérie's escape on Dolan's ship. This became a second number, with Chérie in a glittering evening gown, performing the torch song *Tu n' peux pas t' figurer*. At this late hour the club has come alive. Magnificent cockatoos swing on their perches, delivering the promise of the club's name.[15] Waiters rush through the club, ready to fulfill every wish of the smartly dressed clientele.° Among the guests is the registrar, who hopes for Chérie's sake that Frazer will arrive. As more guests arrive, she glances at the door and at the table reserved under Frazer's name. Her performance becomes more emotionally intense, until Dolan arrives and Frazer's reservation card is removed. Chérie tearfully flees the stage, bringing the audience to its feet demanding an encore. In desperation, Chérie tells Dolan that she will follow him on board his ship. Dolan, however, wants to avoid any sign of romantic involvement — particularly in front of his suspicious wife. He warns Chérie that his ship is no luxury liner, but she does not care. She only wants to leave Papeete. Dolan's second attempt to dissuade Chérie by warning her of his wife's presence is equally futile. All Dolan can say is "Hey, there's also my wife!— Ay ya ay ya ay ya ay ya."

Chérie does, indeed, find herself encountering the jealous Mrs. Dolan, who serves as the catalyst for Chérie's arrival on the atoll. Below the deck Dolan's tyrannical spouse totes a shotgun on her way to Chérie's cabin, where she finds the willful woman reclining in her negligée. A nasty quarrel breaks out between the two women, which Chérie takes in stride, although she does not further provoke Mrs. Dolan by draping her hosiery over the gun's barrel, as suggested in the script.

Chérie's sudden arrival on the atoll means considerable restrictions for the men. Antoine and Giovanni have to move into Stan and Ollie's house which causes obvious inconvenience. Therefore, a house of Chérie's own has to be built. Before the men go to sleep they promise one another, as noted in the script, that no woman shall ever come between them. The same discussion was also filmed while the men clean up the next morning.

Once again, the action was drastically rewritten. Originally, the four men were to bring the bed crashing down thanks to their collective weight. Given Laurel and Hardy's ability to milk a comic idea, this was a fairly weak gag. It was decided to reshape the scene into an extended sight gag sequence: Stan appears in his nightshirt, familiar from earlier Laurel and Hardy films. He's the first to slip into bed, but is soon confronted by Ollie, who points out that they now have guests. Out of courtesy, Stan shoves over to make room for Ollie, Giovanni and Antoine — and crashes to the floor. In the spirit of compromise, Ollie tells him that they will take turns. When one of them wakes up, the other will take his place, a negotiation that only Stan would agree to. It is time for Ollie to go to sleep, so he tells Stan to blow out the candle. When Stan remembers that Ollie will relieve him after waking up, he asks his friend whether he is awake yet. "No!" barks Ollie, and Stan resigns himself to retiring on the chair. At the same moment Oscar the lobster creeps into the room to cuddle with Stan. Stan dozes off and falls noisily off the chair, rousing Ollie, Antoine and Giovanni from their sleep. Resolving not to fall asleep again, he cozies back into his chair, snuggling Oscar. Ollie's snores rattle the hut, and Stan gets an idea. He sets the alarm clock ahead. Just as Antoine and Giovanni join in on Ollie's snoring concerto, the alarm clock rings. The bedmates crawl drowsily out of bed and begin dressing, when Ollie realizes it is still pitch dark. He lights the candle, resets the alarm clock, and slips back into bed. Antoine and Giovanni try to follow him, but Stan has already made himself comfortable. They join forces and throw him out, but to no avail. Stan's finds his way back in the twinkling of an eye, and all four men bicker over a sleeping berth as the scene fades out.

Even after this reworking, Laurel remained unhappy with the script. In the studio he initiated another rewrite and, despite his health, it was one of the comic highlights of *Atoll K*. Ollie's suggestion that he relieve Stan from guard duty is met with Stan's typically innocent approval: "Now that's what I call a sport. Thank you, Ollie. That's a good idea. I sleep, and when you wake up, I sleep again." This dialogue harkens back to *Oliver the Eighth* (1934) and *The Big Noise* (1944), when the two friends agree to sleep in turns to defend themselves from the murderous widow. In *Atoll K*, Ollie's snoring is used to additional comic effect. His thunderous breathing literally shakes the walls, blowing Stan from his chair twice.

To make matters worse, a bat wings its way into the bedroom. Stan clumsily battles the intruder, waking his slumbering bunkmates. Joining forces, the friends try to swat the airborne interloper with a frying pan and ukulele, creating a cacophony that culminates in Ollie hitting his head against a ship's bell. Ollie orders the men to open the window so that the troublemaker can fly out; this solution has the boomerang effect of allowing a flock of bats *in*! This creates even greater havoc, which does not bother Stan at all, since he is curled up in bed with Oscar, fast asleep.

A further continuation of the sleepless night had been developed by Laurel on the Côte d'Azur, but went unfilmed at Billancourt. The next morning, Ollie wakes up with a grotesquely inflated stomach with a mind of its own. Deformation gags such as this are commonplace in Laurel and Hardy's repertoire. For example, the climax of *Below Zero* (1930) has Stan running around with a huge belly, after drinking a barrel of water. In *Going Bye-Bye!* (1934), menacing Butch Long wraps Stan's and Ollie's legs around their necks like a bowtie. But here there was no explanation for Ollie's distended stomach, unlike similar scenes in *They Go Boom* (1929) or *Be Big* (1931), so the scene was deleted from *Atoll K*.

In a new scene Chérie manicures her fingernails after the fitful night at the Café Crusoe, humming a little tune, much to the enjoyment of the men. The four original stowaways prepare themselves for Chérie's invitation to breakfast, but the script differs from what eventually ended up on film. Antoine no longer presses his trousers between hot stones, nor does Stan cut Ollie's hair using a pot. The barber scene suggested by the second treatment promised a "classic" Laurel and Hardy sequence, but its deletion seems wise in retrospect. Instead, the scene now concentrates on morning rituals such as brushing teeth and shaving. As a reminder of the night before, a bat flies out of the cupboard and tangles with Stan's hair. Ollie's toothbrush loses all of its bristles, which he spits out one by one. Stan's approach to grooming, however, is the most satisfying one. As his comrades hog the shaving equipment, Stan ingeniously takes a piece of sandpaper and noisily rubs away his beard, much to the astonishment of his friends.

As scheduled, the breakfast scene was shot, as was the laundry scene where Frazer's photo falls out of Chérie's blouse. But both scenes were rejected in favor of material that placed greater emphasis on Laurel and Hardy. In the new version the foursome timidly surround Chérie at breakfast, shy and speechless. Chérie asks the tongue-tied duo if the cat has their tongue. Stan, naturally, checks his tongue with his hand to see if it is still there. Ollie and Stan sit down to a table that shows a feminine touch for the first time in years. The boys make a half-hearted attempt at the hat-switching routine, something they have done countless times, most memorably in their Oscar-winning short *The Music Box* (1932). Before Chérie serves breakfast, Stan finds Frazer's photo on the ground, picks it up and examines it through a pair of spectacles with one blackened lens. He asks Ollie, Antoine and Giovanni whether they know the man in the photo, but they do not. With great melancholy, Chérie tells them it is "a friend" and tucks the photo into her décolletage. Chérie then cheerily serves up some bouillabaisse, which is not greeted with enthusiasm by the men, who've been eating bouillabaisse for years. The men's disappointment is a relic of a scripted scene, where Antoine jumped out of bed eagerly anticipating Chérie's breakfast, which he is certain will be anything *but* bouillabaisse. This scene was deleted. Now Antoine asks Chérie, "Tell me, was your boyfriend fond of bouillabaisse?" Cherie fondly answers, "Oh! He loved it!" Now the men start to cry sympathetically, but it is hard to say whether they weep for Frazer or for Chérie, whose heart obviously belongs to someone other than the comrades.

Before shooting began at Billancourt, more scenes were scripted and filmed to show Chérie's gratitude. After breakfast Chérie weaves straw hats for the men in the bedroom that Antoine and Giovanni vacated on her behalf. This scene was cut, but we do see the men wearing the hats in the very next scene.

Dutch journalist Simon van Collem visits the set at the Paris Studios Cinéma, January–March 1951. From left to right: Laurel, Hardy, Suzy Delair, Max Elloy, Simon van Collem, Adriano Rimoldi, Michael [aka Michel] Dalmatoff (courtesy Bram Reijnhoudt).

With the exception of a few minor dialogue changes, Frazer's unexpected arrival was shot in Chérie's new house. Inside she has fixed a picture of the Eiffel Tower to make it clear that she is from Paris. When Frazer meets Chérie and her newfound friends he pointedly taunts, "You're not content just to be a singer, you've also got to be the comedian," and wonders if they are playing "Snow White and the Seven Dwarves"—a second nod to the well-known Grimm Brothers fairy tale that the scriptwriters incorporated. In no time Chérie and Frazer are arguing again, only to be interrupted by news of a uranium find.

The official announcement that the atoll is full of uranium was filmed as planned with the senior official, who also acknowledged the sovereignty of Crusoeland on Cap Roux. On that occasion the official name of the atoll, "International Commission for Geodetic Research, Matter 2860, Atoll K," was condensed to a simple "Atoll K." The radio announcements were recorded with various speakers in different languages; unlike the rest of the film, this dialogue would not be dubbed later. The succession of multiple languages shows the news rapidly spreading around the world, in English, French, German, Italian and Spanish. During recording, the producers evidently forgot to let the Italian speaker announce that after a fourteen-day conference, an international commission had been appointed to clarify the sovereign rights of the atoll. There are two English announcers. The younger newscaster has an American accent, while the older one uses British Oxford English. He confuses the island's name as "Atoll H," before calmly correcting himself by stating "Atoll K."

The radio reports reach the atoll, prompting the inhabitants to form a government of their own. Ollie decides to write the constitution on an empty page of the book *Robinson Crusoe*. Here the script is enhanced by another Laurel-and-Hardy gag. Ollie asks Stan to sharpen their rarely used pencil. Stan does it by cranking an oversized pencil sharpener, leaving nothing but a stump. Ollie reacts pragmatically: "This will have to be a short constitution."

Unanimously, the atoll is christened "Crusoeland." The new governmental cabinet is elected according to script, with Stan designated as the people. It is one of the film's sharper points of satire to have "the people" represented by one man ruled by a four-person cabinet. This results in one of Laurel and Hardy's best-remembered dialogue exchanges:

> STAN: What about me?
> OLLIE: Stanley, you are the people!
> STAN: I don't want to be the people.
> OLLIE: What do you mean, you don't want to be the people? There are more of you than there are of us.
> STAN: You mean, there's a lot of me?
> OLLIE: Certainly!
> STAN: Oh, why didn't you tell me? I didn't know.

Having resolved this problem, Ollie alone signs the constitution as president of Crusoeland. According to the script, all inhabitants including Stan were to sign it. In the original version, Stan signed "P" for "people," instead of using his name. All of this was deleted before shooting at Billancourt.

The German radio announcer (Hans Werner = Jean Verner) only appears in the French and the Italian version; Paris Studios Cinéma, January–March 1951 (screen capture from the French version *Atoll K*).

Following a montage of countless people descending upon Crusoeland via all modes of transportation, the script was to cut to Stan and Ollie in their bedroom. At Billancourt this was reshaped into a pure Laurel-and-Hardy scene. Before the duo notices the Scottish bagpiper passing their bungalow, they are busily cleaning their château. Ollie cheerfully pulls a freshly rinsed shirt out of a washtub, while Stan tidies up with an oversized feather duster. Stan raises a cloud of dust that settles on Ollie's clean garment, absent-mindedly remarking, "It's impossible to keep this house clean. Look at that." Suddenly aware of Ollie's frustration and his newly soiled shirt, Stan hurries to apologize: "The dust did it!" This was borrowed from similar scenes in *Helpmates* (1932) and *The Dancing Masters* (1943). Unlike *The Dancing Masters*, the *Atoll K* reworking took full advantage of this comic opportunity.

The initial encounter with the rebellious Alecto in the reconstructed Café Crusoe was basically shot according to the script, including the catalyst for the disaster ahead: the distribution of free liquor. A few new scenes were added for comic punch. The wrapped fender from the wreck of the *Momus* falls on Stan's head. Alecto hits Ollie in the stomach with a tray, and Stan threatens the Cossack with a bottle: "Do that again!" But as Stan swings back the bottle, he breaks it over Antoine's head, leaving Alecto to take Stan's invitation literally: he hits Stan over the head with the tray. Two scenes were dropped. The first would have shown Stan being driven into the ground by Alecto, leaving his friends to pull him out. The other scene was to have shown Alecto comically ejected from the café as a spinning top.

A new scene was added. Ollie threatens to deport Alecto; Stan confirms, "Yes, we'll have you imported." Antoine and Giovanni, however, stop the undertaking. There are no laws on Crusoeland that allow the expulsion of Alecto. This change matches the original dialogue, when the friends protest the pilfering of the café's furniture, only to have the criminals counter that theft on Crusoeland is not forbidden by law. This initiates the alteration to the government's constitution. To make it public, Ollie posts his presidential proclamation at the wreck of the *Momus* (three versions of this had already been shot at Cap Roux).

To demonstrate just how dangerous Alecto is, a new scene that was not part of the original script was written and shot in the studio. At a conspiratorial meeting in Alecto's hut, his devoted followers slavishly bring him a chair and beverages. Alecto explains to them that Crusoeland is ruled by a bunch of idiots, making it easy for him to usurp power and ultimately control the island's limitless natural resources. When one of his henchmen reminds him that the people of Crusoeland are happy and content, Alecto hauls off: "The people! Bah! We'll just tell them they are not happy. They're always ready to believe that. We'll have to organize a few demonstrations just to show them how dangerous it is to live without laws." When he receives notice that Ollie has posted his proclamation, things quickly escalate.

Ollie's naïve belief that his resolute action has put him back in control of the situation is soon shattered. Alecto storms into Stan and Ollie's bungalow with the proclamation tucked under his arm (interestingly, the French version features the banner "Salut"). From there the scripted scenes involving Ollie's incarceration and the myriad mix-ups between Alecto and Ollie were shot as planned. But on Cap Roux the chase outlined in the script was already deemed too long. Consequently, a number of new location shots were filmed to tighten the climax. New scenes were needed to cover the gaps in the plot. At first Alecto puts Ollie under arrest and ponders his next move. When Stan suggests to Ollie that Alecto be hung, Alecto congratulates Stan on his excellent idea which he intends to apply to Ollie and his cabinet. Stan fails to grasp the gravity of the situation and asks Ollie, "What did he say?" to which Ollie replies, "Why don't you keep your big mouth shut?"

As in the script, Alecto promises a short but fair trial, followed by a hanging. Since he considers Chérie too beautiful to be executed, he decides to keep her as his first lady, posting guards in front of Stan and Ollie's house. An addition to the script had Alecto demanding Ollie hand over his presidential outfit of admiral's hat, cape, checked trousers and ceremonial sword. To the friends' horror, Chérie leaves the bungalow arm in arm with Alecto. Later, with the sounds of the gallows being constructed in the distance, Stan peers out the window of the bungalow. A gunshot sends his derby flying, eliminating any last doubts that the four men are prisoners.

In a slight modification to the script, a new scene was shot to make it clear that Chérie hadn't changed allegiances at all. She makes her way to the radio operator's tent in an attempt to contact Frazer. Bewitching Alecto's confederate, she gains access to the radio, contacting Frazer's ship. She informs her ex-fiancé that the new ruler plans to hang her friends. Frazer covers the microphone with his hand and orders the ship to head for the atoll, however, he cruelly decides to rub in the fact that Chérie said he did not need him anymore. His spiteful jab at Chérie can only make the audience wonder what she sees in such an obvious jerk.

The confusing events surrounding the execution were rewritten as well. An additional scene was shot to simplify events to a single walk to the scaffold by the condemned men. The script had already arranged for Alecto to fall through the gallows' trapdoor; the new scene also has Chérie dropping Alecto onto the ground, this time onto a thatch of cactus. Just before Alecto's drop through the trapdoor, a few of his henchmen arrive to inform him that Chérie is a traitor. Suddenly Alecto sees the truth: Chérie has fooled him, and stuck by her friends.

Following the sinking of the atoll, and with Frazer's rescue of Chérie and her friends shot at the Nice studio La Victorine, the final scenes showing the future of the film's five main characters were filmed at the Paris studio. Antoine's fate in the lion's cage, and Giovanni's return to the wooden fence in Italy, had been shot in Marseilles and on Cap Roux, respectively. According to the script, Chérie and Frazer attempt once again to get married, only to start bickering right away. The unnerved registrar waits for a break in the squabbling to hear them both say "I do," finally declaring them husband and wife.

The final scene of the movie was, of course, reserved for Stan and Ollie. The script's original ending, with the duo paying penalties on Stan's inheritance at the tax office, was decidedly uninspired. The reason for paying the taxes is understandable — obviously, Stan and Ollie had been duped by the notary's promise that the island would be tax-free. But Stan's planned final line, "Yes, it was a terrible night!" is just the vaguest reference to Ollie's boastful recollection to Chérie of his rescuing of his comrades on that pitch-black night.

This ultimately unfulfilling ending obviously necessitated a rewrite. Until now the authors had forgotten all about Stan's inherited island, the reason for the boys' odyssey in the first place. So after all their troubles, Stan and Ollie finally arrive at their destination, surrounded by an international cornucopia of supplies: ginger ale, Bordeaux wine, frankfurters and sauerkraut. Frazer has donated a large refrigerator which he promises to restock from time to time. Stan and Ollie begin dreaming of a carefree life with nothing to do but eat and sleep, with nobody to tell them what to do. Of course, such a happy ending will never suffice for a Laurel and Hardy movie. Their idyll is soon ended, since the lawyers have lied about the tax-free island in this version too. A government official taps them on the shoulder and announces that his unnamed government is confiscating the island for unpaid inheritance taxes. The official is accompanied by a group of strongmen who take away all their supplies and food, leaving Stan and Ollie with nothing. Ollie's reaction is the expected one, in the classic Laurel and Hardy tradition: "Well, here's another nice mess you've gotten me into!" As usual, Stan bursts into tears: "Well, I couldn't help it, you're always blaming me for everything!" And thus, the movie *Atoll K* fades out.

At long last, on April 4, 1951, shooting finally came to a close. It was with great relief that the news could finally be announced: after a long delay, *Atoll K* had been finished.[16]

Laurel and Hardy, however, had completed their parts a little bit earlier. Laurel, unsurprisingly, was particularly anxious to leave France for the United States. The scheduled twelve weeks of shooting had stretched into a stay in France of more than eleven months. On April 1, 1951, nearly a year to the day after his departure for France, Laurel left Europe with his wife Ida. It was a particularly appropriate day, the end of a cruel April Fool's joke. His partner Hardy was in less of a hurry, staying to vacation in France with his wife Lucille. On April 23, 1951, the Hardys set out for home aboard the *MS Washington* via the Panama Canal.[17]

While the production of *Atoll K* had been a nightmare for Laurel and Hardy, at least they left one happy person in France. A young artist had an extremely successful international career ahead for himself, one that lasted until his death in 2007. In 1950, pantomimist Marcel Marceau employed a little trick in Paris to persuade his idol Stan Laurel to attend a stage performance, afterward inviting him to a café. Laurel saw Marceau's performance the next day[18] and was so enthusiastic about the young man's pantomime skills that he immediately started to promote Marceau to the French press. As early as 1951 Marceau and his stage character Bip experienced a breakthrough — a guest performance in Berlin planned for four days resulted in a triumphant welcome that lasted two months, making Marceau an internationally renowned artist.

Neither Laurel nor Hardy were completely healthy when they began their journeys home. It took Laurel several months of medical care and a diet of meaty soups and puddings to recover a degree of his former weight. By December 1951 he was able to increase his weight from 114 to 149 pounds, and was finally starting to look like himself again.[19] Hardy's coronary problems, however, had served as a warning to do something drastic about his excessive avoirdupois. His doctor advised him to reduce weight and take it easy. Hardy followed the advice and lost a considerable amount of weight, but quickly regained it when he felt better.[20]

At the beginning of 1952, the two comedians were in shape to perform once again in public. They accepted an engagement for another stage tour through the British Isles, presenting a sketch titled *A Spot of Trouble*, which Laurel had based on their early talkie two-reeler *Night Owls* (1930). The tour commenced

Laurel and Marcel Marceau as Bip in Marceau's Paris cloakroom, 1950 or 1951 (courtesy Bram Reijnhoudt).

at the end of February 1952 in Peterborough. After a four-week stay in Dublin and Belfast, Laurel and Hardy continued their tour through Great Britain until the end of September 1952. Their final performance took place in Cardiff.[21]

After the end of shooting in Paris, Léo Joannon began final editing of *Atoll K*, now called the "biggest super-production of the last years."[22] The initial cut had already commenced during shooting in the area surrounding St. Raphaël. Now it was time to assemble the material in one final push in order to release *Atoll K* in the next months, and then wait for it to hit it big.

8

The Editing

Due to the extensive additional shooting at Billancourt, it was inevitable that the final product would differ significantly from the original script. The script's essential weakness — the paucity of truly strong gags — had been corrected to some degree. Wisely, many more "pure" Laurel-and-Hardy scenes than originally intended were shot at the Paris Studio Cinéma. These scenes gave the editors a wealth of material to work with, allowing them to cut extraneous material and polish sequences in the editing room. But with all this, the director and editor of the film still had a lot of work ahead to turn *Atoll K* into an entertaining film with a sense of style and rhythm. This was not made any easier by the fact that editing had already begun in Paris before shooting was complete, while location work was still underway on the Côte d'Azur. It was not until shooting was complete that studio and location scenes could be combined.

One thing that even the most skillful editing could not overcome was Laurel's abysmal appearance. Nor could it disguise that Laurel's visage changed noticeably between location and studio shots, filmed several months apart. One possibility would have been reshooting all of Laurel's footage but, of course, this was not an option. The schedule and budget had long spun out of control. Due to climate, the production would have had to wait several weeks to redo location shots after the work at Billancourt. And it is impossible to say if reshoots would have made things any better. Laurel had left the hospital in satisfactory condition, but his appearance was even worse than before his hospitalization.

That meant the editors had to make the best with what they had. It is well known that Laurel was deeply involved in the editing process of the team's films for many years. But it seems improbable that he contributed to the editing of *Atoll K*. When he was at the Côte d'Azur, Laurel was probably in no condition to commute between St. Raphaël and Paris. Since shooting at Billancourt stopped only after Laurel's departure for the United States, which is when the lion's share of editing work began, Laurel's involvement is highly doubtful.

Files of script girl Madeleine Longue on the editing process and the cutting continuity no longer survive, so any information on the length of the raw footage as well as the final product remains elusive. Despite this, it is possible to determine with some certainty the actual length of the film after initial editing was completed.

At the end of July 1951, É.G.É. submitted the film to the Centre National de la Cinématographie for the approval of public screening. At this point the film's total length was 2,753 meters, for a running time of 100 minutes.[1] This was the world's first look at *Atoll K*.

The 100-minute version no longer seems to exist. Clocking in at 98 minutes, the English-language version is the longest extant cut of *Atoll K*. Although it is not clear when, where —

or even *if*— this version was ever released, it apparently survives. William K. Everson screened it on February 7, 1967, for the New York–based Theodore Huff Memorial Film Society, and reviewed it for his screening notes.[2] Fortunately, the original-image master materials survive in the collection of the French Archives Françaises du Film in Bois d'Arcy; naturally these rare and delicate items are unavailable for public access.[3] However, some 16mm copies of the 98-minute version circulate among collectors.

In other words, there are significant differences in running time between the longest possible unreleased English-language version, and the various, differently edited and dubbed theatrical versions. These variations are mirrored in the many video and DVD releases of *Atoll K* dating back to the 1980s. In the early 1990s, the French version was released in France as part of the Collection Hollywood [*sic*] Nostalgie series on René Chateau's VHS label. It clocked in at approximately 88 minutes at 25 frames per second (Secam system) corresponding to a 93-minute running time at 24 frames per second. The Italian version *Atollo K* is commercially available on DVD, from an apparently incomplete 16mm copy which runs about 85 minutes at 24 frames per second. The British version, titled *Robinson Crusoeland*, listed at 82 minutes long, differs considerably from the English-language version entitled *Utopia*,[4] despite having exactly the same running time. In the United States, *Utopia* fell into public domain, resulting in countless VHS and DVD releases as well as an earlier issue on Super-8. Another home-movie version that today seems extremely hard to locate is a Super-8 reel called *Out-Takes*, released in the United States around the beginning of 1977, and consisting of scenes snipped from *Utopia*. Finally, the German dubbed version of *Atoll K*, known as *Dick und Doof erben eine Insel* and running 90 minutes, has been available under this title on both VHS and DVD.

The longest conceivable version of *Atoll K* is suggested by the English-dialogue script, which represents the most complete of the three original versions of this film.[5] It contains Suzy Delair's song *Laissez-moi faire* dubbed into English and retitled "Come and Get It." It also includes the Frazer-Chérie dialogue "What time is it?" and "It's twelve fifteen" in the registrar's office and the nightclub, respectively,[6] plus the snippet with the German radio announcer whose only words are "unter dem Namen Atoll K" ("under the name Atoll K"). Both of these bits are also present in the French version (Chérie's song in French, of course), but are absent from the 98-minute English-language version, except for Frazer's question "What time is it?" The English-dubbed song and Chérie response "It's twelve fifteen," however, can also be found in a shorter English-language version of *Atoll K*. In other words, while no print of the 100-minute version seems to be extant, the material from which it was comprised does survive in its entirety in either the unreleased 98-minute English-language version, its shorter version, or the French release version.

During the editing process, the opening of the film was completely rearranged. Chérie Lamour and Antoine are no longer introduced one after the other; Chérie's initial appearance now occurs approximately halfway through the film. It was also decided that introducing Antoine with *two* failed attempts to enter a country would have been one too many, so his appearance as a bearded twin was scissored. Only Giovanni's argument about the wall he is building was retained, to be used later in the story. This is only one example of changes between the different original versions of the film.

Following a title sequence accompanied by Laurel and Hardy's familiar "Ku-Ku" song, *Atoll K* opens with a view of London's Big Ben. After an introductory preamble by an off-screen narrator, we see a plaque informing us that we are at the office of the notaries where

Stan and Ollie are expected shortly. The audience's very first view of Stan, again underscored by the "Ku-Ku" song, is a shocking sight. The opening had been shot between January and March 1951 at Billancourt, when Laurel was emaciated by illness. Once the shock has subsided, Stan and Ollie's encounter with the avaricious lawyers is a well done and original comic sequence, a worthy opening to the film.

Fade to Stan and Ollie at the port in Marseilles. Stan now looks quite healthy, at least in comparison to the previous sequence. The Marseilles scenes had been shot months earlier in August 1950, when Laurel's health had yet to decline. There is no superfluous material in the harbor sequence; instead, the film concentrates on Stan, Ollie and the harbor official who collects the boys' last cent. Stan and Ollie remain at the center of the film for several wonderful minutes. First they get down to business (in their own unique way) on the deck of the *Momus*, foreshadowing the technical hazards that would bedevil them throughout the film. Once they proceed below deck, Stan seems to have aged several years, the cabin scenes having been shot in the Paris studio months later. In the cabin, Ollie finds what will eventually be his presidential outfit, a family of cats creates havoc, Ollie sprays himself with water, and the pair discuss the limited space (considering Ollie's size) within the inflatable lifeboat. This final insult has Stan comforting his offended friend.

In the next scene, Stan and Ollie are quayside loading their cargo onto the *Momus*, under command of Ollie's whistle. Stan suddenly seems rejuvenated by years. When Stan's careless enthusiasm causes Ollie to pratfall onto a watermelon, Stan brushes off his friend's posterior with bushy vegetable leaves. This is the lowbrow Stan we know.

The scenes with Antoine and Giovanni were tightened up in a way not to distract from Stan and Ollie. Antoine's attempt to disguise himself as a monkey using the fur coat of the *Medex* captain fails, as does Giovanni's effort to board the freighter with the help of some harbor workers. The harbor policemen stop to wonder how their intervention has led to such an ironic outcome.

Meanwhile, aboard the *Medex*, Antoine complains to the captain about his hopeless situation. Noticing Stan and Ollie on the neighboring *Momus*, the captain foists Antoine upon them as a machinist. Antoine is dropped onto the yacht, knocking Stan against the starter, the would-be machinist accidentally setting the *Momus* out to the high seas.

Out on the ocean, things slow down a bit. On the deck of the *Momus*, Stan and Ollie discuss whether the course they have taken is correct. In this scene Stan's face is once again gaunt and sickly; these shots were taken on the Côte d'Azur after work in Marseilles was completed, when Laurel's hospitalization became more and more inevitable.

Antoine rings the dinner bell and confesses to Stan and Ollie that he is not a machinist. Below deck we find the cadaverous Stan from Billancourt. A mysterious hand pinches his food and drink, starting an argument between the boys. The ship's engine suddenly fails and Stan and Ollie try to repair the motor on deck, dropping the parts into the sea, only to discover the fuel tank is empty. This time the contrast between Stan's appearance in the cabin and up on deck is less obvious, since this outdoors scene was filmed at a time when Laurel's health had already begun to deteriorate.

On the plus side, the discovery of Giovanni's presence as a stowaway and food thief has been edited, tightening the tempo of the comic sequence. In rapid succession we see the failed attempt to hoist the sail, resulting in Ollie going overboard and Stan tossing him the useless life preserver which sinks to the bottom of the sea.

The scenes involving the spaghetti meal were virtually eliminated (we see Stan, Antoine and Giovanni cleaning their plates when Ollie discovers his pants have been transformed into sails). The lengthy dialogue between the four men, as they discuss their reasons for playing hooky, was also trimmed. However, Giovanni's tale about why he left his home country was retained. As mentioned before, this sequence exists in different variants in the original versions of the film.

The shipmates' battle against the forces of nature is highlighted by Stan's comic encounter with the animated table in the cabin. His attempt to calm the ocean with oil remains intact. He also fights the lifeboat which inflates itself and seems to take on a vicious life of its own. Stan saves himself by puncturing the malevolent rubber raft; this excellent scene is marred by a certain directorial clumsiness — neither the falling flour sack nor its bursting are immediately apparent at first glance. This is a letdown compared to its carefully constructed counterpart in *Helpmates* (1932), in which Ollie, blackened by soot, is covered in billowy white flour. Beyond the technical awkwardness, Laurel's otherwise brilliant performance is hampered by the fact that he appears much older and sicker in these cabin scenes shot in the studio at Billancourt.

Once the storm has calmed and the atoll has emerged from the sea, Stan emerges from the *Momus* a seemingly healthier man. The aftermath of the stormy night was shot at the beginning of September 1950 on Cap Roux, before Laurel's rapid physical decline was anticipated. Stan and Ollie's comic interaction while inspecting the wreck, which disgorges an outpouring of books onto the unfortunate Ollie, was left intact. The scenes following the wreckage, until the reading of *Robinson Crusoe*, were trimmed to approximately two minutes. The rechristening of the four castaways according to Defoe's novel was eliminated, although Ollie is called "Oliver Crusoe" after his election as president.

A couple of unimportant scenes illustrating the castaways' cultivation of the atoll were deleted, including Stan and Ollie fighting for protection from the scorching sun, and the castaways's arduous toting of building materials while Ollie slumbers. Gone too are Ollie's inadvertent radio repair and the resultant scene of bad news pouring in from around the world, convincing the men that life is relatively good on the atoll. There were still enough shots of everyday life on the atoll and the inhabitants' efforts to create an infrastructure to reduce the material to a montage. As the atoll lacks horses, it is up to Stan to don a harness and take over the job of plowing; the seeds, however, are feasted upon by seagulls. Giovanni busily erects accommodations, using Antoine's cooking pot to mix the cement. The off-camera narrator ties the scenes together, creating an effective passage of time: "Nature has supplied them with plenty of fresh water. Man has set to work. So has nature. She has quickly changed a bare rock to an enchanting paradise. Weeks, months, years have passed. Everything is now improved. At last our castaways have earned the right to take a little time off from their hard work."

In the playful scene that follows, Stan lures his pet lobster Oscar out of his hut, leading him out on a huge chain to provide him with a little refreshment. Stan then turns to the ocean and skims a stones on the water with his frying-pan-turned-tennis-racket, taking the viewer (and the plot) from the atoll to Tahiti.

The skillful editing has so far succeeded in transforming the first 42 minutes of *Atoll K* into a diverting and satisfying Laurel-and-Hardy comedy. The editors had adroitly focused attention on Laurel and Hardy, even during the cutaway scenes in Marseilles with Antoine and Giovanni. After this excellent opening, *Atoll K* loses its comic momentum and, unfortunately, never recovers. Nevertheless, some exceptional scenes with Stan and Ollie are sprinkled throughout the rest of the film.

It was now up to the editor to find a creative way to change the scene from the atoll to Tahiti. Once again the filmmakers relied on voiceover. A tenuous connection is made to the men's need for femininity in their little world, as embodied by Chérie Lamour, currently auditioning at the finest nightclub in town. The narrator explains: "This island has become a real paradise. Yes, but a garden of Eden without Eve ... and Adam is bored. Eve! I beg your pardon, Chérie Lamour. As you can see, she's got plenty of brains, and culture. The most glorious girl in Tahiti. And born in Paris, of course. Today is her big day. First of all she's taking an audition at the Cacatoes, the smartest nightclub in town. And also she's expected at the courthouse for an important occasion. She is going to marry Lieutenant Jack Frazer."

Chérie's introduction emphasizes her feminine charms. Her artistic ambitions, unfortunately, create no end of tension between Cherie and her fiancé, Lieutenant Frazer. The conflict is nicely handled through the editing: while Frazer impatiently awaits Chérie's arrival at the registrar's office, his bride-to-be launches into her audition song *Laissez-moi faire*. The lyrics nicely underscore her free-spirited nature, a trait that Frazer little appreciates — as we will soon find out.

After the audition Chérie, contract in hand and three quarters of an hour late, rushes into the registrar's office. The bride and groom vehemently bicker over their different views of a woman's role in married life. Frazer stalks off; heartbroken Chérie optimistically asks best man Captain Dolan to invite Frazer to her performance at the nightclub. Her dramatic, emotional performance is to no avail: the bridegroom does not show up. So Chérie asks Dolan to whisk her away on his ship — Frazer will never see her again. This plot device makes Chérie's encounter with Dolan's jealous, shrewish wife much clearer than in the original script, which introduced Chérie briefly at the beginning only to return to her much later, at which point she is likely forgotten. Mrs. Dolan is now the impetus for Chérie to find herself on the seemingly uncharted, uninhabited atoll.

The scenes shot at Billancourt provided the bridge needed to connect the action on Tahiti to the four comrades' paradise. It also enabled Suzy Delair to perform two memorable songs, as she requested, in an exotic setting. Best of all, it transformed her character from the prostitute Colette of the second treatment and the floozy of the original script into an honest young woman pursuing both her artistic dream and a stable married life. One problem remained: Laurel and Hardy, the film's stars, are offscreen for approximately ten minutes!

Stan and Ollie ultimately reappear, just before Chérie's landing on the atoll. Stan has seen a ship, but failed to inform his island mates. Chérie's arrival is cut so that she suddenly appears in front of Stan outside the cabin. When Stan informs Ollie, Antoine and Giovanni that there is a girl in the kitchen, he looks quite healthy, especially in the shot where he smiles at Chérie. This was shot on Cap Roux.

This reediting of Chérie's arrival allowed further tightening of the action. An off-camera commentary had already described the work that went into cultivating the atoll, so this dialogue was deemed unnecessary. And since the idea of renaming the inhabitants *Robinson Crusoe*-style was abandoned, there was no longer any reason to nickname Chérie "Monday."

As Stan and Ollie escort Chérie to her new abode, Ollie recounts his dramatic, single-handed rescue of the *Momus* during the cataclysmic thunderstorm. Later that night, when Stan and Ollie are forced to share their Billancourt-based dormitory with Antoine, Giovanni and a cadre of bats, Stan appears woefully haggard. His nightshirt and "snakeskin" dressing gown create a skeletal appearance something his standard costume has been able to conceal to a point. Fortunately, the scene with the bats is funny and effective, carefully crafted with comic energy and sound effects that recall Laurel and Hardy's heyday.

The next morning, Stan is not looking much better. The foursome determines that no woman shall ever come between them. That decision is quickly undermined by the men's enthusiastic grooming (Stan noisily sanding down his beard with a piece of sandpaper). The scene efficiently sums up the events that preceded it and propels the plot in a new direction.

The men rush over to Chérie's breakfast table, rags wrapped around their feet to replace their long-worn shoes. The constant seesawing of Stan's physical condition continues: he seems to have recuperated as he runs to the bungalow, but the minute he enters the cabin for breakfast he is again the withered man from the Paris studios. The producers could only hope that audiences would not notice Stan's ever-changing appearance.

Comparing the finished film to the script, the breakfast scene as well as the joint stroll across the atoll to Chérie's new dwelling were retained. (Stan looks much healthier during these location scenes.) The only scene cut was Chérie sewing curtains for her new bungalow.

After the surveyors have swarmed the atoll, Frazer surprisingly appears at Chérie's house, where he is introduced to her friends. This scene was shot in the studio, which means another abrupt change in Stan's appearance. The tiff between the constantly quarreling lovebirds, causing Chérie to adamantly rebuff Frazer's demand that she return with him, was wisely shortened. The subsequent discovery of uranium, as well as the discussion over which country will take control of the atoll, had been filmed in the bay of Anthéor — once again, the fresh air appears to have worked wonders on Stan's health. Nevertheless, Stan stumbles and sits on a rock during this scene, perhaps due to weakness.

By this point we are 70 minutes into *Atoll K* with considerably less focus on Laurel and Hardy during the last 30 minutes. Not only did Chérie's relationship with Frazer demand a large chunk of the running time, but so did the discovery of uranium. Which brought director Joannon to the next challenge: the political implications of the uranium find. The two earlier treatments and two versions of the script tried desperately to resolve ownership of the atoll; in the finished film the solution is quite simple and reasonably acceptable. For the remaining 30 minutes of the film, Stan and Ollie are still the main characters but have even fewer opportunities to engage in their unique brand of comedy. This was the first time in Laurel and Hardy's career that political commentary entered into their film. The politics of the time prevented such an approach in the World War II–era *Air Raid Wardens* (1943), while the military milieu and enemy agents were merely the backdrop for comedy in feature films such as *Pack Up Your Troubles* (1932), *Bonnie Scotland* (1935), *Great Guns* (1941) and *The Big Noise* (1944).

The uranium find is followed by a press conference in Washington, and soon radio reports around the world turn the news of the island's rich resources into a worldwide sensation. News reaches the atoll courtesy of the castaways' portable radio. They quickly decide to create a constitution of their own, electing Ollie as president who will rule over the people of the newly founded "Crusoeland"— the people, of course, consisting only of Stan. Since the plotline has veered away from Stan and Ollie for a few minutes, it is not so obvious that Stan is once again the sickly figure of the Paris studio shooting. The new national flag is hoisted, but there is no sign of the helicopter which flew over the atoll and waved at the inhabitants with its rotor blades. It is doubtful that this deleted scene would have helped the movie.

At this point the script's action was altered heavily in the editing room. Originally the immigration by hundreds of people was to take place after the declaration of sovereignty (during which we catch a few glimpses of the helicopter) and news of the idyllic conditions on the island. Instead, there is a cross-fade from the raising of the flag to the Cap Roux–based travel agency, promoting trips to Crusoeland in English, French, German and Italian.[7] People are desperately clamoring for tickets, a situation mirrored the world over. Everywhere, newspapers with huge headlines in every language trumpet the utopian conditions on the atoll. "In Crusoeland No Laws"; "A Crusoeland libre immigration" (French: "No restrictions of immigrations for Crusoeland"); "In Crusoeland Geld abgeschafft" (German: "No money in Crusoeland any longer"); and "In Crusoeland niente carceri" (Italian: "No prisons on Crusoeland"). The scene shifts to an airport where departures to the atoll are announced in five languages. Every means of transportation imaginable is used to whisk people from around the world to the promised land, though only a few remained in the final edit. We never do see the camel drivers, Eskimos, cowboys, skiers from Switzerland, the Chinese man in his rickshaw, the tandem from Naples, or the Venetian gondola and the requisite wine cask.

Laurel and Hardy's next appearance was also shot in the studio. While Stan and Ollie are tidying up their bedroom (Stan coating Ollie's freshly washed shirt with dust), the first immigrants land on the atoll. A fully costumed Scottish piper and an American Indian march by, accompanied by appropriate music; other ethnic stereotypes, including a bicyclist in striped tricot, were cut.

During the announcement of the new state's sovereignty by the international commission, a healthy-looking Stan applauds in the bay of Anthéor. The restructuring of the earlier scenes made Ollie's radio interview unnecessary, since the earlier radio reports had already drawn throngs of immigrants to the island. All that survives of this filmed scene is a few stills.

In turn, a pan across the island's coast illustrates the speed in which civilization has invaded Crusoeland. A lorry rail has also been built, transporting ore past makeshift tents and native teepees. This rapid development also brings about a decided lack of respect for the government: a mother pragmatically uses the flag to wipe the faces of her brood of children.

The founders of this former paradise have maintained one small oasis of enjoyment, transforming Café Crusoe into a popular meeting place. Ollie's proud statement

The same scene as used in the film. Note the Spanish writing replaced by the German writing "erste Reise nach"; Cap Roux, September 1950 (screen capture from *Utopia*).

Location shot: the bagpiper enters the atoll; Cap Roux, September 1950 (courtesy Sylvette Baudrot).

Location shot: the bicyclist in striped tricot in front of Chérie's bungalow, deleted from the movie; Valescure, September 1950 (courtesy Sylvette Baudrot).

about being the father of all the happy people of Crusoeland, and Stan's rejoinder, were deleted. Instead, a poster in four languages welcomes all to the café, including the riff-raff drawn to the island by its lack of law and order. Even though Alecto dispatches the unsavory hoodlum who tries to prevent Stan from giving away his liquor, the power-hungry Cossack is also the one who spells the end of harmony on the atoll. A few quick scenes demonstrating Alecto's violent and insolent nature were all it took to put this idea across, so the footage with the Lilliputians and the two Greeks who plunder Café Crusoe was deleted. However, one of the two Greeks is still glimpsed in the movie when the enraged crowd, led by Alecto, marches to Stan and Ollie's bungalow.

Stan's weakened physique during the Café Crusoe scenes somehow fit the situation, but it is hard to laugh when a fender falls onto Stan's head and Alecto clobbers him with a metal tray. The introduction of Alecto brings an aura of menace to the film, which seldom yields for the rest of the movie. Alecto incites the people of Crusoeland to rebel against Ollie's government after he tells his henchmen how easy it will be to take power.

The posting of the proclamation proves to be the straw that breaks the camel's back. It was shot in three different versions which were used almost exactly as shot. Yet the reference

Ollie déclare imprudemment que son île ne connaît pas de lois.

Deleted scene: Ollie's interview as president of Crusoeland on Cap Roux, September 1950 (author's collection).

to a gag from Laurel and Hardy's silent short *The Finishing Touch* (1928) was cut. So we do not see Ollie swallow the tacks he put in mouth while hammering up the constitution.

Alecto removes the kid gloves and stages a coup. Ollie mistakes the angry mob storming their cabin for grateful citizens thanking him for stabilizing the lawless conditions of the island. In Billancourt it was decided to drastically cut the protracted political commentary in the script. New scenes were shot in the studio to cover up for the deleted Cap Roux footage. The editing continued in this vein, trying desperately to tone down the alarming heaviness of the script's resolution. Gone were the back-and-forth mix-ups between Alecto and the doomed Ollie, huge chunks of the far too extensive chase, and the many confusing attempts at an execution. Little remained of the elaborate chase other than the men's getaway in the lorries. When Ollie exits his lorry he accidentally pulls a lever that tips the others out of their little dumpsters, making the pursuers aware of the escapees' whereabouts.

Even though this section of the plot had been cut radically, there is still a lack of real comedy. Among the funnier moments is Stan's suggestion to Ollie that Alecto be hung, a proposition that Alecto promptly reverses, thanking Stan profusely for the excellent idea. The triumphant Cossack offers Stan, Ollie, Antoine and Giovanni a farce of a trial and departs with Chérie as his future First Lady.

Nearly all the action for the rest of the film consists of Chérie's efforts to free her friends and summon Frazer for help. Certainly, Chérie's disposal of Alecto's henchmen using a flower, a pepper shaker, and a handbag full of stones is a strong comic sequence. Unfortunately, this basically funny scene is marred when she accidentally knocks out Stan; Laurel's weakened physical state is all too obvious in this scene shot at Billancourt. Instead, strenuous physical comedy is now focused on Alecto rather than Stan and Ollie. His fall through the gallows trapdoor onto a patch of cactus provides a fittingly funny comeuppance for the villainous rogue, but fails to deliver the laughs one expects from Laurel and Hardy's glory days.

Alecto's march on Stan and Ollie's bungalow. At his left one of the Greeks who plundered Café Crusoe in a deleted scene. Far left: Joe [aka Joè] Davray. Cap Roux, September 1950 (screen capture from *Utopia*).

So another nine minutes have passed, and nothing in the climax can compete with the comic strength of the film's first 42 minutes, up to the point at which the thunderstorm first raised the atoll. Now another storm sends the citizens of Crusoeland fleeing the doomed island in boats. As the atoll sinks into the mist, there is little doubt that all of the islands' inhabitants have drowned except for Stan and Ollie and their friends.

There is effective comic irony in having Chérie and her friends find salvation on the very gallows that were to mean their doom, the hangman's scaffold transforming into the perfect life raft. Chérie's obstinate refusal to be rescued by Frazer because, in her opinion, he did not arrive early enough, elevates the comedy. The men, however, are only too eager to get safely onto Frazer's ship. The only bit cut from this scene was Ollie's complaint that Stan had gotten them into another nice mess. His familiar catchphrase would be used to better effect later.

After a quick cross-fade, *Atoll K* devotes its final three minutes to comedy. The narrator takes us through the unfortunate destinies of the film's lead characters. Chérie and Frazer bicker their way through their marriage ceremony. Giovanni ruefully returns to Italy and fulfills the wish of his employer — nailing up the wooden fence, which has apparently already replaced his magnificent brick wall. Antoine's fate is implied with exceptionally dark humor. Socks, suspenders and a snarling lion are all we see of another attempt to escape in an animal's cage.

Fittingly, the movie ends with Laurel and Hardy. A new version of the final scene was shot at Billancourt, improving upon the unsatisfactory finale found in the script. The new ending bridges the beginning of the plot, and summarizes the fate of the once huge inheritance. Stan and Ollie have lost their money to the lawyers in London and harbor officials in

Deleted scene: concrete battle on Cap Roux, September 1950 (author's collection).

Marseilles. They have also lost their "yacht" in the shipwreck. Now the last of their legacy, Stan's island, is confiscated. Ollie's classic line, "Well, here's another nice mess you've gotten me into!" and Stan's trademark, his helpless cry, bring to a close the final feature film appearance of the two great comedians, accompanied by the "Ku-Ku" theme. Fade out.

One of *Atoll K*'s greatest strengths is Paul Misraki's music which, with the exception of Suzy Delair's songs, was recorded under the direction of Marc Lanjean.[8] The songs had been accompanied by Misraki and his orchestra in the Studio Ventura at the beginning of January 1951. The soundtrack proves Misraki to be a brilliant composer with a knack for placing just the right nuance to the action, supporting the atmosphere of the film from beginning to end. The opening music accompanying the credits immediately welcomes the viewer to a joyful event. Among the many remarkable musical ideas, one worth mentioning is the sprightly accompaniment as Stan, Ollie, Antoine and Giovanni escort Chérie to her new home. Furthermore, the musical bridge Misraki employed during Frazer and his surveyor's landing on the atoll is full of atmospheric foreboding.

Compared to the state of the script on the day shooting began, the final edit was something of a miracle. While there were only a few Laurel-and-Hardy gags in the original script, the completed *Atoll K* offers a wealth of inventive and funny scenes featuring the two comedians, who carry the film most of the time. It is possible that Laurel's negative attitude toward the movie (calling it an "abortion"[9]) likely resulted from bitter memories of the circumstances surrounding production, rather than from the film itself.

Unfortunately, the filmmakers never did come up with a way to use the incomparable presence of Laurel and Hardy effectively throughout the longest starring vehicle of their entire

Location shot: Michael [aka Michel] Dalmatoff as Alecto and script girl Madeleine Longue after the concrete battle on Cap Roux, September 1950 (courtesy Sylvette Baudrot).

career. As Laurel and Hardy rarely depended on heavily constructed plots during their hey-day, the complicated storyline of *Atoll K* allowed them limited space for their trademark comedy. This is not surprising; the duo's feature films that burden them with sub-plots, particularly those with a romantic interest, are generally regarded as their weakest. That said, Suzy Delair's charismatic performance and captivating musical performances salvage any extraneous scenes during Stan and Ollie's absence from the screen. In the end, the editing succeeded in maintaining a logical flow of events throughout the movie, no easy task given the muddled structure of the original script.

The character of Chérie not only interacts nicely with Stan and Ollie, but provides an interesting contrast to the type of woman usually found in the world of Laurel and Hardy films. The two comedians generally fared best when dealing with domineering or deceitful females typified by Mae Busch or Anita Garvin; it remains mere speculation how *Atoll K* would have turned out if Chérie had been a foul-tempered nemesis rather than a friend to the boys.

One could easily question the need to team Antoine and Giovanni with Stan and Ollie. Laurel and Hardy need only rely on each other to draw big laughs. But Max Elloy and Adriano Rimoldi as Antoine and Giovanni handle themselves nicely during their scenes at the port in Marseilles, as well as during the theft of food aboard the *Momus* and the nocturnal battle with the bats.

Of course, it was a question of zeitgeist to inject some political satire into the script. The recent past had revealed to the world the brutal, even inhuman, dictatorial regimes that dwelt within civilized Europe. The dream of escaping from state-run paternalism was common at the time, and the thought of joining old friends Laurel and Hardy on such a utopian quest promised to be irresistible. The political aspect of *Atoll K*'s plot pointedly asserts that idyllic conditions, philanthropy and freedom are on shaky ground so long as unscrupulous demagogues such as Alecto continue to incite the public. Combining political commentary with Laurel-and-Hardy comedy ultimately proved elusive — well-structured, properly conceived Laurel and Hardy routines which actually explored political satire were neither written nor shot.

One option that was not available during the editing: *more of Laurel and Hardy*. Very little Laurel and Hardy footage was left to transform *Atoll K* into a genuine Laurel and Hardy vehicle. The only solution would have been to cut the movie radically. The first 42 minutes present a typical Laurel and Hardy comedy around the same length as their penultimate Hal Roach production, *A Chump at Oxford* (1940, U.S. version). However, editing together the subsequent scenes with Stan and Ollie and adding them to the first part of the movie would have been impossible, as all their scenes were interconnected to the complicated plotline of the film's second half. Even if that approach had succeeded, it would have meant a feature film with a running time of less than an hour. Based on the development of the production and the enormous costs it demanded, this would have proved a disaster. An hour-long *Atoll K* could never have been marketed as a true feature film in 1951 — particularly since it had been heralded for more than a year as the "biggest super-production of the last years." The financial risk of achieving disappointing box-office results with such a short film forced the filmmakers to release a feature film of considerable length. As a sub-plot was necessary under such circumstances, it surely had to be a comprehensible one.

Now that the film was completed, the producers would soon learn if they had made the right decision. The upcoming release of *Atoll K* would bring them face-to-face with the reaction of the audience, the critics, and the box-office.

PART II

Atoll K on the Market

9

The French Version of *Atoll K*

To prepare *Atoll K* for release to the French market, all of Laurel and Hardy's dialogue had to be dubbed into French. The French public was already accustomed to dubbings of foreign language films. With the exception of phonetic versions of some of their early sound movies, in which Laurel and Hardy spoke their own lines in French, their American films had been dubbed in France since the 1930s, employing voice actors who varied over time.

Isabelle Kloucowsky had already written dialogue scripts for several film dubbings when she cowrote the French version of *Atoll K* with producer Raymond Eger's brother Jean-Claude Eger. Presumably she also directed the voice recording in the dubbing studio,[1] as she was also a professional dubbing director. Frank O'Neill was employed as Laurel's French voice. His voice was considerably higher than Laurel's original voice, but was considered so perfect for the role that O'Neill had already dubbed Laurel several times previously. Hardy's voice was supplied by Howard Vernon, a Swiss actor recognized for his onscreen appearances as well as his dubbing performances. He was known to dub films in German as well as French, as he spoke both languages fluently.

To stress Stan and Ollie's American origins, their voices were typically dubbed with a U.S. twang. The voice actors would also tend to exaggerate their performances, resulting in a certain amount of comic overacting. Obviously the various producers wanted to stress also the comedic nature of the films. *Atoll K* received the same treatment, as French movie audiences were already familiar with this type of dubbing of Laurel-and-Hardy movies.

O'Neill and Vernon proved to be the ideal pair of voice talents. Together with Isabelle Kloucowsky, they provided an impeccable French dubbing of Laurel and Hardy's roles in *Atoll K*. The slightly exaggerated speaking style avoided tipping the balance into silliness, managing to appropriately capture the character of the team's comedy. Stan and Ollie's French in *Atoll K* is pleasing.

The French release version of *Atoll K* was the first of several variants of the film. The opening titles feature a coarse-meshed, textile background and offer the most comprehensive credits of all known versions. "G. Barnabo" [Guglielmo Barnabò] is listed as an actor, though he does not appear in the French release version. Contrary to other opening credits, only René Wheeler and Pierro Tellini were given credit as scriptwriters. As Klorer and Kohner had bowed out after the second treatment, this was an understandable oversight. That said, it might have been worth mentioning the many others who added to the script. As it is, only Monty Collins's contribution as gag writer was credited in the English version. No mention of John Berry's directing efforts are found in the French opening credits.

The film fades in on a plaque outside the notary's office, which varies from version to version. In the French version it reads, "Bramwell, Bramwell et Bramwell—Notaires—

Correspondants: Paris, Rome, Madrid, Tanger." In contrast, most signage used in the film was created in multiple languages: the inscription on the monkey/lion cage, the fuel gauge of the *Momus*, the sign over the stage exit in Cherié's nightclub, the promotional banners outside the travel agency, the newspapers from around the world, the flight information at the Nice airport, the announcement outside the Café Crusoe, even Oscar's doghouse.

Giovanni's account of why he left Italy was shot in two versions. In the French version Giovanni verbally relates his motives, versus the overlong and overblown flashback scene filmed for the Italian version.

An insert shot was produced for the French version, to serve as a plot bridge between the atoll and Tahiti. After Stan's frying pan lob there is a quick fade to a nautical chart depict-

ing the Pacific ocean. From the bottom left of the map a hand appears holding a pencil, and follows a line northeast to Tahiti and its capital city Papeete. Here, at the Cabaret Cacatoès, the voiceover introduces Cherié as the Eve that the lonely Adams of the atoll are missing.

Above: Howard Vernon, Hardy's French voice in *Atoll K*, 1953 (author's collection). *Right*: Frank O'Neill, Laurel's French voice in *Atoll K*, 1940s (courtesy François Justamand).

After the Washington government official has announced news of the atoll discovery to the journalists, a succession of radio announcers appear in a quick montage, giving radio listeners over the world an account of the news in various languages.[2] None of the announcers were dubbed for the French version. First the female Italian announcer is heard; next is the British announcer (whose slip of the tongue, resulting in "Atoll H" instead of "Atoll K," was cut from the French version). The female Italian announcer returns, followed by a French speaker, then the American, Spanish and German announcers. Finally, the American introduces the Frenchman's announcement of the appointment of an international committee. Oddly, in both shots the French announcer's bespectacled face is obscured in shadows.

The final alternate scene in *Atoll K* occurs when Ollie's French proclamation is posted on the wreck of the *Momus*. To the right of the proclamation a man is working with a shovel, while another man steps into the picture, two women at his arms. The women loosen their grips and the man hits a worker against the head, pushing him behind the proclamation and out of the picture.

Even before Eger submitted *Atoll K* to the Centre National de la Cinématographie requesting a screening license at the beginning of July 1951, Deutschmeister's Franco London approached the French film authority. Franco London feared that American distributors might take advantage of the new, soon-to-be-released Laurel-and-Hardy movie by reissuing the team's old films, causing a glut of Laurel-and-Hardy product which might affect the initial release of *Atoll K*. Since the French government had invested a considerable amount of money into the production of the movie, Franco London asked the authority for special arrangements to avoid economic failure.[3] Franco London, however, had no legal recourse to act against American distributors so the film authority was not able to prevent American reissues either.

As already mentioned, Eger's É.G.É. submitted *Atoll K* on July 25, 1951, to the Centre National de la Cinématographie at a length of 2,753 meters. The resulting running time of 100 minutes later was quoted in a list of French movies scheduled for release in 1951.[4] Yet this version of *Atoll K* only existed a very short time. Immediately after the submission to the authority É.G.É. cut the movie down to 2,661 meters, or a running time of 97 minutes. É.G.É.'s decision was just the beginning of the never-ending trimming of *Atoll K*. Every subsequent version of the movie was shortened from this original cut.

Insert of the map of the Pacific, seen only in the French version of *Atoll K* (screen capture).

On July 27, 1951, only two days after the submission to the Centre National de la Cinématographie, *Atoll K* was approved for public release without any reservations at a length of 2,661 meters. Thereafter it was allowed to be screened not only in France and in Northern Africa, but also in then–French-occupied Saarland and, according to the postwar Allied Occupation Statute concerning Germany and Austria, in those two countries as well. The authority deemed the chances of marketing the film in France, as well as its export, favorably.[5]

French distributor Sirius, who published a trade ad for *Atoll K* and other movies on its upcoming release schedule in the trade paper *Le Film Français* on the same day *Atoll K* had been approved by the French authority,[6] was still concerned about the box-office chances of the film at this length. A few days later Sirius ordered it cut to 2,441 meters, or a running time of only 89 minutes.[7] However, in France, this still would not be the last word on *Atoll K*'s running time.

A few weeks after the official approval, and after many months of production delays and sales promotion, the movie was finally ready to be seen by the public. The premiere was planned to take place at a venue that would attract attention and create a certain connection with the shooting on the Côte d'Azur. Although this was a French-Italian coproduction with an emphasis on the French version's release, the world premiere took place neither in France or Italy, but in Monte Carlo. It can only be guessed whether Monaco was chosen because of Stan's dream of being a Monegasque citizen in the first treatment of the script.

The world premiere of *Atoll K* took place at the venerable Cinéma d'Été in Monte Carlo on September 10, 1951. By this time the running time of *Atoll K* had slightly increased to 93 minutes or 2,535 meters, which approximately corresponds to the French sound negative stored at the Archives Françaises du Film.[8] This now served as the ultimate length of the French version.

French proclamation.

The events surrounding the Monegasque premiere and the audience and critical response is unknown. So it cannot be said for sure if any of the film's stars attended the premiere. One thing, however, is certain. Laurel and Hardy had already returned to the United States months ago and had no interest in another visit to France.

It is impossible to determine exactly which scenes were cut for pre-release prints of the French version, prior to its premiere in French cinemas. What is known is the contents of the version screened on September 10, 1951. For the Monte Carlo premiere, seven minutes of the original 100 minutes were cut. This 93-minute version corresponds to the running time of the VHS offering released in France in the early 1990s, which is virtually identical to the French dialogue script.[9] The cuts made for the official French version demonstrate a further attempt to focus the action on Laurel and Hardy. With the exception of one scene, only sequences without the two comedians were removed.

The first cut came following Antoine's attempt to leave the *Medex* disguised as a monkey. Gone were his comments to the harbor police about the strange laws that prohibit stateless people from going on land while monkeys are allowed to do so. While this is effective dialogue, it was not absolutely necessary to the plot.

Furthermore, most of the dialogue between Stan, Ollie, Antoine and Giovanni on the deck of the *Momus*—in which they explain why they're running away from the world's troubles—was cut. While we are already familiar with Antoine's motives, Giovanni's rationale remains obscure. Since it was decided to team the boys with two other fellows, it would have helped to have Giovanni's presence better explained. The viewer is left to guess that Stan and Ollie are not happy to pay taxes after their experiences with the notary, but it is their emphatic "We don't like taxes!" which directly leads to the abolition of taxes in Crusoeland.

The French version also cuts two short scenes conveying everyday life on the rapidly populating atoll: the bustling construction of an infrastructure, including the lorry trail, and a shot of a mother wiping her children's face with the Crusoeland flag. The loss of the latter shot is especially regrettable, as the disrespectful use of the flag fits the satirical tone of the film. Instead, the viewer is now invited into Café Crusoe, where the Cossack Alecto soon appears for the first time.

The most substantial cutting involves Alecto, whose villainy is played down in the French version. His conspiratorial meeting with his cronies after the uproar in the Café Crusoe has been completely eliminated. This particular deletion glosses over much of Alecto's maliciousness and political dangerousness.

Following the overthrow, the French version eliminates Chérie's walk through the camp to the radio operator's tent, and her flirtatious attempt to lure him away so that she can contact Frazer. Unfortunately, Chérie's conversation with her piqued ex-fiancé, as well as Alecto's gleeful audit of the hangman's ropes for Stan, Ollie, Antoine and Giovanni, were also removed. These cuts did not help the plot. As Chérie and her comrades are rescued by Frazer in the final minutes of the film it remains unclear, without the deleted scenes, why Frazer is in the right spot at the right time. Even more incomprehensible is Chérie's complaint that she does not want to be rescued by Frazer, because he did not arrive quickly enough. This remark suggests that she was indeed waiting for Frazer, and that he did not arrive purely by accident.

Eventually, Stan and Ollie's final scene faced the scissors. As soon as the pair try to make themselves at home on Stan's island, a policeman appears and confiscates their new homeland due to insufficient payment of taxes. Ollie scolds Stan who starts to weep, and thus the movie ends. In contrast to the French version, the final cut of *Atoll K* shows that the official did not come alone. Acting on orders, a couple of strongmen take away all of Stan and Ollie's food and supplies. With this element missing, showing the boys totally bereft of everything but the clothes on their back, the ending loses considerable comic impact.

After the Monte Carlo premiere it was time to release *Atoll K* to the French public, who had supported the production with their tax francs. Franco London, who was to sell the feature film worldwide, had prepared a lovingly designed promotional booklet on heavy stock and with a cardboard cover, in French, German and Spanish languages. A map of Crusoe-land graces the cover, and inside President Ollie greets the reader. There are many stills from *Atoll K* throughout, among them the deleted mortar battle between Stan, Ollie, their comrades and the mob. As in the opening titles of the French version, Tellini and Wheeler are given credit as scriptwriters.

Meanwhile, distributor Sirius was busily preparing paperboard mats, posters, lobby cards and, most likely, promotional ideas for cinema owners.[10] In the end three posters were designed, each considerably different from the other, but all focusing on Laurel and Hardy and Suzy Delair. The first poster, illustrated by designer Pierre Pigeot, presents, in a stylized manner, Stan and Ollie along with Antoine and Giovanni cultivating the atoll, while Chérie approaches the atoll in a rowboat. The second poster, designed by Deseto and probably of Italian origin, presents a scenario far removed from the actual content of the movie: Chérie is seen as an Hawaiian beauty with grass skirt and a lei. Stan and Ollie are fishing at the shore, while Antoine and Giovanni reside in the background. The third poster is again by Pigeot, and is even more colorful. In front of a couple of suggested movie scenes, Chérie is placed in her stage attire alongside Stan and Ollie. Antoine and Giovanni can be spotted as tiny figures, who would only be recognized by those who had already seen the film.

Music publishers were active, too. Even before the release of *Atoll K* in French cinemas, Paris publisher Éditions Musicales Imperia issued differently designed sheet music featuring both songs Suzy Delair performed in the movie. Other publishers distributed the songsheets in Belgium and Switzerland, too. Two of the covers show caricatures of Stan and Ollie paddling in a canoe to the atoll on which Chérie stands.[11]

The French premiere of *Atoll K* did not take place in Paris as reported in some French Laurel-and-Hardy literature.[12] In fact, it took place in Bordeaux on September 25, 1951, where *Atoll K* was praised as "the funniest movie on the atomic age" and was set to open at the local cinema Olympia.[13] Unfortunately, the daily box-office results did not live up to expectations. Though high hopes surrounded the drawing power of Laurel and Hardy, *Atoll K*'s run at the Olympia ended on October 1, 1951.[14]

Detailed box-office reports from the early 1950s are rarely to be found in international movie trade papers. Not so in France, where such reports were a matter of course due to the French movie crisis. The reports, however, did not cover the entire country — a huge task at the time — but they did report on new movies playing in major French cities.

These overviews often reported the number of screenings per cinema, its capacity, the price of admission, the attendance, as well as the box-office gross. Data for the French version is summarized in appendix 5 of this book. This provided valuable information on the marketing prospects of new movies, enabling cinema owners to keep on top of trends.

From September 25 to October 1, 1951, *Atoll K* drew 11,000 audience members to the Olympia, grossing approximately 1,560,000 old francs, the peak result during this period among the nine movie theatres of Bordeaux.[15] In spite of this, the film was canceled at the Olympia, although it did not disappear from Bordeaux completely. In late November or early December 1951, the film was screened at the smaller cinema Étoile. Approximately 2,500 moviegoers attended. The Étoile charged the comparatively low admission of 100 old francs, only slightly more than the then minimum hourly wage of 78 old francs, leading to a gross of 252,000 old francs. In that week, *Atoll K* reached the second-lowest rank of local cinema revenues. Consequently, the movie was canceled.[16]

The reaction of the Bordeaux press to the Olympia premiere was lukewarm at best, and

VOUS Y CONNAITREZ
LE CALME ET LA PAIX...

Two illustrations from the 1951 French Franco–London brochure. Top: Alecto surrenders on Cap Roux after the deleted concrete battle. Bottom: Alecto and the mob during the thunderstorm preceding the sinking of the atoll (author's collection).

1951 French poster art (first version) for *Atoll K*, art by Pierre Pigeot (author's collection).

1951 French poster art (second version) for *Atoll K*, art by Deseto (author's collection).

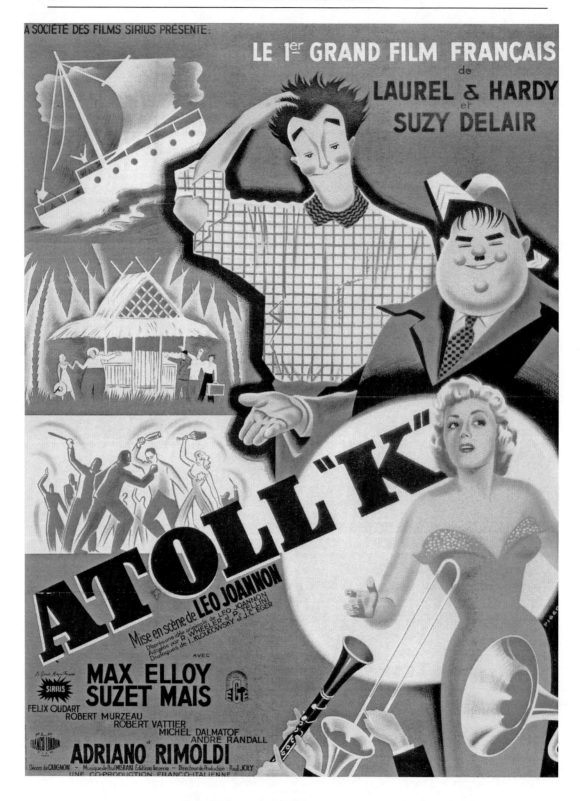

1951 French poster art (third version) for *Atoll K*, art by Pierre Pigeot (author's collection).

Cover of the 1951 French Imperia partiture of the song "*Laissez-moi faire.*" Note the misprinted song title "*Laissez vous faire*" (author's collection).

did not conceal the fact that the critics were expecting much more. One of the disappointed critics, who was nevertheless delighted by Suzy Delair's songs, wrote[17]:

> [As the movie had been shot in France,] this "change of scenery" nurtured hope for something entirely new in the cinematic world of Laurel and Hardy. Wrong again! On the contrary, it seems those responsible tried to stuff every joke and far-flung gag into *Atoll K* that the likeable two comedians had ever used in their old movies. The only new thing is the pretense for Laurel and Hardy's escapades.

Atoll K still had to wait for its Paris premiere. Instead, its next stop was Marseilles. "The kings of laughter in their latest movie shot in Marseilles" and "A whirlwind of joy" were the headlines used to fill the medium- to large-sized cinemas Club, Majestic and Odéon from October 10, 1951, onward.[18] That the film had not been entirely shot in Marseilles was conveniently overlooked on this occasion. *Atoll K* played just one week, but achieved better box-office results than its first week in Bordeaux. Some 20,000 filmgoers paid roughly 2.58 million old francs admission.[19] Did the advertising of the Marseillian shooting draw the crowds?

At long last the Paris premiere of *Atoll K* was announced for October 17, 1951, at the first-release cinemas Ermitage, Max Linder and Olympia.[20] In Paris, the film did not even score a modest success. Box-office results were reported only for the medium-sized Max Linder theater. Compared to the grosses of other Paris cinemas over that period, revenues were disappointing. In the French capital, with its millions of inhabitants, no more than roughly 7,500 visitors viewed *Atoll K* during 35 screenings in its first week at the Max Linder. The Olympia, too, did not hold more than this number of screenings.[21] All in all, the Max Linder grossed approximately 1.4 million old francs.[22] The following week saw another 35 screenings at the Max Linder, but the audience dropped to roughly 3,700 paid attendees,[23] garnering approximately 680,000 old francs. Consequently, the Max Linder canceled *Atoll K*, as did the Olympia.[24]

Nevertheless, *Atoll K* did not vanish from Paris as quickly as the cancellations at the Max Linder and Olympia seem to suggest. The movie was shown until at least mid–November 1951 at the Ermitage,[25] where it had also opened on October 17, 1951. The Paris premiere was followed by a second release on November 21, 1951, at the Moulin Rouge, but was canceled there as early as November 28, 1951.[26] Either *Atoll K* had been leased for just one week, or the modest grosses of 1.1 million old francs from 7,000 attendees over 28 screenings were not satisfying enough to extend its run another week.

During *Atoll K*'s initial Paris run, correspondent Mosk (Gene Moskowitz) of the U.S. trade paper *Variety* attended a screening on November 13, 1951. His resultant review created several myths reflected in future Laurel and Hardy literature.[27] It had been assumed that Mosk had reported on the French premiere of *Atoll K*, which had in fact occurred many weeks earlier.[28] Furthermore, his listing of a 100-minute running time was definitely incorrect. Presumably he had culled this information from internal notes on the final cut of the movie. Last, but not least, Mosk's review was likely responsible for *Atoll K*'s belated arrival on American movie screens. When it opened in the United States three years later, the movie had been mutilated. The first two sentences seemed to seal the film's fate:

> An improper mixture of fantasy, satire and slapstick does not leaven this into palatable comedy for upper case U.S. slotting. With comics Stan Laurel and Oliver Hardy in the cast and an exploitable theme this could do for special situations and dualers.

But the *Variety* review did concede that *Atoll K* had at least three effective Laurel and Hardy scenes: Giovanni's theft of food in the galley, Stan's fight against the inflatable lifeboat, and his encounter with the sliding table in the cabin. But in the end, Mosk's opinion was that Laurel and Hardy were lacking their usual zest. To make matters worse, he also pointed out director Joannon's slack comic pacing and the ineffective editing of Laurel and Hardy's gag sequences. Finally, according to Mosk, Suzy Delair did not contribute more than two chansons and "abundant beauty."

The French trade papers' reaction to *Atoll K* reflected neither the Bordeaux press's reservations nor Mosk's acerbic review from *Variety*. In its short review the trade paper *La Cinématographie Française* did not mention a single negative aspect of the film, but (quite rightly) lauded the lavish production of *Atoll K* and (less justifiably) Joannon's skillful handling of the many gags. The rest of the review praised the actors' performances.[29] The 1952 annual *Index de la Cinématographie Française* collected the trade paper's complete 1951 reviews of French feature films including *Atoll K*.[30] As the index was frequently consulted by the French movie industry, the overwhelmingly positive review seemed more like a cleverly placed advertising tactic.

Competing trade papers did much the

Advertisement for the Paris premiere of *Atoll K* at the cinemas Ermitage, Max Linder and Olympia on October 17, 1951 (author's collection).

same. Like *La Cinématographie Française*, the trade paper *Le Film Français* represented the interests of the French movie industry. It too praised the movie and predicted strong box-office.[31] Therefore, it's not surprising that the distributor's paper *La Voix du Cinéma* ignored *Atoll K*'s flaws. It happily reported that Laurel and Hardy's gags were as joyful as in their pre-war days.[32]

Approximately six weeks after the Paris premiere, the cinema owner's trade paper *L'Exploitation Cinématographique* provided a more honest appraisal, in its section "Form Your Own Opinion." Cinema owners, obviously, were especially interested in hearing the box-office prospects of *Atoll K* from reliable sources. Negative reviews of *Atoll K* poured in[33]:

"Wavers between political satire and Western parody. Childish situations based on ballyhoo. Any humor is efficiently extinguished."

"Mixture of ingredients that have lost their original flavor."

"To me, a kind of a nightmare."

Atoll K is screened at the Paris cinema Moulin Rouge, November 1951 (courtesy Benedetto Gemma).

"Too often one cannot laugh at all. There is neither rhyme nor reason in the whole thing, which lacks any originality."

"Just more proof that even the most talented artists will not be able to rescue a clumsy plot filled with tiresome comedy."

"Unwatchable!"

The merciless comments came from reviews in various papers such as *Aux Écoutes, Le Canard Enchaîné, Le Figaro, Franc Tireur, Libération, Le Parisien Libéré* and *Semaine de Paris.* They could not have been more different from the trade papers' reviews if they tried.

The review in the journal *Education Nationale* was equally ruthless. They found the stiff dialogue, paucity of gags and the setting of the movie unworthy of Laurel and Hardy, and advised moviegoers of all ages to avoid *Atoll K,*[34] though it overlooked the fact that neither Laurel nor Hardy performed *en travestie* in *Atoll K,* a trademark of Laurel's in several earlier films[35]:

> Laurel and Hardy are always a surefire with people who like to laugh.... Nevertheless, it is a pity to overuse certain gags. For example, Laurel and Hardy in drag is nothing more than old hat.

The critic of the *Journal du Dimanche* furrowed his brow[36]:

> What in hell has lured Laurel and Hardy onto this atoll? Unfortunately, this adventure adds nothing to their fame, though the story is rather enjoyable.... The whole thing is sometimes plausible and somewhat pleasant, nevertheless, the next moment one feels bored, because the script is lousy and the dialogue entirely banal. There is a bad smell that comes with this incoherent production.

Of course, the critics quoted in *L'Exploitation Cinématographique* had written more in-depth reviews than the rather vicious excerpts suggest. The big Paris daily newspaper *Le Figaro* elaborated on their unhappiness with the film[37]:

> The movie wavers between political satire and Western parody employing childish situations based on ballyhoo. Any humor is efficiently extinguished. The second bananas are either acting badly or overacting, their style of comedy turns out to be simply distressing. Fortunately, a chase that employs many extras livens the whole thing a little bit. The only favorable sequence is Laurel and Hardy's journey across the ocean.... The gags are tied together expertly ... and for a few minutes we are able to recognize our funny boys with their classic antics. However, the famous entertainers have lost much of their verve.

Simone Dubreuilh roasted *Atoll K* in the daily newspaper *Libération*[38]:

> Laurel, Hardy and Suzy Delair on a uranium-loaded desert island: kindling for comedy, you would think. Unfortunately, you are wrong.... Today Laurel and Hardy are two touching gentlemen who try hard to make us laugh. Sometimes they succeed with their old, well-proven tricks.... But more often we cannot laugh. Much too often the two comedians are lacking inspiration and originality.
>   Léo Joannon has made a film from elements that do not match.... [H]e has simply tied together old gags hastily knocked up into an incoherent patchwork of scenes.... The unfortunate technical inadequacy and the casting of second-rate actors who have no concept of their profession do not help the movie at all.... It is considerably harder to produce an excellent movie comedy than a first-rate drama. But most importantly, there are simply no successful comedies made from international ingredients. Movie comedies only live through the actors who represent the typical character of their country.

Simone Dubreuilh's last remark pinpointed the essential problem with international coproductions, a concern that was picked up by others critics, too. Of course, there are exceptions to that rule — for example, 1952 launched the extremely successful French-Italian series of *Don Camillo* movies starring Fernandel and Gino Cervi. The *Nouvelles Littéraires* critic Georges Charensol also voiced his concerns about coproductions, but saw a greater problem in Laurel's physical appearance (which he contrasted with the "surprising well and healthy appearance" of Hardy. He also complained that the movie, in his opinion, had too few effective scenes to offer[39]:

> Unfortunately, they have been put into a meager and tiresome plot which hardly does honor to the contributors to this French-English-Italian-American coproduction.... [P]roducers are desperately searching for new markets, hoping to develop them by means of international coproductions. Therefore, they have to employ secondhand plots and ... to dub actors who cannot be called upon to speak French, English and Italian.
>
> Coproductions of the type to which the movie industry is increasingly resorting are a dangerous matter in my opinion.... All important works of art have a home country, and the long-lasting creations of the cinema have always given us personalities of distinctive ethnic character....
>
> Nevertheless, *Atoll K* still comes up with two or three genuinely funny scenes ... but funny ideas and their realization are poles apart. The ideas within *Atoll K* appear to be adapted, pretentious and handled in a way that not much of them is left over.

Arguably the most detailed and forgiving review, infused with an understanding of the team of Laurel and Hardy, was contributed by the critic Tachella in the movie magazine *L'Écran Français*. He, too, condemned the weaknesses of the script. However, he largely refrained from commenting on the political aspects of *Atoll K*, which he found surprisingly tame in spite of his magazine's proximity to the French communists. Tachella wrote[40]:

> *Atoll K* ... is the first French movie of the famous American team Laurel and Hardy who, to put it bluntly, act in their usual well-proven style of simple laughter and ambitionless farce; in other words, enjoyable and healthy entertainment. Léo Joannon hit the spot by allowing Laurel and Hardy full rein and not to impose another kind of comedy upon them. Yet, we are disappointed. It is not sufficient to simply remain true to a tradition. Joannon fails to adequately transpose the tradition visually. The happy medium would have demanded a solid, ample and weird farce.
>
> ... It would have been decidedly better to let Laurel and Hardy take care of themselves and not to team them up with two others such as Max Elloy and Adriano Rimoldi.... These two partners add precisely nothing to the movie. Instead, they keep on spoiling Laurel and Hardy's comic effect; in other words, exactly what makes us laugh.
>
> ... Unfortunately, the script gets lost in needless extravaganzas, banal "surprises" and pseudo-psychological complications.... The end of the film is ... arranged with completely conventional, arbitrary, and hard-to-believe moments of suspense which we cannot laugh at....
>
> Laurel and Hardy have grown old. But we love them still the same.... At the same time, it has long been well known that nothing is more difficult for a clown than to conceal his wrinkles. The wrinkles defeat the comical effect, so that we find ourselves laughing out of sympathy....
>
> Suzy Delair ... strains against a difficult role, as her "creative" side is stressed.... To place Suzy Delair between Laurel and Hardy would have increased the comic potential of these three artists tenfold. Now we laugh only at Laurel and Hardy, not at the ensemble. The authors simply ignored that a movie based on Laurel and Hardy's comedy cannot cull laughter from a subplot excluding Laurel and Hardy. Instead, the authors employed two more comedians who should dare not call themselves comedians. Elloy and Rimoldi are plainly unable to counter Laurel and Hardy's comedy....
>
> But we should take all this with a pinch of salt.... If you love Laurel and Hardy you will have to see *Atoll K*. Despite its shortcomings the movie is much better than the screen vagabonds' last American features....

Renowned French movie periodicals such as *Cahiers du Cinéma, Cinéclub, Positif* and *Revue du Cinéma* did not acknowledge *Atoll K* with even a single word, even though they were familiar with Laurel and Hardy's popularity among all classes of the French populace. Their silence may be the result of their lack of respect for director Joannon, thus preferring to ignore him.

Atoll K opened not only in Paris on October 17, 1951, but also in at least six more cinemas in the French cities of Lille, Lyon and Nancy. In Lille, as well as in Lyon, the movie played for no more than a week, while its run in Nancy was extended for a second week. Until the end of October 1951, *Atoll K* was seen in these three cities by 45,000 cinemagoers.[41] In Toulouse, *Atoll K* proved to be considerably more successful when it was screened for just under 10,000 attendees in the days before Christmas 1951.[42] In fact, the brand-new Laurel-and-Hardy movie outdid the box-office results for the local rerelease of *Laurel et Hardy conscrits* (*The Flying Deuces*, 1939), which by mid–November had been seen by close to 5,700 paying customers.[43] Later, in early March 1952, *Atoll K* was screened at two cinemas in Nice for a week at a time, attracting approximately 10,000 movie lovers.[44]

During its all-important first run in French cities, *Atoll K* turned out to be an under-performer. In November 1950, distributor Sirius had predicted total revenues in France of 180 million old francs for the first two years after *Atoll K*'s release.[45] Ultimately, the grosses Sirius had hoped for were never matched by box-office results. Cinema receipts had to exceed the distributor's sales revenues, as the cinema owners only had to pay the agreed rental fees to Sirius — but not their share of the profits. In turn Sirius, due to its contractual obligations, had to share its proceeds with the coproducers. Under such circumstances it would take huge audiences for Sirius to cover their portion of production costs, let alone make a profit.

According to a survey covering the period from September 25, 1951, to March 11, 1952, *Atoll K* had been seen in France by at least 112,541 filmgoers, providing a total gross of 16,535,187 old francs, which today is roughly the equivalent of $1.74 million U.S.[46] This amount would not have represented at least ten percent of Sirius's prognosis. However, the trade papers' reports only represent the minimum revenues, as only an extract of the total French grosses had been covered. Very likely *Atoll K* had been screened in many provincial French cinemas from late autumn 1951 on, as well as in the Saarland and in Northern Africa, maybe also in some of the smaller Paris cinemas on which the trade papers usually did not give an account. In any case, at the beginning of October 1951 Sirius had taken out an ad for *Atoll K* in the trade paper *Ciné France Afric* for the distributing region of Northern Africa.[47]

In comparison, an autumn 1950 report had Sirius stating grosses from Joannon's movie *Le 84 prend des vacances*— from which *Atoll K* had been partly refinanced — at 200 million old francs (today well over $28.65 million U.S.) for the first two years after its release. A few months later, at the end of 1950, Sirius reported additional revenues of 132 million old francs from that same film, which today corresponds to approximately $18.9 million U.S.[48] Apparently, *Atoll K* failed to generate similar revenues during a comparable period. Presumably the producers would have to wait much longer to cover their expenses of roughly $2 million U.S. (today more than $27.5 million U.S.). This scenario puts *Atoll K* as a financial flop during its first French release. But such a debacle cannot be claimed offhandedly for *Atoll K*. Not only is a complete overview of the film's grosses missing, but also the overview for the first two years upon which Sirius had based its forecast.

In any case, Sirius managed to keep the movie in its distribution program for several years, and in 1958 submitted a request to the Centre National de la Cinématographie to extend the commercial use of *Atoll K* until the end of 1959. The license was granted.[49] However, this does not necessarily suggest solid financial success based on satisfying, long-running box-office results. In the end, it cannot be determined exactly how long Sirius kept *Atoll K* in distribution.[50] In later years another distributor, Cinédis, took control of *Atoll K*.[51]

The home-movie audience had to wait until the beginning of the 1990s for the French version of *Atoll K* to be released on VHS. This version is long out of print, and there has been no reissue on DVD to date. In December 1997, distributor Télédis, a member of the Paris-based Gaumont group, secured the U.S. copyright on the VHS presentation of *Atoll K*'s French version.[52]

Although *Atoll K* did not turn out to be the blockbuster the French film industry hoped for, memories of the shooting on the Côte d'Azur were kept alive, at least in St. Raphaël. In August 1990, the municipality of St. Raphaël commemorated the 40th anniversary of *Atoll K*'s arrival in their community. The event, staged in collaboration with the French Laurel-and-Hardy club *Têtes de pioches* (named after the Laurel-and-Hardy feature *Block-Heads*, 1938), included French Laurel-and-Hardy look-alikes as well as seven citizens of St. Raphaël who recounted their personal experiences surrounding the production of *Atoll K*.[53]

Finally, February 2006 saw the release of a French CD compilation of Suzy Delair's movie chansons titled *Lady Paname*, featuring her two *Atoll K* chansons, *Laissez-moi faire* and *Tu n' peux pas t' figurer*.[54]

10

The Italian Version *Atollo K*

Italian filmgoers were also accustomed to the dubbing of Laurel and Hardy into their native tongue. In contrast to the French version, *Atollo K* (as it was christened in Italy) had to be almost entirely dubbed into Italian. The Italian actors had, with the exception of the Italian radio announcer, spoken their lines in French. Fortunately, Suzy Delair's songs remained in French, so her original, charming performances were retained for *Atollo K*. Further maintaining the international flair, the radio announcers' commentary went nearly undubbed. The news of the appointment of an international commission had to be dubbed into Italian, however, as no Italian speaker had been filmed delivering these lines. Consequently, the French announcer now changed nationalities to Italian.

Once editing of *Atollo K* was completed, the Roman dubbing studio Compagnia Doppiatori Cinematogràfici (C.D.C.) was assigned to produce the Italian dub of the movie. It was an excellent choice. In Italy, as well as France, there had been various voice artists who had come to represent Laurel and Hardy. The finest team of all proved to be Mauro Zambuto for Laurel and Alberto Sordi for Hardy. Shortly after the end of World War II the pair successfully dubbed nearly all of Laurel and Hardy's sound films. As in the French versions, Laurel and Hardy were given a slightly comic tone and distinctly American accent. Zambuto also provided Laurel with a considerably higher voice. Most important, they captured Laurel and Hardy's distinctive characters, proving that quality dubbing can have true artistic merit.

Sordi even met the comedians in person when Laurel and Hardy traveled to Italy in June 1950. At that time it had been reported that Sordi would once again provide the voice for Mr. Hardy, this time in the upcoming Italian version *Atollo K*. Although Sordi had other commitments throughout the spring and summer of 1951, he nevertheless considered it an honor to dub Hardy anew. Sordi had gained fame as Hardy's Italian voice to such a degree that he developed a music-hall act around it. Before Sordi walked on stage he announced from behind the scenery that Hardy's voice incarnate was to appear. He then performed his Hardy parody in costume with all of Ollie's famous mannerisms intact.[1]

Every now and then, when a dubbing studio and the dialogue director carefully cast even the smallest role with great care, the picturegoer can enjoy an uncompromised cinematic experience. This was the case with *Atollo K*. Rosetta Calavetta as Chérie, Lauro Gazzolo as Antoine, Giulio Panicali as Giovanni, Gualtiero De Angelis as Frazer, Olinto Cristina as Alecto and Carletto Romano as Giovanni's employer all offered exceptional vocal performances. Of course, voice actors can only be at their best if the studio strives to create the right atmosphere. Without it, a dubbing can come across as sterile and artificial. In this respect C.D.C. left nothing to be desired, and *Atollo K* turned out to be a fully satisfying effort.

Atollo K differs in several ways from the original English and French versions. Unfortunately,

Atollo K only survives in a damaged version which is missing several scenes.[2] This makes a complete reconstruction of the Italian version almost impossible. Yet the dialogue script of the Italian version is still in existence.[3] It practically mirrors the English version and includes Giovanni's verbal account of why he left Italy. Variations between the Italian, the English and the French dialogue scripts include two additional, but unused, narrator commentaries which were designed only for the Italian version. The first one was to be spoken during the wild ride from the Marseilles harbor. The second one refers to the scene in which Frazer's photo is found on the floor during breakfast. Finally, Antoine's first name was changed to its Italian counterpart Antonio. The order in which the radio announcers speak differs from the French version as well. The Italian speaker starts the sequence, followed by the British announcer (minus his "Atoll H" slip of the tongue) before returning to the Italian speaker. The American takes over, before the Italian-dubbed French speaker is heard. After a few words by the German announcer and the American speaker, the dubbed French announcer continues with the news of the appointment of the international commission.

Today it is impossible to say what the 1951 opening credits of *Atollo K* looked like.[4] The

Laurel and Hardy's Italian voices in *Atollo K*, Alberto Sordi [left] and Mauro Zambuto, during the dubbing of *Saps at Sea* (1940), late 1940s (courtesy Benedetto Gemma).

original material is lost, and the available opening credits (underscored with Misraki's music) are presumably the shortest of the three original versions. None of the scriptwriters, nor Joannon's role as scenarist are mentioned. In contrast to the coarse-meshed, textile background used in the other versions, *Atollo K*'s opening credits feature four crudely drawn caricatures of Laurel and Hardy. While the drawings do relate to the movie, they lack any artistic value.

According to the revised script, the plaque "Notaio" had been inserted right after the opening credits,[5] but this shot is missing from the surviving copy of *Atollo K*. Perhaps the most significant difference between *Atollo K* and all other known versions of the movie is the flashback to Giovanni's dispute with his wealthy employer. Consequently, there is no verbal recollection from Giovanni on the deck of the *Momus*.

Suzy Delair's Italian voice in *Atollo K*, Rosetta Calavetta, 1953 (courtesy Benedetto Gemma).

The flashback is used in *Atollo K* to accommodate Italian actor Guglielmo Barnabò, who appears alongside his compatriot Adriano Rimoldi as Giovanni's employer. Though Barnabò has only this short scene in the film, he was given prominent credit on the 1951 Italian lobby cards. This was obviously a ploy to position the film as a true French-Italian coproduction to the Italian public. In reality, there are only two Italian actors with prominent roles in *Atollo K*: Rimoldi and Luigi Tosi as Lieutenant Frazer. Barnabò has no more than two lines, even fewer than Vittorio Caprioli (lawyer Poltroni), whose name had not been highlighted.

Atollo K is also the only

Giovanni and his employer, a scene only used in *Atollo K* (screen capture from *Atollo K*).

version to show Ollie in full presidential garb fixing the (Italian) proclamation to the wreck of the *Momus*. The action taking place to the right of the proclamation differs from the French version. In *Atollo K* two men are working with a pickaxe, when they make way for a third man who traverses through the picture from the left bottom to the left top. However, in *Atollo K* it is again the French proclamation that Alecto slams down onto Ollie's head.

Other changes are barely noticeable at all. For example, the shrieks and exclamations during the nocturnal fight with the bats are clearly dubbed in the Italian version, with bats visible, while they are heard from off-camera in the French version.

The French release of the movie had likely been pushed forward due to the financing of the French government. In any case, Gastone Tomassini, head of the coproducing Fortezza, requested the Italian license for *Atollo K* from the Roman Ufficio Centrale per la Cinematografia on October 9, 1951, more than two and a half months after French approval. A short summary of the film's storyline was submitted, along with the Italian dialogue script. The summary mistakenly places Chérie's nightclub, named Cacatoa Club in the Italian version, in Tangiers, Morocco, rather than Papeete on the isle of Tahiti. Tomassini stated the film's length was 2,667 meters — a running time of approximately 97 minutes, slightly shorter than the English 98-minute version. This was nearly the same length as the original French version before it was shortened to its official 93-minute theatrical release version. Two days after Tomassini's submission, *Atollo K* was officially approved for Italian release; shortly afterward the trailer submitted by Fortezza, running 80 meters, was approved as well.[6]

Without the availability of the version presented by Fortezza to the Ufficio Centrale per la Cinematografia, there is no way of knowing what was removed from the final cut of 2,753 meters to reduce *Atollo K* to 2,667 meters. Comparison between the Italian dialogue script and the dialogue script of the 98-minute English version suggests that the two versions were essentially the same. In that case, the only variances might have been a reordering of the radio announcers and slightly different opening credits. Assuming the shortened opening credits on currently available prints are indeed the original 1951 credits, this could explain the difference in timing between the Italian and English versions.

There is no evidence that *Atollo K* ever screened in Italian cinemas at a length of 2,667 meters. The existing, choppy print of *Atollo K* clocks in at 85 minutes, making it nearly 12 minutes shorter than the copy submitted to the Italian film authority on October 11, 1951. Distributor Minerva, who purchased the screening rights from Fortezza, announced a running time of 90 minutes (rounded up, in all likelihood) in its promotional campaign book.[7] When *Atollo K* opened in Rome in April 1952, it ran just 88 minutes.[8] Another source claims an even longer running time of 102 minutes,[9] but any evidence is missing. Such a version would have run longer than the original final cut of 100 minutes.

Though the contents of the 88-minute Italian version cannot be absolutely verified, the damaged 85-minute copy of *Atollo K* suggests some segments that are obviously missing.

The first noticeable gap occurs right after the opening credits and after a short glimpse of London's Big Ben, when secretary Miss Pringle enters the notary's office. Conspicuous by its absence is the introductory narration and the Italian language plaque "Notaio."

The fragmented *Atollo K* does contain Antonio's debate with the harbor police, which was cut from the French version. Cut from the Italian version, however, is the two officials' observation on the absurdity of Antonio's and Giovanni's situation. Also missing is Captain Bonnet's discussion with Antonio on the hopelessness of his situation on the *Medex*. Even the crucial moment when the captain bids Stan and Ollie "good morning" and foists Antoine upon

them is missing. There-
fore, the dialogue between
the captain and Stan and
Ollie starts with Ollie's
query on how to start the
engine of the *Momus*.

The scene in which
Stan, Ollie, Antoine and
Giovanni find themselves
stranded on the atoll is
clearly incomplete. Com-
pared to the French ver-
sion, the damaged *Atollo K*
is also missing Chérie's
introduction by the narrator, as well as her audition
at the Cacatoa Club. It is
also lacking Frazer's impatient anticipation of his
bride's arrival. Existing
prints have the action
abruptly cutting to Chérie's
arrival at the registrar's

Atollo K is the only version in which Ollie in person fixes the proclamation to the wreck of the *Momus* (screen capture from *Atollo K*).

office, where Frazer yanks her onto the chair beside him. So Chérie literally drops into the
action, while the other main characters had been properly introduced, her last name of Lamour as well as her Parisian origin remain unknown. The viewer is never told that Chérie and
Frazer are living in Tahiti or why they are quarreling with each other. Above all, Chérie suddenly holds a bridal bouquet which had been handed to her by best man Captain Dolan,
another victim of the print's tattered state.

A huge gap occurs when, following the writing of Crusoeland's constitution and Stan's
election as "the people," the action suddenly cuts to the bagpiper who leads the parade of
immigrants in front of Stan and Ollie's bungalow. Missing is the hoisting of the Crusoeland
flag, the newspaper reports luring legions from around the world to the island, and Stan covering Ollie's freshly laundered shirt with dust during their housecleaning.

Still found in the incomplete *Atollo K*, but cut from the French version, is the remarkable scene in which a mother dries her children's faces with the flag of the new state. Furthermore, Alecto's conspiratorial meeting with his henchmen is an integral part of the Italian
version, underlining the dangerous nature of the Cossack. And while Chérie's distress call
from the radio operator's tent is missing from the French version, Italian moviegoers witnessed
this scene as early as 1951.

According to the Italian dialogue script the commentaries used in the other versions were
also meant for *Atollo K*. Nevertheless, the current print indicates at least one variation: no
narration accompanies Misraki's music during the montage of the castaways' cultivating of
the atoll. The only voice we hear is Giovanni counting out the seeds he is planting, one by
one. Two commentaries scheduled for the Italian version, during the *Momus*'s pell-mell departure from Marseilles and at the end of the breakfast scene between Chérie and the four men,

were omitted during production. Presumably the two other commentaries used in the French version, up until Chérie's first appearance, are lost due to material damage. Consequently, both Stan and Ollie's arrival at the notary and Chérie's sudden appearance at the registrar's office are choppy and incomplete. As a result we do not hear the narrator until the very end of the Italian version, when Frazer rescues Stan, Ollie, Antonio, Giovanni and Chérie from their gallows-turned-lifeboat. The contents of this commentary mirrors the corresponding narration used in the French version.

The final missing footage is also the most serious loss: Stan and Ollie's final scene. After Stan and Ollie have finally arrived on the inherited island, Stan speaks his last two lines before the movie abruptly cuts to the "Fine" title, inadvertently providing Stan and Ollie with a happy ending. The actual ending of the film can only be reconstructed with the help of the Italian dialogue script. The viewer is deprived of an unexpected yet all-too-typical situation for the boys, when Stan and Ollie's food and supplies are confiscated to comic effect.

A few days after licensing for *Atollo K* was approved, Rome-based distributor Minerva asked the movie authority for a license for the use of comprehensive promotional material. This consisted of four different posters, another large advertising graphic, a set of 16 lobby cards, paperboard mats and the aforementioned trailer, which was now probably a bit longer than at the time of its licensing.[10] With the exception of a few ad mats, the distributor spotlighted Barnabò—despite his tiny role—alongside Laurel and Hardy, Suzy Delair, Rimoldi, Elloy and Tosi. This can only be seen as another publicity ploy to make the moviegoers believe in a large-scale involvement of Italian actors in this production.

The first colorful poster was designed by Deseto. Aside from the language change to Italian, it is identical to the second French poster described in the previous chapter. In all likelihood Deseto was also responsible for a second large poster in landscape format. In it, the five main characters of *Atollo K* take center stage, with Stan busy fishing. An influx of new immigrants descend upon the island via ships, plane and parachutes. Particularly interesting is the well-armed warship—a relic of Joannon's outline and the first treatment? The third poster places Chérie front and center on the island, framed by Laurel-and-Hardy caricatures used previously in a September 1950 issue of the French trade paper *Cinématographie Française*. The fourth poster is perhaps the most unusual, depicting scenes nowhere to be found in *Atollo K*—although they certainly capture the essence of the film. A man at the tax office literally has the shirt taken off his back. Another gentleman expresses his disbelief at newspaper reports on the island paradise. A third man plugs his ears to block out the noise of the big city. Finally, a gangster and his sweetheart are seen forcing their way of life onto the island. Then there is one last colorful piece of promotion, with Stan's and Ollie's heads placed on a mushroom cloud rising over four Hawaiian beauties better suited for Laurel and Hardy's classic *Sons of the Desert* (1933) than *Atollo K*.

The distributor also supplied cinema owners with its information sheet (*Notizie Minerva*) and a campaign book. Both provided a synopsis of *Atollo K*, but it seems doubtful that the author ever saw the finished film. There are details only to be found in the script, not in the final cut. In fact, Minerva's promotional materials actually fudged new details, suggesting that Frazer had two-timed Chérie. According to Minerva, Antoine did not meet his end in the lion cage, but succeeded in boarding another ship. Ollie's radio interview on Crusoeland after the approval of the island's sovereignty had indeed been shot, as well as his proud statement, "We are the perfect government, because we do not have laws." But this scene had been left on the editing room floor. Finally, Stan and Ollie had to queue up at the tax office in the script, but not in the finished film. Minerva was in good company when it came to inconsistencies — in late summer 1951 the Italian distributor's association Unitalia picked up the alleged end of the movie from Minerva's press material in its overview of Italian productions for the year.[11]

Minerva, like all distributors the world over, had plenty of taglines — good and bad — at hand: "Don't you want to stop hearing about war? Are you tired of modern day life? Are you fed up with paying taxes? Then join Oliver Hardy and Stan Laurel on *Atollo K*!" "Stanlio and Ollio find uranium and cause a world's earthquake of laughter." "*Atollo K* is an unerring satire on modern day life as well as a miniature edition of Stanlio's and Ollio's inexhaustible humor." Thus, moviegoers were lured with South Seas escapism and by the master comedians themselves. Last, but not least, the campaign book featured an eye-catching full-color cover and tips for advertising efforts. For local first releases, cinema owners were advised to drive a car festooned with Laurel-and-Hardy jumping-jacks through the main streets of their town — the jumping jacks having movable extremities so that the Hardy dummy could do Ollie's famous tie-twiddle. Stilt-walkers dressed up as clowns should walk up and down the sidewalks, carrying trumpets, megaphones and *Atollo K* posters. The foyers of the cinemas should be decorated in full South Seas style, with cardboard palm trees and mock torches leading into the auditorium, accompanied by posters and artwork depicting Suzy Delair framed by Laurel and Hardy caricatures. Furthermore, the distributor suggested staging an *Atollo K* contest in local newspapers, in partnership with a local retailer or to promote a new product. The most inventive results were to be rewarded by Minerva. Contestants should be invited to write down their thoughts on the following theme: "An American, an Englishman, a Frenchman and an Italian have landed on Atollo K, and its load of uranium. Who will snap it up in which way, and why?"

Further exhibition approvals had to be expedited overnight when Minerva requested licenses from the Italian licensing authority on October 23, 1951, for screenings in the cities of Brescia and Carrara,[12] where *Atollo K* was likely shown on October 25, 1951.[13] In any case, it was not long before the trade paper *Cinematografia* reported that Minerva would soon release *Atollo K* to Italian cinemas.[14] Between November 1 and December 15, 1951, the film played in (at the very least) Bologna, Genoa, Naples, Palermo and Turin. Critics were far from ecstatic, reacting with polite restraint at best. In Bologna, *Atollo K* was judged "mediocre," but elsewhere it was deemed "reasonably neat."[15] The 2,000-seat Bari cinema Galleria screened the movie March 18–20, 1952, taking in a comparatively meager 450,000 lira, then corresponding to roughly $700 U.S.[16] The box-office was even poorer in Padua, where *Atollo K* played just two days at the Concordia, taking in no more than 170,000 Lira or approximately $300 U.S.[17] The critic for the trade paper *L'èco del cine e dello spettacolo* joined the chorus of poor reviews after the movie's premiere at the Roman cinema Quattro Fontaine, where it played April 12–20, 1952.[18]

According to *Cinematografia's* monthly market observation in ten selected Italian cities (Bari, Bologna, Florence, Genoa, Milan, Naples, Padua, Palermo, Rome and Turin), Laurel and Hardy's newest movie played for a mere 36 total screening days at various cinemas in April 1952. This placed *Atollo K* third from the bottom in a list of 69 movies which had premiered that month, the leader being *Don Camillo* (*Le Petit Monde de Don Camillo*; Julien Duvivier, 1952) with 304 screening days.[19] The same results played out during May, June and July of 1952. Throughout each of these three months the movie lasted no more than 39 days in the ten selected cities, after which no further screenings were reported in the trade papers.[20]

Scenes which do not appear in the movie. 1951 *Atollo K* poster art (author's collection).

Atollo K was mentioned one last time in August 1952 by *L'èco del cine e dello spettacolo.*[21] Alberto Sordi, Hardy's Italian dubbing voice, remembered that the movie "did do very bad" in Italy.[22]

A Roman Catholic film critic barely found the film worth mentioning in the 1951 volume *Segnalazioni cinematografiche del centro cattolico.* It was tersely summed up as "a sorry, mediocre effort." In the concluding "moral evaluation," it judged the movie unsuitable for children and continued[23]:

> Taken apart, the plot appears to be harmless. Although everything is softened by the comic approach, some scenes cause reservation due to situations that are a bit too bawdy. Therefore, screenings [for] juveniles are not advised as it is only fit for grownups.

At this time it became clear that *Atollo K* would not receive the opportunity to be screened at parochial events. Catholic film criticism of the time would judge movies on this suitability as well. Their ratings had enormous consequences for movie-theater bookings, a situation no longer extant in Italy. In those days parochial statements were more or less the law for the country's many believers. So it cannot be ruled out that the Catholic church's few words had an enormous impact on the poor financial performance of *Atollo K.* The

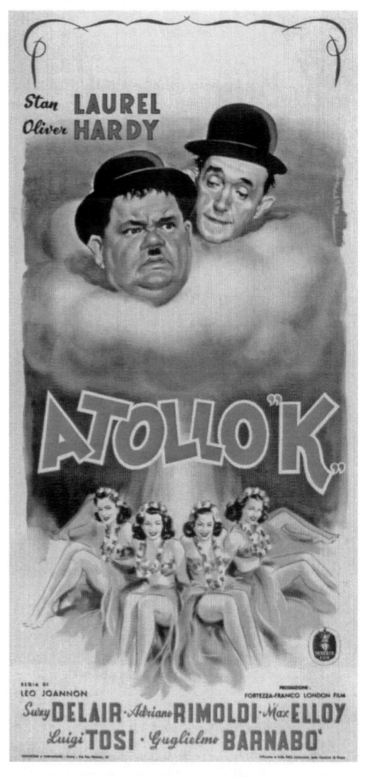

Hawaiian beauties on Crusoeland. 1951 *Atollo K* poster art (courtesy Benedetto Gemma).

poor response to the film could not be counteracted when, for example, the movie magazine *Novellefilm* published a retelling of *Atollo K*'s plot in July 1952, renaming Alecto "Miguel."[24]

The journal *Filmcritica* failed to live up to its name when it published a summary of *Atollo K*, minus any critique.[25] Other larger movie journals did not even mention the film.[26] In the end, Minerva's aggressive advertising campaign yielded only moderate results. The movie papers were unanimous in their view that *Atollo K* was far from a success. The following review from the movie magazine *Intermezzo* was nothing short of an execution[27]:

> This is a movie of missed opportunities. It could have easily developed inventive ideas into successful results. Instead, the story of the stateless man vanishes into thin air on the atoll. The two famous comedians are nothing more than old. The traces of the illness Laurel suffered during the shooting are all too obvious. The movie is promoted as an Italian one, but has no more than two Italian extras. Mysteries of international contracts! The photography, Misraki's music and the Italian dialogue are entirely weak.

After a screening at the Milan cinema La Spezia in May 1952, Paolo Locori's disillusion was apparent in the movie magazine *Hollywood*. Full of nostalgia for the heyday of slapstick, he wrote[28]:

> Comedy has changed in the last few years, developing into a new style. In doing so it has left behind the classic themes of the golden days of Charlot [Charlie Chaplin], Harold Lloyd and Ridolini [Larry Semon] that we remember so vividly. At that time actors as well as directors knew how to make the public laugh, but also how to touch their hearts. Today the public is satisfied to listen to the platitudes of a certain Bob Hope or to admire Danny Kaye.
> The era of "pie-into-the-face-movies," which brought roars of laughter to our fathers, is over. With its passing the true comedians have gone, too. Today, comedians spring up like mushrooms, thrusting themselves in the nation's movie theaters.
> In his recent movie, director Joannon nevertheless relies on two aces of comedy who have already made the whole world laugh: Stan Laurel and Oliver Hardy. This director, who is little known to us, leans on the two stars rather superficially. In fact, the lack of any "je ne sais quoi" is all too obvious. Sometimes the film appears to have been completely abandoned. In vain one searches for the easiness, the esprit and the inventiveness which have distinguished many movies of the comedy genre.
> *Atollo K* could have been something special — possibly what the director had in mind. Instead, it relies on the observation of a government that rules by two principles: no laws and no taxes. Nevertheless, the utopia of this kind of government is not given full due in the movie. Therefore, Léo Joannon cannot be spared from the criticism that he has not been the master of the situation.
> Stan and Ollie's presence is not enough to lift the movie from its mediocrity. Even worse, Stan Laurel appears to be very tired, and his expressive face has lost its former freshness. At least Oliver Hardy is himself again.
> The efforts of the French actress Suzy Delair and the Italian Luigi Tosi better remain unmentioned.

The incomplete nature of all current prints of *Atollo K* does not seem to be the result of a fire in Minerva's vaults, which destroyed the distributor's stock. Two rereleases followed the film's initial release in 1951, each accompanied by new promotional material. At the beginning of April 1963, Roman movie merchant Umberto Momi submitted a trailer measuring 80 meters to the Italian movie authority. The highlights of this reel were the *Momus* tossing on the raging sea, a conversation among the four shipmates, the nocturnal bat fight, Stan with Oscar, a conversation with Chérie, the violent encounter with Alecto in the Café Crusoe, and the flight of the inhabitants of Crusoeland during the sinking of the atoll.[29] Momi received the exhibition license in early May of 1963. At the time, *Atollo K* reportedly ran (as in 1951) 2,667 meters.[30] However, it is quite possible that the 1951 release information was reused in 1963 without any further question. But the 1963 licensing procedure does seem to suggest that the then-available copy of *Atollo K* was still intact. From around 1964 onward, a 16mm copy of the damaged distributor's print came into circulation, remaining the longest existing copy of the Italian version to this day.

The advertising material for *Atollo K's* first rerelease consisted of new lobby cards with no mention of the distributor, but announcing Laurel and Hardy in an "explosive laughing bomb." These cards depicted several scenes from the movies against a brown background, alongside a portrait of Stan in his bowler and Ollie wearing Chérie's bast hat. The smiling pair are pointing to the proclamation fixed to the wreck of the *Momus*. Unlike the proclamation in the film, the one used here erases any mention that there would taxes on Crusoeland. Presumably this rerelease was accompanied by a poster showing Stan and Ollie during the thunderstorm, as a wave breaks up the *Momus*. According to the poster, the promised "laughing bomb" exploded.

The poster for the second rerelease presents a cartoon portrait of Stan and Ollie as true "Robinson Crusoes," posing with a goat on a tiny tropical island against a white background — more holidaymakers than castaways. The same motif was used on the lefthand side on a new set of lobby cards, with the rest of them devoted to scenes from the movie. Again, the rerelease cards prepare the moviegoer for an "Atomic Bomb of Laughter." One card depicts Stan pointing to the proclamation while Ollie, in profile, looks on as he did on one of the 1951 Minerva lobby cards. In fact, Stan's pose comes from a publicity photo without Ollie, which did not show the proclamation at all. The original photo had Stan pointing to the wreckage of the *Momus*, indicating his opinion that it is still in good shape — moments before it collapsed in a heap.

Years later, in the mid–1970s, the 16mm copy of the damaged *Atollo K* print was the basis of Italian home-movie distributor Gaf Film's Super-8 release. The latter one resurfaced in 1992 on VHS, this time published by Center Video. Of course, with another distributor came yet another version of *Atoll K*. Gaf Film's variation on *Atollo K* was cut even further. Instead of the already truncated 85-minute running time, the Gaf print is another ten minutes short!

Of course, the Gaf version lacks everything already missing from the incomplete *Atollo K*. The opening credits clock in at a mere twelve seconds, featuring only one of the hastily drawn caricatures and mentioning only Laurel and Hardy and co-stars Suzy Delair, Adriano Rimoldi and Max Elloy.

The scenes in the Marseilles harbor were severely cut by Gaf Film. Antonio's aborted escape in the monkey cage and his banishment back to the *Medex*, as well as Giovanni's attempt to board the freighter, are both missing. That means Antonio's history remains unknown in the Gaf version, providing no reason for the captain of the *Medex* to foist him on Stan and Ollie.

The Super-8 version also omits scenes of the astonished Stan, Ollie, Antonio and Giovanni discovering they have landed the *Momus* on the atoll. Instead it cuts directly from the island's emergence from the sea to Stan and Ollie sitting on the deck of the marooned wreck.

As in the incomplete 16mm print, the Gaf version also cuts abruptly from Stan's skipping of the stones to the disastrous wedding ceremony. But this time the entire second nightclub scene is missing, as is Chérie's conversation with Captain Dolan about taking her aboard his freighter. This means that both of Chérie's songs are missing from the Super-8 version.

Instead the film cuts from Chérie's words to Dolan in the registrar's office to Mrs. Dolan scanning the horizon for an island. Even worse, the Gaf version cut Stan, Ollie, Antonio, and Giovanni's spoiled sleep and their nocturnal fight against the swarm of bats—a strong comic scene whose omission is fairly unbelievable.

Gaf also eliminated any evidence of Alecto's political dangerousness. Not only is his conspiratorial meeting with his henchmen missing, but so is his rabble-rousing march across the island to Stan and Ollie's bungalow.

A more curious omission is Gaf's deletion of the scene in which Chérie fills her bag with stones and grabs the pepper shaker and flower. We do see her wield these weapons outside Stan and Ollie's bungalow, but with no idea of where or how she got them. Further trims removed any indication that Chérie had knocked out five of the pursuers to cover her friends' escape. The already shortened chase was shortened further, so that the runaway foursome no longer tumble out of the lorry cars, falling at the feet of their pursuers.

And there was one last bit of editing still to come. The film returns to Chérie's and Frazer's second attempt at marriage at the Papeete registrar's office, but there is no trace of Antonio's and Giovanni's eventual fates (an echo of the deletion of their introductions at Marseilles). As Stan and Ollie's final appearance in *Atollo K* survives only in an extremely truncated form, the viewer is left with the erroneous impression that Chérie and Frazer took center stage in the film's final moments.

Eleven years passed until this home-movie mistake was corrected. In 2003, Italian DVD

Lobby card of the second *Atollo K* rerelease, 1960s. A compilation of different scenes (courtesy Benedetto Gemma).

The aforementioned lobby card of the second rerelease used a candid shot of Stan pointing at the wreck of the *Momus* combined it with...

label Elleu released a value-priced (7 Euro) DVD of the fragmented, 85-minute version of *Atollo K*. Remarkably, the print contained both the Italian and English-language soundtrack, the English track being derived from the U.S. version, *Utopia*. This meant large sections of the film would go silent while viewing the English option, since *Utopia* is even more incomplete than the choppy *Atollo K* (more on that in chapter 12).

... a shot already used for a 1951 *Atollo K* lobby card (author's collection).

The incomplete Italian version, and most notably its mutilated final moments, understandably left Italian Laurel-and-Hardy enthusiasts unsatisfied. So they came up with something special for the meeting of the Sons of the Desert tent "Noi Siamo le Colonne" on the occasion of the fortieth anniversary of Stan Laurel's death, February 23, 2005. Enzo Garinei and Giorgio Ariani, who have been Laurel and Hardy's Italian voices since 1985, were invited to Modena. On May 27, 2005, they redubbed the intact ending of Atoll K into Italian[31]: "Bene, ecco un altro pasticcio in cui mi hai cacciato!" ("Well, here's another nice mess you've gotten me into!")

11

The English-Language Version of
Atoll K, Robinson Crusoeland

The third original version of *Atoll K* was produced in English for English-speaking markets, and is the only version featuring Laurel and Hardy's native tongue. Since both comedians spoke with their own voices during the shooting, none of their dialogue, naturally, was dubbed. They spoke English, and so did also the British and American radio announcers — the American announcer filmed at Billancourt reports the appointment of the commission. All other roles, with the exception of all radio announcers, had to be dubbed, as were Suzy Delair's two songs. According to the opening credits of the English-language version, the English dialogue was written by Monty Collins (died June 1, 1951), John Klorer (died July 15, 1951) and Isabelle Kloucowsky, who had already been responsible for the French dialogue. Yet Klorer's contribution seems doubtful, as he bowed out of *Atoll K* before scripting was completed and filming commenced. This is pretty much all that is known about the English-language dubbing of *Atoll K*; the dialogue director, the dubbing studio, even the voice talents remain unknown to this day.

Laurel and Hardy's biographer John McCabe describes the English-language dubbing as "flat, toneless Chicago accents."[1] But even today there is question over whether this comment truly applies.[2] It is still unclear whether Paul Frees was the English-language narrator[3] or Antoine's voice — or if Frees was even involved in the dubbing.[4] If Frees did indeed portray Antoine, he could take credit for the sole acceptable piece of dubbing, which is not surprising. After all, Frees was something of a vocal jack-of-all-trades. He lent his voice to a host of U.S. cartoon characters, including Disney's Professor Ludwig Von Drake as well as the animated counterparts for John Lennon and George Harrison in the Beatles cartoon series from the 1960s.

In any case, the English-language dubbing of *Atoll K* obviously relied on American voices, as no British English (with the exception of the British radio announcer) is to be heard in the movie. This corresponds to the information found on the leader of the existing 16mm copy of the 98-minute English-language version mentioned in chapter 8. It contains the French-language note "son américain" ("American Sound"), but not "son anglais" ("English Sound.") Furthermore, the English-dialogue script, dated July 29, 1951, bears the French stamp "Dialogues américains" ("American Dialogue"), but not "Dialogues anglais."

While the Italian dubbing of *Atollo K* shows that the C.D.C. took great care in preparing a proper adaptation, the exact opposite is true of the English-language dubbing. It is distressing to hear the artless, uninspired recitals of the English dialogue, the one exception being the role of Antoine.

Yet the dubbers and their listless readings are just the first of many flaws in *Atoll K*'s disastrous dubbing into English language. The sound has been recorded in an entirely sterile atmosphere, with no audible distinction whether the action takes place indoors or in the open air. Instead, all we hear is the stuffy studio atmosphere. Even worse, the audio provides a visual example of how to destroy a dubbing job: on several occasions the sound is out of synch with the picture, the low point being the horrific handling of both of Suzy Delair's songs. In the English-language version, Delair's songs are not only out of synch and totally lacking in atmosphere, but performed by a totally lackluster English-language voice actress. Instead of charm, all we feel is impatience. If it were not for Laurel and Hardy's sterling voices, there would be little interest in a botch job that barely merits discussion. To do it justice, *Atoll K* should be redubbed anew into English in a sympathetic, artistic manner.

Aside from the dubbing, *Atoll K*'s English-language version provides a few variations from the other, previously discussed versions. For starters, its opening credits run longer than other known versions. The design is identical to the French version, but provides less information. The scriptwriter credits differ completely. Alongside Wheeler and Tellini, who are given credit in the French version, Klorer and Kohner are listed as well — although they had left the project after completing the second treatment. This is the first time we see Monty Collins credited for contributing "gags."

The plaque outside Bramwell's London office simply reads "Bramwell, Solicitor" in the English-language version. Oddly, this sign does not appear in the 98-minute English-language version nor in the familiar American version *Utopia*, but in the British *Robinson Cru-*

Voice actor Paul Frees, 1960s. Did he contribute to the dubbing of the English version? (author's collection).

soeland and in the German release of *Atoll K*, due to the fact that the German variant was based on the English-language version. (More on this in chapter 14.) Presumably an error in the editing room places the French plaque in most English-language versions, regardless of the length. Otherwise the multilingual shots of the monkey/lion cage, the fuel gauge, Chérie's checkroom, newspapers, travel information and the advertisement in front of the reopened Café Crusoe are an integral part of the English-language version.

As in the French version, Giovanni verbally explains his reasons for running away to sea, meaning that his employer does not appear in the English-language version. The order of the radio announcers varies slightly from the French version: the American speaker begins, followed by his Spanish colleague and then by the Italian woman, before the French announcer takes over. From this point the American announcer does most of the reporting, including the final announcement of the appointment of the international commission, with a brief interruption from the British speaker and his slip, "Atoll H." In contrast to the other two original versions, the German speaker is missing completely.

Unlike the Italian version, Ollie is not seen posting the English proclamation. Otherwise, the surroundings resemble the French version, with a slight variation from the other original versions: a man with a shovel and two other men are working to the right of the picture, when the brute from the French version appears with two women on his arms. This time they walk differently through the picture, and the workers make way for them. The lout with the two women pushes the shovel-bearing worker out of the picture, as he does in the French version. Finally, there are again four voiceover commentaries placed as in the French version and nearly identical with the exception of an irrelevant variation.[5]

Although *Atoll K* had been dubbed into American English, it was not initially released in the United States. Instead it was launched in Europe. Titled *Robinson Crusoeland*, it first saw light in cinemas in Great Britain.

But, strangely, the marketing history of *Atoll K*'s English-language version does not start in Europe, but in the U.S. On September 20, 1951, Bookbinder, as president of his enterprise All Star and the man who masterminded the production of the movie in 1949, submitted the English-dialogue script for the 100-minute version of *Atoll K*'s final cut to the Motion Picture Division of the New York Education Department, requesting a license to release the movie.[6] Bookbinder had already been prompted to cut the film to a length of 8,188 feet, or a running time of approximately 91 minutes. The structure of this cut remains unknown. The same day, the authority approved *Atoll K*'s release.[7]

On October 3, 1951, Laurel wrote in a letter that *Atoll K* was to be released in the United States under another title during December of that same year[8]: "I think the picture we made in France is to be released here in December — they are changing the title, so as soon as I do hear, will let you know and when it plays in your Metropolis, you will see Babe and me with a bunch of Wild Foreigners!"

In late December 1951 or early January 1952, Laurel and Hardy, who were soon to embark on their second postwar British stage tour, were interviewed by Erskine Johnson. The subject was their revival on American television, which reportedly saw the boys showered with offers. Though the TV showings of their old two-reelers did not net the comedians a single dime, they did win the team a whole new generation of fans. During the interview Erskine referred briefly to *Atoll K* and to Laurel's stay at the Paris hospital. Laurel now reported that the movie was set to be released in the United States during the current

The English version proclamation (screen capture from *Utopia*).

winter season.[9] Yet it would be another three years until Laurel and Hardy's final movie had its American premiere. Most likely *Variety*'s November 21, 1951, review of *Atoll K*'s French version created second thoughts about an immediate American release.

Since *Atoll K*'s English-language version was completed and ready for release, it still made sense to book it in cinemas as quickly as possible. Why not start in the United Kingdom? The British exhibitors were more likely to have consulted domestic trade papers, not the U.S. *Variety* review or those in the French and Italian journals. For the time being, Franco London in Paris could hope that no negative reviews had preceded *Atoll K*. Therefore, Franco London entered into a contract with International Film Distributors, Ltd. [International Film] to exploit the movie in the United Kingdom.

Though complete opening credits under the title *Atoll K* had been provided, the movie was retitled *Robinson Crusoeland* for the British market, and presumably for the entire territory of the day's British Empire. Whether or not the new title was an attempt to minimize financial risks resulting from negative American, French and Italian reviews is a matter of speculation.

However, as in France and Italy, the distributors had no intention of releasing the 100-minute version of *Atoll K* in Great Britain. Instead it was cut down to 8,500 feet for a

1952 British *Robinson Crusoeland* poster art (courtesy Glenn Mitchell).

running time of 94 minutes and 27 seconds. Afterwards, distributor International Film submitted *Robinson Crusoeland* to the London British Board of Censors licensing the movie for public distribution without demanding further cuts and without any further reservations on November 12, 1951, classifying it "U."[10] Which scenes were cut from *Atoll K* to trim the submitted print by five and a half minutes cannot be determined since this version is not known to survive today.

International Film remained busy, organizing trade shows to showcase *Robinson Crusoeland* at the beginning of January 1952,

Distributor's label of the 1952 British version *Robinson Crusoeland* (screen capture from *Robinson Crusoeland*).

in London and other major British cities. To advertise the film, conventional lobby cards were created from stills, with the title and distributor information printed in the basebar of each still.[11] The distributor also commissioned promotional illustrations to be published by the trade press. The design was culled from Minerva's 1951 Italian *Atollo K* promotional graphics, showing Stan and Ollie engulfed in a cloud alongside a quartet of Hawaiian beauties, with the motto "Get away from it all ... to an island paradise!" The poster had a slightly cartoonish feel, with Stan and Ollie's faces given a strange, almost Martian-like, tinge of green.[12] When *Robinson Crusoeland* was later distributed in Britain by E.J. Fancey Productions, Inc., this design was dumped in favor of a rather cheaply made poster depicting caricatures of Stan and Ollie aboard a ship bearing the title of the movie.

International Film's trade shows took place between January 3 and 10, 1952. On January 3, *Robinson Crusoeland* played in London (Studio One), Birmingham (Futurist Theatre), Leeds (Tower Cinema) and Manchester (Oxford Picture House), on January 4, in Cardiff (Park Hall Cinema), Newcastle (Essoldo Theatre) and Sheffield (Cinema House), on January 8, in Glasgow (La Scala Cinema) and finally on January 10, in at least one other British cinema.[13] On January 4, 1952, the trade paper *To-Day's Cinema* praised *Robinson Crusoeland*[14]:

> The film is produced on a lavish scale with big island locations, two catchy ditties and plenty of celebrated clowning from Laurel and Hardy in their own original style. Be it Stan wrestling with an inflated life raft or Ollie encountering bats, the team provoke plenty of chuckles with their succession of time-honored gags. Plenty of noisy action is available in the film's climax which has Stan and Ollie almost dangling from a rope's end, and it makes a fitting finale to the whole zany plot.

The critic was further impressed by the pace of the action, Suzy Delair's charismatic performance, the performances of the movie's main costars alongside Laurel and Hardy, as well as Joannon's good direction. His final verdict: "Grand attraction for star devotees and rib-tickler for the popular hall."

The trade paper *Daily Film Renter* was equally benevolent[15]:

Refreshing general laugh-maker that will be especially welcomed by the faithful fans ... Laurel and Hardy are their inimitable selves with the inevitable "another fine mess you've got me in..." fade out ... Max Elloy and Adriano Rimoldi do good work as the comedy pair's adventurous companions.

A couple of days later, however, trade paper *Kinematograph Weekly* posted a decidedly more lukewarm review, pointing out that *Robinson Crusoeland* was also suitable for children[16]:

Generously mounted slapstick comedy ... headed by popular American comedians, Stan Laurel and Oliver Hardy.... The co-stars never waver ... but an unnecessary strain is put on its cast and its audience by excess footage. It would have been twice as good if it had been a third shorter. Star and title pull is, however, considerable. Acceptable light fare for industrial and family halls.
    The picture has quite a witty story, but refuses to leave well alone. Bright cracks at taxation, democracy and dictatorship, staged against colorful backgrounds, are all too frequently bogged down in a welter of obvious slapstick. Stan Laurel and Oliver Hardy improvise effectively and help to absorb the padding.... Incidentally, there is still time to trim its sails.

This final suggestion was a broad hint to further cut the movie prior to its public release. The trade paper's critics, as well as the reviewer of the British Film Institute's *Monthly Film Bulletin*, had seen *Robinson Crusoeland* at the trade-show length of 8,621 feet (approximately 96 minutes).[17] In other words, the movie was now roughly two minutes longer than the version submitted to the British Board of Film Censors. Interestingly, *Robinson Crusoeland*'s trade-show version included both of Suzy Delair's songs,[18] although the first of them is missing from the 98-minute English-language version of *Atoll K*.

When International Film issued its advertising material to cinema owners, the distributor had complied with *Kinematograph Weekly's* urgent recommendation. Prior to the official British release, *Robinson Crusoeland* had been shortened substantially, albeit not for a third of its 100 minutes, but for nearly 14 minutes running time from the trade-show version. Thus International Film reported *Robinson Crusoeland*'s length as 7,509 feet or 82 minutes in its distributing documents.

For decades the search for a copy of *Robinson Crusoeland* seemed to have been in vain. Recently a nearly complete print of the 82-minute version has resurfaced. But, despite the

similar running times, it is now beyond a shadow of a doubt that *Robinson Crusoeland* differs significantly from its U.S. counterpart, *Utopia*.[19] *Robinson Crusoeland* is yet another edit unlike *Utopia*. Overall, it appears that the further editing of *Robinson Crusoeland* put the stress on a comprehensible plot, sometimes even at the expense of Stan and Ollie's scenes. Nevertheless, the two comedians remain strongly in the middle of the interest, as many non–Stan-and-Ollie scenes had also been cut.

Title of the 1952 British version *Robinson Crusoeland* (screen capture fom *Robinson Crusoeland*).

1952 British *Robinson Crusoeland* lobby card (courtesy Chris Seguin).

Robinson Crusoeland opens with International Film's label presenting the distributor's name and flying brants. The credits are nearly identical to those of the 98-minute English-language version *Atoll K.* The only difference is the film title itself which has been recreated graphically after the typeface "Atoll K." International Film's credits for the scriptwriters underwent a strange metamorphosis. According to these opening credits, Frederick Kohner did not team up with the other writers — his brother, movie agent P. (Paul) Kohner did. In fact, Paul Kohner had nothing to do with *Atoll K*'s script. His role, on behalf of Bookbinder, was merely to *find* a scriptwriter for the film. This misinformation seems to be the result of a typo confusing the first letter of Frederick Kohner's given name. This inevitably caused a domino effect; elsewhere in Europe "P. Kohner" was also credited as one of the scriptwriters.

As mentioned earlier, Bramwell's English notary plaque appears immediately after the few shots of London. There are no cuts until the moment when Giovanni falls out of the sail aboard the *Momus.* But, presumably, the further scenes until the beginning of the thunderstorm (Giovanni discovered as stowaway, his outburst of fury and the introductions to each other) underwent an even heavier editing than in the American version *Utopia* which is discussed in the following chapter.[20]

The first regrettable loss is the tightening of scenes depicting the four castaways cultivating the island. Antoine's search for his cooking pot (Giovanni has pinched it to mix concrete) is missing as are a few glimpses of Stan in front of his newly constructed home. We are left wondering where things came from, especially the bungalow adjoining Oscar's lobster-doghouse. The original commentary telling us of the years of toil spent settling the atoll has also been cut, leaving the false impression that the islanders miraculously transformed the barren rock into an island paradise overnight.

Such cuts, however, do not affect the plot of the movie, nor does the removal of Chérie's audition at the nightclub. The voiceover no longer introduces her as the most glamorous girl in Tahiti, who comes from Paris and has "plenty of brains and culture" but only as the Eve desperately missing from the atoll. This tightened section still provides a smooth transition, taking Chérie directly from the nightclub to the wedding chamber where her announcement of her newly signed contract provokes the bridal bickering.

Therefore, Chérie's second song appears to be her first one. The British distributor decided not to employ its weak English-language dubbing, but to rely on Suzy Delair's excellent original French performance, a truly artistic advantage. Whether the distributor made up his mind for this change after the British trade shows from early 1952 remains unclear.

Aside from a few minor cuts, Chérie's clash with the captain's wife is also retained. The trims include Mrs. Dolan making her way down to Chérie's cabin (she suddenly appears out of nowhere) and forcing Chérie at gunpoint to climb into the rowboat.

The breakfast scene inside Antoine's and Giovanni's cabin includes an added insert shot missing from the 100-minute version of *Atoll K*, and is only to be found in *Robinson Crusoeland*. In its original edit, the scene leaves it up to the viewer to decide whether the men are

1952 Canadian *Robinson Crusoeland* lobby card with pasted-on still (courtesy Chris Seguin).

Frugal British rerelease poster art for *Robinson Crusoeland* (courtesy Bram Reijnhoudt).

crying for Chérie or for Fraser when she surprises the castaways with yet another pot of bouillabaisse. But the British version attempts to provide a different reason for the men's tears, as would the German version (see chapter 14). As Chérie places the pot on the table, there is a quick flashback to Oscar's kennel — showing the frying pan Stan's pet lobster had bathed in before Chérie's arrival. These few frames from the earlier scene are a clumsy attempt to suggest that Oscar has ended up in the soup. In reality, Oscar is not mentioned at all during the breakfast scene in any of *Atoll K*'s original versions.

Minor trims versus wholesale cutting seem to have been the mandate of *Robinson Crusoeland*'s editors. Arriving at Chérie's new home, her remark "As warehouses go, it's a funny one" is gone, necessitating the removal of Antoine's line "Did you really think we were building a refrigerator?" Later Frazer arrives on the atoll — his confrontation with Chérie is softened somewhat in *Robinson Crusoeland*. Barging into Chérie's happy reverie, he wonders whether she is playing Snow White and the Seven Dwarves. His taunt, "You're not content just to be a singer, you've also got to be the comedian," is cut. Also missing, in contrast to the English-dialogue script, is the German announcer following the Washington press conference. Of course, neither edit will be noticed by the audience.

At this point the edits to *Robinson Crusoeland* begin in earnest. Gone are the scenes with Stan and Ollie cleaning house, the arrival of various ethnic stereotypes outside their cabin, and the onslaught of humanity onto Crusoeland. The action continues from the moment the mother dries her children' faces with the flag. Consequently, there is neither the arrival of the countless immigrants nor the recognition of Crusoeland's sovereignty. Surprisingly, these cuts barely affect the plotline.

Even more substantial cuts concern the action in the reopened Café Crusoe, excising, once again, lengthy scenes featuring Laurel and Hardy (the scenes aboard the *Momus* preceding the thunderstorm plus the scene discussed in the previous paragraph). Cut from this sequence are the newcomer to whom Stan hands over two free bottles of liquor, and the gangster who expects a profit from the liquor he brought to the Crusoeland. Alecto's arrival at the bar and his gruff dismissal of the gangster were also deleted. Instead, Alecto appears from nowhere to drag Chérie to his side, leading the viewer to assume that Stan and Ollie want to "import" Alecto to defend Chérie's honor. All in all, Alecto's level of menace is severely downplayed in *Robinson Crusoeland* (moreso than even the French version). Missing, too, is the conspiratorial meeting with his henchmen.

Furthermore, a few of Alecto's inflammatory declarations have been deleted. Having overthrown Crusoeland's government in Stan and Ollie's bungalow, he arrests the cabinet — with the exception of Chérie whom he wants to put under his "personal protection." Though he announces that Stan, Ollie, Antoine and Giovanni will be hanged in *Robinson Crusoeland*, he does not proclaim that the gallows will soon be erected. This version also eliminates Alecto's personal inspection of the ropes that will hang the doomed men. None of these changes affect the coherence of the plot, but they further downplay Alecto's despotism.

Finally, Stan and Ollie's final scene has been kept intact (unlike the French version), giving British audiences one last opportunity to fully experience Laurel and Hardy together.

When the first reviews of trade-show screenings of *Robinson Crusoeland* were printed in mid–January 1952, the trade papers were unable to provide a definitive release date in Great Britain. A specific date was still to be determined. Nevertheless, *Robinson Crusoeland* was soon in the news. On January 28, 1952, the visibly recuperated Stan Laurel and his partner arrived at Southampton on board the *Queen Mary*, to commence their aforementioned British tour.

After landing, Laurel and Hardy were greeted on the dock by Hawaiian-garbed girls, not unlike the South Seas beauties depicted on International Film's promotional materials for *Robinson Crusoeland*. Of course, the Hawaiian girls arrived thanks to the distributor. The opportunity to combine the arrival of the two comedians to the United Kingdom with publicity for their current movie was not to be missed, especially since Laurel and Hardy's

1952 British "faces" publicity for *Robinson Crusoeland* (author's collection).

reception at Southampton was filmed by newsreel cameras. In other words, Laurel and Hardy's appearance would soon be seen on cinema screens across the country, courtesy of a Movietone newsreel released on January 31, 1952.[21] In it, Laurel and Hardy flirt with the Hawaiian girls; one of them kisses Laurel on the cheek and in return he presents her with a lollipop. Hardy suggests they should take the girls out to see *Robinson Crusoeland* that afternoon. "Good idea," replies Laurel.

This does not mean that *Robinson Crusoeland* was actually playing on movie screens on January 28, 1952, either in Southampton or in London, Laurel and Hardy's next stop. The official release of the movie was announced by the trade papers at the beginning of February, still without an exact date. Laurel and Hardy's current British tour coincided nicely with this timing.[22]

At the end of February 1952, *Robinson Crusoeland* was advertised on the cover of *To-Day's Cinema*. Not later than mid–March 1952 the movie was screened at Portsmouth's Essoldo Theatre, at least half a year earlier than assumed until now.[23] The presentation came complete with the necessary publicity. For the campaign International Film's public relations manager ordered human-sized papier-mâché replicas of Laurel and Hardy's famous faces, including bowler hats and the inscription *Robinson Crusoeland*. The oversized heads were introduced in London, where the distributor had its head office, and men were hired to walk up and down Picadilly Circus wearing them.[24] They made for appropriately eye-catching street-level publicity, especially in busy shopping areas. For one occasion the distributor also provided smaller Laurel-and-Hardy heads for sidewalk exploitation. Regardless of their size, the comedian's papier-mâché heads were called "faces" by the British advertisements.[25]

The large-scale heads seemed to inspire similar publicity internationally in future years. When *The Bohemian Girl* (1936) premiered as *Dick und Doof werden Papa* ("Dick and Doof as Daddies") in the Federal Republic of Germany in August 1957, the German distributor employed comparable items. This was repeated with enormous success years later, when *Jitterbugs* (1943) was released to German cinemas in 1965 as *Dick und Doof und die Wunderpille* ["Dick und Doof and the Wonder Pill"].[26]

On the occasion of the Portsmouth premiere, the "faces" visited a hospital and a football match, among other places.[27] The owner of the Essoldo resorted to other unorthodox methods to promote *Robinson Crusoeland*. Instead of using International Film's promotional trailer, he produced a trailer of his own using a well-known radio announcer.[28] The Portsmouth promotional campaign was so successful that the manager of the Essoldo partook in the annual "Showman's-Credit-Award" contest,[29] like many of his colleagues with similar *Robinson Crusoeland* campaigns over the course of the year.[30] All of this was supported by Laurel and Hardy's ongoing personal appearance tour.[31]

At the end of April 1952, *Robinson Crusoeland* started a run at Liverpool's Scala Cinema, where the movie had been screened four months earlier during the initial trade shows. While Laurel and Hardy look-alikes strolled the streets of Liverpool, a local dance hall arranged a *Robinson Crusoeland* evening, presumably to the mutual benefit of both the cinema owner and the manager of the dance hall. The dance hall's orchestra put on funny clothing and, accompanied by the Laurel and Hardy "faces," walked across town playing music.[32]

At around the same time, *Robinson Crusoeland* played at the Maidstone Central. Reporting on the event said[33]:

> Utilising the giant papier-mâché heads of the two stars, a parade around the town was arranged, a window tie-up with the local toy shop finalized, and window space next door to the theatre garnered for extra display. A painting competition was also sponsored.

British cinema owners ordered so many of these giant heads from the distributor that the manufacturer could not keep up with the demand. For a short time, delivery of the "faces" bypassed International Film and went directly to the exhibitors, in order for them to employ the papier-mâché heads on time.[34] All this ballyhoo yielded tremendous fruit, bringing "sensational opening and follow-up business" and labeling *Robinson Crusoeland* a "huge grosser."[35] From the end of May until June 1952, the box-office at the Cambridge Rex allowed the distributor to boast: "International's movies defeat the weather." Similarly successful activities took place at the cinemas Park Hall, Broadway and Granby in Cardiff, Hammersmith and Reading, respectively. Of course, these local efforts resembled their well-proven predecessors. There were slight variations, of course, with balloons and vouchers given away for reduced admissions. Other joint campaigns with local pubs offering reduced admissions to dance halls or similar amusements — but not dealing directly with the movie — were offered. Free comic books, too, were distributed to children.[36]

Robinson Crusoeland remained part of British cinema programs until at least the end of October 1952. The trade papers continued to report on noteworthy advertising campaigns — for example, in the towns of Horsham, Oldham and Stornoway, as well as the London district of Islington — essentially pointing out how box-office results benefited from good P.R.[37] The success of these local publicity strategies may be the reason that International Film, with two exceptions, found it unnecessary to place large-sized advertisements in British trade papers.

International Film also sold *Robinson Crusoeland* to at least one other distributor, London-based Butcher's Film Service Ltd.[38] For years it was believed that another distributor, Equity, rereleased *Robinson Crusoeland* in the United Kingdom under the title *Escapade*.[39] But this was not the case. As early as February 29, 1952, Equity arranged an *Escapade* trade show at the London G.B. Theatre. *Escapade* was simply a compilation of the Laurel and Hardy shorts *Oliver the Eighth* (1934), *The Chimp* and *The Music Box* (both 1932).[40]

Robinson Crusoeland left its mark outside the cinemas, too. It showed up in narrative form in *Super Cinema Annual 1953*, which claimed to be "the finest family fun book of the year" and had been published continuously for years. Under the headlines "Laughs Galore with Laurel and Hardy" and "You Just Can't Help Laughing at Stan and Olly," an unknown author retold the tale of *Robinson Crusoeland* as a children's story, interpolating a few extra details.[41] His retelling contained a couple of peculiarities, which is somehow fitting considering the number of modifications, adaptations and variations of *Atoll K* created along the way. The author provided fresh dialogue for Stan, Ollie and other characters that is nowhere to be found in the movie *Robinson Crusoeland*. According to the retelling the duo was not received by the lawyers Bramwell, Bonnefoy and Poltroni, but by Mr. Frogg, Mr. Toad and Mr. Tadpole. The most remarkable aspect of this reimagining, however, is the complete disappearance of Chérie. As there is no leading lady, there is no bride for Lieutenant Fraser. Instead, he arrives on the atoll as one of the surveyors. In the end he rescues the four male castaways simply because he is looking for a free lobster dinner! Gone, too, is Alecto's murderous attempt to hang Stan, Ollie, Antoine and Giovanni. Instead, Alecto and the islanders flee to boats as the castaways simply float away on a wooden platform. Furthermore, Antoine is saved from his darkly humorous fate in the lion cage and is left searching for a home country. Finally, the readers of *Super Cinema Annual* were informed that all of Stan and Ollie's belongings are confiscated the minute they arrive on the island.

With all this going on, it cannot really be said that *Robinson Crusoeland* was a genuine flop in the United Kingdom. At the same time, the film's reception does not seem to suggest that it left any kind of lasting impression in London or in the country's other large cinemas. If the film had been a box-office triumph, the trade papers would likely have heralded its success in the big cities. In contrast to the attention the British trade papers originally paid to *Robinson Crusoeland* (though, surprisingly, the date of the official British release was never disclosed), *Monthly Film Bulletin* as well as F. Maurice Speed's *Film Review* yearbooks kept mum on the movie to a large extent. Both publications made a habit of reviewing every film released in Great Britain, but in the case of *Robinson Crusoeland* they confined themselves to either announcing the upcoming movie (*Film Review*) or promising a review that never followed (*Monthly Film Bulletin*).[42]

Nevertheless, the movie continued to be part of the cinema programs in smaller theaters throughout the provinces, with profitable box-office proving the old maxim "every little bit helps." Beyond the United Kingdom, International Film further marketed *Robinson Crusoeland* throughout the British Empire which, in 1952, still included Australia, Canada, Cyprus, Jamaica, Ghana, Hong Kong, Malaysia, Nigeria, and Rhodesia.

In 1964, *Robinson Crusoeland* was bestowed a delayed honor in Great Britain. The movie had not been screened in the United Kingdom for many years when the National Film Theatre, run by the British Film Institute, organized three special presentations in the London Millbank Cinema, with the Laurel-and-Hardy two-reeler *Brats* (1930) as a prelude. This was part of a limited retrospective of Laurel-and-Hardy feature films. On Laurel and Hardy's final goodbye to the silver screen, the insightful John Minchinton wistfully wrote[43]:

> This was the last Laurel and Hardy film, a rarity which is rarely shown. Made in France under trying conditions it is a rather tragic yet heroic gesture. The boys retained their flair to the end, triumphing over Laurel's illness and other adversities to produce moments of their own particular wonder, such as Stanley innocently making a sandwich of Ollie's hand—complete with ketchup. This film, a dying fall, somehow adds to their endearment.

Decades later, with the video age long underway, *Atoll K* made a reappearance in Great Britain—on VHS, heavily cut, and not under the familiar U.K. title. *Robinson Crusoeland* seems to have vanished without a trace. Thus, every video offering in the U.K. is the American version, *Utopia*. Between 1992 and 2005 countless videotapes and, later, DVDs were released in the United Kingdom—Orbit Films/Storm PLC (1992) and Classic Entertainment (2005) among them—but always with the same contents and inferior picture and sound quality.

Among the worldwide flood of *Utopia* DVDs one oddity is particularly worth mentioning. Manufactured in 2005 in either Belgium or the Netherlands, the movie features Dutch subtitles but no hint of the originating distributor. The cover also bears the title *Robinson Crusoeland*, with a running time of 70 minutes. The inscription on the disc itself states a duration of 75 minutes. Regardless of the time, anyone hoping to insert the DVD and discover the long-elusive version of *Robinson Crusoeland* is due for a disappointment. This is yet another of countless copies of *Utopia* which, by the way, clocks in at 80 minutes. Let us file this disc as a chief contender for the "exceptionally scanty quality" award.

12

Utopia in the
United States of America

More than three years had passed since Bookbinder had received approval for public release of *Atoll K* from the Motion Picture Division of the New York Education Department. Perhaps it was hoped that in the intervening years the fast-paced film business would have forgotten *Variety*'s ruthless review of November 1951, which deemed the movie unsuitable for America's larger cinemas. Of course, there is always the chance that one's past can catch up with one, which is probably the reason for retitling *Atoll K* in the United States as well.

But by 1954 Bookbinder had abandoned the idea of marketing the movie he launched so many years ago.[1] On November 24, 1954, New York film merchant George J. Waldman asked the aforementioned film authority to approve the retitling of *Atoll K* to *Utopia*, receiving approval approximately one week later. At the beginning of December 1954, Waldman ordered substitute seals for *Utopia* and, by mid–December, he was finally licensed to duplicate three copies of the film for distribution purposes.[2]

At the time of Waldman's request, *Utopia* still seemed to have the 91-minute (8,188 feet) running time presented at the end of September 1951, when *Atoll K* was first licensed in New York. Actually, following the British example, the movie had been cut long ago to a running time similar to *Robinson Crusoeland*'s — thus preventing any possible reservations in the trades that the film might be too long. But *Utopia* and *Robinson Crusoeland* are two entirely different edits, as stated in the previous chapter.

In contrast to the lengthy opening credits of the original English-language version *Atoll K*, the coarse fabric background was removed for *Utopia*. Instead, the much shorter credits are presented over snippets of footage from the movie, with Stan and Ollie introduced over a close-up of their conversation aboard the *Momus*. Interestingly, there is no director credit. Berry's suspected communist sympathies do not seem to be the reason for his omission — his name already did not appear in the opening credits of the 98-minute English-language version *Atoll K*. And Leo Joannon had no apparent cause to be politically suspect in the United States.

In editing *Atoll K* down to the 82-minute *Utopia*, the distributor obviously tried to remove as many non–Laurel-and-Hardy scenes as possible to concentrate on the two comedians. Nevertheless, some Laurel-and-Hardy scenes were trimmed from *Utopia*. The original editors in Paris already had to overcome the challenge of piecing *Atoll K* into a comprehensible film. Removing a 18 minutes from the 100-minute final cut ran a further risk of destroying any semblance of a coherent plot. But this is exactly what happened in the American cut. As early as 1967, William K. Everson consequently called *Utopia* a "mutilation."[3]

Compared to its British counterpart *Robinson Crusoeland*, with which it shares an approximate running time, *Utopia* feels like it was edited with a dull axe versus the delicate and thoughtful scissoring *Robinson Crusoeland* received.

A scene found in both *Robinson Crusoeland* and in the final cut of *Atoll K*, but cut from *Utopia*, is the conversation between Antoine and Captain Bonnet after the harbor policemen have thwarted Antoine's attempt to escape in the monkey cage. Fortunately, neither this dialogue nor the conversation between the policemen who have come between Giovanni and freedom are necessary to the plot, and so they are not missed. Later, Giovanni's explanation aboard the *Momus* of why he is running away from Italy is reduced to a single sentence, leaving his motives obscure. In *Utopia* he merely states that he is playing hooky from a world where he is "always being told what to do and then how to do it."

Like *Robinson Crusoeland*, *Utopia* also misses scenes depicting the four castaways cultivating the island, among them Antoine's search for his cooking pot, as well as Stan in front of his newly constructed home. But *Utopia*'s omission of one delightfully comic touch — Stan pulling his pet lobster out of the hut with the help of a heavy chain — is a particularly sad loss, since this scene fits well with Laurel's comic sensibilities.

Chérie's introduction marks the beginning of the wholesale cutting that would have a serious impact on *Utopia*. Here is where the U.S. version begins to stray from the U.K. edit. *Robinson Crusoeland*'s voiceover introduces Chérie as "Eve," but deletes the fact that she is auditioning at the smartest nightclub in town — information that is kept in *Utopia*. While the song which wins her the nightclub contract has also been cut from *Robinson Crusoeland*, the British version offers an arguably stronger link between the introduction of Cherie and her tardy arrival at her own wedding. *Utopia*, on the other hand, promises the audience a glimpse of Cherie's audition before abruptly cutting away.

In *Utopia*, all we see of the audition is Chérie gesturing to a clearly bored nightclub manager. Cut to the registrar's office where Chérie and Frazer fail to get married. Captain Dolan is seen in only two quick glimpses, in the background in the wedding chamber and at the end of the scene at the registrar's office door. This important character is reduced to little more than a silent extra — his handing of the bridal bouquet to Chérie and his conversation with her after the aborted ceremony are gone completely. After a few words from the registrar, Chérie tells Dolan that Frazer will never see her again, even though she does not know exactly what she will do next.

The disappearance of Dolan — here and in subsequent scenes — is especially damaging to *Utopia*, since it muddies all of Chérie's motives for running away and completely obscures how she came to arrive on the island. Chérie's urgent plea to Dolan to take her aboard his ship is missing and, consequently, her grand nightclub performance in which she waits wistfully, but in vain, for Frazer. Dolan's virago of a wife, and his desperate moan about how his wife will react to Chérie, have been completely erased. So there is no clash between Chérie and Mrs. Dolan, and no argument between the captain and his wife about Chérie being left to row to the island alone. The audience sees a quick view of the island through a telescope (who is holding it?), a shot of a boat, and a cheerily waving Chérie bidding adieu from a rowboat. How did she get there? Who took her? Why drop her off here? We are left wondering.

One might argue the necessity of the two songs. Yet Chérie's audition at the Cacatoes-Club and the capricious singer's contract are the very reasons for the squabble between the tempestuous not-quite-newlyweds. Chérie's eagerness to tell her fiancé about the contract has far less importance in *Utopia*. While this is acceptable, it is downright disturbing to send her directly from the registrar's office to the atoll in a span of 20 seconds.

Immediately prior to Chérie's arrival at the boys' hut, a scene focused on Stan's naïve stupidity has been trimmed. Antoine and Giovanni no longer remark on Stan's dumbness, leaving a gap. The movie misses a reaction to Stan's innocent ineptitude — typical for a Laurel-and-Hardy movie (the comment was retained in *Robinson Crusoeland*). In this case, his vacuity has shot down the opportunity to leave the atoll behind.[4]

While *Utopia*— unlike *Robinson Crusoeland*— did not touch Frazer's dialogue upon entering Chérie's bungalow, more cuts occur after Frazer's discovery of uranium and his conversation with Stan, Ollie, Antoine and Giovanni over which nation will take possession of the island. In *Atoll K* there follows a press conference in a ministerial office, announcing the newly discovered atoll to a throng of reporters. This scene is nowhere to be found in *Utopia* (it remains, however, in *Robinson Crusoeland*). Instead, a number of hands grasp at photos and documents spilling out of a folder labeled "Atoll K." The radio announcers report on the discovery of the island but not the enormous uranium find — this negates one of the main reasons why crowds of emigrants set out for Crusoeland: the hope of capitalizing on the island's rich resources, alongside the forgiving political conditions (the newspapers failed to report the uranium find as well). Crusoeland's sovereignty remains clear, however, since the American radio announcer reports the appointment of an international commission to decide the island's fate. Unlike the British release, the American version *Utopia* preserves this sequence of events, starting with Stan and Ollie's housecleaning until the recognition of *Crusoeland's* sovereignty, all of which is missing from *Robinson Crusoeland*.

Utopia suffers the same substantial cuts concerning the action in the reopened Café Crusoe as *Robinson Crusoeland*, excising, for another time in *Utopia* (after the scenes aboard the *Momus* preceding the thunderstorm), lengthy scenes with Laurel and Hardy.

While *Robinson Crusoeland* omits, after the overthrow of government, a couple of Alecto's statements in Stan and Ollie's bungalow, they are nearly intact in *Utopia*. *Utopia* deletes, however, Alecto's suggestive remark in Stan and Ollie's bungalow that he prefers not to hang Chérie, but to put her under his "personal protection."

The events surrounding Chérie's radio S.O.S. were cut twice for *Utopia*, again differing from *Robinson Crusoeland*. The first cut eliminates Frazer's comments that he did not deliberately set out for the atoll

1954 Welch's Grape Juice advertising in *Utopia* (screen capture from *Utopia*).

and his reproach that Chérie does not need him. These cuts do not change the film dramatically, but they do paint Frazer in a gentler light than in *Atoll K's* final cut; *Robinson Crusoeland* had provided a similar change during Frazer's and Chérie's encounter in her bungalow. Alecto's call to organize the execution of Stan, Ollie, Antoine and Giovanni within the next hour has also been removed, further softening his anarchic character.

Fortunately, Stan and Ollie's final scene, which had been severely abridged in the French version, remains untouched in *Utopia*, just as it had been in *Robinson Crusoeland*. Our final screen visit with the boys is, thankfully, complete.

However, other strange happenings occur in *Utopia*. While Antoine prepares the meal in the galley of the *Momus*, he pours the boys a drink to propose a toast. In the original version he pours red wine from an unlabeled bottle. In *Utopia*, an insert shot transforms the wine into a bottle of Welch's grape juice, removed by a hand that belongs to someone other than Max Elloy. This early form of product placement is hugely overused in film productions today, but was a relatively rare occurrence in the 1950s (one of the most blatant early examples was the Marx Brothers' final film, 1949's *Love Happy*). In many ways it resembled the placement of a sponsor's product in TV programs of the time. *Utopia*'s U.S. distributor presumably charged a hefty sum for this placement, hoping to boost the movie's revenues

1954 *Utopia* lobby card with Chérie knocking down more mobsters [deleted scene] (author's collection).

Visible patch work on the 1954 *Utopia* poster art (courtesy Scott MacGillivray).

outside the box-office. In 1954 Welch's grape juice was already an established, popular product well-suited to this type of promotion. From 1951 on Welch's had been advertised so successfully on TV that, in 1955, they took over sponsorship of Walt Disney's *Mickey Mouse Club* and, years later, the popular cartoon series *The Flintstones.*[5] All that is missing from this strange addition to *Utopia* is Alfred Hitchcock appearing to mock the sponsor, as he did from October 1955 onward in his highly acclaimed TV series *Alfred Hitchcock Presents* and *Alfred Hitchcock Hour.*[6]

In the United States, *Utopia* had been taken under the wing of Philadelphia distributor Exploitation Productions. They promoted the movie at 80 minutes, even though it clocked in at two minutes more and, according to the press, should play for 83 minutes. Exploitation Productions provided a large-sized campaign book for theater owners, without mentioning the director or producer by name, but offering trivia for the press as well as a summary of the plot. The promotional material consisted of paperboard mats with close-ups of Laurel and Hardy, suggesting both men were in better physical condition than they would actually be seen in the movie. The mats depicted the Hawaiian beauties known from the British *Robinson Crusoeland* graphics and the Italian *Atollo K* publicity, but the exotic lovelies are not employed on the *Utopia* poster or on the full-color lobby cards. The lobby cards replace the grass-skirted girls with a photo of Chérie, attractively attired in beachwear.

Like the film, the poster for *Utopia* is something of a patchwork. The separate picture and type elements were produced on different sheets of paper, then clipped out and glued

Foreign agents disguised as an international commission? 1954 *Utopia* publicity shot. Hardy shaking hands with Charles Lémontier (author's collection).

onto unused poster paper. The reproduction of this clumsy collage could not conceal the elements from which it was cobbled together.

The distributor's press blurb for one of the stills provided another curiosity. Ollie is presented in his presidential outfit with his copy of *Robinson Crusoe* tucked under his arm, at the very moment the chairman of the international commission approves Crusoeland's sovereignty by handshake. The photo's caption suggests that *Utopia*'s U.S. distributor had not seen the movie themselves; the text describes a rather intriguing situation found neither in the script nor in the movie: "*Atoll K*— Greeting a delegation of foreign agents disguised as an international commission is Oliver Hardy."

Exploitation Productions also provided a black-and-white drawing aimed at children, showing Stan and Ollie stranded on the atoll. Cinema owners were advised to hold a coloring contest with the drawing, and to arrange a pie-eating contest under the slogan "If you were in Utopia how many pies could you eat?" Furthermore, patrons were encouraged to write essays based on their ideas of utopia or to appear dressed up as Laurel and Hardy. The best efforts would be rewarded. Along with the information that *Utopia* was Laurel and Hardy's first new movie in years, Exploitation Productions came up with a number of advertising catchphrases, none of them particularly ingenious: "Eat, Sleep and Laugh: Utopia," "Have the Time of Your Life: Utopia" and "Get Away from Taxes: Utopia."

Finally, the distributor produced a hundred-second trailer, without announcer voiceover but punctuated with captions that cleverly wove together short scenes from the film to intrigue and dazzle the viewer. The trailer begins with the boys' entrance at the notary, accompanied by the announcement, "They're back!" Next Stan and Ollie disembark from the stranded *Momus* and tear their jackets, as they did in *Berth Marks* (1929). Another caption states: "In Their First NEW Comedy Feature In Years." Cut to Stan on the atoll, with his name superimposed beneath him. Ollie is introduced in much the same way, as he pratfalls onto the watermelon aboard the *Momus*. While Stan, Ollie, Antoine, Giovanni and Chérie walk across the atoll, the name of the distributor and the title *Utopia* are shown. The trailer then cuts to Ollie conversing with Stan about life on the open sea. Antoine's lion cage follows, although with the rather misleading caption "More Fun Than A Circus." After Alecto hits Ollie on the head with a tray and the bats have swarmed the castaways, there is another caption: "New 80 Minute Comedy Riot." The trailer ends on Ollie moaning his classic "Well, here's another nice mess you've gotten me into!" before the names of the two comedians, the movie's distributor and title concludes the reel.

Despite the lively trailer, the trade paper *The Exhibitor* was underwhelmed. The lack of enthusiasm is evident in a few dry words[7]: "A lot of money was spent on production, but the slapstick antics of Laurel and Hardy will appeal most to the kids."

And then, at long last, *Utopia* made its debut in U.S. cinemas. New York movie merchant Waldman kept the marketing momentum going. Exploitation Productions arranged the U.S. premiere of Laurel and Hardy's latest movie for the very day the distributor received the license for duplicate prints for *Utopia* from the Motion Picture Division of the New York Education Department. On December 14, 1954, *Utopia* premiered at the New York Globe cinema on a double bill with an hour-long documentary, *This Is Your Army* (John J. Gordon). According to his daughter Lois, Stan Laurel was less than happy about the U.S. screenings, having assumed to his relief that *Atoll K* was to be shown only in Europe.[8] However, Laurel himself wrote in a letter dated October 3, 1951, that the film was to be released soon in the United States. Both comedians relayed the same story, without any further comment, in an interview published at the beginning of 1952.[9]

While the *New York Times* critic discussed the documentary in favorable detail the next day, he had only a few words for *Utopia,* none of them positive. Of course, Stan and Ollie did not inherit the atoll as he claimed[10]:

> The Messrs. Laurel and Hardy herein are awkwardly involved in some hectic silliness on a South Seas atoll they've inherited. Mlle. Delair is called on merely to be strident, muscular and amorous in the English-language-dubbed farce. Oliver Hardy is the standard globular and exasperated type he has portrayed so many times before. Mr. Laurel appears woefully haggard. No wonder. The boys never should have left home.

Soon afterward, *Variety* also reported on *Utopia,* reprinting an excerpt from the November 21, 1951 review. This time they were slightly more appreciative, omitting the earlier review's crushing introductory sentences. A few new lines even seemed to recommend the movie, but not without reservations: "Old Laurel and Hardy routines seem to lack their previous zest. Hardy's resigned double-takes and the Laurel crying do not register for heavy yocks."[11]

In January 1955 *Utopia* also played as second feature to *Blackboard Jungle* (Richard Brooks, 1955) in two large, downtown Los Angeles cinemas: the State and the Hollywood RKO Pantages Theatre. The double bill played May 11–31, 1955, at the RKO Pantages, and was extended an additional week at the State, until June 7, 1955.

When the *Los Angeles Times* checked out *Blackboard Jungle* on May 12, 1955, the reviewer found a few words to comment on *Utopia,* too. It could not recommend it: "Foreigners' voices are dubbed—badly. The film gets off with some welcome chuckles but grows progressively worse."

Variety published another *Utopia* review the same day; the reviewer had watched the film the previous day in Hollywood. Again the trade paper was less than enthusiastic:

> It's the first new film for the comedy team in a decade (their last was *The Bullfighters* at 20th Century-Fox' [in] '45) and there's little, if any, evidence of a change-in-format from their previous pix. Film's a sure-pleaser for the Laurel and Hardy following and okay as supporting fare for most situations, albeit overlong at 83 minutes.... Laurel and Hardy trademarks abound throughout—the slapstick, Stan's predicaments and his accompanying whines, Ollie's weight problem (he's heavier yet) and such. Performance-wise, they're the same team that worked those Metro two-reelers [years ago].
>
> Film ... carries no producer and director credit; nor does the pressbook. They needn't feel ashamed, however. *Utopia* is not what the title implies nor is it art. But it's in the Laurel and Hardy groove.

On May 22, 1955, the *Los Angeles Times* published another review under the headline "Laurel and Hardy's Latest Utopia Lost." This ends with a wisp of nostalgia:

> One of the strangest of recent exhibits is *Utopia....* Chaotic result. A René Clair might have made an acceptable social satire out of this, but what materializes on the screen is simply bumbling chaos. As for the stars, Oliver Hardy holds up as his usual grumpy self, but the lovable Stan Laurel appears cruelly emaciated by his long illness. It is all too plain that *Utopia* is destined to be the last of the Laurel and Hardy comedies. For the many happy hours they have given us, our grateful thanks.

In the United States—Laurel and Hardy's homeland—*Utopia* was no blockbuster. The relatively few copies Waldman ordered for the New York release demonstrates that he, too, did not have high expectations.[12] As Scott MacGillivray found out, *Utopia* had a hard slog ahead in the nation's smaller cinemas. In 1956 the owner of Chicago's Empress Theatre, facing lackluster box-office after a five-day run, came up with an unique solution to boost receipts: he advertised *Utopia* as an Abbott & Costello comedy! It is very likely that Laurel and Hardy never learned of this, but there was irony in the way that they would once again be supplanted by the comedy team that usurped them in 1941 with the phenomenal success of *Buck Privates* (Arthur Lubin).[13]

In autumn 1957, Exploitation Productions considered releasing *Utopia* as half of a double bill with a reissue of the horror movie *Dementia* (John Parker, 1955), retitled *Daughter of Horror*.[14] Afterward, in late autumn, *Utopia* played in Boston for a short time.[15] In September 1957 another distributor, New York's Realart Film Exchange (a subsidiary of American International Pictures), made arrangements to acquire *Utopia*.[16] Yet it remains unclear whether this distributor actually released the film.

Utopia's poor reception in the United States has long been the matter of a great deal of speculation. By the 1960s it was rumored that codirector John Berry was the cause for its obscurity — McCarthy-era distributors would have avoided like the plague any film associated with a suspected communist sympathizer.[17] However, the fact that there had been no official word on Berry's contribution to *Atoll K* seems to contradict this theory. Being marketed by a relatively unknown distributor like Exploitation Pictures does not explain it either. When, in 1958, Robert Youngson failed to align his now-legendary compilation *The Golden Age of Comedy* with a major distributor, he sold it to the insignificant Distributors Corporation of America — and scored a phenomenal success. The screening rights were promptly purchased by 20th Century–Fox, who played up Youngson's two previous Oscar wins and subsequently earned a tidy profit.

Utopia, on the other hand, was never accepted by a major distributor. What is worse, it was never submitted for copyright in the United States until the 1980s.[18] This made *Utopia* fair game, resulting in countless offerings on the 16mm and 8mm collector's market. Nevertheless, until the mid–1970s, *Utopia* still seemed to be something of a rarity.[19] In 1977 something truly exceptional hit the U.S. home-movie market: a company called Matinee Memories released a plain box labeled in red, handwritten text "Laurel + Hardy Out-takes." Inside was a 400-foot Super-8 reel (running approximately 20 minutes) containing scenes cut from the English-language version of *Atoll K* for *Utopia*, as well as a few scenes familiar from *Utopia*.[20]

The dawn of the video age in the early 1980s spelled the end of the Super-8 home-movie market. But it marked a new era for *Utopia*. Since the title was public domain, it seemed everyone could release it in the United States without copyright concerns. Soon the market was flooded with VHS releases, most of them with inferior picture and sound. *Utopia* quickly became the most easily available Laurel and Hardy film, found in supermarket bargain bins across the country. In Europe, most VHS releases of *Utopia* came from Great Britain.

The only thing that set these countless VHS releases apart was the packaging. Most were totally unimaginative, often having nothing to do with the film itself. The occasional release featured colored stills from *Atoll K* as cover art. One of the most interesting photos appeared on the Congress Video Group release, depicting Stan and Ollie in front of microphones following the recognition of Crusoeland's sovereignty by the international commission. Next to Ollie stands the reporter Osborne who, according to the script, interviewed Ollie on the unique nature of the island state. Another curiosity was offered by New Age Video, Inc., in 1988. Under the heading "Popcorn Classics," *Utopia* was packaged like a popcorn bag, accompanied by a ration of microwave popcorn. The label on the tape includes the overblown banner "Greatest Film Classics," a designation which, in this case, can certainly be disputed.

The tangled mess of such offerings became even messier with the introduction of DVDs. *Utopia*—like countless other public domain titles—was suddenly everywhere. The packaging

1988 Popcorn Classics video cover for *Utopia* (author's collection).

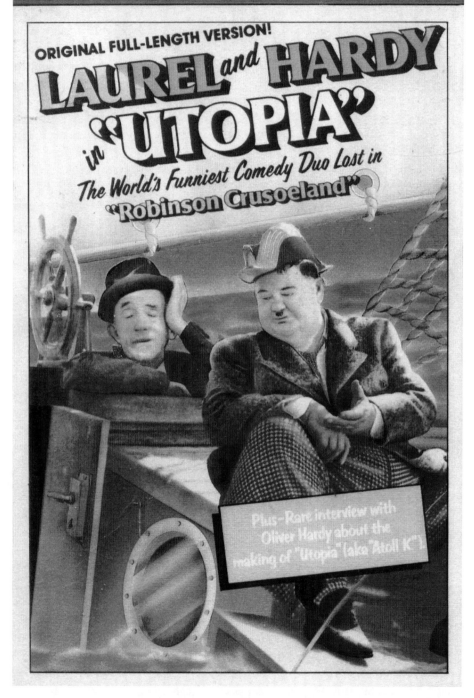

1986 Hal Roach Studios Film Classics, Inc. video cover for *Utopia* (author's collection).

could be extremely deceptive: artwork for two of these DVDs was culled from *Way Out West* (1937) and *Swiss Miss* (1938). The previous chapter already makes mention of the odd *Robinson Crusoeland* DVD. Another DVD, published in Europe in 2005, also merits special mention. More on this in the final chapter.

In the United States, *Utopia* also received television airplay as episode 23 of the syndicated *Laurel and Hardy Show* (premiering 1986). This resulted in yet another oddity. Paul Misraki's music from the opening and closing credits was replaced by music from Laurel and Hardy's Roach feature *Block-Heads* (1938).[21] Obviously this was an attempt to register copyright for an edition that had been slightly altered from the public domain version. Indeed, Hal Roach Studios — which had nothing to do with the production of *Atoll K* and *Utopia*— requested and received U.S. copyright for their modification of *Utopia* in summer 1986. Therefore, in the same year, Hal Roach Studios was able to print their copyright entry on press photos from the film, as well as on the cover of their VHS release in September 1986 under the label "Hal Roach Studios, Film Classics Inc." According to the cover, *Utopia* was presented in its "original full-length version" adding that Laurel and Hardy, "the world's funniest comedy duo," was "lost in *Robinson Crusoeland*." This time the tape's label boasted "Award Quality Movie Greats," although neither *Atoll K* nor *Utopia* had actually ever won any awards. This particular tape also features a surprisingly good print of *Utopia*, offering a couple of

Scene from "UTOPIA", © 1950
Hal Roach Studios, Inc., renewed 1986, "THE LAUREL & HARDY SHOW" #23, © 1986 Hal Roach Studios, Inc. All Rights Reserved

1986 Hal Roach Studios *Utopia* lobby card with copyright notation for "The Laurel and Hardy Show #23." Note the alleged 1950 *Utopia* copyright and its 1986 "renewal," neither of which occurred (courtesy Peter Mikkelsen).

COLORING CONTEST

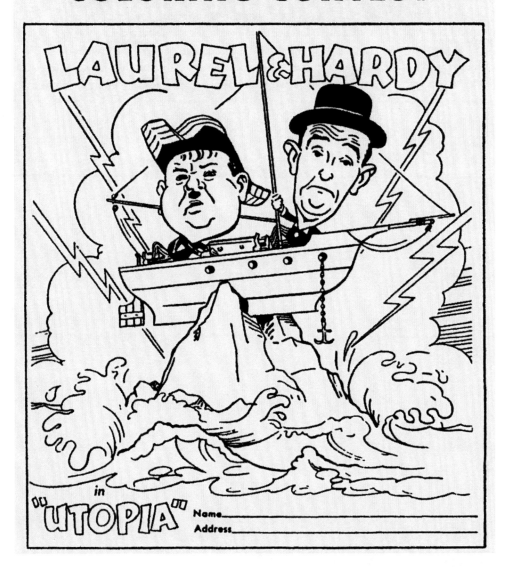

Coloring Contest sheet from the U.S. pressbook *Utopia* (courtesy Scott MacGillivray).

peculiarities. The Welch's grape juice insert has been removed. And, as in the *Laurel and Hardy Show* presentation, the opening title cards and music are lifted from the earlier Laurel and Hardy film *Block-Heads*, integrating the familiar *Utopia* clips. Meanwhile, Misraki's music stops abruptly with the fade in of "The End." This exceptional tape also includes the June 10, 1950, interview with Oliver Hardy from the TV series *Ship's Reporter*, titled "Tribute to a Star."

The Hal Roach Studios were not the only ones to pursue copyright on Laurel and Hardy's final film. As already mentioned, French distributor Télédis secured U.S. copyright for *Atoll K*'s French VHS version at the end of 1997.[22]

An intriguing example of what could be salvaged from the mutilation that became *Utopia* was proven in recent years. Skillful editing and imaginative use of music combined selected scenes from *Utopia* with Louis Armstrong's final hit, *What a Wonderful World.* The uplifting yet melancholy tune perfectly aligns with the whimsical, but somehow poignant, nature of the aging comics' final film. One of the clip's most appealing moments cleverly matches footage of Stan and Ollie shaking hands with the notaries to the lyrics "I see friends shakings hands, saying how do you do," while Stan, knocked out by Chérie's rock-filled bag, waves his "I love you." This delightful video was posted on youtube.com under the title *What a Wonderful Utopia,* before being withdrawn from circulation in mid–September 2006.[23]

13

Atoll K Throughout the World

Like news of the discovery of Crusoeland, the marketing and distribution of *Atoll K* spread across the world. The findings on the myriad international releases presented here are far from exhaustive,[1] but it would seem that each country's variant was a curiosity all of its own.

Ideally, a chronological examination would start with the German version of *Atoll K*, which was released in December 1951. However, this version is of particular interest — especially given the variations currently available on DVD — so the final chapter of this book is reserved for the German release.

Franco London prepared an exceptional promotional brochure in the Spanish language, and it did not take long for *Atoll K* to reach Spain. In December 1951, distributor Chamartín received permission from the Spanish board of censors to screen *Atoll K* (retitled *Robinsones Atómicos* ["Atomic Robinsons"] and dubbed into Spanish) in Spanish cinemas.[2] The length submitted to the board of censors and running time in theaters are, unfortunately, unknown.

Robinsones Atómicos' Spanish premiere apparently took place on January 17, 1952, at the Saragossa Cine Corso.[3] Two days later it debuted at the Bilbao Cine Consulado, eventually opening at the Madrid theater Palacio de la Música on March 29, 1952.[4] *Robinsones Atómicos* played across Spain; throughout 1952 it screened, for example, in Elche (Costa Blanca) and in Santoña (Cantabria). Again there were promotional events, including free balloons for children, and hackneyed catchphrases such as "the biggest jumble of the century" and "the best holiday movie."[5] The Spanish poster shows Stan, Ollie, Antoine and Giovanni with the hangman's noose around their necks, moments before Alecto signals their demise — hardly the expected comic moment from a Laurel and Hardy movie.

In spring 1952, distributor Eagle-Lion Film decided to release *Atoll K* to the Danish public. Eagle-Lion had purchased the British version, which was subsequently licensed for release (along with the trailer) by the Danish movie authority at the end of May 1952. The license requested no further cuts (the submitted version ran roughly 93 minutes), but, for reasons unknown, the film was shortened somewhat. The result still ran approximately ten minutes longer than the official British version, *Robinson Crusoeland*.[6]

In Denmark, as in other nations across Europe, Laurel and Hardy were still revered by the public. Laughter is the international language, a fact Eagle-Lion emphasized when they announced *Gøg og Gokke paa atom øen* ("Gøg and Gokke on the Atomic Island"): "Here they are again in their latest laughing romp. You will burst from laughter, when you experience the rip-roaring adventures of the two comedians. Have fun!"

The premiere of *Gøg og Gokke paa atom øen* (with Danish subtitles by Willy Breinholst, a well-known humor writer in Denmark, and Hartvig Andersen) took place on August 1, 1952, at the Copenhagen cinema Carlton. The box-office was impressive enough to ensure an extended run until August 19, 1952.[7]

The Danish poster is far more inviting than the rather macabre Spanish poster. It features a charming caricature of the two comedians fishing, while a bikini-clad Chérie approaches the atoll in a canoe — a motif seemingly borrowed from Deseto's French-Italian *Atoll K* poster. Once again the distributor's information lists P. Kohner as scriptwriter; as noted earlier, this was American movie agent Paul Kohner, who had not contributed a single word to the film's script. This error was probably lifted from British promotional material, without further verification.

The press reaction to the Danish premiere of *Gøg og Gokke paa atom øen* was truly benevolent, reflecting the affection Denmark held for "Gøg and Gokke" (translation: "Cuckoo and Clout").[8] The critics did not dwell on the appearance of the aging duo, instead proclaiming that Laurel and Hardy had once again proven themselves to be masters of comedy.[9] Overlooking the weak plot and the wretched English-language dubbing, one reviewer suggested the audience merely sit back and enjoy Laurel and Hardy's artistry:

> Well, they are back again, the two jokers.... Only Laurel and Hardy are allowed to speak in their own voices, the rest are dubbed so they speak when their mouths are closed — or vice versa, it doesn't really matter.... They set off for the island and fool around in the good, old-fashioned way, and have a lot of fun on the way. Thus goes the first half of the picture until Laurel and Hardy more or less disappear into the background and, amongst others, the sweet singer Suzy Delair turns up on the island. After that there it isn't so much fun anymore. Some satire comes in, but this isn't really Laurel and Hardy's strong suit. Still, they are back on the screen, and the fun has begun again, but the first half of the film was the best.

Another critic commented on Hardy's record-breaking heft and Laurel's pitiful appearance, again demonstrating a true fondness for the team:

1952 Spanish *Robinsones Atómicos* poster art (author's collection).

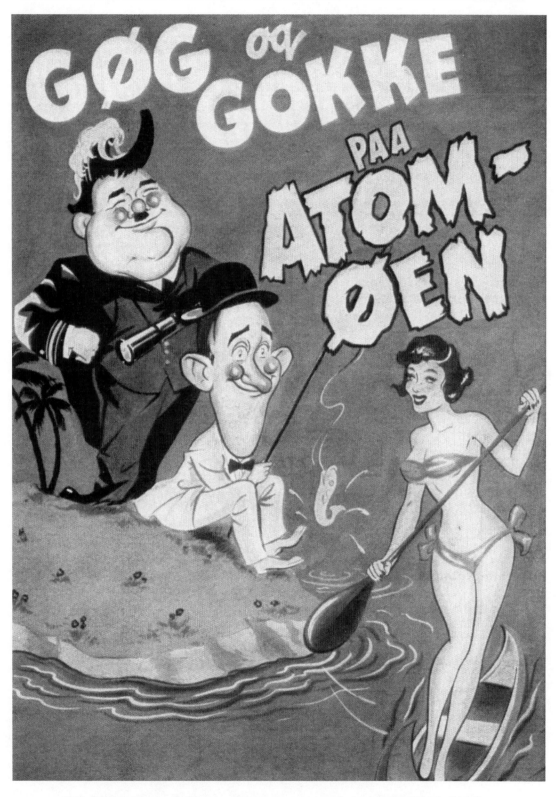

1952 Danish *Gøg og Gokke paa Atom-øen* poster art (courtesy Dr. Ulrich Rüdel).

It has been some time since we last saw [Laurel and Hardy], and they have changed since then. Ollie is fatter and rounder than ever before, and the skinny, sad-faced Stan looks very old, though he is only 62 years old. You really wish him a well-earned vacation on the South Seas island where ... the major part of the film takes place. The humor does not seem to have changed.

Yet another critic bowed before Laurel and Hardy's comic skill, despite attributing their roots to the Mack Sennett school which they had never attended. (In fact, Hardy shot just one film at Sennett's studio, *Crazy to Act*, in 1926 — twelve years after he made his film debut.) The reviewer went on to call *Gøg og Gokke paa atom øen* a "grand comedy":

[In the new Laurel and Hardy movie] all the old slapstick traditions of Mack Sennett are observed. Few comedians today, such as Laurel and Hardy, have learned their lesson from the days when Sennett released an avalanche of remarkable comedies to the cinemas.... You might talk about the pessimistic tendencies when the society [on Crusoeland] meets its ruin, and [Laurel and Hardy] are just barely rescued from the gallows — some scenes are practically macabre, but the main impression is of two skillful and trained comedians who are having a great time. The only complaint would be that they are surrounded by a group of mediocre actors. Only Suzy Delair manages to rise to the occasion and plays along fine with the comedians.

In Canada, the British version *Robinson Crusoeland* premiered no later than October 30, 1952, sharing a double bill with *All Because of Sally* (aka *Sally and Saint Anne*, Rudolf Maté, 1952) at the Toronto cinemas Esquire, Midtown and Odeon.[10] The film had been licensed for public release in mid–July 1952 by the Ontario Film Review Board, on the condition that children would be accompanied by their parents. *Robinson Crusoeland* doesn't seem to have been a major attraction at the aforementioned theaters; the program was changed a couple of days later. From there the film screened in the city's smaller cinemas and likely moved on to other towns across the country. A few years later, in 1955, 16mm copies of *Robinson Crusoeland* were also distributed in Canada.[11]

1952 Canadian *Robinson Crusoeland* advertising (courtesy Chris Seguin).

So, surprisingly, *Atoll K* entered the North American continent considerably earlier than the U.S. premiere of *Utopia* in December 1954. At that time, Canada was still formally considered a British territory, finally attaining constitutional independence from Great Britain in 1982. So the distribution and marketing of the film were a continuation of the British efforts; International Film sold *Robinson Crusoeland* in Canada just as it had in Great Britain. (International Film did, however, prepare different lobby cards for Canada.)

With the advent of home video, the film soon became available on VHS in Canada. As no copy of *Robinson Crusoeland* could be secured, Vancouver-based Premiere Entertainment International Ltd. offered a tape with the familiar American version *Utopia*. Perhaps the most unusual Canadian sighting occurred when the French version of *Atoll K* was given an open air screening on August 3, 2003, by the Musée National des Beaux-Arts du Québec, introduced by film historian Yves Laberge. It remains unclear whether the French version had already been shown publicly in Québec in the early 1950s.[12]

In 1952, Swiss distributor Royal Films offered all three original versions of *Atoll K* (christened the "Atomic Bomb among the Comedies") to the Federal cinema owners. Both the French and Italian version could play without subtitles in Switzerland; German-speaking citizens, however, were not offered a German dub of the movie. Instead they saw the English-language version with French and German subtitles. Allegedly each version was 2,700 meters long, making them nearly as long as the 100-minute final cut which went unreleased until then.[13] However, this running time seems doubtful. It is more likely that Royal Films took the length from the European producer's internal fact sheet, which did not necessarily align with the films as finally presented.

In the Netherlands, as in Denmark, *Atoll K* appears to have been enthusiastically received. In this case the British version, *Robinson Crusoeland*, retitled *Robinson Crusoë & Co*, was released. In early April 1953, the Amsterdam Cinema Royal, with its 1,162 seating capacity, enjoyed such favorable box-office during its four daily screenings that the film was held over for an additional week. The Rotterdam Capitol did the same. The success of *Robinson Crusoë & Co* was noted on an advertising by its distributor, Nederland.[14]

In 1988, Laurel and Hardy's final film was made available on VHS in the Netherlands. Again, no copy of *Robinson Crusoeland* had been located, so the Springtime Film B.V. tape titled *Atoll K/Utopia* contained the inevitable U.S. version of the movie (with Dutch subtitles). Among the countless VHS releases of *Utopia* to flood the market, this one is unusual: it misspells composer Paul Misraki's last name "Marisky," and gives credit to John Berry as Joannon's codirector. As with most copies of *Utopia*, it opens with the distributor's credit Exploitation Productions Incorporated and the clip introducing Stan and Ollie on the deck of the *Momus*. From there the coarse meshed textile background from the English-language *Atoll K* takes over, before fading in on the familiar *Utopia* for the remainder of the tape.

The search in Mexico leads to the rumor that *Atoll K* screened there as early as December 1950—an obvious impossibility, given that the film was only halfway through shooting by that date. In reality, Mexican audiences were seeing *Bonnie Scotland* (1935) under the title *Había una vez dos héroes* ("Once There Were Two Heroes").[15] The film would finally premiere in Mexico on November 28, 1956, at the Mexico City Teatro Metropolitan.[16] Large-sized advertisements for *Los dos Robinsones* ("The Two Robinsons") announced that El Gordo y el Flaco ("the Fat One and the Thin One," as Laurel and Hardy were known in Mexico), "the best comedians ever," were returning to the silver screen "in their 1956 super-production." The running time for the movie (which, by 1956, was already five years old—the

Le film comique et atomique de l'année

Suzy Delair
Adriano Rimoldi

LAUREL
et HARDY

Die Atombombe
unter den Lustspielen

ATOLL-K

Une grande production de LÉO JEANSON

1952 Swiss *Atoll K* advertising. Note the misspelling "Jeanson" instead of "Joannon" (author's collection).

1953 Dutch *Robinson Crusoë & Co* advertising (courtesy Bram Reijnhoudt).

distributor's attempt to make it more current?) was promoted as a hefty two and a half hours, and included four cartoons: two *Tom and Jerry* and two *Donald Duck*.[17] The lobby cards promised "nonstop laughter"" with the "kings of laughter," and picturegoers were invited, "Accompany us to Crusoeland and forget all your problems!"

The Mexican distributor did not release the Spanish-language version of *Atoll K* that had already been dubbed in Spain, providing Spanish subtitles instead. But which version of *Atoll K* opened at the Teatro Metropolitan? It is unlikely that the distributor used either the French or Italian version. In fact, an examination of one of the paperboard mats, as well as the lobby

1956 Mexican *Los Dos Robinsones* advertising (author's collection).

1956 Mexican *Los Dos Robinsones* lobby card. Bottom right: note the colored version of the 1954 U.S. black-and-white drawing for children (author's collection).

cards prepared by Mexican distributor Jorge M. Dada[18] suggests that they had been culled from publicity material prepared by U.S. distributor Exploitation Productions for the American release of *Utopia* at the end of 1954. The portraits of Laurel and Hardy shown on the Mexican material are exactly the same as those in the U.S. campaign book and poster. One of the Mexican paperboard mats also showed the Hawaiian girls from the U.S. material, seen earlier in the 1952 British advertising material for *Robinson Crusoeland*, and originating in the Italian *Atollo K* publicity. The Mexican lobby cards also integrate the coloring contest illustration from *Utopia*'s promotional kit. All this presents fairly strong evidence that it was the 82-minute U.S. version *Utopia* that was released in Mexico.

Los dos Robinsones' successful run at the Teatro Metropolitan extended until December 18, 1956. From there, the film moved to cinemas across the country. The critic for the daily newspaper Excelsior praised the venerable team and their latest effort[19]:

> To see the large number of children in the cinema resembles a travel through time. They are the descendants of the youngsters who themselves flocked to the cinemas [to watch the two comedians.] ... Indeed Laurel and Hardy have become exceptionally thin and thick, respectively ... but they have remained the same master comedians who turned generations of moviegoers into their fans.... Their gags [and] their mishaps ... are no less funny and contagious than long ago, when the team was 30 years younger.

1961 Polish *Flip i Flap na bezludnej wyspie* poster art by Marian Stachurski (author's collection).

1977 Czechoslovakian *Laurel a Hardy zdedeli ostrov* lobby card (courtesy Dr. Ulrich Rüdel).

Atoll K finally arrived behind the European Iron Curtain in June 1961. State-run distributor Centrala Wynajmu Filmów released the French version with Polish subtitles, retitled *Flip i Flap an bezludnej wyspie* ["Flip and Flap as Islanders"]. It is possible that the then-current head of the Polish communist board of censors ordered cuts to the film.[20] The film was promoted to moviegoers with a colorful poster drawn by Marian Stachurski, but public reaction was lukewarm.[21] Four decades later the considerably shorter U.S. version, *Utopia,* was released in Poland on DVD; the cover design features a publicity still from the boys' earlier classic *Way Out West* and the slightly amended title *Flip i Flap Utopia.* Those unfamiliar with the Polish presentation of foreign movies should prepare themselves for an unusual experience. A Polish voiceover runs over the original English-language track of the movie, the standard Polish substitute for full dubbing. The announcer does not lip synch each role individually or change his voice according to character, but narrates in a rather impassive monotone throughout the movie.

Before there were perestroika and glasnost, *Atoll K* also played Czechoslovakia. Beginning in January 1977, a 90-minute edit was titled *Laurel a Hardy zdedeli ostrov* ("Laurel and Hardy Inherit an Island"). No further details are known of this version.[22]

Although details on all of *Atoll K*'s foreign releases remain, by necessity, sketchy (research could continue for years in every corner of the world), one thing is certain: *Atoll K* was anything but the financial misfire it is commonly believed to be. Indeed, the film enjoyed widespread distribution and the reviews unearthed during research universally fail to condemn the film as a failure.

14

The German Version of *Atoll K*, *Dick und Doof erben eine Insel*[1]

Unlike the French-, Italian- and English-language variations, the German version of *Atoll K* cannot be considered another "original" version — but it is of unique interest thanks to its relative availability and the distinct differences it offers compared to the originals and the mutilated *Utopia*. Furthermore, it received special attention in terms of marketing in the European marketplace, the German audience being particularly important to the producers from the very beginning. Today's view of *Atoll K* as a financial fiasco is quickly disproved by the record of the reception the film garnered in Germany (West Germany), where it was anything but a flop. The German version was marketed not only in the Federal Republic of Germany, but also in Austria. (As mentioned in the previous chapter, there is no indication that this version was shown in quadrilingual Switzerland.[2]) Although Laurel and Hardy were well-known in the German Democratic Republic (East Germany), it appears that *Atoll K* was never shown there. In fact, their movies were not launched there until 1963, and even then screenings were infrequent. In comparison, the team's films enjoyed countless showings in the Federal Republic of Germany from 1949 until 1970.

Laurel and Hardy's popularity in Germany had been immediate and enormous, from 1928 onwards, soon earning them the German marketing nickname "Dick und Do(o)f" ("Fat and Dumb"). The name may not have been flattering but it did stick; it first appeared in 1929 in promotional material prepared by distributor Parufamet. German audiences quickly knew the duo by this moniker; even legal action by German distributor M-G-M (associated with Parufamet until the early 1930s, at which point it took over the distribution of Laurel and Hardy's films) aimed at prohibiting the use of "Dick und Doof"[3] fizzled out by 1937. During the Nazi era, until 1938, the team enjoyed popular success and critical praise in Germany, even from fascist newspapers. A few short years after World War II, a major Laurel-and-Hardy boom was initiated in the theaters of the Federal Republic of Germany. *Atoll K* was slated to play an important role in this revival. Indeed, film trader George H. Bookbinder's Munich-based companies Bookfilm International Corporation and All Star Pictures Sales Corporation partially funded the film. Bookbinder had been also responsible for the Laurel-and-Hardy renaissance in the German movie industry from autumn 1949 onward.

Within the series of reissues scheduled for this German revival, *Atoll K* was something special — after all, it was Laurel and Hardy's "new" film. In 1950, German distributor Prisma (whose proprietor, Franz Sulley, would later contribute to the production of the highly successful German *krimis* [crime films] of the 1960s "Edgar Wallace" series) had tremendous box-office success with the German Laurel-and-Hardy dubbings of *Hinter Schloss und Riegel* and

Lange Leitung (*Block-Heads*, 1938) which had been purchased as Franco London productions. Curiously, *Hinter Schloss und Riegel* was not the long-lost German phonetic version of *Pardon Us* (1931), but the German version of the French-dubbed *Sous les verrous*— a compilation of *Any Old Port* (1932), *Pardon Us* and *One Good Turn* (1931). When the German press reported in April 1950 that Laurel and Hardy were to start shooting *Atoll K* in May, along with French comedian Bourvil as a "European coproduction of laughter,"[4] Prisma immediately secured an option for the new movie's distribution rights.[5] At the end of August 1950, Laurel and Hardy were quoted in German newspapers, promising that they wanted to shoot the movie "in record time and to visit Germany afterwards to get to know their German friends."[6] By this time there had already been considerable setbacks in the schedule, with countless more on the horizon. The scheduled "record time" of twelve weeks stretched into nine months, and Laurel and Hardy never made it to Germany. German reports on the shooting of *Atoll K*, like those in France, stressed that production was running smoothly. Shedding some light on Laurel and Hardy's career and their style of comedy, one report emphasized the "side-splitting team's comedy under the blistering Mediterranean sun."[7] It also admired Suzy Delair's wardrobe designed by Jacques Fath and advised the readers to look out for a flamboyant hat.[8]

Prisma kept busy keeping interest alive in the project, in hopes of cashing in on Laurel and Hardy's lasting popularity. The distributor had already announced that *Atoll K* would be ready at the end of August 1950, although at that time only shooting in Marseilles had been completed. For its winter 1950/51 season, Prisma announced the film yet again, emphasizing once more that it was the first Laurel-and-Hardy film shot in Europe: "A super contingent of European comics as well as the attractive Suzy Delair."[9] At the beginning of May 1951, Prisma released more news along the same lines,[10] about a month after shooting had been completed.

In fact, the various production delays forced Prisma to keep interest in *Atoll K* alive for more than a year and a half, until its German premiere at the end of 1951. Prisma was more than happy to promote Suzy Delair's participation, as she was tremendously popular in Germany. With the release of *Unter falschem Verdacht* (*Quai des orfèvres*; Henri-Georges Clouzot, 1947), which successfully premiered in October 1948 in Berlin, she became a favorite of German moviegoers.[11] The actress was often noted by the German movie press, who regularly published prominent photographs of her.[12]

Later, the positive impact of Suzy Delair's appearance in *Atoll K* was boosted by the popularity of her 1949 feature film *Lady Paname* (Henri Jeanson). *Lady Paname* was one of the French films to be presented at the first Berliner Filmfestspiele in 1951, better known internationally as Berlinale. The festival was the scene of the film's German premiere, and Suzy Delair's appearance at the premiere resulted in tremendous attention and excellent reviews.[13] Suzy Delair was very impressed by her Berlin trip, taken at a time when Berlin was still suffering the ravages of World War II and far from its eventual reconstruction. She remembers:

> The screening of *Lady Paname* to the German public turned out to be an enjoyable experience. However, it was strange to see the famous Kurfürstendamm of the formerly glorious Berlin in ruins covered with flowers and flowerpots filled with geraniums here and there. A fountain, a column of water and, near Hitler's former bunker in the Soviet zone of occupation, a Russian soldier who did not seem to realize the chaos during the change of guards accompanied by whistle signals provided a strange apocalyptic setting that reminded me somehow of Claude Debussy's *Jardin sous la pluie.*

By mid–May 1951, Prisma had acquired *Atoll K*'s screening rights from Paris-based Franco London.[14] Once the contract was signed, the distributor immediately announced that Laurel and Hardy's latest film would finally be released to German cinemas in October 1951.[15] This turned out to be another case of wishful thinking. As the German movie market had favored German dubbings of foreign movies since the 1930s (a preference that had intensified following World War II), *Atoll K* needed to be dubbed. Prisma commissioned the same dubbing studio to produce the German version of *Atoll K* that had previously dubbed the recent Laurel-and-Hardy reissues *Hinter Schloss und Riegel* and *Lange Leitung*. These German versions originated from the Internationale Film–Union AG, Studio Remagen [IFU], which had been founded by the Section Cinéma in the 1940s French-controlled zone of postwar Germany. The foundation had been initiated by French movie official Marcel Colin-Reval.[16] In the 1950s, the IFU grew up to be one of the leading dubbing studios in the Federal Republic of Germany, highly regarded for its first-rate work. In September 1951, Prisma contracted the IFU to create a German version of *Atoll K* and its trailer for an all-inclusive fee of 40,000 Deutsche marks.[17] The equates to approximately $110,000 U.S. by today's standards, far exceeding the average cost of a modern-day feature film dubbing in Germany.

IFU received the English-dialogue script to prepare the German rough translation in mid–September 1951, by which time the Wiesbaden-based Freiwillige Selbstkontrolle der Filmwirtschaft [FSK] had already set an examination date on the distributor's request. After the end of World War II, from mid–1949 on, the FSK controlled all film releases in the Federal Republic of Germany. The authority examined the English-language version of *Atoll K* at a length of 2,481 meters (well over 90 minutes) and, with the help of the German rough translation, approved the movie for children under 16 years of age. At the same time it was prohibited from public screenings on holidays such as Easter and Christmas, a common practice at the time.[18]

A few days after the FSK license was issued, Prisma's leading dramatic and dubbing supervisor, Dr. Franz Biermann, emphasized the importance of this new, high-profile production, making it plain that *Atoll K* demanded a "particularly diligent dubbing." In fact, he went out of his way to point this out at every opportunity. Scrutinizing the English-language version, Bierman was nothing short of shocked, and he demanded to see the French version as well, for further comparison. In a letter dated September 28, 1951, he revealed his deep concerns to the IFU and outlined his solutions to improve the film and its marketability[19]:

> The bad reviews [of *Atoll K*] were based on the poorly dubbed American version of the film, so that no one could get an idea of the acoustic charm of Suzy Delair's voice.... Further, in the American version dissolves ... are only preliminary or entirely missing....
>
> The film consists of three sections, only loosely connected by voice-over narration. The middle part does not fit in at all and is quite weak. Essentially, it puts a halt to the *Dick und Doof* plot line and prematurely tires the audience. There is a risk that the film does not sufficiently stimulate the audience anymore in the third part, since even this section has severe pacing problems and does not quite bring its main protagonists to their full effect, like the really excellent first third does....
>
> The movie tries to link together the three incoherent parts by means of a commentator. The voice-over narration is only a makeshift solution.
>
> Thus, the dubbing has the difficult task to enhance the film's pacing in the last third by editing and to dilute the second part's embarrassing clumsiness. Strategically adding weight to the narration is considered the main remedy for these problems, so that some parts of the plot, upon further editing, may be clarified by the narration....
>
> All scenes in the Suzy–Frazer section (songs and wedding) are to be cut accordingly. Any padding needs to be removed, the point of the scenes needs emphasis. One owes this to the German audience of the *Dick und Doof* films.

Biermann felt the need for dramatic revisions and created a checklist requesting the following "changes or improvements, respectively":

- The opening commentary should explain the term "atoll" during the opening credits and in doing so, allude to the bikini fashion.
- It should be shown how Giovanni gets on board Laurel and Hardy's ship.
- Text should emphasize when Antoine, in the cabin, takes the butcher's knife in his hands.
- One of the shots of the atoll emerging from the ocean should be deleted.
- Heavy editing of the Chérie–Frazer section (songs and wedding scene) while expanding the commentary.
- Laurel's first falling off the chair due to Hardy's snoring should be cut to make the effect more plausible.
- The worn toothbrush in Hardy's hand should be shown, by means of a trick shot if necessary.
- Frazer's arrival on the atoll should be heavily edited and explained by commentary.
- The scenes in the inn and during the conspiracy should be edited to accelerate the pace.
- The scenes of Chérie knocking some men unconscious should also be slightly edited.

Biermann's requests and his industry profile shattered Prisma's hopes of releasing *Atoll K* to the West German cinemas in October 1951. The acceptance of the German version was now postponed until the beginning of December 1951. Appropriately, Prisma arranged promotional dates and pre–Christmas trade shows in Düsseldorf, Frankfurt/Main, Hamburg, Munich and Berlin. At the beginning of October 1951, Franco London submitted an English-language copy to Prisma for the reediting and dubbing. The one was 2,693 meters and ran more than 98 minutes.[20] This was the longest English-language version known to exist, exceeding the 2,481-meter version Prisma had submitted to the FSK. Soon afterward, the official 2,561-meter French version was delivered to the IFU.[21] Of course, neither the English-language nor French-language versions had the additional scene Biermann had requested, in which Giovanni weasels his way on board the *Momus*. In truth the scene had never been shot, as Prisma would learn.[22]

Separate music and effects tracks were also supplied, so there was no need to compose and record new music for the German dubbing. There was also an extra audiotape of

Hardy's German voice Hermann Pfeiffer, early 1950s (author's collection).

Suzy Delair's songs, which were heavily emphasized by Biermann even though he recommended cutting several of Chérie's scenes.

In addition to his editing requests, Biermann also had specific ideas regarding the quality of the German dubbing. Werner Völger, who was supervising *Atoll K*, was considered both an expert sound-dubbing director and a specialist at creating superior German dialogue. Völger had often worked with dialogue writer Wolfgang Schnitzler, known for his elegant and witty texts. Schnitzler, due to his "excellent linguistic gag ideas," was therefore Biermann's favored candidate as Völger's coauthor. He was also given the task of translating Chérie's lyrics.

German dubbings of the 1950s and early 1960s are often of remarkable artistic quality. Ambitions were high, and the pool of excellent voice actors from stage and screen was tremendous. Since the German film industry essentially needed to be reinvented after World War II, dubbing was a welcome source of income, and talented actors did not consider it a comedown to lend their voices to famous foreign colleagues. The German version of *Atoll K* particularly benefited from this attention to quality. Perhaps most importantly, Laurel's voice was supplied by Walter Bluhm, a comic actor who was soon to be known as "the German voice of Stan" (Bluhm had, in fact, performed this function since 1937; by 1938 the Nazi regime had started to limit the import of American films until completely prohibiting them in autumn 1940). Bluhm's fame as "Stan" easily surpassed that of his excellent work on stage and in supporting roles in films such as *Liane, das Mädchen aus dem Urwald* (*Liane, Jungle Goddess*;

Eduard von Borsody, 1956), let alone his other countless dubbing assignments (such as Mr. Stringer in the early 1960s British *Miss Marple* films starring Margaret Rutherford). Like Italian Alberto Sordi, who was comfortable dubbing Oliver Hardy, Bluhm grew to be forever associated with Laurel. In the 1970s, Bluhm, who died in 1976, occasionally appeared publicly as Stan Laurel. In 1975 he also redubbed nearly all of Laurel and Hardy's feature films one last time.[23] In *Atoll K*, Bluhm speaks in a different manner from his familiar approach. At times his voice is higher than usual, even squeaky at times, which presumably mirrors Frank O'Neill's high-pitched voice in the French version, which Bluhm and director Völger had studied.

In contrast, the casting of Hardy's German voice was less consistent. *Atoll K* features Hermann Pfeiffer, previously an actor in pre-war German Ufa films and a singer as well. In 1953, Pfeiffer became the official voice of Hardy.[24] Like Bluhm he frequently worked in dubbing studios, before becoming a TV director in later years.

Suzy Delair's German voice Edith Teichmann, early 1970s (author's collection).

INTERNATIONALE FILM-UNION A. G.
STUDIOS REMAGEN

REMAGEN (Rhein), den   19. November 19 51
Fernruf 263

VERTRAG

Zwischen der **Internationalen Film-Union A. G.,** Synchronisations-Abteilung Remagen, oder deren Rechtsnachfolgerin — beide im folgenden „Filmfirma" genannt —

und Herrn/Frau   Walter Bluhm, Berlin, Steglitz, Brentanostrasse 54

andererseits — im folgenden „der Filmschaffende" genannt — wird folgender Vertrag geschlossen :

1. Der Filmschaffende steht der Filmfirma

   als   Sprecher

   für die Rolle :   Doof(Stan Laurel)

   in dem Film mit dem Titel :

           "Atoll K"

   zur Verfügung.

2. Die Vertragszeit beginnt am   16. November 1951   und endet

   a) am   20. November 1951

   b) mit Beendigung der Rolle

   c) sobald die Tätigkeit als   wie obenstehend

   in dem Film, für den er engagiert ist, nicht mehr erforderlich ist.

3. Der Filmschaffende erhält ein Honorar von

   DM   725.--   in Buchstaben :   Siebenhundertfünfundzwanzig

   als Pauschale für die Dauer seiner Mitwirkung an der Synchronisation des Films.

   DM   --   in Buchstaben :   --
   für jeden Aufnahmetag.

   Sollten Nachaufnahmen vorgenommen werden, so erhält der Filmschaffende bei Tagesgage für jeden Tag seiner Mitwirkung die Hälfte des Tageshonorars. Bei Pauschalabschluß erfolgt entsprechende Umrechnung des Honorars auf die Nachaufnahmetage, wobei je Tag ebenfalls die Hälfte von der Filmfirma zu zahlen ist.

                                        Bitte wenden !

Bluhm's *Atoll K* contract [face] as Stan's German voice, dated November 19, 1951 (author's collection).

Young actress Edith Teichmann dubbed Suzy Delair, offering an impeccable singing and voice-over performance. Her singing may not have been in the same class as Suzy Delair's, but she was convincing nevertheless. The difference between the two musical interpretations would only be noticed by those who compared the German dubbing directly to the French version — only on close inspection does Edith Teichmann's German singing, which is sometimes slightly out of synch, catch the viewer's eye.

Carl Voscherau, the German voice of Michel Dalmatoff's Alecto, also merits special mention. Voscherau's playfully robust voice was frequently employed when hefty, dyspeptic characters needed to be dubbed. A prime example is British actor James Robertson Justice from the successful 1950s–60s British *Doctor* movies, originally starring Dirk Bogarde.

Along with the many experienced voice actors like Bum Krüger (who dubbed both Captains Bonnet and Dolan), Hans Nielsen's contribution as the German voices of Giovanni and lawyer Poltroni is particularly noteworthy. Nielsen was also an internationally known actor, seen onscreen, for example, in crime dramas such as *Scotland Yard jagt Dr. Mabuse* (*Scotland Yard vs. Dr. Mabuse* aka *Scotland Yard Hunts Dr. Mabuse*), directed by Paul May.

Only a few production files on German dubbings from the 1950s survive today. Fortunately, information on *Atoll K*'s German version is available. This gives us an idea of the salaries paid, which were substantial compared to today's going rates. The rough translation cost 400 Deutsche marks. Völger charged 1,200 Deutsche marks for his dialogue script and another 2,500 DM for directing. Schnitzler's contribution to the dialogue script came to 1,200 Deutsche marks plus 200 DM for his German translation of Suzy Delair's songs. The salaries for all 39 dubbing roles, which were cast with 22 voice actors by the IFU, totaled 7,890 Deutsche marks. Bluhm's share was 725 DM for 137 takes and Pfeiffer earned 675 DM for 196 takes. Bluhm's considerably higher fee was due to his status as an established dubbing artist. In comparison, however, Nielsen took in the highest earnings on a per-take basis — receiving for just 57 takes the same 675 DM that Pfeiffer earned.

The recording sessions took place from November 17–19, 1951, at the IFU's Remagen studio; a previous engagement prevented Bluhm from participating earlier. In the end IFU delivered a solid, if not quite flawless, German dubbing — nearly exactly the careful product that Biermann demanded. The opening title cards were designed by well-known German cartoon studio Fischerkoesen. Writing credits were limited to Tellini (his first name Piero mistakenly reads "Pietro," yet another of the endless variations in each version's opening credits) and Wheeler, a listing that is closer to truth than the respective credits on the English-language version.

In spite of Biermann's numerous suggestions to tighten the film, IFU's 90-minute version remains substantially longer than the standard, butchered release *Utopia*, containing scenes virtually unknown in the United States and also in the United Kingdom due to the decades-long unavailability of *Robinson Crusoeland* prints.

IFU's working print was the English-language version, which at that time still included the English notary plaque "Bramwell, Solicitor." The German-version *Atoll K* and the British version, *Robinson Crusoeland,* remain the only available versions of the movie with this plaque intact.

Prior to Chérie's introduction, the German version shows the men at work building homes on the atoll, with stonemason Giovanni pilfering Antoine's cooking pot. Stan is seen standing in front of the recently erected houses and later pulling his chained-up pet lobster Oscar out of a kennel, its roof inscription readable in the German version.

Both of Chérie's nightclub performances have been retained, as has Captain Dolan's role as best man and Chérie's confidant — unlike *Utopia*, where Dolan's role is virtually nonexistent. Antoine's and Giovanni's comment on Stan's stupidity is kept in, following Stan's innocent remark about waving at the passing ship. The German-version also keeps the Washington press conference, the impetus for the mass immigration to Crusoeland.

The events inside Café Crusoe, with the gangster wanting to sell his liquor and the resulting riot, are nearly intact. This important scene had been edited severely for *Robinson Crusoeland* and *Utopia*, meaning the loss of some excellent Laurel-and-Hardy footage. Despite the cuts to the German version, Alecto comes across as much more vicious here than in *Robinson Crusoeland* and *Utopia*. In the Café Crusoe, Alecto answers Chérie's question of what he'll have with a blunt "You!" — which she, in turn, answers with a slap in the face (as seen in *Robinson Crusoeland* and *Utopia*). When he exempts Chérie from the execution with the promise of putting her under his "personal protection," the leering innuendo is in perfect keeping with his brutal nature. His cruelty is confirmed later, when he malevolently announces Stan's, Ollie's, Antoine's and Giovanni's execution within the hour as Chérie frantically tries to contact Frazer. Prisma had no desire to jeopardize FSK's strict conditions for approving release to juveniles. A designation of "unsuitable for young audiences" would have meant the loss of a great deal of Laurel and Hardy's traditional audience, severely affecting the box-office. However, the distributor did not see these scenes with Alecto as problematic, and was proven right. The FSK did not demand their removal. Most likely, Alecto's lasciviousness would have eluded small children.

Prisma's dramatic advisor Biermann also had no problem retaining the complete radio conversation between Frazer and Chérie, during which Frazer cannot resist making a snide remark or two. Clearly, Biermann saw this as important to maintaining a coherent plot.

The removal of ten minutes from *Atoll K*'s final cut for the German version did not result in any drastic gaps in the plot. After Antoine has been seized by the harbor police, the German version omits Captain Bonnet's comments that Antoine has experienced this all over the world. *Atoll K*'s original cut includes a second conversation between Antoine and the captain on the deck of the *Medex*; this exchange has been shortened for the German version. Thus Bonnet, without any further conversation, leaves the forlorn Antoine sitting alone on the deck. On Biermann's request the IFU also removed one of the scenes of the emerging atoll.

As in the French version (chapter 9), Stan, Ollie, Antoine and Giovanni's conversation about why they are running away from it all has been severely cut. Antoine and Giovanni join Stan and Ollie without explanation; it remains unclear to the viewer why Giovanni is a stowaway. Worse still, Stan and Ollie's rationale for playing hooky (Ollie: "Taxes!" Stan: "Yeah, we don't like taxes!") has been scissored, weakening the setup for the socio-political satire to follow.

Chérie's audition at the nightclub is still part of the German version; her song *Laissez-moi faire* (in German: "Lass mich nur machen," which translates into "Let me have a go") has not been shortened by a verse as Biermann had suggested. The nightclub has been renamed Kakteen-Bar ["Cactus Bar"], though it should probably have been translated into Kakadu-Club (as in the original versions), since there is not a cactus to be seen in the club's interior.

Most of the footage that occurs between Stan's skipping of the stones to Tahiti and Chérie's arrival on the island underwent several cuts. Two short scenes were tightened, the first being Frazer's impatient anticipation of his fiancée's arrival at the registrar's office. The second cut has Chérie, still at the registrar's office after the aborted wedding, asking Dolan to persuade Frazer to come to the club that evening. In the German version the scene ends on a mournful Chérie, eliminating two short pieces of dialogue found in *Atoll K*'s final cut. Dolan: "I'll give him the message, but you know him better than I do." Cherie: "Oh, well then, he'll show up, I'm sure." Prior to the fade-out she glances optimistically into the camera. Again, these cuts do not affect the coherence of the plot.

However, Chérie's second performance at the nightclub was cut considerably, and even restructured to some extent. Her song *Tu n'peux pas t'figurer* (German: "Ja, mein Mund," translating "Yes, My Mouth") lasts less than a minute, compared to the two and a half minutes in the original version. Although the IFU had been given separate music and effects tracks, the song "Tu n'peux pas t'figurer" required a new arrangement to create an effective abridgement.

The sequence of events in the nightclub was altered dramatically, eliminating most of the original's emotional impact. At first a Chinese employee collects napkins that have been used by the guests. Scenes of the registrar and his wife waiting for other guests and welcoming them with a garland of flowers, and the wife shushing him during Chérie's performance are gone; instead, the German version cuts to Dolan entering the club. The registrar beams on his arrival, obviously hoping his entrance brings good news for Chérie. Cut to a table reserved under Frazer's name at the sold-out club. There follows a rather baffling sequence in which other naval officers enter, only to be greeted by looks of skepticism and disappointment from the registrar. In fact, Dolan actually enters *twice*, his initial entrance intercut with the arrival of two other officers. Surprisingly, the IFU had copied two of the previous shots and, contrary to the original final cut, assembled them in a double sequence. Entirely missing is Dolan making his way through the club to the bar, where he informs the owner that Frazer is not coming, as well as Chérie's imploring look to Dolan. Now the club manager removes Frazer's reservation sign immediately after the registrar's doubtful look and his chat with Dolan. Dolan catches Chérie's eye and shrugs his shoulders, signaling an abrupt end to her song (it would run another 30 seconds in the original edit). Ignoring a standing ovation, Chérie retires to her dressing room in tears (a reaction shot from the registrar was also cut). Events in Chérie's dressing room were trimmed as well; the manager no longer asks her for an encore. There is only a very short conversation between her and Dolan, overlaid by a new commentary at Biermann's request: "Look what you've done, Chérie. Now he has sailed away."

Later on, Chérie's clash with Dolan's wife aboard the freighter is tightened. The captain's wife still discovers the atoll through her telescope, but below deck Chérie no longer taunts Mrs. Dolan as she searches for her nylons. Instead, there is a quick cross-fade to Dolan's freighter and Chérie's banishment to the dinghy.

The order of the radio announcers reporting on the discovery of Atoll K (following the Washington press conference) remains the same as in the English-language version. The German announcer, who appears in both the French and the Italian versions, is missing from the German version—instead, both the American and British announcers are dubbed in German. The landing of boatloads of immigrants on the shores of Crusoeland was slightly reduced. Sadly, the provocative moment with the mother disrespectfully wiping her children's faces with the national flag was cut, just as it was in the French version. There is instead a quick cut to the outside of the newly reopened Café Crusoe, then inside to the harried Antoine serving bouillabaisse. (In the original versions he comes into the scene with his tray before beginning to serve.)

Alecto's conspiracy to overthrow the atoll's government, which had already been subject to cutting in the English-language and French versions, was also removed from the German version. The film cuts to an insert shot of Ollie's proclamation (in German) immediately after the tumultuous events in Café Crusoe. (The insert is unsigned and fills the entire frame, since only the English-language, French and Italian versions of the proclamation were shot on Cap Roux.)

Alecto's *High Noon*–style march on Stan and Ollie's bungalow was also cut. In the German version he tears down the proclamation and, in no time, appears to confront the government — we do not see him incite his fellow rabble-rousers along the way.

While these cuts downplayed Alecto's role, the German version offers an acceptable balance between a comprehensible plot and the subsequent focusing of *Atoll K* on Laurel and Hardy. The film's greatest loss is the poignant strength of Chérie's torch-song performance.

Most of Biermann's suggested changes were disregarded, avoiding the damage his requests might have inflicted on this version. The scene in which Ollie's gale-force snoring twice knocks Stan off his chair remains unchanged, and the proposed trick shot of the worn toothbrush was likewise ignored.

A few surprising alterations do make their way into the film, presumably on Biermann's request. The excuses employed by the three lawyers to bilk Stan and Ollie out of most of the inheritance differ only slightly from the original, as stated in chapter 7. But the audacity of their excuses is highlighted in the German version. Bramwell begins: "To save taxes we have already paid the taxes for you." Bonnefoy follows: "These ones and our fees permit us to deduct from the inheritance," whereupon Poltroni continues with a litany of bogus taxes: "There are income taxes, succession taxes, accession taxes, inheritance taxes, property taxes, bachelor taxes, expense taxes and freeway taxes." Bramwell steps in to reassure Stan and Ollie: "Only the usual deductions."

In contrast to the original versions (but in a much more effective manner than attempted in *Robinson Crusoeland*), the German version sees Stan's pet lobster Oscar as the chief ingredient in Chérie's bouillabaisse. Antoine: "Did you cook the lobster that has been tied down outside?" Chérie: "Yes, he was terrific." At this, Stan, Ollie, Antoine and Giovanni start crying. On top of that, the German version dubs Stan crying "My Oscar!" as he dips a potato into the stock pot. The German commentary adds: "Forget about Oscar." In the original version Oscar is not mentioned at all; instead the men shed tears for either Frazer or Chérie after discovering Frazer's photo.

Later, in the Café Crusoe, a bottle-wielding Stan dares Alecto, "Do that again!" (after the Cossack has hit Ollie over the head with a tray). But in the German version his threat is changed to "Drop it," effectively killing the point of the joke (since Alecto then immediately clobbers Stan).

One last change was incorporated, when the island finally sinks into the ocean. In the original versions Stan, Ollie, Chérie, Antoine and Giovanni are the sole survivors. But the German version insists that no one really got hurt: "Do not worry! No human being was hurt. Of course, everyone was saved. The atoll only disappeared the way it once emerged. That is typical for atolls."

While it may forever remain IFU's secret why they decided Oscar had to be cooked, it is obvious to some degree why the German version downplayed the doom of the atoll. The distributor wisely satisfied any FSK censorship concerns over youth protection, which would have seriously affected attendance.

But the new German commentary is the biggest drawback of the German version. As requested, dubbing director Völger recorded more than the four commentaries originally found in the English-language and French versions. Actually, Biermann's idea of "strategically adding weight to the narration ... so that some parts of the plot, upon further editing, may be clarified by the commentator" was not a bad one. Yet that type of commentary runs the risk of describing the action on the screen. That is exactly what happened at the IFU. The German narrator Richard Münch, an established theater actor and cabaret artist with an appealing voice, does an admirable job, but was forced to adhere to Völger's and Schnitzler's German dialogue script.

The clumsiness of the German narration is evident from the beginning. Münch starts by explaining the term "atoll" during the opening credits, before making an obvious "bikini" reference to the atoll of the same name. The commentary continues with a weak pun, suggesting that the atoll is smaller than the smallest island, and "therefore a-toll"—meaning, in German, "not too amazing."

During the introductory glimpses of London, further commentary was added, imagining how nice it would be in the age of the atom bomb to dream of a desert island. This addition might be acceptable, but the following lines spoken during the emergence of the atoll are hardly necessary: "If we were Dick and Doof ... we would take [it] for the inherited island. But it is not. The ... phenomenon is an atoll."

On the other hand, Münch's comments accompanying Frazer and Chérie's combative wedding ceremony are felicitous. They nicely bridge the compressed sequence of events, their bickering fading into the background while the narrator summarizes their dialogue. Their actual conversation is only heard for a few moments, when Frazer angrily asks Chérie whether she plans to continue working after the marriage.

Yet it is simply unnecessary to tell us at the end of Chérie's cloakroom scene that it is her fault that Frazer left. Even without this pointer it is obvious by Frazer's non-attendance that the ex-groom had not waited for Chérie.

A couple of other commentaries are equally pointless, including the lengthy explanations during Chérie's clash with Mrs. Dolan. Dolan's final words in Chérie's cloakroom ("That sounds like fun") trigger this protracted commentary: "And it will be fun. Friday has come and the ship is put to sea. A truly black Friday. Here comes the captain's wife. Nice, but strict. She wears the breeches, you know what I mean. What is she up to? What did she spot? Of course, our island! It cannot be anything else. The film needs to keep moving on as a true film has to do. Somehow we have to return to our friends, and so we do. This aggressive lady has drawn up an evil plan. Guess where she goes." As Mrs. Dolan has spotted the atoll through her telescope, is it really necessary to tell the audience what she is looking at? And it sounds downright awkward (and slightly apologetic) to have Münch say the film has to keep moving to return to "our friends." But there's more: as Chérie sets off in her rowboat and Dolan barely manages to prevent his wife from shooting her, the narrator adds, "That was a narrow escape, and we almost lost our Eve." Finally, as if further explanation is necessary, we are informed: "The island Chérie is heading for is, of course, the atoll of the four castaways."

Münch's commentary during the surveying of the atoll and Frazer's arrival at Chérie's bungalow is especially intrusive. They push Mısraki's atmospheric music into the background, and simply state the obvious: even though the viewer soon will learn about the rich uranium sources thanks to the Geiger counter, we are told, "Confidentially, the island is loaded with radioactive rocks, in Latin: uranium. But at the moment still no one knows."

As Stan, Ollie, Chérie, Antoine and Giovanni float on the scaffold following the sinking

1951 German *Atoll K* poster art by Olaf Iversen (author's collection).

of the atoll, the narrator is simply wasting his breath when he announces, "The atoll has vanished, and the friends are still alive thanks to the scaffold." Later, as the narrator reveals the comrades' individual destinies, Giovanni's fate receives this attempt at humor: "[He] returns to his home country Italy. Accidentally, he is out of a job, so he nails up the world with planks." In reality, Giovanni has torn down the stone wall and now builds a wooden fence for his employer.

Völger's *Atoll K* trailer was narrated by Hans Nielsen. The voice-over is another case of overkill: "Stop! Attention! Wait! Stop all! Listen! No further step! Do not move! Hold your breath, until you have seen this! The cinematic event! The film! *Atoll K* ... murder ... the total experience! A comic film, an atomic film! *Atoll K*!" The distributor's advertisements boasted headlines that blared: "The movie to relax [to] COMPLETELY."[25]

At the end of November 1951, earlier than originally scheduled, Prisma accepted the German dubbing.[26] Still there were time pressures. To exploit the Christmas season in the Federal Republic of Germany as well as in Austria, the distributor had to organize trade shows on the Allies' request, at the very least in, the Federal Republic. These took place in five cities from December 11 to 17, 1951— Düsseldorf, Frankfurt am Main, Hamburg and Munich.

Along with Franco London's German language *Atoll K* brochure, Prisma provided a campaign book, paperboard mats, lobby cards and a colorful poster for the movie (which was also to be called *Atoll K* in the Federal Republic of Germany). Designer Olaf Iversen's poster presents Stan, his lobster Oscar, Ollie and Chérie on a stylized atoll. The distributor also offered

1951 German *Atoll K* showcase publicity art by Olaf Iversen (author's collection).

a wall-sized outdoor poster as well as a cabinet display featuring an atoll, a young lady in a bikini and Iversen's drawing of Stan, Ollie and Chérie, bearing following successive headlines: "Bikini is an atoll," "An amazing Bikini," and "However, this is *Atoll K*." Making use of Prisma's contemporary lobby cards, *Atoll K* was called "the laughing sorrow buster." Indeed, the German people could use a "sorrow buster"—in 1951 the Federal German economic miracle still was a long time coming, with the young German postwar state still suffering the consequences of World War II. Most Germans could barely take care of necessities, let alone fork out money for movie tickets.

Following the example of the Italian distributors, Prisma's press department did not seem to have watched *Atoll K* too closely. At the end of Prisma's synopsis for cinema owners, the movie's final sequence is described this way: "Dick and Doof are waiting at the tax office counter section 'penalties for delay.'" This scene had been shot at Billancourt, but rejected in favor of the film's eventual "another nice mess" ending on the inherited island.

As soon as the German version of *Atoll K* was ready, Prisma promptly moved into Austria. The West German dubbing was released in Vienna on December 14, 1951, even prior to the trade shows and the release of the movie in the Federal Republic of Germany. Retitled *Die beiden Robinsons auf Atoll K* ("The Two Robinsons on Atoll K"), the film was distributed by Tirol-Film in Austria. One critic who attended the Vienna premiere suggested that the plot offered "favorable occasions for the appearance of the two comedians which, however,

never do attain the root of the political satire. Despite the broader scope offered, for example, by the scenes shot in Marseilles, the direction is hardly different from one of the team's previous films. Nevertheless: plenty of laughs."[27] The Austrian Catholic *Filmschau* only found a "shallow, unambitious slapstick comedy" which "still results in bright effects employing a host of banal grotesque scenes as well as lively gags and excellent facial expressions from the indestructible team."[28] Years later, in approximately 1960, Viennese distributor Favorit rereleased *Die beiden Robinsons auf Atoll K* to Austrian cinemas, broken into four parts which, according to critics, "are standing side by side completely senseless": *Stan und Olly erben eine Insel* ["Stan and Ollie Inherit an Island"], *Stan*

Suzy Delair as Chérie. 1951 German *Atoll K* lobby card: "The laughing sorrow buster" (author's collection).

und Olly als Robinson ["Stan and Ollie as Robinson"], *Stan und Olly sollen hängen* ["Stan and Ollie Are Up to Be Hanged"] and *Stan und Olly: Abenteuer auf Atoll K* ["Stan and Ollie: Adventure on Atoll K"].[29]

Atoll K opened in the Federal Republic of Germany on December 21, 1951, at both the Munich Grosskino im Kongress–Saal des Deutschen Museums and at the considerably smaller Gabriel-Lichtspiele.[30] The Federal German Catholic *Film-Dienst*, in contrast to today's view, often saw Laurel and Hardy's comedy as a "breach of tastefulness."[31] *Atoll K*, however, was better received than usual, earning a lengthier review. This particular critic obviously enjoyed the satirical elements and expressed a rare appreciation for Joannon's direction[32]:

> For the first time Dick and Doof dabble in satire and parody, thus injecting a more profound sense into their inexhaustible gags and their grotesque clowning, without sacrificing comedy. Careful direction and photography, partly employing neo-realistic stylistic devices as well as felicitous special effects, lift the Dick and Doof movie beyond their usual standard. Tightening of a couple of scenes would be to the movie's advantage. Dick and Doof movie with satiric ambitions, accessible for more mature kids, too.

In the end, *Film-Dienst*, without having seen the uncut version of the film or the distributor's preliminary work, demanded even further tightening — unintentionally complimenting Prisma, who had already prearranged the trimming of non–Laurel-and-Hardy scenes. René Albouze's special effects, cherished by *Film-Dienst*, have to be judged in more realistic fashion. They are serviceable, of course, but cannot hold a candle to the works of renowned American special-effects artists Willis O'Brien (*King Kong*; Ernest B. Schoedsack, Merian C. Cooper, 1933) or Ray Harryhausen (*The Seventh Voyage of Sinbad*; Nathan Juran, 1958).

The reviewer for *Evangelischer Film-Beobachter*, *Film-Dienst*'s Protestant counterpart, was equally positive, though he was known to condemn Laurel and Hardy's films as "humiliatingly stupid."[33] The Protestant reviewer praised *Atoll K*'s entertainment value[34]:

> Even moviegoers who do not care for this kind of cultivated ballyhoo will have to admit that this movie is above the standards of Laurel and Hardy films. Despite the story's overall bawdiness it is not just another rough-house comedy ... which means a lot these days. Sometimes a certain morality comes through ... though it may be hidden in a raw and not too tasteful hull.... In this way the viewer enjoys a certain moral benefit. Naïve minds who attend simply to laugh ... will have sufficient reason for laughter. Box-office of suitable theatres will not miss out.

Trade paper *Der Neue Film* still found Laurel and Hardy's antics "appealing," but rightly questioned expanding the duo to a foursome by including Antoine and Giovanni.[35] Some critics resented the fact that the script and direction abandoned the political satire halfway, expressing disappointment that the movie failed to free Laurel and Hardy from their familiar surroundings. Reviewers suggested that Laurel and Hardy's "side-splitting seafaring" as well as the pace "are interrupted ... by subplots including political parody and ... by an overdone accumulation of implausibilities."[36] The reviewer at *Die Welt* noted that the "serious social problem of possession" had been well addressed.[37] The *Frankfurter Rundschau* felt that the most important thing was that "the audience laughs, laughs, laughs."[38]

The *Hamburger Morgenpost* proceeded further[39]:

> Dick and Doof need a long time to warm up in their crazy slapstick movie, before they are revved up to launch a parody on Hollywood western vehicles. Unfortunately, the appealing new gags sometimes flop, which is not surprising after 25 years of comedy team work. Maybe they felt the same way, thus leaving the juiciest comedy to capricious French singer Suzy Delair.

Despite reviews such as these, the response from the Federal German daily press was basically positive. When the movie premiered in Cologne at the beginning of January 1952, local critics emphasized that adults would find reason to laugh at *Atoll K*, even though the film was geared to adolescents.[40] But they were quick to point out that Laurel and Hardy's latest film distinctly differed from their earlier Roach comedies: "While Laurel and Hardy's characteristics in earlier films play a role within the plot, *Atoll K*'s plot seems only to present the characteristics. The film teems with scenes emphasized by director Joannon as 'especially typical.' Sometimes Laurel and Hardy stick a little to close to 'type' ... Nevertheless, the film is an undiluted pleasure for all Dick und Doof fans."[41] In this, the *Uelzener Allgemeine Zeitung* agreed: "The viewer is happy with the antics of the two comedians."[42]

In its 1951–52 program, Prisma announced *Atoll K* as "Dick and Doof in the conflicts of world politics. An international coproduction of mirth."[43] It promoted a "hurricane of laughter," stating that its "audience [was] weak from laughter."[44] Following trade previews, the film was well received at its Munich premiere, but receipts waned at the end of February 1952 — screenings decreased and audience reaction was poor.[45] But *Atoll K* recovered: in April 1952 business was satisfactory and the film was still screening in rural and urban cinemas. The film played at least until July 1952 and stayed in Prisma's program until the autumn of that year, with good to very good box-office.[46]

This did not mean that the film then disappeared from German cinemas. At a Munich screening in early 1954, *Münchner Merkur* summed up the film: "The old ideas are long in need of repair, but Oliver Hardy and Stan Laurel exhibit so many funny routines that you cannot help laughing, despite any resistance."[47]

Any collector of German Laurel-and-Hardy movie posters will be familiar with distributor NWDF (Nordwestdeutscher Filmverleih und Vertrieb) or NWDF-Unitas (Nordwestdeutscher Filmverleih und Vertrieb — Unitas), created under the auspices of Erich J. A. Pietrek. His own boss since 1957, Pietrek entered the distribution business as early as 1933. After working for two other West German Laurel-and-Hardy distributors who eventually went bankrupt, Pietrek acquired every Laurel-and-Hardy title he could, often rechristening them with the *Dick und Doof* label to appeal to a juvenile audience. His success with Laurel and Hardy reissues led to *Atoll K* becoming *Dick und Doof erben eine Insel* ("Dick and Doof Inherit an Island") in 1958. The rerelease poster, newly designed by Pietrek's graphic artist Heinz Bonné (the man responsible for the boys' apparent high blood pressure in the NWDF posters), promoted the film as "Stan Laurel and Oliver Hardy's last movie, the only one shot in Europe."[48]

Pietrek was a master of weather-beaten promotional clichés, which he put to good use for *Dick und Doof erben eine Insel*. He advertised Laurel and Hardy as "indestructible masters of extreme comedy" presenting "a quick succession of comic adventures ... in a series of never-ending slapstick situations." "Dick and Doof ... battle their way against the audience's roars of laughter" and "They are leading an assault of the laughter muscles" were just two more examples.

Admittedly, Pietrek's formula worked. The marketing left potential audiences blind to the flaws of the movie. *Dick und Doof erben eine Insel* played successfully for years, as spotlighted by a review from a Düsseldorf engagement in 1964: "Nonstop waves of joy in the sold-out cinema. Lucky souls who secured a ticket enjoyed this side-splitting romp."[49]

As Pietrek kept *Dick und Doof erben eine Insel* in business for roughly a decade, he became increasingly concerned over Laurel's unhealthy appearance in the film. His solution was to substitute stills from *Dick und Doof in der Fremdenlegion* (*The Flying Deuces*, 1939) for *Atoll K* lobby cards, and had lobby cards from *Dick und Doof in der Fremdenlegion* relabeled with the title *Dick und Doof erben eine Insel.*

Film recycling was another one of Pietrek's trademarks. Time and time again he cobbled together something new out of past successes; he was especially fond of *The Flying Deuces.* By mid–1972 Pietrek showed no hesitation in mixing up lobby cards of *Dick und Doof in Afrika*, his eleven-minute version of *The Flying Deuces* previously released in 1964, with stills from *Atoll K* stills, none of them showing Laurel.[50]

Earlier, in 1965, Pietrek had commissioned the IFU to assemble another one of his compilations. *Superschau des Lachens* ["Super Show of Laughter"] was cheaply stitched together from the German-dubbed versions of Laurel and Hardy's features *Babes in Toyland* (1934), *Atoll K* and *The Flying Deuces*,[51] awkwardly linked with a commentary written by Helmut Harun and spoken by well-known German cabaret artist Jürgen Scheller. From mid–1966 onward, Pietrek profited nicely from his latest compilation—quite nicely, in fact, since he only paid the IFU 8,000 Deutsche marks for the reworking.[52]

The *Superschau des Lachens*, also known as *Dick und Doof—Superschau des Lachens*, starts with the storyline from *Babes in Toyland*, with Stan delivered to the evil Barnaby's house as his "bride." This is followed by a condensed version of *Atoll K*, which represents fifty percent of the compilation's running time. Afterwards Ollie falls in love with Georgette in *The Flying Deuces*, only to learn that his beloved is already married. At the beginning of *Superschau des Lachens* the narrator introduces the duo who "belong together like film and cinema," characterizing them thusly: "Oliver Hardy ... the super manager, who outwits himself overeagerly, the bull in his own china shop ... Stan Laurel, the dumb little brother, the eternal scapegoat." The abridged *Atoll K* was tied together with seven more commentaries. During the sinking of the atoll we're told, "Do not worry, all of our friends have been rescued"—a barely subtler approach than Münch's original commentary.

The trailer, also voiced by Jürgen Scheller, boasted the usual exaggerations, inflating the 83-minute *Superschau des Lachens* to 100 minutes. "Hundred minutes packed with comedy, hundred minutes of nonstop laughter! A super show of laughter with the supermen of comedy, Stan Laurel and Oliver Hardy.... An anthology of the most fantastic gags from the 30-year career of the incomparable comedians, Dick and Doof" read some of the ballyhoo, a claim made credible by the timespan represented by the compilation's extracts.

To promote *Superschau des Lachens*, Pietrek and his graphic artist Bonné put scissors and glue to good use. Stan's sickly appearance in *Atoll K* led Pietrek to cut and paste photos of Stan's younger self onto lobby cards for *Dick und Doof erben eine Insel*. This gave the marketing materials for *Superschau des Lachens* a consistent look, but made Laurel's appearance in the actual film more of a shock to unsuspecting audiences.[53]

The NWDF-Unitas head was once again satisfied. The daily press welcomed the compilation: "Fans of the unforgettable comedy team are again allowed to feast on their slapstick antics and laughingly pay tribute to their stunning comedy.... Nonstop series of slapstick events and comic adventures.... A film accurately called 'super,'" reported the Bielefeld papers *Westfalenblatt* and *Freie Presse*, among others.[54]

The critic for the *Evangelischer Film-Beobachter* overlooked the compilation, but the Catholic *Film-Dienst* did review it, although it gave the film short shrift. Under the headline "Unpretentious Hubbub Entertainment for All," it went on to read: "Only the person who expects little and does not object to ballyhoo will be entertained by *Superschau des Lachens*."

1958 German *Dick und Doof erben eine Insel* poster art by Heinz Bonné (author's collection).

1965 German *Superschau des Lachens* poster art by Heinz Bonné (author's collection).

1958 German *Dick und Doof erben eine Insel* lobby card (author's collection).

The critic deemed Laurel and Hardy's "usual slapstick" to be more boring than entertaining. Instead, he emphasized the profound comedy of *Dick und Doof erben eine Insel.*[55]

Box-office remained strong, although *Film-Sonderdienst Ott* warned against the danger of reissues: "Dick and Doof have retained their attraction. Do not overfeed the market with too many of these old excavations."[56] In late summer 1966 the film steadily reported "very good business."[57] *Superschau des Lachens*, described as "Dick and Doof's collected work" by the *Erlanger Tageblatt*, remained in West German cinemas at least until July 1967.[58]

Pietrek also sold *Superschau des Lachens* to Austria, where it was distributed by Favorit beginning in the autumn of 1966. The Catholic Austria movie critic dismissed it in one sentence: "The familiar, naïve slapstick which, due to this piling up, is more wearisome than amusing."[59]

At the very beginning of his career as an independent distributor, the entrepreneurial Pietrek sold *Dick und Doof erben eine Insel* to the Federal German Berlin 16mm film dealer Bruno Schmidt and later, in 1965, to Atlas Schmalfilm ("Atlas 16mm film"). Then, when the market for Super-8 sound home movies emerged, Pietrek was ready. Around 1978, a two-part home-movie version was released by Ufa/ATB. With a total running time of roughly 38 minutes, this was simply a collection of extracts that offered little indication of the complete film's structure.

In the 1960s, Pietrek also took *Dick und Doof erben eine Insel* into Scandinavia (Denmark, Finland, Norway and Sweden) and Iceland, offering the English, French and German versions for distribution.[60] The film apparently remained successful enough to allow Pietrek to refuse offers from the KirchGroup to acquire the German version in the 1970s. Consequently, *Atoll K* was missing from the KirchGroup's highly successful German TV half-hour series *Dick und Doof* from 1970–73 (and the redubbed feature retrospective), as well as the 1975–80 series of Laurel-and-Hardy feature films labeled *Lachen Sie mit Stan und Ollie* ("Laugh with Stan and Ollie"). Both series were aired by Zweites Deutsches Fernsehen (ZDF). In 1985, Pietrek ultimately let go of the film. *Atoll K* or *Dick und Doof erben eine Insel*, aired for the first time on German TV on September 8, 1991, on media mogul Leo Kirch's pay–TV channel Premiere. By this time nearly all of available Laurel-and-Hardy films had long since aired on Federal German TV.

In the end, Pietrek, who died in autumn 1989, posthumously arranged for the TV premiere of the German version of the duo's final film.[61] This led Kirch's video label Taurus to finally release *Dick und Doof erben eine Insel* on VHS in 1996. Beginning in 1998, this video was sold by Kinowelt Home Entertainment GmbH who, unfortunately, failed to secure the DVD rights for their impressive series of Region-2 Laurel and Hardy DVDs launched in 1999. Tobis Home Entertainment took advantage of this omission to release, in 2004, a DVD featuring both the German version *Dick und Doof erben eine Insel* and *Utopia*. The print of *Utopia* was particularly good, a refreshing alternative to the countless shoddy offerings of this version. This being *Atoll K*, however, there naturally had to be a few new oddities with this release. From the very

1965 German *Superschau des Lachens* lobby card made from the previous card with a rejuvenated Laurel (author's collection).

beginning, the KirchGroup's opening credits trumpet their restoration of Laurel and Hardy's films from the Hal Roach library —*Atoll K* had nothing to do with the Roach studios. As the film fades in, a newly created title card credits Exploitation Produktions Incorporated (properly spelled Exploitation Productions Incorporated). Finally, Misraki's version of Laurel and Hardy's theme song over the end titles is disrupted by "On to the Show," a Leroy Shield composition from the Roach era. Will the tampering with *Atoll K* ever stop?

Atoll K may not have been a genuine blockbuster in the German-speaking European market, but it was far from a flop. In fact, *Atoll K* turned out to be a profitable bet for both distributors and theater owners for many years, a claim that many Laurel-and-Hardy films cannot accurately make. In this respect *Atoll K* mirrors Laurel and Hardy's final 20th Century–Fox feature. Though today *The Bullfighters* (1945) has a less than stellar reputation, it was a box-office hit in the United States and remained in worldwide distribution until 1947. It continued to be offered to cinemas until the 1990s, making it the team's only 20th Century–Fox film to remain in constant circulation for more than fifty years.[62]

Thus ends our archaeology — or should I say atollology? — of *Atoll K*. Against all odds, and just as they did in over a hundred misadventures, Laurel and Hardy persevered. These two comic gentlemen had no need to be ashamed of their final film together.

Appendix 1: Filmography

The Final Cut

Atoll K, 1951

Length: 100 minutes (2,753 meters); sound; black and white; *script provisionally finished*: August 1950, with ongoing changes until the end of shooting; *period of shooting*: August 7 through October 10, 1950, and January 12 through April 4, 1951; Laurel-and-Hardy scenes had been finished a couple of days when shooting completed on April 4, 1951; *shooting on location*: August 7, 1950 through circa mid–August 1950 (harbor of Marseilles), August 16 through October 10, 1950 (Agay, Anthéor Bay, Cap Roux, Valescure near St. Raphaël, coastal area of Cap Roux and St. Raphaël as well as airport of Nice); *studio shooting, water basin of the studio La Victorine (Nice)*: approximately early October 1950 (most of the scenes on deck of the *Momus*, Ollie's fall into the ocean, additional scenes of the *Momus*, the scaffold floating on the sea); *recording of music at the Paris Studio Raymond Ventura*: January 11, 1951 (Suzy Delair's songs "Laissez-moi faire" and "Tu n'peux pas t'figurer"); *studio shooting at the Paris Studios Cinéma (Billancourt)*: January 12 through April 4, 1951 (the remaining studio shooting).

Producing enterprises: É.G.É. (Paris), Universalia (Rome; only 1950), Les Films Sirius (Paris; also French distributor), Franco London Film S.A. (Paris; also worldwide marketing), Fortezza Film (Rome; also Italian marketing); *producers*: Raymond Eger (É.G.É.) and uncredited Salvo d'Angelo (Universalia; only 1950), Henri — aka Henry — Deutschmeister (Franco London Film S.A.), Gastone Tomassini (Fortezza Film), George H. Bookbinder (movie marketeer, New York); *executive producer*: Paul Joly; *set secretary*: Paulette Boréal; *idea and first outline*: Léo Joannon; *first treatment*: Raymond Eger, Léo Joannon, Alex Joffé, Jean Levitte; *second treatment*: John — aka John D.— Klorer, Frederick — aka Friedrich — Kohner, René Wheeler, Pierro — aka Piero — Tellini; *script:* René Wheeler, Pierro — aka Piero — Tellini; *script collaboration and additional gags*: Monty — aka Monte — Collins; *uncredited script collaboration*: Léo Joannon, Alex Joffé, Stan Laurel, Jean Levitte, Tim Whelan; *dialogue of the French version*: Isabelle Kloucowsky — aka

Kloukowski, Jean-Claude Eger; *dialogue of the English-language version*: John — aka John D. Klorer, Monty — aka Monte — Collins, Isabelle Kloucowsky — aka Kloukowski — *dialogue of the Italian version*: ?; *director*: Léo Joannon (the complete shooting on location at the Côte d'Azur and the studio shooting at La Victorine as well as studio shooting at the Paris Studios Cinéma without Laurel and Hardy), John Berry (uncredited; studio shooting of the Laurel-and-Hardy scenes at the Paris Studios Cinéma), Alfred Goulding?; *first assistant director*: Pierre Franchi; *second assistant director*: Pierre Nivollet; *production manager*: Maurice Hartwig; *assistant production managers*: André Rameau, Jean Piette; *location manager*: Pierre Charron; *script girls*: Madeleine Longue, Sylvette Baudrot (second unit); *artistic and technical advisers*: Paolo Moffa, Isabelle Kloucowsky — aka Kloukowski; *technical manager*: René Moulin; *director of photography*: Armand Thirard; *cameraman*: Louis Née; *operative cameraman*: Jean Dicop; *second cameraman*: Robert Florent; *stills photographer*: Henri Moiroud; *editor*: Raymond Isnardon; *editor assistant*: Monique Isnardon; *recording director*: Pierre — aka Pierre–Louis — Calvet; *sound recordist*: René Moreau; *boom operator*: Maurice Dagonneau; *music*: Paul Misraki; *lyrics*: André Hornez, Paul Misraki; *arrangement of the songs*: Wal Berg; *conductor of the song recording*: Paul Misraki; *conductor of the score*: Marc Lanjean; *set designer*: Roland — aka Jean-Roland — Quignon; *set designer assistants*: Raymond Gabutti, Paul Moreau; *props and pyrotechnical effects*: René Albouze; *make-up and hairdressing*: Carmen Bresle, René Daudin, Michèle Péguéro; *Suzy Delair's wardrobe*: Jacques Fath; *wardrobe supervisor*: Jean Zay; *wardrobe mistress*: Simone Pinoteau; *chief electrician*: René Touillaud; *transports*: Dedé Cretel (Transports S.T.A.B.); *public relations*: Georges Cravenne, Michel Ferry.

Cast: Stan Laurel (Stan Laurel), Oliver Hardy (Oliver Hardy), Julien Maffre (Laurel's stand-in), Victor Decottignies (Hardy's stand-in), Claude May (Miss Pringle), André Randall (lawyer Phineas Bramwell), Robert Vattier (lawyer Yves Bonnefoy), Vittorio Caprioli (lawyer Pietro Poltroni), Lucien Callamand (harbor official who collects the last of Stan and Ollie's money), Olivier Hussenot (Monsieur

233

Bonnet, captain of the *Medex*), Max Elloy (Antoine), Adriano Rimoldi (Giovanni Coppini), Guglielmo Barnabò (Giovanni's Italian employer, Italian version only), Suzy Delair (Chérie Lamour), Philippe Richard (manager of the Cacatoes-Club), Luigi Tosi (Lieutenant Jack Frazer), Félix Oudart (mayor and registrar of Papeete), Titys (his deputy), Palmyre Levasseur (registrar's wife), Robert Murzeau (Captain Mike Dolan), Suzet — aka Suzy — Maïs (Martha Dolan), Henri Cote (surveyor discovering the uranium find), Charles Lémontier (senior official who approves the sovereignty of the atoll), Maurice Pierrat (bespectacled French radio announcer, dubbed into Italian for the Italian version), Hans Werner — aka Jean Verner — (German radio announcer, English-language and French version only), Jean Maxime (sailor in the Café Crusoe who receives two bottles of liquor from Stan), Nicolas Amato (Rub-Out Raymond, hoodlum who wants to sell the liquor), Michel — aka Michael — Dalmatoff (Alecto), Guy Henry (Alecto's henchman in white cowboy shirt), Jo — aka Joè — Davray (Alecto's henchman with waistcoat and hat who reports that Ollie fixed the proclamation), Roger Legris (radio operator Higgins), Hubert Deschamps (policeman who confiscates Stan's inherited island and the boys' belongings), extras: harbor workers in Marseilles and residents of the region Var/St. Raphaël as crowd which emigrates to Crusoeland.

Notes About the Final Cut

So far the actors of the following roles could not be identified definitely:

1. the two harbor policemen in Marseilles
2. Frazer's chief officer Bosun and best man alongside Captain Dolan
3. Alecto's henchman in plaid shirt, without hat — first guard in front of Stan's and Ollie's bungalow (Franck Maurice?)
4. Alecto's hatless henchman in plaid shirt, second guard in front of Stan's and Ollie's bungalow (Gilbert Moreau?)
5. the radio operator on Frazer's ship
6. the radio announcers, with the exception of Maurice Pierrat and Hans Werner — Jean Verner
7. the reporters

It has been claimed that Simone Voisin contributed to the film. Did she play the mother who dries the faces of children with the Crusoeland flag, or one of the background women who pass by the proclamation in the English-language and the French version?

Atoll K was financed, among others, by the movie marketeer George H. Bookbinder who for years sold Laurel-and-Hardy movies in postwar Germany through his Munich enterprises *Bookfilm International*

Corporation and *All Star Pictures Sales Corporation*. According to the Danish and English (British) credits, Paul Kohner contributed to the script. This, however, is unfounded. Probably a yet unknown Italian director was called in for the shooting at Billancourt.

The supposed working titles *Atoll* and *Entente Cordial* seem doubtful as Léo Joannon's 1949 outline bears the headline *"Atoll K."*

Atoll K borrowed ideas from the following Laurel-and-Hardy movies: *Twice Two, Bonnie Scotland, Saps at Sea, Towed in a Hole, Come Clean, Helpmates, Berth Marks, Hog Wild, Dirty Work, Oliver the Eighth, The Big Noise, The Music Box, The Dancing Masters* and *Why Girls Love Sailors*.

Original Versions

Atoll K

Length: 93 minutes (2,553 meters); French version, only Laurel and Hardy were dubbed into French; *located*: Gaumont/Télédis (Paris).

World premiere: September 10, 1951 (Cinéma d'Eté, Monte Carlo, Monaco); *French premiere*: September 25, 1951 (Olympia, Bordeaux); *French premiere*: October 17, 1951 (Ermitage, Max Linder and Olympia, all in Paris); *Commission de Controle des Films Cinématographiques (French board of movie approval)*: file no. 9,841, July 27, 1951 (length: 2,661 meters), without reservations for France and Northern Africa, also for Saarland, Germany and Austria; *distributor*: Sirius (France and Northern Africa).

Dubbing studio: Lax? (on the studio compound of Billancourt, Paris); *dialogue of the French version*: Isabelle Kloucowsky — aka Kloukowski, Jean-Claude Eger; *dubbing director*: Isabelle Kloucowsky — aka Kloukowski; *voice actors*: Frank O'Neill (Stan Laurel), Howard Vernon (Oliver Hardy).

Video: Collection Hollywood Nostalgie, René Chateau; *order no.* 3330240034914; *date of release*: c. early 1990s (running time of the video: 89 minutes); *U.S. Copyright Office, Washington*: file no. PA-891–351 for Télédis (Paris), December 10, 1997 (video edition only)

Note: Longer prerelease versions of the official French version could not be located. However, the Archives Françaises du Film in Bois d'Arcy hold a copy of the original French sound (2,691 meters = 98.35 minutes).

Atollo K, aka Atollo "K"

Length: originally approximately 97 minutes (2,667 meters), later on 88 minutes; version dubbed into Italian, including the last radio announcer, with the exception of Suzy Delair's songs and the other radio announcers' parts; *located*: Museo Nazionale del Cinema, Turin (85 minutes, incomplete copy).

Italian premiere: October 25, 1951 (unknown cinemas in Brescia and Carrara), April 12, 1952 (Quattro Fontane, Rome); *Ufficio centrale per la cinematografia (Italian board of movie approval)*: file no. 10,701, October 11, 1951 (feature film, 2,667 meters), and file no. 10,701, October 17, 1951 (trailer, 80 meters), each without reservations; *distributor no. 1*: Minerva; *distributors no. 2 and 3*; two rereleases prior to 1964; *16mm distributor*: ?; approximately from 1964 on; *dubbing studio*: Cooperativa Doppiatori Cinematografici (Rome); *Italian dialogue and dubbing director*: ?; *voice actors*: Mauro Zambuto (Stan Laurel), Alberto Sordi (Oliver Hardy), Lauro Gazzolo (Max Elloy), Giulio Panicali (Adriano Rimoldi), Rosetta Calavetta (Suzy Delair), Cesare Polacco (Philippe Richard), Gualtiero De Angelis (Luigi Tosi), Mario Besesti (Felix Oudart), Giorgio Capecchi (Maurice Pierrat), Carletto Romano (Guglielmo Barnabò), Olinto Cristina (Michel — aka Michael — Dalmatoff), Pino Locchi (Alecto's hatless henchman in plaid shirt — Gilbert Moreau?).

Super-8: Gaf Film; *order no.* 356; *date of release*: mid–1970s (74 minutes).

Video: Center Video; *order no.* 7505207; *date of release*: 1992 (running time of the video: 71 minutes; running time according to the cover: 90 minutes).

DVD: Elleu Multimedia Srl; *order no.* 88–7476–142–2; *date of release*: 2003 (running time of the video: 82 minutes; running time according to the cover: 85 minutes).

Notes: As the Italian actors spoke their lines in French during the shooting they, too, had to be dubbed into Italian.

So far I have located neither the 97-minute Italian version nor a complete copy of the 88-minute version.

Distributor Minerva stated the length as 90 minutes in its 1951 propaganda campaign book. According to another source, *Atollo K* had a length of 102 minutes; that would have been even longer than the final cut. This, however, is unfounded.

Center Video is a video copy of Gaf Film's super-8 version.

The Elleu-DVD contains the silent short *The Home Wrecker* with the Signet Films label. In fact, this is the Stan Laurel short *Smithy* (1924).

Atoll K

Length: 100 minutes; English-language version, all roles dubbed into English language, except Laurel and Hardy and the radio announcers; *located*: ?

Dubbing studio: ? (Chicago or Los Angeles?); *dialogue of the English-language version*: John — aka John D. — Klorer?, Monty — aka Monte — Collins, Isabelle Kloucowsky — aka Kloukowski; *dubbing director*: ?; *voice actors*: Paul Frees? (commentator or Max Elloy?)

Notes: Klorer's contribution to the dubbing seems doubtful, as he left *Atoll K* even before the provisional finishing of the script and before shooting began. He also died on July 15, 1951, in Los Angeles.

Paul Frees' contribution to the dubbing remains unclear.

The English-dialogue script bears the stamped date July 29, 1951. The slightly cut English-language version had been presented for the first time to a censorship board on September 20, 1951. At that time the movie presumably had been dubbed into English, most likely in the United States.

So far the 100-minute version has not been located.

English-language Versions

Atoll K

Length: 98 minutes; the longest English-language version known to exist; *located*: private hands.

Premiere: unknown, however, internal screening to *The Theodore Huff Memorial Film Society,* New York/USA, on February 7, 1967.

Video: Springtime Film B.V., Amsterdam; *order no.* 750; *date of release*: 1988 (running time of the video: 80 minutes); *title*: *Atoll K/Utopia*.

Notes: Some 16mm copies of this version do circulate among collectors. There is also a shorter version on 1952 3M film which includes the English-language version of Chérie's first song. The video contains the nearly complete opening credits of the 98-minute version, however the remainder of the film is the severely cut version *Utopia*.

Robinson Crusoeland

Length: 96 minutes, later on 82 minutes; British version in Great Britain and the British Empire, different from *Utopia*; *located*: ?

British trade shows (8.621 feet = 96 minutes): January 3, 1952 (Studio One, London; Oxford Picture House, Manchester; Scala Cinema, Liverpool; Futurist Theatre, Birmingham; Tower Cinema, Leeds), January 4, 1952 (Cinema House, Sheffield; Essoldo Theatre, Newcastle; Park Hall Cinema, Cardiff), January 8, 1952 (La Scala Cinema, Glasgow), January 10, 1952 (cinema and town unknown)

British premiere (7.509 feet = 82 minutes): from mid–March 1952 on at the latest, Essoldo (Portsmouth); *British Board of Film Censors (British board of movie approval)*: file no. 16.086, November 12, 1951, without reservations "U" (94 minutes 27 seconds); *distributor no. 1*: International Film Distributors, Ltd., marketed by Butcher's Film Service Ltd.; *distributor no. 2*: E. J. Fancey Production, Inc.

Notes: The 1952 British trade showing of the 96-

minute version contained both of Suzy Delair's English language–dubbed songs, while the 82-minute version omits the first song, but contains the original French version of the second song. There is an unlabeled Belgium DVD titled *Robinson Crusoeland* with Dutch subtitles that is claimed to run 70 minutes according to the cover and 75 minutes according to the label on the disc, but contains the U.S. version *Utopia* running 80 minutes.

Robinson Crusoeland's formerly presumed rerelease title *Escapade* in fact is the title of a program compiled from Laurel and Hardy's sound shorts *Oliver the Eighth*, *The Chimp* and *The Music Box*, which had been distributed in Great Britain by the distributor Equity from spring 1952 on, approximately the same time as the official British release of *Robinson Crusoeland*.

Utopia

Length: 82 minutes; U.S. version, different from *Robinson Crusoeland*; *located*: KF 15 (Munich), at present the version offering the best picture and sound quality.

American premiere: December 14, 1954, The Globe (New York/United States of America); *State of New York, Education Department, Motion Picture Divison* (*American board of movie approval*): file no. A 68391, September 20, 1951, without reservations, titled *Atoll K* (movie: 8.188 feet = circa 91 minutes; trailer: 149 feet); *State of New York, Education Department, Motion Picture Divison, Change of Title Affidavit*: file no. A 68391, November 20, 1954, without reservations, titled *Utopia* (82 minutes); *State of New York, Education Department, Motion Picture Divison 2*: file no. S 44.680, December 6, 1954; *distributor no. 1 (1951)*: All Star Productions Corporation, not distributed; *distributor no. 2 (1954)*: Exploitation Productions, Inc.; *distributor no. 3 (1957)*: Realart Film Exchange?; *16mm distributor (1982)*: Thunderbird; *Super-8*: Matinee Memories; *date of release*: beginning of 1977 (400 feet); *title*: Laurel + Hardy Out-Takes.

Video and DVD: Since the mid–1980s, countless videotapes and DVDs have been published in the United States, Great Britain, Canada, the Netherlands and Poland, all running 80 minutes. On most the picture and sound quality is exceptionally inferior. Among these are:

- *Video*: Hal Roach Studios Film Classics, Inc.; *order no.*: V 1011; *date of release*: September 1, 1986; *U.S.-Copyright*: file no. PA-307-779 (U.S. Copyright Office, Washington), September 2, 1986, in favor of Hal Roach Studios' The Laurel and Hardy Show no. 23 version.
- *Video*: Springtime Film B.V., Amsterdam; *order no.* 750; *date of release*: 1988; *title*: Atoll K/ Utopia.
- *DVD*: Tobis Home Entertainment; *order no.* 82876 61999 9; *date of release*: October 25, 2004;

Freiwillige Selbstkontrolle der Filmwirtschaft (FSK; *German board of movie approval*): *title*: Dick und Doof erben eine Insel, Atoll K (Utopia).

Notes: It is not certain whether the Super-8 reel *Laurel + Hardy Out-Takes* contains Suzy Delair's first English-language-dubbed song and the German radio announcer, both of them missing from the 98-minute English-language version of *Atoll K*. The videotapes mentioned are of good quality; however, they are outmatched by the Tobis DVD's picture and sound quality by far. The Hal Roach Studios video does not contain the Welch's Grape Juice promotional insert. It comes with Hardy's June 10, 1950, Ship's Report interview as bonus, titled here "Tribute to a Star." The Springtime-Film video also contains *Utopia*, but according to the tape's label it is incorrectly said to run 84 minutes. The cover credits John Berry as Joannon's codirector. The video opens with the familiar *Utopia* opening credits, beginning with the distributor's information (Exploitation Productions Incorporated) followed by a clip introducing Stan and Ollie on deck of the *Momus* before cutting to the nearly complete opening credits featuring a coarse-meshed, textile background from the English-language version *Atoll K*. The rest of the tape contains the *Utopia* cut. Due to a writing error, Tobis's DVD information on the distributor reads: Exploitation Produktions Incorporated.

Other Versions in chronological order of their national premieres (the list is not internationally exhaustive)

The versions mentioned below are not available with the exception of the non–Austrian German-language versions and the Second Polish version.

German dubbing (feature film)

Length: 2,481 meters (90 minutes).

Voice recording: November 17–19, 1951; *dubbing studio*: IFU, Remagen (Federal Republic of Germany); *executive producer*: Eugen Berger; *rough translation*: Philip H. Heister; *dialogue script*: Werner Völger, Wolfgang Schnitzler; *lyrics*: Wolfgang Schnitzler; *dubbing director*: Werner Völger; *musical adaptation*: Conny Schumann; *editor*: Edith Kandler; *sound*: Werner Strötzel; *sound effects*: Manfred R. Köhler; *main titles and insert of the proclamation*: Studio Fischerkoesen.

Voice actors: Richard Münch (narrator), Walter Bluhm (Stan Laurel), Hermann Pfeiffer (Oliver Hardy), Erdmuthe Dilloo-Caspary (Claude May),

Hans Nielsen (Vittorio Caprioli, Adriano Rimoldi), Wolf Martini (André Randall, Charles Lémontier, British radio announcer), Anton Reimer (Robert Vattier, Max Elloy, Lucien Callamand), Bum Krüger (Olivier Hussenot, Robert Murzeau), Günther Heising (the taller harbor policeman, second reporter), Wimm — aka Wim — Schroers (the smaller harbor policeman, voice from the loudspeaker in the radio operator's tent), Werner Kusch (Frazer's best man Bosun, radio operator on Frazer's ship), Edith Teichmann (Suzy Delair, including the songs), Max Eckard (Luigi Tosi), Gerhard Geisler (Felix Oudart, Henri Cote), Margarete Melzer (Suzet — aka Suzy — Maïs), Leopold Reinecke (first reporter), Alf Marholm (third reporter, Maurice Pierrat, Nick Amato), Wolf Lossen (fourth reporter, Roger Légris), Hermann Stein (American radio announcer), Carl Voscherau (Michel — aka Michael — Dalmatoff), Kurt Schmidt-Schindler (Jean Maxime); *trailer commentator:* Hans Nielsen

Austria: *Die beiden Robinsons auf Atoll K;* four-part version from 1960 on, rerelease title: *Stan und Olly erben eine Insel, Stan und Olly als Robinson, Stan und Olly sollen hängen, Stan und Olly: Abenteuer auf Atoll K; located:* ?

Austrian premiere: December 14, 1951 (Vienna); *distributor no. 1 (1951):* Tirol-Film; *distributor no. 2 (from 1960 on):* Favorit-Film; *Austrian board of movie approval:* permitted for adolescents (all federal states).

Federal Republic of Germany: *Atoll K,* aka *Atoll "K"* aka *Dick und Doof auf Atoll K;* rerelease title from 1958 on: *Dick und Doof erben eine Insel; located:* KF 15 (Munich).

German trade shows: December 11, 1951 (Alhambra, Düsseldorf; Turmpalast am Eschenheimer Turm, Frankfurt/Main; Esplanade-Theater, Hamburg; Filmtheater am Sendlinger Tor, Munich); December 17, 1951 (Marmorhaus, Berlin).

German premiere: December 21, 1951 (Grosskino im Kongress-Saal des Deutschen Museums und Gabriel-Lichtspiele, Munich).

Distributor no. 1 (1951): Prisma; *Freiwillige Selbstkontrolle der Filmwirtschaft (FSK, German board of movie approval):* file no. 3.243, September 26, 1951, permitted for adolescents under 16 years, no permission for general holidays (2,441 meters; *FSK-Trailer (83 meters):* file no. 3.783, January 24, 1952, permitted for adolescents under 16 years, no permission for general holidays.

Distributor no. 2 (1958): NWDF; *FSK:* file no. 3.243a, 5. December 1958, permitted for 6-year-old children, no permission for general holidays.

Distributor# 3 (1960): NWDF-*Unitas; FSK:* -

16mm distributor no. 1 (1957/58): 16 mm distributor Bruno Schmidt; *title: Dick und Doof auf Atoll K.*

16mm distributor no. 2 (1965): Atlas Schmalfilm; *title: Atoll K.*

Super-8: Ufa/ATB, *order no.* 339, 340 [two parts, 240 meters = approximately 38 minutes]; *date of release:* circa 1978; *titles: Dick und Doof. erben eine Insel, Dick und Doof. Unkraut vergeht nicht.*

TV 1: September 8, 1991, Premiere (Pay TV); *title: Dick und Doof erben eine Insel.*

TV 2: November 16, 2003, Kabel 1 (private TV channel, no subscription required); *title: Dick und Doof erben eine Insel.*

Video 1: Taurus-Video GmbH; *order no.* 1,367; *date of release:* April 22, 1996; *FSK:* file no. V 5,294, September 13, 1995, permitted for 6-year-old children; *certified and approved as: Laurel und Hardy erben eine Insel.*

Video 2: Kinowelt Home Entertainment GmbH; *order no.* 1,367; *date of release:* from August 1998 on; *title: Laurel und Hardy erben eine Insel.*

DVD: Tobis; *order no.* 82876 61999 9; *date of release:* October 25, 2004; *title: Dick und Doof erben eine Insel, Atoll K (Utopia).*

German dubbing: *Superschau des Lachens*; compilation from the Laurel and Hardy feature films *Babes in Toyland* (1934), *Atoll K* and *The Flying Deuces* (1939), using extracts of the German dubbed version *Atoll K*

Length: 2,260 meters (83 minutes).

German voice recording of the commentary: end of August 1965; *dubbing studio (arrangement of the extracts):* IFU, Remagen; *executive producer:* Horst H. Roth; *commentary:* Helmut Harun.

Narrator and trailer commentator: Jürgen Scheller.

Federal Republic of Germany

Superschau des Lachens aka *Dick und Doof-Superschau des Lachens: located:* KF 15 (Munich).

German premiere: circa June 1966; *distributor:* NWDF-Unitas; *FSK:* file no. 34.682, October 7, 1965, permitted for children six years old, no permission for general holidays; *FSK trailer (75 meters = 2 minutes 45 seconds):* file no. 34.683, October 7, 1965, permitted for 6-year-old children, no permission for general holidays.

Austria

located: ?

Austrian premiere: circa autumn 1966; *distributor:* Favorit-Film; *Austrian board of movie approval:* permitted for adolescents (all federal states).

Spain

Robinsones Atómicos: *length*: ?; *version*: Spanish dubbed version, version used unknown; *located*: ?

Spanish premiere: January 17, 1952 (Cine Corso, Saragossa); *Spanish board of film censors*: December 1951; *distributor*: Chamartín

Denmark

Gøg og Gokke paa atom øen: *length*: 93 minutes; *version*: Danish-subtitled English-language version; *located*: ?

Danish premiere: August 1, 1952 (Carlton, Copenhagen); *Danish board of movie approval*: file no. 40.902 and 40.969, May 20 and 27, 1952 (2,535 meters) as well as file no. 44.388, March 20, 1953 (2,495 meters); *distributor*: Eagle-Lion Film

Danish subtitles: Willy Breinholst, Hartvig Andersen.

Canada

Robinson Crusoeland: *length*: 82 minutes; *version*: British version of the English-language version; *located*: ?

Canadian premiere: October 30, 1952 (Toronto: Esquire, Midtown and Odeon); *Ontario Film Review Board (Canadian board of movie approval, Ontario; 35 mm)*: July 14, 1952, PG (parental guidance suggested); *Ontario Film Review Board (16mm)*: January 19, 1955, PG; *distributor*: International Film Distributors, Ltd.

Atoll K: *length*: 93 minutes; *version*: French version; *located*: Gaumont/Télédis (Paris).

Canadian premiere: August 3, 2003? (Musé national des beaux-arts du Québec, Québec), open air.

Note: So far it cannot be verified whether the French-version *Atoll K* premiered in Canada as early as 1951/52.

Switzerland

Atoll K: *length*: 2,700 meters?; *version*: French-and-German-subtitled English-language version, French version, Italian version; *located*: ?

Swiss premiere: 1952; *Swiss board of movie approval*: ?; *distributor*: Royal Films.

Notes: The length reported seems to be doubtful, as there is no evidence of an original version at this length. So far the screening of the German dubbed version in Swiss cinemas cannot be verified.

The Netherlands

Robinson Crusoë & Co.: *length*: 82 minutes; *version*: Dutch subtitled British version *Robinson Crusoeland*; *located*: ?

Dutch premiere: April 1953 (Cinema Royal, Amsterdam; Capitol, Rotterdam); *Dutch board of movie approval*: ?; *distributor*: Nederland.

Mexico

Los dos Robinsones: *length*: 82 minutes?; *version*: Spanish-subtitled American version *Utopia*?; *located*: ?

Mexican premiere: November 28, 1956 (Teatro Metropolitan, Mexico City); *Mexican board of film censors*: file no. 22.859 A?, date: ?; *distributor*: Oficinas Jorge M. Dada.

Poland

Flip i Flap an bezludnej wyspie: *length*: 93 minutes (2,553 meters); *version*: Polish-subtitled French version; *located*: ?

Polish premiere: June 1961; *Polish board of film censors*: ?; *distributor*: Centrala Wynajmu Filmów.

Note: The Polish version is said to have been cut on request of the communist board of film censors.

Flip i Flap — Utopia: *length*: 82 minutes; *version*: Polish-subtitled American version *Utopia*, also with Polish voice-over; *located*: Mayfly.

DVD label: Mayfly; *date of release*: mid–2005.

Czechoslovakia

Laurel a Hardy zdedeli ostrov: *length*: 90 minutes?; *version*: ?; *located*: ?

Czechoslovakian release: January 1977; *Czechoslovakian board of film censors*: ?; *distributor*: Ustredni pujcovna filmu

Note: A Czech DVD under the same title has been announced at a length of 83 minutes. Most likely, this will be another *Utopia* offering, this time with Czech subtitles. Further details are unknown.

Appendix 2: Information in Opening Credits and Distributors' Data

This overview provides an impression of the inconsistency of official information. Proper names written in capitals in the informations are rendered in the usual upper and lower case. Accents or similar orthographic signs may be missing, not having been used in the official credits.

Opening Credits

French-version *Atoll K*, 1951 (1 min 45 seconds)

Credits are running over a coarse-meshed textile background.

Laurel et Hardy
et Suzy Delair
dans
Atoll K
Mise en scène
de Léo Joannon
Adaption: René Wheeler, P. Tellini
d'après une idée originale de Léo Joannon
Dialogue: Isabelle Kloucowsky, Jean-Claude Eger
avec
Max Elloy
Suzy Maïs
Félix Oudart, Robert Murzeau, Luigi Tosi, Michel Dalmatoff, A. Randall, R. Vattier, C. May, R. Légris, O. Hussenot, Caprioli, C. Lémontier, G. Barnabò
et Adriano Rimoldi
Directeur de la Photographie: Armand Thirard
Caméraman: Louis Nee
1er assistant: Jean Dicop
2ème assistant: Robert Florent
Décors de: Roland Quignon
Assistants: R. Gabutti, Paul Moreau

Ingénieur du Son: Pierre Calvet
Assistants: René Moreau, M. Dagonneau
Montage: Robert Isnardon
Assistante: Monique Isnardon
1er Assistant Réalisateur: Pierre Franchi
Régisseur Général: Maurice Hartwig
*Script-Girl*s: Madeleine Longue, Sylvette Baudrot
Régie: André Rameau, Jean Piette, Pierre Charron
Maquillage: Carmen Bresle, René Daudin, Michèle Péguéro
Photographie: Moiroud
Costumes: Zay
Conseillers Artistiques et Techniques: Paolo Moffa, Isabelle Kloucowsky
Directeur de Production: Paul Joly
Musique: Paul Misraki
Paroles des Chansons: André Hornez, Paul Misraki
Editions Impéria
Tourné à Paris-Studios-Cinéma, Billancourt
Enrigistrement Sonore: Western-Electric (S.I.M.O.)
Laboratoires G.T.C.: Joinville-St. Maurice-Nice
Visa de Censure: no. 9.841
Une Co-Production Franco–Italienne
É.G.É, Sirius, Franco London Film, Fortezza Film
Edition Mondiale: Franco London Film
Producteur Délégué: Raymond Eger

Italian-version *Atollo K*, currently available version (47 seconds)

Credits are running over caricatures.

Una coproduzione italo francese
Fortezza Film
Franco London Film
É.G.É.-Sirius
Stan Laurel Oliver Hardy
in
ATOLLO K

con Suzy Delair, Adriano Rimoldi, Max Elloy
Vittorio Caprioli, Luigi Tosi, Félix Oudart
consigliere artistico e tecnico: Paolo Moffa
dir. produzione: Paul Joly
scenografia: R. Quignon
montaggio: R. Isnardon
aiuto regia: P. Franchi
fotografia di Armand Thirard
regia di Léo Joannon

English-language version *Atoll K*, 1951 (2 min 7 seconds)

Credits are running over a coarse-meshed textile background.

Franco London Film presents
Atoll K
Starring Laurel and Hardy
and Suzy Delair
Screenplay: J. Klorer, F. Kohner, R. Wheeler, P. Tellini
Based on an idea by Leo Joannon
Dialogue: John Klorer, Monty Collins, I. Kloucowsky
Gags by Monty Collins
with: M. Elloy, M. Dalmatoff and A. Rimoldi
Director of Photography: A. Thirard
Cameraman: L. Née
Art Director: R. Quignon
Sound: P. Calvet
Editor: R. Isnardon
Technical Adviser: I. Kloucowsky, P. Moffa
Production Manager: P. Joly
Music: Paul Misraki
Lyrics: A. Hórnez, P. Misraki
Sound Recording System: Wide Range, Western Electric (S.I.M.O.)
Directed by: Leo Joannon
Associated Producers: Raymond Eger, Fortezza Film, Films Sirius

Shortened English-language version, *Robinson Crusoeland*, 1952 (1 min 30 seconds)

Aside from the title the credits are identical to the English-language version above.

Shortened English-language *Utopia*, 1954 (44 seconds)

Credits are running over movie clips.

Exploitation Productions Incorporated
Stan Laurel Oliver Hardy
UTOPIA
also in the cast Suzy Delair, M. Elloy, M. Dalmatoff, A. Rimoldi

Screenplay: J. Klorer, F. Kohner, R. Wheeler, P. Tellini
Based on an idea by Leo Joannon
Dialogue: John Klorer, Monty Collins, I. Kloucowsky
Gags by Monty Collins
Music: Paul Misraki
Associated Producers: Raymond Eger
Fortezza Film Film Sirius
Wide Range Western Electric Sound

German-version *Atoll K*, later on *Dick und Doof erben eine Insel*, 1951 (1 min 49 seconds)

Credits are running over a newly shaped, partly animated background.

Dick und Doof erben eine Insel (Atoll K)
Hardy als Dick
Laurel als Doof
in Atoll K
mit Suzy Delair
und Max Elloy, Suzet Mais, Felix Oudart, Robert Murzeau, Luigi Tosi, Adriano Rimoldi, Dalmatoff
Drehbuch: René Wheeler und Pietro Tellini nach einer Idee von Léo Joannon
Musik: Paul Misraki
Kamera: Armand Thirard
Bauten: Roland Quignon
Schnitt: Isnardon
Eine Gemeinschaftsproduktion der
Franco–London Films S.A., Fortezza Films, Films Sirius, Films É.G.É.
Regie: Léo Joannon
Deutsche Bearbeitung:
Internationale Film-Union AG, Studio Remagen, Tonsystem Klangfilm
Buch und Regie der deutschen Fassung: Werner Völger
Liedertexte und Buchmitarbeit: Wolfgang Schnitzler
Ton: Werner Strötzel
Schnitt: Edith Kandler

Distributors' Data

Minerva, *Atollo K*, 1951

Minerva Film presenta
Una produzione
Fortezza — Franco London Film
Regia di Léo Joannon
con
Stan Laurel — Oliver Hardy
e
Suzy Delair — Adriano Rimoldi — Luigi Tosi
Guglielmo Barnabò — Max Elloy

Personaggi ed interpreti
Stan Laurel: Laurel

Oliver Hardy: Hardy
Suzy Delair: Chérie
Adriano Rimoldi: Giovanni
Luigi Tosi: Frazer
Guglielmo Barnabò: Il Sindaco
Max Elloy: Antonio

International Film Distributors, Ltd., *Robinson Crusoeland*, 1952

Starring Laurel and Hardy
and Suzy Delair
Screenplay: J. Klorer, R. Wheeler, P. Tellini and P. Kohner
Production Company: É.G.É.-Universalia
Director: Leo Joannon
Scenario: René Wheeler, P. Tellini
From an idea by: Léo Joannon
Editor: Robert Isnardon
Cameraman: Armand Thirard

The Cast
Stan: Stan Laurel
Ollie: Oliver Hardy
Chérie Lamour: Suzy Delair
Antoine: Max Elloy
Mme Dolan: Suet Maïs [Note: "Suet" (instead of "Suzet"), an obvious writing error.]
Le Maire/Mayor: Felix Oudart
Captain Dolan: Robert Murzeau
Lt. Frazer: Luigi Tosi
Alecto: Dalmatoff
Giovanni/Halo: Adriano Rimoldi

Danish version: Eagle-Lion Film, *Gøg og Gokke paa atom øen*, 1952

Eagle-Lion Film praesenter
Stan Laurel Oliver Hardy
GØK OG GOKKE PAA ATOM ØEN (*Atoll K*)
med
Suzy Delair
Max Elloy

Luigi Tosi
Adriano Rimoldi
Iscenesaettelse: Léo Joannon
Manuscript: John Klorer, R. Wheeler, P. Tellini og P. Kohner
Fotografering: A. Thirard
Musik: Paul Misraki
Danske tekster: Willy Breinholst og Hartvig Andersen

Personerne
Stan: Stan Laurel
Ollie: Oliver Hardy
Antoine: Max Elloy
Giovanni: Adriano Rimoldi
Chérie Lamour: Suzy Delair
Løjtnant Frazer: Luigi Tosi
Alecto: Dalmatoff
Dolan: Robert Murzeau
Fru Dolan: Suzet Maïs
Le Maire/Mayor: Felix Oudart

Franco London Films' Advertorial Booklet, in French, German and Spanish language, 1951; for example, German version

Eine Co-Produktion der Franco London Films S.A.— Films É.G.É. Films Sirius — Fortezza Film
Regie: Léo Joannon
Drehbuch: René Wheeler und Piero Tellini nach einer Idee von Léo Joannon
Dialoge: Isabelle Kloukowski und Jean Claude Eger
Kamera: Armand Thirard
Ton: Pierre Calvet
Bauten: Roland Quignon
Montage: Isnardon
Musik: Paul Misraki
Künstlerischer und technischer Berater: Paolo Moffa
Herstellungsleiter: Paul Joly

Note: Except for the language, the different versions of the booklet are identical.

Appendix 3: Alternative Sequences

Commentaries

The final cut of *Atoll K* contains four voice-over commentaries. The first comes immediately after the opening titles, over images of London (where it's always teatime). The second commentary is heard over the scenes of Stan, Ollie, Antoine and Giovanni farming and building on the atoll. Following that, the announcer takes us from Stan's skipping of stones to Tahiti, where we meet Chérie. Finally, as the film comes to a close, the announcer explains the final destinies of Antoine, Giovanni, Chérie and Frazer, up until Stan and Ollie's arrival on the inherited island.

Of course, the narration on each foreign version varies by language. The English-language version eliminates the counting of seeds ("901, 902, 903, 904, 905") while Giovanni sows. According to the Italian-dialogue book, two more commentaries had been planned which don't exist in the English-language or French versions. The first was to be spoken during the wild ride out of the Marseilles harbor. The second was to occur during the breakfast scene in which Frazer's photo is discovered on the floor. Before the fellows and Chérie set out for the alleged warehouse, the Italian commentary was to inform the viewer of the construction of Chérie's bungalow and her upcoming move into it. The scenes are found in the only existing, damaged copy of *Atollo K*; although the soundtrack is complete, there is no commentary.

Actually, the offscreen narration in the damaged print of *Atollo K* isn't heard until the very end of the movie, when Stan, Ollie, Antoine, Giovanni and Chérie are adrift on the scaffold. The final commentary on the main characters' fates corresponds to *Atoll K*'s final cut. It's obvious that the introductory voiceover, before Stan and Ollie's arrival at the lawyer's office in London, is missing due to print damage. Furthermore, it's interesting that, in contrast to the English-language and French versions, there is no commentary over the scenes showing the group cultivating the atoll.

Notary's Plaque

French version: "Bramwell, Bramwell et Bramwell — Notaires — Correspondants: Paris, Rome, Madrid, Tanger"

Italian version: Inscription planned: "Notaio." Due to the material defect the plaque is not to be seen in the existing copy of *Atollo K*. A photograph of this plaque is not available.

English-language version: "Bramwell, Solicitor." The French plaque is used in both the 98-minute English-language version *Atoll K* as well as in *Utopia*. The English plaque is seen both in the British version *Robinson Crusoeland* and in the German version *Atoll K*, the latter being based on the English-language version.

Promotional Insert

The *Welch's Grape Juice* promotional insert is seen only in the U.S. release, *Utopia*. The hand reaching for the labeled bottle obviously does not belong to Antoine. This insert has been removed from the 1986 Hal Roach Studios Film Classics, Inc. video release of *Utopia*.

Giovanni's Report Aboard the Momus

English-language (except *Robinson Crusoeland*?), French and German versions: Giovanni tells his comrades aboard the *Momus* why he left Italy. However, this scene has been cut down beyond recognition in the French and German versions.

Italian Version: Giovanni's oral report has been replaced by a lengthy flashback depicting an argument with his employer.

Map Insert

This insert was produced for the French version only. After Stan's frying pan serve, there is a fade to a nautical chart of the Pacific, zeroing in on Tahiti. From the bottom left of the insert a hand holding a pencil appears, moving to the top right to point out the capital of Papeete.

Nocturnal Battle Against the Bats

The Italian-version *Atollo K* misses tiny bits of Ollie's, Antoine's and Giovanni's exclamations, which are intact in the English-language and the French versions.

Radio Announcers

Depending on the version, the radio announcer making the final statement (informing the castaways of an international commission having been appointed to determine sovereign rights to the atoll) is either American English, French or Italian. The German speaker is missing from both the English-language and German versions.

According to the English-dialogue book, the complete announcements are as follows [respective announcer in brackets]:

Attenzione, attenzione [Italian speaker]
Stunde für Stunde haben wir unsere Hörer [German speaker, Hans Werner aka Jean Verner]
al corriente de las difficultades [Spanish speaker]
riscontrate dalle grandi potenze [Italian speaker]
pour trancher le problème soulevé [French speaker, Maurice Pierrat]
The recent discovery in the Pacific [American speaker]
of an island which will be known henceforth as Atoll H, I beg your pardon, Atoll K. After a fortnight of conference [British speaker]
the great powers, in a joint statement issued today, announced the appointment of an international commission to decide which nation will be awarded sovereignty rights over the island which was emerged from the ocean only a short time ago and will be known as Atoll K [American speaker]."

Differing from the dialogue book, the German speaker does not precede his Spanish colleague, but follows him saying "unter dem Namen Atoll K" instead of "Stunde für Stunde haben wir unsere Hörer." The line "riscontrate dalle grandi potenze" mistakenly reads "discontrate dalle grandi potenzi" in the dialogue book.

The following overview outlines the restructuring of the radio announcer scenes in each version:

French version

Italian speaker
British speaker [only the first part of his announcement, without his slip of the tongue]
Italian speaker
French speaker (Maurice Pierrat)
American speaker
Spanish speaker
German speaker (Hans Werner aka Jean Verner)
American speaker
French speaker (Maurice Pierrat)

Italian version

Italian speaker
British speaker (only the first part of his announcement, without his slip of the tongue)
Italian speaker
French speaker (Maurice Pierrat, however, Italian-dubbed)
American speaker
Spanish speaker
German speaker (Hans Werner aka Jean Verner)
American speaker
French speaker (Maurice Pierrat, however, Italian dubbed)

English-language version, also *Robinson Crusoeland* and *Utopia*

American speaker
Spanish speaker
Italian speaker
French speaker (Maurice Pierrat)
American speaker
British speaker (with his slip of the tongue, "Atoll H" instead of "Atoll K")
American speaker

German version

The scene corresponds to the English-language version which formed the basis of the German version. However, the German speaker is missing. The American, the British and the French speakers are dubbed into German.

Ollie's Proclamation

French version

The camera fades in on the French proclamation, already fixed to the wreck of the *Momus*. To the right of the proclamation is a man working with a shovel, while another man steps into the picture with a sailor's hat on his head, with two ladies on his arms. The woman on his left wears a skirt without a pattern, while the other woman wears a long spotted skirt. The ladies release themselves from his arms as he hits the worker against the head, pushing him behind the proclamation and out of the picture.

Italian version

Ollie, in presidential garb with admiral's hat and cape and with his back to the camera, posts the Italian-language proclamation. Afterward, two workers with picks appear, giving way to another man who crosses from the bottom right of the picture to the top left.

English-language version

Similar to the French version, but with an English-language proclamation. At the right-hand side of the screen there are two more workers alongside the worker with the shovel, when the man with the sailor's hat and two women appear. The man and the women go through the scene differently from the French version, as the worker with the shovel makes them wait. As in the French version, the man with the sailor's hat pushes the worker out of the picture.

German version

The German proclamation is a simple insert short, filling the entire screen and missing Ollie's signature.

Therefore there the workers and the gruff passersby aren't included in the scene.

Multilingual Inscriptions

Several shots use multilingual props and signage so that alternative shots were not needed. The monkey/lion cage in the harbor, fuel gauge of the *Momus*, inscription of the nightclub's stage exit, newspaper reports, outdoor signage of the travel agency, airport departure information, and announcement plaque in front of the Café Crusoe are written in three or even five languages. Oscar's lobster hut bears inscriptions in three languages, none exactly the same: "Beware Ferocious" above the entrance, "Chien méchant" (French: "Biting Dog") on the rooftop and "Attenti al cane" (Italian: "Beware the Dog!") on the left side wall. However, the Geiger counter bears a French inscription only.

Different Names

Due to the differences in language, the name of the nightclub at which Chérie performs varies among the original versions: Cocatoes-Club (English-language version), Cabaret Cacatoès (French version) and Cacatoa Club (Italian version). Each translates to the same: Cockatoo-Club. The German version, however, deviates from the rest: Kakteen-Bar ("Cactus Bar").

The names of the main characters remained the same among the original versions and the German version. A slight variation in the Italian version only: Antoine was renamed Antonio.

Appendix 4: Scenes Cut from the 100-Minute Version

French-version Atoll K *(93 minutes)*

- Antoine's discussion with the harbor policemen as to why stateless men are prohibited going on land while monkeys are allowed to do so
- Dialogue on the deck of the *Momus* as to why Giovanni left Italy and establishing that Stan and Ollie do not like taxes
- A mother wiping her children's face with the Crusoeland flag.
- Alecto's conspiratorial meeting with his cronies
- Chérie's walk through the camp to the radio operator's tent, her flirtatious attempt to lure him away, and her conversation with Frazer
- Alecto's gleeful audit of the hangman's ropes
- On Stan's island a couple of strongmen taking away all of Stan and Ollie's food and supplies

Note: The structure of the preceding French cuts (2,661 meters and 2,441 meters respectively) is unknown.

Italian-version Atollo K *(85/88 minutes)*

- Short glimpses of London after the view of Big Ben until Miss Pringle enters the notary's office
- The harbor policemen's observation on the absurdity of Antoine's and Giovanni's situation
- Captain Bonnet's discussion with Antoine on the hopelessness of his situation
- Captain Bonnet foisting Antoine upon Stan and Ollie
- After the storm Stan, Ollie, Antoine and Giovanni becoming aware that they are stranded on the atoll
- Chérie's introduction by the narrator
- Chérie's audition at the nightclub
- Frazer's impatient anticipation of his bride's arrival

- Hoisting of Crusoeland's flag
- Recognition of Crusoeland's sovereignty and the newspaper reports
- Legions from around the world landing on Crusoeland
- Stan and Ollie's housecleaning
- Commentaries until the final phase of the movie
- Stan and Ollie's final scene after Stan's last two sentences

Note: The structure of the preceding 2,667-meters Italian cut is unknown.

English-Language version Atoll K *(98 minutes)*

- Chérie's audition at the nightclub as well as the first scenes in the wedding chamber
- The German radio announcer

English-Language version Robinson Crusoeland *(82 minutes)*

- Cuts, details unclear: Giovanni being discovered as a stowaway, his emotional outburst at being found and the men introducing each other, as well as the men's conversation on deck of the *Momus* after the spaghetti meal
- Commentary telling of the years of toil spent settling the atoll
- Antoine's search for his cooking pot which Giovanni has pinched to mix concrete
- Stan in front of his newly constructed home
- Second part of Chérie's introduction
- The complete scenes dealing with Chérie's audition at the nightclub as well as the first scenes in the wedding chamber

- Mrs. Dolan making her way down to Chérie's cabin
- Mrs. Dolan forcing Chérie at gunpoint to climb into the rowboat
- Arriving at Chérie's new home, her remark, "As warehouses go, it's a funny one," and Antoine's line, "Did you really think we were building a refrigerator?"
- After Frazer's arrival in Chérie's new home, his taunt "You're not content just to be a singer, you've also got to be the comedian"
- the German radio announcer
- Recognition of Crusoeland's sovereignty and the newspaper reports
- Legions from around the world on their way to Crusoeland
- Stan and Ollie's housecleaning
- Stan handing over two free bottles of liquor to a newcomer, which a gangster wants to prevent, because he has come to Crusoeland to sell liquor
- Alecto's arrival at the Café Crusoe and his gruff dismissal of the gangster, as well as his shooting of bottles of liquor
- Alecto's conspiratorial meeting with his cronies
- Alecto announcing that the gallows will soon be erected, asking for Ollie's presidential outfit and for Chérie to accompany him
- Alecto's gleeful audit of the hangman's ropes

Note: The structure of the preceding 91-minute English-language cut is unknown.

English-Language version Utopia *(82 minutes)*

- Captain Bonnet's discussion with Antoine on the hopelessness of his situation
- The harbor policemen's observation on the absurdity of Antoine's and Giovanni's situation
- Giovanni's oral report on deck of the *Momus* (merely stating that he is playing hooky from a world where he is "always being told what to do and then how to do it")
- Antoine's search for his cooking pot which Giovanni has pinched to mix concrete
- Stan in front of his newly constructed home
- Stan pulling his pet lobster out of the hut with the help of a heavy chain
- Second part of Chérie's introduction by the narrator
- Chérie's audition at the nightclub as well as the first scenes in the wedding chamber
- Captain Dolan's appearance, aside from two silent appearances in the wedding chamber
- Chérie's grand nightclub performance
- The complete action on board Captain Dolan's freighter, except the view through a telescope

- Antoine's and Giovanni's remark on Stan's dumbness
- Press conference in Washington
- The German radio announcer
- Stan handing two free bottles of liquor to a newcomer which a gangster wants to prevent, because he has come to Crusoeland to sell liquor
- Alecto's arrival at the Café Crusoe and his gruff dismissal of the gangster as well as his shooting of bottles of liquor
- Alecto's conspiratorial meeting with his cronies
- Alecto wanting to put Chérie under his "personal protection"
- Frazer stating that he did not deliberately set out for the atoll and giving reproaches that Chérie does not need him
- Alecto's call to organize the execution of Stan, Ollie, Antoine and Giovanni within the next hour

Note: The structure of the preceding 96-minute English-language cut is unknown.

German-version Atoll K — Dick und Doof erben eine Insel *(90 minutes)*

- Captain Bonnet's comments that Antoine has experienced rejection all over the world
- Captain Bonnet's discussion with Antoine on the hopelessness of his situation
- One of the shots during the atoll's emerging from the ocean
- Cuts of the discussion on deck of the *Momus* after the spaghetti meal, Antoine and Giovanni joining Stan and Ollie without explanation, Stan and Ollie's rationale for playing hooky (Ollie: "Taxes!" Stan: "Yeah, we don't like taxes!")
- Chérie awaited urgently in the anteroom of the wedding chamber
- Dialogue at the end of the scene in the registrar's office (Dolan: "I'll give him the message, but you know him better than I do." Cherie: "Oh, well then, he'll show up, I'm sure")
- Prior to the fade-out of the scenes in the registrar's office, Chérie glancing optimistically into the camera
- Chérie's second song "Ja, mein Mund" ("Tu n'peux pas t'figurer") lasting less than a minute, compared to the two and a half minutes, for example, in the French version
- In the nightclub, the registrar and his wife waiting for other guests and welcoming them with a garland of flowers (and his wife shushing him during Chérie's performance)
- Chérie's imploring look to Dolan

- The removal of Frazer's reservation sign and the registrar's doubtful look
- The manager asking Chérie for an encore
- On Dolan's freighter, Chérie getting out of bed and searching for her nylons
- The German radio announcer
- The landing of boatloads of immigrants on the shores of Crusoeland slightly reduced

- A mother wiping her children's face with the Crusoeland flag
- In the Café Crusoe, Antoine coming into the scene with his tray before beginning to serve
- Alecto's conspiratorial meeting with his cronies
- Marching on Stan and Ollie's bungalow, Alecto inciting the inhabitants of Crusoeland to rebel against the government

Appendix 5: French Box-Office Reports, 1951–1952

Overall results of the screenings of the French-version *Atoll K* covered by the French movie trade papers for the period September 25, 1951, through March 11, 1952, appear below in chronological order. Records show that 112,541 visitors watched the movies in selected cinemas and paid 16,691,021 or 16,535,187 old French francs. This is certainly not the complete gross of the French version. Presumably, the movie was also screened in other French cities, and in the Saarland and Northern Africa. Such market reviews either had not been published or do not survive.

In two cases the information on the capacity varies.

Abbreviations used in the following table:

    fr: old French francs

    NC: not counted

City	Cinema	Capacity	Admission, fr	Period of Screening	Visitors	Grosses, fr
Bordeaux	Olympia	1,788	?	Sept.25– Oct. 1, '51	10,852	1,561,490
	Étoile	400 or 600	100	Nov. 20–26, '51	?	?
				Nov. 27– Dec. 3, '51	2,556	251,595; 2nd start
Marseilles	Majestic	935	130–150	Oct. 10–16, '51	7,099	956,150
	Odéon	1,800	130–175	Oct. 10–16, '51	8,690	1,186,260
	Club	375	?	Oct. 10–16, '51	?	?
				Oct. 17–23, '51	4,288	465,980
Lille	Cinéac	800	85–120	Oct. 17–23, '51	11,027	1,159,360
	Rexy	880	100–130	Oct. 17–23, '51	8,461	906,540
Lyon	Français	850	120–160	Oct. 17–23, '51	?	546,330
	Royal	650	160–180	Oct. 17–23, '51	4,624	720,866
				Oct. 24–30, '51	4,186	653,190
	Tivoli	935	150–180	Oct. 17–23, '51	9,296	1,306,260
Nancy	Empire	1,061	?	Oct. 17–23, '51	7,904	1,018,860
Paris	Ermitage	834	?	Oct. 17–23, '51	?	?
				Oct. 24–30, '51	?	?
				Oct. 31 through at least Nov. 13, '51	?	?
	Max Linder	765	200	Oct. 17–23, '51	7,484	1,496,800 (35) or 1,392,024 (35)
				Oct. 24–30, '51	3,647	729,400 (35) or 678,342 (35)
				Oct. 31, '51		canceled
	Olympia	1,900 or 1,870	180–220 or 220–250	Oct. 17–23, '51	NC	NC (32) or NC (35)
				Oct. 24–30, '51	NC	NC (32) or NC (35)

City	Cinema	Capacity	Admission, fr	Period of Screening	Visitors	Grosses, fr
				Oct. 31, '51		canceled
	Moulin Rouge	1,620	150–220	Nov. 21–27, '51	7,112	1,066,800 (28)
				Nov. 28, '51		canceled
Nice	Forum	1,100	150–180	Mar. 5–11, '52	NC	396,000
	Variétés	950	150–180	Nov. 5–11, '52	5,552	885,160
Toulouse	Variétés	2,025	?	Dec. 19–25, '51	9,763	1,383,980

Chapter Notes

Chapter 1

1. Newsreel *Welt im Film*, no. 131. C.f. for the first British stage tour A. J. Marriot, *Laurel & Hardy: The British Tours* (Blackpool, UK: A. J. Marriot, 1993), 157, 158, 284, 286–289.

2. *Mein Film* no. 538, April 17, 1936, 14.

3. 1957 advertising material of German distributor Centfox for *Dick und Doof: Schrecken der Kompanie* (*Great Guns*, 1941), 4.

4. C.f. Jolande Wiegands (Bram Reijnhoudt), *All Aboard for Paris* in "Laurel and Hardy in Europe," *Blotto* no. 19/20 (Hilversum 1993), 897–901. The French form for the Laurel-und-Hardy-Club membership application is reproduced on p. 897, while the photo of the club emblem can be found on p. 899. The four club rules are listed on p. 901. Nothing is known about Austrian or Italian participants.

5. Ban by the Film-Prüfstelle Berlin ["Board of Film Censors, Berlin"] on May 8, 1936, file no. 42,400, confirmed by the Film-Oberprüfstelle Berlin ["Supreme Board of Film Censors, Berlin"] on June 13, 1936, file no. 7,819. Among other things it is reasoned: "Considering the dishonesty of the film, which essentially paints an inaccurate picture of refusable gypsy life in corny form, makes it impossible to see it as a work of art. The film exhausts itself to a depiction which … is not perceived by the audience as a parody … which in its inner overall attitude does not have a place in our state…. The film is below the threshold of attitude which responsible censorship has to draw as a limit of artistic activity."

6. Columbia, M-G-M, Paramount, RKO, 20th Century–Fox, Universal, United Artists and Warner Brothers.

7. *Mein Film* no. 5, January 30, 1948, 14.

8. Vienna's landmark cathedral, St. Stephan.

9. Bookbinder started his activities with *Abenteuer auf hoher See* (*Saps at Sea*, 1940); c.f. letter from the Office of Military Government for Germany—U.S., Information Services Division, Motion Picture Branch, U.S. Army, Munich, to Bookbinder dated September 27, 1949, in file no. 240 of the Freiwillige Selbstkontrolle der Filmwirtschaft [FSK; "Voluntary Self Control of the Film Industry"].

10. *Film-Echo* no. 51, December 19, 1953, 1,300.

11. Kretschmer's letter from Paris, dated October 9, 1952, to Vera Kaiser, Bookbinder's Munich representative, on some Laurel and Hardy films; in the archives of the author.

12. Randy Skretvedt, *Laurel and Hardy: The Magic Behind the Movies* (Beverly Hills: Moonstone Press, 1987), 418. In 1964 Deutschmeister together with the German production Deropa Film und Fernsehen GmbH successfully launched four-part adaptations of adventure stories in the pre–Christmas period of the Zweites Deutsches Fernsehen ("second German TV channel"). The so-called "Adventsvierteiler" ("four-part stories for the holiday season") lasted until 1983. Each production ran six hours in four parts. In the first years the productions were adapted from classic adventure stories. Deutschmeister co-produced Daniel Defoe's *Robinson Crusoe* (1964), Miguel de Cervantes y Saavedra's *Don Quijote von der Mancha* (*Don Quixote de la Mancha*, 1965), Robert Louis Stevenson's *Die Schatzinsel* (*Treasure Island*, 1966), Mark Twain's *Tom Sawyers und Huckleberry Finns Abenteuer* (*Tom Sawyer and Huckleberry Finn*, 1968) and James Fenimore Cooper's *Die Lederstrumpf-Erzählungen* (*The Deerslayer, The Last of the Mohicans, The Pioneers, The Pathfinder, The Prairie*; 1969).

13. Emilio Lonero and Aldo Anziano, *La storia della Orbis-Universalia: Cattolici e neorealismo* (Cantalupa [Turin]: Effatà Editrice, 2004), 14, 144, 145, 190. *Atoll K* is not mentioned in this book.

14. According to no. 2 of the special conditions ["Publicité"] of the contract between Les Films É.G.É. and script girl Sylvette Baudrot, July 15, 1950.

15. Previously Joannon had worked as a film producer. Whether he contributed funds to *Atoll K* and, therefore, he was assigned to direct the movie for that reason, must remain a speculation.

16. Letter of the Comité des Avances a l'Industrie Cinématographique de Centre National de la Cinématographie dated December 26, 1950, in the collection of the Bibliothèque du Film, CN 881.

17. In the collections of the Bibliothèque du Film, Paris: CN 1,359, and its script collection *Atoll K*.

18. In the files of Sylvette Baudrot.

19. C.f. Skretvedt, 418.

20. See, for example, Richard Bann's filmography in Leonard Maltin, Leonard, ed., *The Laurel & Hardy Book* (New York: Curtis Books, 1973), 301.

21. In Western Europe also known as "zakouski," from the Russian "zakouska."

22. Joannon's original version is quite confusing: Ollie is first mentioned after the first third of the outline and it is only revealed later that he arrived on the atoll together with Stan. The crate is only brought into play toward the end of the outline: the boys had used it as a craft on the sea. It remained their ship substitute and was apparently used by Ollie for his quest for matches after their arrival on the first atoll.

23. It is not known whether Joannon saw the British Ealing comedy *Passport to Pimlico* (Henry Cornelius, 1949), when it opened in France on October 26, 1949, under the title *Passeport pour Pimlico* (*Index de la Cinématographie Française* 1951, Paris 1952, 231; *La Saison Cinématographique 1948/49*, Paris 1984, 160). In this movie the British government cuts off the entire supply of the London suburb Pimlico to starve out its inhabitants. The people of

Pimlico had declared their independence from Great Britain when evidence surfaced that the suburb belonged to the Duchy of Burgundy. During the blockade, Londoners throw parcels with food over barbwire fences, and — similar to the famous air lift of Berlin — aircrafts supply milk and cattle, too.

24. This is the treatment summarized by Randy Skretvedt in 1987 (420, 421) and by John McCabe in 1989 (*Babe: The Life of Oliver Hardy*, London: Robson Books, 1989, 176). Apparently McCabe did not have access to the same information as Skretvedt. As it is certain now that the treatment was written by Joffé, Levitte, Eger and Joannon, it must have been the basis of the later efforts of John Klorer, Frederick Kohner, Piero Tellini and René Wheeler, whom Skretvedt credited. Skretvedt worked from an English version of the treatment (from the collection of the University of Southern California, Los Angeles) not assigned to any authors.

25. The 18-page treatment was submitted to the French Centre National de la Cinématographie. The envelope is stamped "É.G.É." The script collection of the Bibliothèque du Film holds yet another copy of this treatment comprising 22 instead of 18 pages. Nevertheless, both copies are virtually identical. The 22-page version was written on a different typewriter and split into more paragraphs than the 18-page version. As far as contents go, there are only two minor discrepancies. In very few occasions three periods rather than one are used at the end of sentences. In contrast to page 17 of the first copy, page 22 (penultimate line) of the second copy says "frère jumeau" rather than just "frère" in the first copy, effectively making "twin brothers" out of Stan and Ollie (which they are not, of course). There is a simple explanation of the existence of two slightly different copies of the first treatment: they were just needed in the age before Xerox machines. Duplicates had to be made by means of typewriters. More than one original and four carbon copies could not be produced at once, since the amount of carbon paper loaded in a typewriter was limited. The 18-page version of the treatment seems to predate the 22-page version, as this bears an additional stamp next to the one of "É.G.É.," referring to *Atoll K*. Apparently it was not available at the early stage of work on the plot.

26. From the head of Laurel's letter from Paris dated May 6, 1950, to his niece Nellie Busby.

27. McCabe, *Babe*, 174.

28. Ibid. In a letter dated May 6, 1950, Laurel wrote to his niece Nellie Busby that he intended to travel to England in September or October of the same year after the shooting in Cannes or Nice.

29. Helmut Müller in *Abendpost* (Frankfurt am Main), October 15, 1950.

30. Files on a part of the financing in the collection of the Bibliothéque du Film, Paris. Regarding the organization of the authority, c.f. *Filmpost Archiv* no. 20, November 16, 1948, category A 02, 2–4.

31. Document no. 437 of the Commission d'Agrément et d'Étude des Scénarii, according to no. 2 of the special conditions ["Publicité"] of the contract between Les Films É.G.É. and script girl Sylvette Baudrot, July 15, 1950. Also c.f. letter of Centre National de la Cinématographie dated September 6, 1950, on the financing of the film, in CN 881, Bibliothéque du Film

32. According to Skretvedt (417), Laurel and Hardy were only approached in March 1950 regarding the production of *Atoll K*. Elsewhere it is stated that they received the offer in winter 1949/50: Fred Lawrence Guiles, *Stan* (New York: Stein and Day, 1980), 212. According to McCabe (*Babe*, 174), the producers first approached them at the beginning of January 1950.

33. The contract with Al and Elsie Loukinen could be canceled on monthly term and had been signed on April 3, 1950. The rental was to be paid to Ben Shipman in Laurel's favor; the copy of the contract is in the files of the author. Therefore, it seems doubtful that the Laurels left the United States as early as April 1, 1950, thus claimed by Ida Laurel in McCabe (*The Comedy World of Stan Laurel*, New York: Doubleday, 1974, 80). At the moment there are no hints that the Laurels signed the contract in blank and left it to Shipman to conclude the agreement.

34. Possibly this explains the date "March 1950" in Skretvedt (417).

35. Ida Laurel has claimed that even upon the Laurels arrival in France there was not any kind of plot. C.f. McCabe (*The Comedy World of Stan Laurel*, 80).

36. Skretvedt, 422. It has been claimed that the new authors tried for three months to create an effective plot for *Atoll K* before Laurel and Hardy — in the middle of June 1950 after Hardy's arrival in Paris — got in contact with the newly engaged scriptwriters to discuss the treatment. According to Frederick Kohner, *The Wizard of Sunset Boulevard: The Improbable Life of Paul Kohner* (Palo Verde: Morgan Press, 1974), 217 [page number from the German edition], this author had been hired in March 1950 to work on the script for *Atoll K* from April 1950 on, in Paris, together with other writers.

37. Scott MacGillivray, *From the Forties Forward* (Lanham: Vestal Press, 1998), 138.

38. C.f., for example, James Agee's script *The Tramp's New World*, written for Charlie Chaplin at that time. It was published in John Wranovics, John, *Chaplin and Agee*, 2005. *The Tramp's New World* depicts Chaplin's tramp in a post-atomic utopian setting.

39. *La Stampa*, June 23, 1950; interview by Benedetto Gemma with Carlo Croccolo, December 14, 2002.

40. E. Cantini in *La Settimana Incom* no. 13 (April 1, 1950), 26.

41. *Abendpost* (Frankfurt am Main), April 14, 1950; *Die Verleiher melden* ["Distributors' Report"], supplement for *Der Neue Film* no. 18 (May 1, 1950).

42. *L'Héroïque Monsieur Boniface* (*The Heroic Mr. Boniface*; Maurice Labro, 1949), *Casimir* (*Three Feet in a Bed*; Richard Pottier, 1950), *Uniforms et grandes manoeuvres* (René le Hénaff, 1950) and *Boniface somnambule* (*The Sleepwalker*; Maurice Labro, 1951).

43. *Paris-Match* no. 58 (April 29, 1950). In the daily paper *Nice Matin*, April 25, 1950, Macario and Fernandel are identified as Laurel and Hardy's partners in *Atoll K*. The Île de Levant is located 60 kilometers due southwest of Cap Roux (on the Côte d'Azur), situated on the Liguric Sea, the holiday island Port Cros being its eastern neighbor.

44. *La Stampa*, June 23, 1950; *Il Tempo*, June 27, 1950.

46. *Hollywood* (Milan) no. 254, 29. July 1950, 2.

46. Nevertheless, years later Fernandel took leading roles alongside Bob Hope in *Paris Holiday* (Gerd Oswald, 1958) and Heinz Rühmann in *Your Money or Your Life* (*La bourse et la vie*; Jean-Pierre Mocky, 1966), two mediocre movies.

47. Cantini.

48. *Nice Matin*, April 25, 1950.

49. C.f. Wes D. Gehring, *Laurel & Hardy: A Bio-Bibliography* (New York: Greenwood Press, 1990), 270.

50. Skretvedt, 421.

51. Mangan tells Hardy he "met Stan just a short time ago, a couple of months ago as a matter of fact," and discussed the new film with him. Guiles (213) incorrectly claims that Laurel and Hardy and their wives commenced their journey together. In fact, Hardy and his wife followed in June 1950.

52. Published in the United States at the beginning of

September 1986 as part of the Hal Roach Studios, Film Classics Inc. *Utopia* videotape, order number V 1.011. Published in Germany on June 2, 2004, as part of the fifth DVD of *Laurel & Hardy: The Platinum Collection # 2* (order no.: CMBOX 006/CMLH 0010). The director of *Ship's Reporter* was Jack Vincent. The exact air date is unknown. Possibly the series was a program filler.

53. *Cinema* (Italy) no. 43, July 30, 1950; c.f. also Skretvedt, 419.

54. *Louella Parsons* in *The Lowell Sun*, April 13, 1950, 39.

54. He is also reported to have worked on Lloyd's feature films *Safety Last!* and *Why Worry?*, both directed by Fred C. Newmeyer and Sam Taylor in 1923, as well as on the Harry Langdon feature film *Tramp Tramp Tramp* (Harry Edwards, 1926).

56. McCabe (*Babe*, 176). However, the exact nature of Whelan's contributions still remains unclear.

Chapter 2

1. This is explicitly indicated on a press photo. *Mein Film* (Austria) no. 18 (May 8, 1950), 2.

2. C.f. pictures reproduced on the title page of the French daily newspaper *La Patrie*, April 16, 1950; in the German trade paper *Film-Echo* no. 18 (June 3, 1950), 409; and in the German film journal *Film und Mode Revue* no. 11, 1950 (early June 1950), 3.

3. *Film und Mode Revue* No. 11, 1950, 3.

4. *Film-Echo* no. 17 (May 2, 1950), 402, and *Illustrierte Filmwoche* no. 23 (June 3, 1950), 382. *Kassenschlager für Ihr Haus* ["Box-Office Hits for Your House"], reproduced in *Filmblätter* no. 33 (August 18, 1950), 670.

5. Kohner, 216. The extensive Paul Kohner Agency collection, comprising, among other things, 155,000 pages of documents, does not contain any materials relevant to *Atoll K*, as a study of the very detailed index published by the Stiftung Deutsche Kinemathek, Berlin (1995) reveals.

6. Kohner, 217–219.

7. The U.S. TV show *This Is Your Life* (in which Laurel and Hardy also appeared) dedicated an episode to Frederick Kohner's sister-in-law Hanna Bloch-Kohner in 1953. The episode contains no mention of Frederick Kohner or his work on *Atoll K*, nor did Frederick Kohner appear as a guest.

8. Kohner (218) claimed that two French and three Italian authors had been hired.

9. Klorer had written scripts for the movies *This Love of Ours* (William Dieterle, 1945), *Good Sam* (Leo McCarey, 1948) and *Tension* (John Berry, 1950), while the busy Kohner was soon to work with Norman Z. McLeod on his 1952 movie *Never Wave at a WAC*. Tellini, too, had already written a script for William Dieterle's 1950 film *Vulcano* and soon thereafter contributed to *Fünf Mädchen und ein Mann* (*A Tale of Five Cities*; Emil E. Reinert, Wolfgang Staudte, 1951). Wheeler had contributed to the important film *Jour de Fête* (Jacques Tati, 1949) and brought his literary abilities to *Fanfan le tulipe* (*Fan-fan the Tulip* aka *Soldier of Love*; Christian-Jaque, 1952).

10. According to Lucille Hardy Price's personal notes, June 17, 1950.

11. Kohner, 218.

12. Ibid., 219.

13. Explicitly indicated on a press photo, as well as *Radio Cinéma Télévison* no. 24 (July 2, 1950), 11. Skretvedt (421) most likely confused the train station with the one the Laurels arrived at two months earlier.

14. Literally "The Big Night of Paris," a public event popular in Paris at that time.

15. *Radio Cinéma Télévison* no. 24 (July 2, 1950), 11. Possibly Laurel and Hardy appeared in a pantomime piece not described in more detail. The show was produced by Henri-François Rey. In the studio André Hugues and Pierre Court [aka Albert] were responsible for the program, which was hosted by Robert Chazal. The shows are believed lost.

16. C.f. Skretvedt, 420–422.

17. Interview with Sylvette Baudrot.

18. Skretvedt (422) reports that the meeting took place in the Hôtel Georges V at the Champs-Elysées. Laurel and Hardy, however, did not stay there; their Hôtel Prince de Galles was located in the Avenue Georges V.

19. Skretvedt, 422. In his Paul Kohner biography, Frederick Kohner (218) claimed that three different scripts of *Atoll K* had been presented to Laurel and Hardy. However, this is a contradiction to the original plan that Kohner, Klorer, Tellini and Wheeler should work out own versions separately, before condensing them into a collective version.

20. Skretvedt, 422.

21. Perhaps the authors sought a solution by referring to a similar structure in Buster Keaton's classic *Three Ages* (Buster Keaton, Eddie Cline; 1923). In that film Keaton had based his complex love story in the Stone Age, in ancient Rome and in the present day. Laurel and Hardy's last M-G-M film, *Nothing but Trouble* (1944), may have served as an inspiration as well, since it presents a long line of cooks and butlers.

22. First published by the Berlin Büchergilde Gutenberg. The book was published in France in 1934 as *La Vaisseau Fantôme* by E. Flammarion in Paris. It was published the same year in Great Britain (Chatto & Windus, London) and in the United States (by Alfred A. Knopf, New York) as *The Death Ship*. In Italy it was published in 1950 as *La Nave Morta* (Longanesi, Milan). C.f. Edward N. Treverton, *B. Traven: A Bibliography* (Lanham, Maryland: Scarecrow Press, 1999), 22 (no. 31–35), 24 (no. 55).

23. Cover letter to the second treatment, in the collection of the Bibliothéque du Film. Lucille Hardy Price's personal notes from August 4, 1950, suggest that the Korea War, which had started on June 25, 1950, may have been a reason to delete the navy scenes. However, this remains doubtful. The second treatment had still been revised some time before Laurel and Hardy left for Italy (June 22, 1950). In this version, the navy had already been eliminated.

24. C.f. Skretvedt, 422.

25. Kohner, 219.

26. For example: *Boom Goes the Broom* (Charley Chase, 1939), *The Heckler* (Del Lord, 1940), *Cold Turkey* (Del Lord, 1940) and *General Nuisance* (Jules White, 1941).

27. *La Stampa*, June 23, 1950; *Il Secolo XIX*, June 23, 1950.

28. According to Lucille Hardy Price's personal notes, June 22–24, 1950. *Crik & Crok a Sanremo*, c.f. *La Stampa*, June 23, 1950. On the trip to Italy, the stationmaster arranged for an unscheduled delay of some hours in Ventimiglia just to have the opportunity to personally meet the two actors.

29. According to Lucille Hardy Price's personal notes, June 25, 1950. According to Giancarlo Governi, *Due Teste Senza Cervello* (Turin: ERI, 1985), 94, Laurel and Hardy lodged in the *Hotel Excelsior di Roma*. However, the location shown by him is the Grand Hotel. Laurel and Hardy also signed autographs on the reverse on one of the Grand Hotel's postcards.

30. *Il Tempo*, June 27, 1950. Walter Chiari and "movie"-padre Andrew Felix Morlion (in 1931 he founded the Brussels-based DOCIP [*Documentation Cinématographique de la Presse*]) also attended.

31. These shows, too, are believed to be lost.

32. According to Lucille Hardy Price's personal notes, June 28, 1950, they were granted an audience with Pope Pius XII in the Vatican the same day; c.f. Governi, 94. However, the Italian newspaper *Il Tempo*, June 27, 1950, reported that Laurel and Hardy left Italy for Paris on the morning of the same day. Probably the audience took place in the morning of June 26, before Laurel and Hardy headed for the Casina Valadier. According to the October 2006 letter of the Prefect of the Prefettura Della Casa Pontificia ["Prefecture of the Pontifical Household"] to the author, no records of Laurel and Hardy's reception in audience from June 1950 were found. The archives of the Vatican *L'Osservatore Romano* did not answer my query. Contemporary Roman newspapers do not seem to have reported on this occasion.

33. C.f. report in *C'est la Vie* no. 35 (July 4, 1950), cover and 4.

34. According to Lucille Hardy Price's personal notes, July 16, 1950.

35. *La Cinématographie Française* no. 1,376 (August 12, 1950), 13. This source reports that Laurel and Hardy took the train to St. Raphaël. According to Skretvedt (422), Laurel and Hardy traveled to the Côte d'Azur to work on the script with Monty Collins and Tim Whelan. Collins' and Whelan's changes first appeared in the revised version of August 1950.

36. *Le Provençal*, August 6 and 7, 1950, pp. 2 and 3 of both issues. This is a contradiction to Skretvedt (422) who says that Laurel and Hardy left Paris on July 16, 1950.

37. *Cinémonde* no. 838 (August 28, 1950), 10.

38. *Le Provençal*, August 7, 1950, 2.

39. *Le Provençal*, August 9, 1950, 2.

40. *Le Soir Illustré* no. 961 (November 23, 1950), 5.

41. *Le Provençal*, August 8, 1950, 2.

Chapter 3

1. *Hollywood* (Milan) no. 254 (July 29, 1950), 2.

2. *Cinémonde* no. 836 (August 14, 1950), 4.

3. *La Cinématographie Française* no. 1,376 (August 12, 1950), 13.

4. *La Cinématographie Française* no. 1,440 (November 3, 1951), 16.

5. Radio interview of Benoît Duteurtre with Suzy Delair, aired by Radio France on March 11, 2006, within the program *Etonnez-moi, Benoît*.

6. *La Cinématographie Française* no. 1,376 (August 12, 1950), 13, and *Cinémonde* no. 836 (August 14, 1950), 4. Previously photos had been staged together with *Atoll K* director Joannon.

7. *Le Provençal*, August 6 and 7, 1950, p. 2 of each issue.

8. *Le Provençal*, August 8, 1950, 2.

9. *Le Provençal*, August 11, 1950, 2.

10. *La Cinématographie Française* no. 1,381 (September 16, 1950), 25; Skretvedt (422) tells of six days.

11. Bendetto Gemma's interview with Carlo Croccolo in March 2007. According to this distributor, *Minerva* is even said to have contracted Croccolo for *Atoll K*.

12. *La Cinématographie Française* no. 1,375 (August 5, 1950), 13. The article mentions that Thirard had just returned from shooting in Brazil. However, it is also possible that Thirard had worked with Henri-Georges Clouzot on a film with the working title *Brazil*, resulting in a confusion with the country.

13. From the files of Sylvette Baudrot.

14. The U.S. DVD *Playtime* (Criterion, order no.

CC1650D, 2006) contains a bonus interview with Sylvette Baudrot.

Chapter 4

1. *La Cinématographie Française* no. 1,375 (August 7, 1950), 13.

2. Carl Macek, "The Great Utopia Controversy," in *The History of Laurel and Hardy*, ed. Ron Haydock (Sherman Oaks, CA: E-Go Enterprises, 1976), 49.

3. In the collections of the Bibliothèque du Film, Paris: CN 1.359, and its script collection *Atoll K*, with the cover inscription "Découpage" ("script separated into scenes").

4. Date on the cover of the "scénario définitif," in the collections of the Bibiliothèque du Film: CN 1.359.

5. *La Cinématographie Française* no. 1,360 (April 22, 1950), 8.

6. *La Cinématographie Française* no. 1,368 (June 17, 1950), 6–7, and *Le Film Français* no. 288/289 (Spring 1950), 28–29.

7. *La Cinématographie Française* no. 1,373 (July 22, 1950), 3.

8. *La Cinématographie Française* no. 1,374 (July 29, 1950).

9. *Cinémonde* no. 834 (July 31, 1950), 9.

10. *L'Écran Français* no. 272 (September 25, 1950), 17; *Cinémonde* no. 838 (August 28, 1950), 11; *Deutsche Film Illustrierte* no. 31 (August 1, 1950), 3. *Cinémonde* erroneously calls Laurel's double "Maffic" and Hardy's stand-in "Decohignies" without revealing their first names. However, the *Deutsche Film Illustrierte* reports the full name of Hardy's stand-in as "Victor Decottighnies," even though the correct spelling of the last name is "Decottignies."

11. *La Cinématographie Française* no. 1,375 (August 5, 1950), 13.

12. According to Ida Laurel (in McCabe, *The Comedy World of Stan Laurel*, 80, and Guiles, 212), shooting started in Paris. This is not true, as the shooting in the Paris studios only took place from January 1951 on. The production notes also refer to the period of shooting and reported to the Centre National de la Cinématographie that shooting had started on August 7, 1950. The work in the studios could not possibly have predated this. Moreover, French trade press did not report such an early beginning of studio shooting.

13. É.G.É.'s letter dated July 26, 1951, to the Centre National de la Cinématographie, file no. 9,841; *La Cinématographie Française* no. 1,376 (August 12, 1950), 17. Thus contrary to Ib Lindberg, Bjørn Rasmussen, and Janus Barfoed, *Laurel & Hardy* (Copenhagen: Det Danske Filmmuseum, 1970) (76), who claim that shooting started at the Nice studio *La Victorine* (There are also a couple of typos in their filmography concerning last names: [Raymond] Elger instead of Éger, [Jean] Dikop instead of Dicop and [Maurice] Dragonneau instead of Dagonneau.) Skretvedt (422), without naming the source, reports that shooting began on August 8, 1950.

14. Centre National de la Cinématographie letters dated September 6 and December 22, 1950, in the collections of the Bibliothèque du Film: CN 881. Among the tasks of the authority was the control of the funding and the income from movies, c.f. *Filmpost Archiv* no. 20 (November 16, 1948), section A 02, 4.

15. *Cinémonde* no. 838 (August 28, 1950), 11.

16. *Le Provençal*, August 6, 1950, 2.

17. Actually "Momos," but used in the Latin form

throughout the movie, though the Roman mythology did not know a god with that name and such tasks.

18. *Le Provençal*, August 6, 1950, 2.

19. *La Cinématographie Française* no. 1,376 (August 12, 1950), 17.

20. Maybe Monty Collins is the author of this scene. There is a photo showing him and Laurel on the set of this scene in Billancourt.

21. However, "P" in *The Bullfighters* does not mean "people," but the U.S. city of Peoria.

22. Charles Barr, *Ealing Studios* (Berkeley: University of California Press, 1998), 199; *Index de la Cinématographie Française 1951*, 231. The movie was first shown at the Cinema Windsor in Nice, before a successful opening at the Parisian Broadway on December 7, 1949, that made it the talk of the town. C.f. Francis Koval, "British Films in Europe," *Sight and Sound* 20 no. 1 (May 1951), 11.

Chapter 5

1. *Intermezzo* (Milan), May 1, 1952.

2. In contrast to the other versions of the script, the Italian version includes only a very few deletions and annotations.

3. Skretvedt, 423.

4. Interview with Sylvette Baudrot. "Jaf" is French slang for buffet.

5. C.f. letter dated August 28, 1950 in McCabe's *Babe: The Life of Oliver Hardy*, 178. However, she does not mention Suzy Delair's interpreter Isabelle Kloucowsky.

6. C.f. ibid.

7. According to the radio interview by Benoît Duteurtre with Suzy Delair, aired by Radio France on March 11, 2006, as part of the program *Étonnez-moi, Benoît*, Laurel and Hardy's relationship during the shooting at the Côte d'Azur had deteriorated to the effect that they did not talk with each other. This, however, is a contradiction to all known reports of Laurel and Hardy's friendship lasting for many years after the end of their Hollywood career and which Hardy stresses in the June 10, 1950, *Ship's Report* interview.

8. Therefore, speculations of color footage of *Atoll K* should come to an end. According to Willie McIntyre, *The Laurel and Hardy Digest: A Cocktail of Lore, Love and Hisses* (Largs: W. McIntyre, 1998), 35, several projectionists have reported on the "dreadful colors" of *Atoll K*. Nevertheless, there are numerous examples of movie buffs and persons professionally related to cinema erroneously recalling special color effects in movies that definitely do not have any color footage.

9. William K. Everson, *The Films of Laurel and Hardy* (Secaucus: Citadel Press, 1967), 211. C.f. Evenson's "screening notes" on *Atoll K*: http://www.nyu.edu/projects/wke/notes/titles/atollk.htm. Missing only the concluding remark, they are identical to the *Atoll K* text in his book.

10. Skretvedt, 424.

11. *L'Écran Français* no. 272 (September 25, 1950), 17, 20.

12. Ibid. and *Cinémonde* no. 840, September 11, 1950, 13.

13. *L'Écran Français*, no. 272 (September 25, 1950), 17, 20.

14. *Var Matin*, August 20, 1990. *L'Écran Français*, no. 272 (September 25, 1950), 17, 20, however, reported that Laurel and Hardy stayed at the Marseilles Hôtel Bristol during the shooting on Cap Roux. Yet this is not the fact. Otherwise Laurel and Hardy would have had to travel the

130 kilometers from Marseilles to Cap Roux and back each day, instead of only a few kilometers from St. Raphaël.

15. Interview with Sylvette Baudrot.

16. *La Cinématographie Française* no. 1,381 (September 16, 1950), 25; Adriano Rimoldi's letter dated September 18, 1950, to his brother, mailed from St. Raphaël, c.f. Nico Orengo, in *La Stampa* (category: Societá & Cultura) no. 188 (August 15, 1991). The whereabouts of the letters is unknown. In any case they were not handed over to one of the three important Italian film institutes in Bologna, Rome or Turin.

17. Adriano Rimoldi's letter dated September 18, 1950, to his brother, mailed from St. Raphaël. C.f. Orengo.

18. French title: La chauve-souris.

19. *La Cinématographie Française* no. 1,391 (December 16, 1950), 17.

20. Interview with Suzy Delair.

21. *La Cinématographie Française* no. 1,380 (September 9, 1950), cover and 23.

22. C.f. McCabe, *Babe: The Life of Oliver Hardy*, 178, 179.

23. *Le Provençal*, August 12, 1950.

24. McCabe, *Babe: The Life of Oliver Hardy*, 178, and Ida Laurel in McCabe, *The Comedy World of Stan Laurel*, 80, 81.

25. Photos in the collection of Sylvette Baudrot.

26. McCabe, *Babe: The Life of Oliver Hardy*, 178, and Ida Laurel in McCabe, *The Comedy World of Stan Laurel*, 80, 81. Ida Laurel explicitly told McCabe of a pencil sharpener. Whether she referred to the one Stan uses in the movie to transform Ollie's pencil into a stump (causing Ollie to remark, "Well, this will have to be a short constitution") remains unclear.

27. Interview by Bertrand Tavernier and Berry's filmography in Bertrand Tavernier, *Amis Américains: Entretiens avec les grands auteurs d'Hollywood*, Institut Lumière/Actes Sud, 585 (filmography), 591 (interview). Interview by Christian Viviani in *Positif* no. 436 (June 1997), 58. The possibility that Berry did not consider his contribution to *Atoll K* newsworthy cannot be excluded.

28. Lonero/Anziano, 14, 150.

29. Unitalia Rom, *La Production Italienne 1950–1951*, no. 13–18 (August-September 1951), 108.

30. *L'Écran Français*, no. 272 (September 25, 1950), 17, 20.

31. Skretvedt, 423, only offers a detail of the photo.

32. C.f. McCabe, *The Comedy World of Stan Laurel*, 81.

33. C.f. Betty Goulding in Skretvedt, 424.

34. According to Ida Laurel in McCabe, *The Comedy World of Stan Laurel*, 81.

35. Skretvedt, 424.

36. Guiles, 214, without sources.

37. *La Cinématographie Française* no. 1,379 (September 2, 1950), 13, and no. 1,380 (September 9, 1950), 23.

38. The Laurel and Hardy shot is reprinted in Aping, 240.

39. Letter to his brother, mailed from St. Raphaël. C.f. Orengo.

40. Sylvette Baudrot and *La Cinématographie Française* no. 1,383 (September 30, 1950), 51.

41. Laurel's letter dated December 1, 1950 to Fred Karno Jr. According to Ida Laurel in McCabe, *The Comedy World of Stan Laurel*, 82, this should have happened after Laurel's return from the hospital. As Laurel only took part in shooting in Paris after his hospital stay, she erred. This is contrary to John McCabe, Al Kilgore, and Richard Bann, *Laurel and Hardy* (New York: E. P. Dutton, 1975), 397. These authors claimed that Laurel continued shooting at the Côte d'Azur after his hospital stay.

42. C.f. McCabe, *The Comedy World of Stan Laurel*, 82.

This difference of weight was mentioned by McCabe previously in his book *Mr. Laurel and Mr. Hardy*, 219, repeated by Jack Scagnetti, *The Laurel & Hardy Scrapbook* (New York: Jonathan David, 1976), 89. In McCabe, *Babe: The Life of Oliver Hardy*, 177, McCabe some 25 years later claimed a starting weight of 170 pounds.

43. Date according to É.G.É.'s production information, July 26, 1951, accompanying application of passing to the Centre National de la Cinématographie, July 10, 1951, file no. 9,841. In contrast *La Cinématographie Française* no. 1,399 (January 13, 1951), 13, reported October 15, 1950. *Cinémonde* no. 848 (November 6, 1950), 6, said that the crew and the actors had returned "today" to Paris to continue shooting. The information of the production seems to be preferable.

44. Ida Laurel in McCabe, *The Comedy World of Stan Laurel*, 82.

45. *Cinémonde* no. 848 (November 6, 1950), 6.

46. *La Cinématographie Française* no. 1,399 (January 13, 1951), 13, and no. 1,391 (December 16, 1950), 12.

47. According to Adriano Rimoldi's letter dated September 18, 1950 (c.f. Orengo), the studio work was scheduled for a month.

48. *Paris-Match* no. 98 (February 3, 1951), back cover.

49. In his letter dated December 3, 1950 (using his recent hotel address in Paris), to Nellie Busby, Laurel writes that he has just been released. Even though Laurel's dates seem to be slightly contradictory, he may not have been released mid–November 1950, as Skretvedt, 425, claims. There is no information at the American Hospital of Paris on the precise dates. According to letters from the hospital dated February 17 and 27, 2006, there could not be found evidence in its files that Laurel had been treated there in 1950 and/or 1951. The inquiry referred as well as to Laurel's legally approved last name, Jefferson (Laurel was born as Arthur Stanley Jefferson), and Kitaeva (Ida Laurel's last name before she married Laurel). It remains unclear whether Laurel checked into the hospital under a pseudonym, took his documents of treatment with him after his release, or whether the documents have been weeded out, thus no longer existing.

50. *La Cinématographie Française* no. 1,399 (January 13, 1951), 13.

51. Interview with Suzy Delair.

52. C.f. Kohner, 219 ($3 million U.S.), and his estimation to Skretvedt, 420 ($2 million U.S.).

53. France gave up these countries. Morocco and Tunisia became independent in 1956, and Algeria in 1962.

54. Committee's letter dated December 22, 1950, in the collection of the Bibliothéque du Film: CN 918. One time the letter refers to three and a half million old francs and another time to 3.6 million old francs. As the sum of the old and the new credit were figured out with 12.6 million old francs, the amount of 3.6 million old francs seems to be authentic. Franco London's list of countries did not survive.

55. Committee's letter dated December 26, 1950, in the collection of the Bibliothèque du Film: CN 881.

56. Committee's letter dated January 23, 1951, in the collection of the Bibliothèque du Film: CN 882, 921.

Chapter 6

1. Laurel's letter to his niece Nellie Busby, in The Stan Laurel Correspondence Archive Project, http://www.lettersfromstan.com.

2. C.f. Laurel gag photo in Everson,18; Laurel and Hardy gag photo in McIntyre, 13.

3. For promoting *Utopia* in the United States, a shot of this inscription was used as a press photo, showing Spanish instead of the German text that appears in the movie. Presumably, this was the original version of the inscription.

4. The German expression "Abfahr" ("departure") is orthographically incorrect. It should read "Abfahrt."

5. *L'Écran Français* no. 272 (September 25, 1950), 20.

6. An inquiry at the studio did not lead to information about the precise date and duration of shooting at La Victorine.

7. C.f. *Pardon Us* (1931), *Beau Hunks* (1931), *Way out West* (1937), *Swiss Miss* (1938) and *The Flying Deuces* (1939).

8. Letter from Roy Tomlinson in *Bowler Dessert* no. 65 (Winter 2005/06), 60: "Tragedy in *Atoll K.*"

9. *La Cinématographie Française* no. 1,386 (October 21, 1950), 8.

10. *La Cinématographie Française* no. 1,390 (December 9, 1950), 8, 9.

11. *Cinémonde* no. 848 (November 6, 1950), cover and 6.

12. *La Cinématographie Française* no. 1,391 (December 16, 1950), 12.

Chapter 7

1. Laurel's letter dated December 1, 1950, to Fred Karno Jr.

2. *La Cinématographie Française* no. 1,399 (January 13, 1951), 13. On Thursday, January 11, 1951, the New York Times reported that shooting was to be continued on "Monday," which would have been January 15, 1951.

3. Laurel's letter to Booth Coleman, in The Stan Laurel Correspondence Archive Project, http://www.lettersfromstan.com.

4. *La Cinématographie Française* no. 1,403 (February 3, 1951), 4; no. 1,406 (March 3, 1951), 19.

5. *Ciné Revue* no. 9, March 2, 1951, p. 11.

6. *La Cinématographie Française* no. 1,408 (March 17, 1951), 7. The trade paper did not publish the complete photo. Yates and Michael Dalmatoff are missing on the left.

7. *La Cinématographie Française* no. 1,407 (March 10, 1951), 22. Wayne's next movie was the boxing film *The Quiet Man* (John Ford, 1952). Herbert Yates kept busy and held a press reception in February or March 1951 at the Paris hotel Georges V. He did not forget to mention that *Rio Grande* was due to be released soon in France.

8. C.f. Orengo.

9. Gagman Monty Collins died on June 1, 1951, soon after the completion of shooting. On July 15, 1951, John Klorer, the scriptwriter who had bowed out of the project mid–1950 and reportedly contributed to the dialogue of the English version, also passed away.

10. For example: *Le Face A Main* no. 4 (January 27, 1951), back cover; *Die Filmwoche* no. 7 (February 17, 1951), 92. Many years later, another candid shot was used in 1978 for an Italian reissue lobby card of the program *Ronda di mezzanotte* consisting of the Italian-dubbed short subjects *The Midnight Patrol* (1933), *Busy Bodies* (1933) and *Oliver the Eighth* (1934). Obviously, the program has nothing to do with *Atoll K.*

11. That day Laurel and Hardy, together with Elloy, Rimoldi, Suzy Delair and composer Misraki, were photographed at the Studio Ventura. The photo was published in *La Cinématographie Française* no. 1,400 (January 20, 1951), 40, and in the Belgian movie magazine *Ciné Revue* no. 4 (January 26, 1951), 9. Another picture similar to this one bears the date January 11, 1951.

12. The respective pages of the script that have been added later are marked "Collins."

13. *La Cinématographie Française* no. 1,402 (February 3, 1951), 4.

14. *Ciné Revue* no. 3 (January 19, 1951), 16, 17.

15. *The New York Times*, December 9, 1950, 29, reports that "Mademoiselle Coco," a French-speaking gray African parrot, had his movie debut in *Atoll K*. However, it is unknown whether the article "Parrot Can't Talk Way In" was merely lighthearted propaganda. According to the script, there was no speaking parrot nor is there the slightest hint that such a scene had been shot. The birds of the club definitely do not speak.

16. *La Cinématographie Française* no. 1,411 (April 7, 1951), 14, and Sylvette Baudrot's notes, according to which the shooting ended that day. Skrevedt, 417, reports "March 1951."

17. McCabe, *The Comedy World of Stan Laurel*, 80, 83; Skretvedt, 425. Ida Laurel had claimed that she and her husband left for France on April 1, 1950. However, the Laurels did not rent their Santa Monica apartment until April 3, 1950. C.f. the tenancy contract and chapter 1.

18. *Der Spiegel* no. 1 (1954), 24. Marceau reported that he persuaded a theater electrician to cause a short-circuit in Laurel's hotel room. During the repair the electrician raved about Marceau and gave Laurel two tickets for Marceau's next show, which Laurel attended. At a café after the show, Marceau paid for four bottles of champagne in honor of Laurel. As Laurel also intended to visit Marceau's next day's performance, the pantomimist engaged a photographer to shoot Laurel's reactions in the auditorium without attracting attention. Marceau later claimed that he had learned tremendously from these photographs.

19. Laurel's letter to an unknown addressee, dated December 6, 1951. According to another letter to Betty Healy (who played Stan's wife in *Our Relations*, 1936), dated October 3, 1951, he already weighed 144 pounds. Both letters in The Stan Laurel Correspondence Archive Project, http://www.lettersfromstan.com.

20. McCabe, *Babe: The Life of Oliver Hardy*, 180, 181.

21. A. J. Marriot, 162–164, 292–295.

22. *La Cinématographie Française* no. 1,412 (April 14, 1951), 6.

Chapter 8

1. 100.65 minutes, to be exact. Length according to É.G.É.'s production information July 26, 1951, from the screening license request of the previous day to the Centre National de la Cinématographie, in Centre National de la Cinématographie, file no. 9,841.

2. C.f. his "screening notes": http://www.nyu.edu/projects/wke/notes/titles/atollk.htm. The Theodore Huff Memorial Film Society was founded in 1951 as The Film Circle and later renamed after the Charlie Chaplin biographer Theodore Huff. It is an association of movie collectors and professionals active in the film industry.

3. According to the archive's letter to the author dated September 29, 2005, the following *Atoll K* materials in the archive's collection, with unclear lengths of opening credits, are not available to researchers:

- the original English-language camera negative: 2,698 meters (98.61 minutes)
- the original French sound: 2,691 meters (98.35 minutes)
- the English-language sound negative: 2,553 meters (93.31 minutes)
- the French sound negative: 2,535 meters (92.66 minutes).

4. More in chapter 11.

5. In the files no. A 68,391 of the Education Department, Motion Picture Division, New York.

6. Picture and sound from this shorter English-language version of *Atoll K* are found on 1952 3M 16mm film as a supplement to an Australian print of *Robinson Crusoeland* printed on Kodak safety film from the same year. More in chapter 11.

7. The German text has apparently been pasted over the Spanish text.

8. É.G.É.'s production information July 26, 1951, in Centre National de la Cinématographie, file no. 9,841.

9. McCabe, *Mr. Laurel and Mr. Hardy*, 219.

Chapter 9

1. The French dubbing was probably produced by the French enterprise Lax, with whom Kloucowsky worked closely. Lax rented atelier rooms on the compound of the Billancourt studios on a regular basis.

2. The radio announcers' lines differ somewhat from the French-dialogue script.

3. Franco London's letter dated July 10, 1951, to the Centre National de la Cinématographie, in Centre National de la Cinématographie, file no. 9,841.

4. *Le Film Français* no. 373–374 (Autumn 1951), 20.

5. É.G.É.'s request July 25, 1951, and the result of the session of the Commission de Contrôle des Films Cinématographiques July 27, 1951, in Centre National de la Cinématographie, file no. 9,841.

6. *Le Film Français*, no. 359 (July 1951), 3. The advertisement for Northern Africa was published in *Ciné France Afric* no. 40 (October 1951), 3.

7. Sirius's letter dated August 7, 1951, to the Centre National de la Cinématographie, in Centre National de la Cinématographie, file no. 9,841.

8. The length in meters is not stated. For example, without revealing sources, Roland Lacourbe, *Laurel et Hardy* (Paris: Editions Seghers, 1975), 196, and Jacques Lorcey, *Laurel et Hardy* (Paris: Editions PAC, 1984), 254, report a running time of 99 minutes. There is no evidence, however. Both authors appear to have culled the location of the first screening from the *Cinématographie Française*. Other Danish (Poul Malmkjaer, *Hr. Gøg og Hr. Gokke* [Copenhagen, 1986], 64, however, disclosing a length of 98 minutes) and Italian Laurel-and-Hardy books (Marco Giusti, *Stan Laurel, Oliver Hardy* [Florence: Il Castoro Cinema, 1978], 130; José Pantieri, *I Magnifici Laurel & Hardy* [Forli: Centro Studi Cinetelevisivi, 1986], 175; and Camillo Moscati, *Stanlio e Ollio* [Genoa: La Coppa della Risita/Lo Vecchio, 1989], 115) seem to rely on Lacourbe and Lorcey. Governi, 139, again reported a length of 98 minutes. Bjørn Rasmussen's and Janus Barfoed's filmography in Lindberg, 176, repeats information from *La Cinématographie Française* including the running time of 93 minutes.

9. Compared to the dialogue script there are only five slight variations: Stan and Ollie's conversation before they descend into the cabin of the *Momus* for the first time, Stan questioning the space available in the lifeboat, the friends' conversation with the captain of the *Medex*, some exclamations during the nocturnal bat hunt and, as already mentioned, some of the news reports from the radio announcers.

10. The French pressbook could not be found in major European movie archives or among Laurel and Hardy collectors. As Franco London's promotional booklet does not

contain advertising tips for the exhibitors, it seems doubt-ful that Sirius used it for its propaganda campaign.

11. The cover for "Laissez-moi faire" misprints the title of the song: "Laissez vous faire."

12. Lacourbe and Lorcey.

13. *Sud-Ouest*, September 24 and 25, 1951.

14. *Sud-Ouest*, October 1, 1951.

15. *La Voix du Cinéma* no. 77 (November 1951), 8. Olympia's capacity and cost of admission is not dis-closed.

16. *Le Film Français* no. 385 (January 11, 1952), 18; *La Voix du Cinéma* no. 79 (January 1, 1952), 18.

17. *Sud-Ouest*, September 29, 1951.

18. *Le Provençal*, October 10, 1951. The advertisement refers only to the Majestic and the Odéon. *La Voix du Cinéma* no. 77 (November 1951), 20, reports that *Atoll K* was also screened at the Club. The price of admission is un-known.

19. *La Voix du Cinéma* no. 77 (November 1951), 8, 20. There is no report on the box-office results of *Atoll K*'s first week at the Club.

20. *Le Figaro*, October 16 and 17, 1951; *Libération*, Oc-tober 16, 1951; *Opéra*, October 17, 1951; *Radio Télévision* no. 364, October 14 to 20, 1951, cover. There is no further in-formation on the booking of *Atoll K* at the Ermitage. Re-ports on Olympia's capacity and admission fees vary be-tween 1,870 and 1,900 seats and 180 to 220 old francs or even 220 to 250 old francs, respectively: *La Cinématogra-phie Française* no. 1,439 (October 27, 1951), 8; *Le Film Français* no. 376 (November 9, 1951), 14.

21. The reports on the number of screenings at the Olympia vary between 32 and 35: *La Cinématographie Française* no. 1,439 (October 27, 1951), 8; *Le Film Français* no. 376 (November 9, 1951), 14.

22. *La Cinématographie Française* no. 1,439 (October 27, 1951), 8. According to *Le Film Français* no. 376 (November 9, 1951), 14, the total gross was 1,496,800 old francs.

23. *La Cinématographie Française* no. 1,440 (November 3, 1951), 2. According to *Le Film Français* no. 376 (Novem-ber 9, 1951), 14, the total gross was 729,400 old francs. According to the overview for the week starting October 31, 1951, *Atoll K* was replaced at the Max Linder as well as at the Olympia by the feature film *Le voyage en Amérique* (Henri Lavorel, 1951) which proved much more successful: *Le Film Français* no. 377 (November 16, 1951), 10.

24. *La Cinématographie Française* no. 1,441 (November 10, 1951), 4. *Atoll K* is no longer mentioned.

25. *Le Film Français* no. 372 (October 26, 1951), 22; *Va-riety*, November 21, 1951, 6.

26. *Le Film Français* no. 380 (December 7, 1951), 10, and no. 381 (December 14, 1951), 8.

27. *Variety*, November 21, 1951, 6, 18.

28. Richard Bann in Maltin, 300, dates both the French and the Italian premiere to November 21, 1951. Referring to the French version, this information was obviously repeated by Skretvedt, 417; Scott Allen Nollen, *The Boys: The Cinematic World of Laurel and Hardy* (Jefferson, NC: McFarland, 1989), 135, and Mark Potts and David Shephard, *What Was the Film When...? The Films of Laurel and Hardy* (Nantwich: Wonderbooks Design, 2001), 197. All seem to have equated the date of the premiere to the publication date of *Variety* containing the *Atoll K* review. MacGillivray, 138, reports "November 1951."

29. *La Cinématographie Française* no. 1,440 (November 3, 1951), 16.

30. *Index de la Cinématographie Française 1951*, 44, 45.

31. *Le Film Français* no. 372 (October 26, 1951), 16.

32. *La Voix du Cinema*, no. 76 (October 1, 1951), 12.

33. *L'Exploitation Cinématographique*, no. 66 (Novem-ber 1, 1951), 162.

34. *Education Nationale*, November 15, 1951.

35. In *Duck Soup* (1927), *Why Girls Love Sailors* (1927), *Sugar Daddies* (1927), *That's My Wife* (1929), *Another Fine Mess* (1930), *Twice Two* (1933), *Babes in Toyland* (1934), *A Chump at Oxford* (1940; European version), *Jitterbugs* (1943) and *The Dancing Masters* (1943). Hardy performs in drag just once, in *Twice Two*.

36. *Journal du Dimanche*, October 21, 1951.

37. *Le Figaro*, October 19, 1951.

38. *Libération*, October 22, 1951.

39. *Nouvelles Littéraires*, November 1, 1951.

40. *L'Écran Français*, no. 328 (October 24–30, 1951), 8.

41. *Le Film Français* no. 375 (November 2, 1951), 17, 20, and no. 376 (November 9, 1951), 20.

42. *La Voix du Cinéma* no. 80 (February 1, 1952), 13.

43. *La Voix du Cinéma* no. 77 (November 1, 1951), 20.

44. *Le Film Français* no. 397 (March 21, 1952), 22. The number of visitors at the Forum has not been reported.

45. Distributor's objective according to its letter dated November 17, 1950, to the Comité des Avances à l'Indus-trie Cinématographique of the Centre National de la Ciné-matographie, referred in the commission's letter dated De-cember 22, 1950, in the collection of the Bibliothéque du Film: CN 918.

46. According to the slightly different reports, the grosses may have totaled 16,691,021 old francs.

47. *Ciné France Afric*, no. 40 (October 1951), 3. The competing trade paper *Filmafric* did not run advertisements for *Atoll K* in 1951 or in 1952.

48. Distributor's objective and statement of success ac-cording to its letters dated September 6 and December 21, 1950, to the Comité des Avances a l'Industrie Ciné-matographique of the Centre National de la Cinématogra-phie. According to the session of the commission Decem-ber 26, 1950; in the collection of the Bibliothéque du Film: CN 881.

49. Centre National de la Cinématographie's letter dated November 24, 1958, to the distributor authorizing the right to sell the movie until November 29, 1959, in Centre National de la Cinématographie, file no. 9,841.

50. According to the *Index de la Cinématographie Française 1961 and 1962* (pp. 951, 1,076 respectively) Sirius remained the French and Northern African distributor. From 1963 onward, *Atoll K* was not mentioned by the index. The movie had been mentioned a final time in *Répértoire Général des Films* of 1959 (297), distributed by Sirius. However, the yearbooks *La Saison Ciné-matographique* from 1959 to 1961 report that *Atoll K* had been distributed by C.F.D.C. as 16mm as well as 35mm copies (pp. 289, 329, 300 of the respective years). From 1962 onward, the film is not mentioned in either of these yearbooks. C.F.D.C. is the abbreviation for the Paris-based Compagnie Française de Distribution Ciné-matographique. The surviving copy of the French version's dialogue script bears the stamp of the name and the address of the Paris distributor Télédis on its cover. Probably this copy had been sent in the late 1950s to the German dis-tributor Erich J. A. Pietrek, where it was found at the end of the 1980s.

51. According to Lacourbe, 194.

52. U.S. Copyright Office, file no. PA-891–351, entry December 10, 1997.

53. *Var Matin*, August 19 and 20, 1990.

54. Label: Accord, order no.: 476 8416. The recording of *Laissez-moi faire* used on the CD differs from the ver-sion heard in the movie. The CD features a live recording in which Suzy Delair is accompanied by a small band.

Chapter 10

1. C.f: Governi, 95, 96.

2. The collection of the Turin Museo Nazionale del Cinema holds two incomplete copies of *Atollo K*. The 35mm copy has a length of 2,314 meters and the 16mm copy 923 meters which means a running time of 84.58 minutes and 84.12 minutes, respectively. Very likely they are identical to the DVD presentation of *Atollo K*.

3. In the files of the Ufficio centrale per la cinematografia, file no. 10,701.

4. In the files of the Ufficio centrale per la cinematografia no evidence could be found as to whether the presently available opening credits belong to the first Italian release of *Atollo K* or whether they have been reshaped for the rerelease. Furthermore, the author of the Italian dialogue could not be substantiated with the help of the files.

5. Instructions for the different notary plaques on page 7 of Sylvette Baudrot's shooting script, but in this case misspelled "Notario."

6. Request of October 9, 1951, and license of October 17, 1951, in the files of the authority, file no. 10,701.

7. Information in Minerva's 1951 propaganda campaign book. This length has also been mentioned by *Segnalazioni cinematografiche del centro cattolico* Volume XXX —1951, Rome, second edition 1951, 162.

8. *L'èco del cine e dello spettacolo* no. 23 (April 30, 1952), distributor's index p. 141.

9. *Intermezzo* (Milan) no. 7–8 (April 30, 1952), 11.

10. Minerva's request dated October 16, 1951, and its undated letter on the propaganda material, received by the authority on October 24, 1951; in the files of the authority, file no. 10,701. The poster and the photos were submitted a week later. According to Minerva's propaganda campaign book, the trailer had a length of 90 meters.

11. *Unitalia Rome*: *La Production Italienne 1950–1951* no. 13–18 (August–September 1951), 108, 109.

12. Distributor's letter, in the files of the authority, file no. 10,701.

13. Date of release according to information of the Italian authority Anica on *Atollo K* on the website of the Associazione, Nazionale Industrie Cinematografiche Audiovisive e Multimediali (Italian Association of Cinematographic Audiovisual and Multimedia Industries), http://www. anica.it/arc/1951/51mm7728.thtml. Bann, in Maltin, 300, states the date of the Italian premiere as November 21, 1951. The author's inquiries to Italian newspapers such as *Brescia Oggi*, for example, for the date and the local cinema, remained unanswered.

14. *Cinematografia* no. 11 (November/December 1951), 14. According to page 45 of this issue, *Atoll K* had premiered in October in Paris.

15. *Cinematografia* no. 12, December 1951/January 1952, p. 58; without information on the length.

16. *L'èco del cine e dello spettacolo* no. 23 (April 30, 1952), 18.

17. Ibid.

18. *L'èco del cine e dello spettacolo* no. 25 (May 31, 1952), 10.

19. *Cinematografia* no. 4 (April/May 1952), 35. *Atollo K* received no screening in Milan and was shown for just two days in Padua. The longest run was seven days in Turin.

20. *Cinematografia* no. 5 (May/June 1952), 38; no. 6 (June/July 1952), 42; no. 7 (July/August 1952), 75.

21. *L'èco del cine e dello spettacolo* no. 30/31 (August 31, 1952), distributor's index p. 178. From no. 32 (September 15, 1952), *Atollo K* is no longer mentioned.

22. According to Sordi in Governi, 95.

23. Volume XXX —1951, 162. When contemporary Italian Catholic movie criticism brushed off a movie it often confined itself to such short statements.

24. Retelling by Giorgio Guglieri in no. 240 (July 26, 1952), 5–7. The magazine basically published retellings, but no reviews.

25. Volume II no. 9 (October 1951), 148.

26. For the period 1951–1952: *Bianco e nero*, *Cinema*, *Rivista del cinematografo* and *Sipario*.

27. *Intermezzo* (Milan) no. 7–8 (April 30, 1952), 11.

28. *Hollywood* (Milan) no. 350 (May 31, 1952), 23.

29. Momi's letter dated April 5, 1963, in the files of the authority, file no. 10,701.

30. Both licenses dated May 2, 1963, with length information, in the files of the authority, file no. 10,701.

31. The Italian dialogue used for this occasion, with the exception of Ollie's final line, is not identical to the Italian dialogue script which surfaced in autumn 2006 during the research for this book.

Chapter 11

1. McCabe, *Babe: The Life of Oliver Hardy*, 177.

2. Randy Skretvedt did not detect such an accent, and presumes that the dubbing has been recorded in Los Angeles.

3. Bann in Maltin, 300; Nollen, 137, who also seems to hark back to Bann.

4. MacGillivray, 141. However, Randy Skretvedt did not identify Paul Frees in any role in the English-language version. He is familiar with Frees' voice.

5. This refers to the second commentary. We do not hear Giovanni count the seeds as he sows.

6. Bookbinder did not submit a request to the Los Angeles Production Code Administration. Today the files of the Production Code Administration are housed at the Beverly Hills Margaret Herrick Library, Academy of Motion Picture Arts and Sciences.

7. Requests and original license in the files of the authority, file no. A 68,391.

8. Letter to Betty Healy in The Stan Laurel Correspondence Archive Project, http://www.lettersfromstan. com.

9. *The Independent Record* (Helena, Montana), January 3, 1952, 4 (column "In Hollywood"). However, statements that Laurel stayed at the hospital for three months in summer 1950 during the shooting were false. He was hospitalized for six weeks after the location shooting in October and November 1950.

10. File no. 16,086. The files do not exist anymore. "U": "Universal"—, that is, "suitable for all." C.f. British Board of Film Classification, http://www.bbfc.org.uk.

11. MacGillivray, 146, seems to have confused the Canadian lobby cards with the British ones. The latter ones do not bear pasted-up photos.

12. A poster with blue, green and skin-toned color scheme is located in the collection of the George Eastman House, Rochester, New York. Instead of the imprint "At long last their first NEW big comedy in years!" the distributor is mentioned along with the license of approval ("U"). The collection of the George Eastman House also holds a large, folded poster depicting Ollie in his presidential outfit. Currently it may not be unfolded due to its brittle condition. Whether this mimics Deseto's French-Italian *Atoll K* poster cannot be verified without a careful comparison. For the time being, both British posters are unavailable for reproduction.

13. *Daily Film Renter* 25 no. 6,275 (January 2, 1952), cover; *Kinematograph Weekly* 418 no. 2,324 (January 10, 1952), and 419 no. 2,328 (February 7, 1952), 30.

14. *To-Day's Cinema* 78 no. 6,412 (January 4, 1952).

15. *Daily Film Renter* 25 no. 6,277 (January 7, 1952), 5.

16. *Kinematograph Weekly* 418 no. 2,324 (January 10, 1952), 22, and 419 no. 2,328 (February 7, 1952), 30.

17. C.f. alongside *Kinematograph Weekly* and *To-Day's Cinema, Monthly Film Bulletin* 19 no. 217 (February 1952), 25.

18. *To-Day's Cinema* 78 no. 6,412 (January 4, 1952).

19. The copy had to be examined carefully as it had been assembled by a private collector using various sources. The bulk is an Australian 16mm positive on 1952 Kodak safety film, titled *Robinson Crusoeland,* and has several gaps due to material defects. Missing footage was bridged using elements from a dupe of *Utopia* on 1954 3M film. The print was further augmented by footage from an obviously cut English-language dupe on 1952 3M film titled *Atoll K.* The latter print contains Chérie's complete first song missing from the 98-minute English-language version; most likely there are alternative cuts of this version. Maybe the 91-minute English-language version *Atoll K* had been used in this special case, which Bookbinder had submitted on September 20, 1951, to the Motion Picture Division of the New York Education Departments.

20. The gap caused by material defects of the *Robinson Crusoeland* copy had been replaced by the respective *Utopia* scenes. This results in an additional running time of approximately 90 seconds longer than quoted in the British distributor's documents. Cutting this sequence in half would indeed mean a running time of 82 minutes.

21. No. 56,695.

22. *Daily Film Renter* 26 no. 6,291 (February 7, 1952), 10.

23. *To-Day's Cinema* 78 no. 6,451 (February 28, 1952), and 78 no. 6,463 (March 17, 1952), 2. According to MacGillivray, 137, *Robinson Crusoeland* is said to have been released in the United Kingdom in September 1952. The author's request for a precise release date has not been answered by the daily newspaper *Portsmouth News.*

24. *Kinematograph Weekly* 420 no. 2,333 (March 13, 1952), 28. Holloway's graphic artist Daines had designed the "faces."

25. The human-high version of the "faces" measured five feet, the smaller version three feet: *Kinematograph Weekly* 422 no. 2,340 (May 1, 1952), 35.

26. C.f. Aping, 291, 395 (with illustrations). In *Dick und Doof werden Papa* the feature *The Bohemian Girl* was presented as a dream within the short subject *Their First Mistake* which framed the feature film.

27. *To-Day's Cinema* 78 no. 6,463 (March 17, 1952), 2; *Daily Film Renter* 25 no. 6,306 (March 15, 1952), 13. The campaign was led by Harold Baldwin.

28. *To-Day's Cinema* 78 no. 6,466 (March 20, 1952), 10. The announcer was Peter Noble, also the editor of the *British Film Year Book.*

29. *Kinematograph Weekly* 421 no. 2,337 (April 10, 1952), 28.

30. *Kinematograph Weekly* 424 no. 2,352 (July 24, 1952), 31: Oldham; 425 no. 2,356 (August 21, 1952), 35: Islington and Horsham; 428 no. 2,367 (November 6, 1952), 31: Stornoway.

31. *Daily Film Renter* 26 no. 6,321 (April 17, 1952), 5.

32. *To-Day's Cinema* 78 no. 6,492 (April 29, 1952), 23. Frank Law was responsible for the campaign. The band was conducted by Eddie Shaw.

33. *Kinematograph Weekly* 422 no. 2,340 (May 1, 1952), 35; *To-Day's Cinema* 78 no. 6,503 (May 14, 1952), 11; *Daily*

Film Renter 26 no. 6,332 (May 14, 1952), 2. *Robinson Crusoeland* is said to have been screened in Dublin during Laurel and Hardy's 14-day engagement at the local Olympia Theater which commenced on May 27, 1952: Marriot, 186, 293.

34. *To-Day's Cinema* 78 no. 6,475 (April 22, 1952), 8.

35. *To-Day's Cinema* 78 no. 6,504 (May 15, 1952), 2.

36. *To-Day's Cinema* 78 no. 6,513 (May 28, 1952), 11, as well as no. 6,519 (June 6, 1952), 15, and no. 6,535 (June 30, 1952), 2; *Kinematograph Weekly* 424 no. 2,353 (July 31, 1952), 20.

37. *Kinematograph Weekly* 424 no. 2,352 (July 24, 1952), 31; 424 no. 2,353 (July 31, 1952), 20; 425 no. 2,356 (August 21, 1952), 35; and 428 no. 2,367 (November 6, 1952), 31.

38. According to International Film's three-page campaign book, in the collection of the British Film Institute. Perhaps there was a personal connection between the two distributing enterprises. One of International's directors was H. D. Butcher; c.f. Peter Noble, ed., *The British Film Year Book,* 4th annual ed. (London: Gordon White, 1952), 54.

39. According to Richard Bann in Maltin, 301.

40. *To-Day's Cinema* 78 no. 6,451 (February 28, 1952), 5. According to *To-Day's Cinema* 78 no. 6,465 (March 19, 1952), 10, the official premiere had not taken place until March 1952. The contents of the program were reviewed in *Kinematograph Weekly* 420 no. 2,335 (March 27, 1952), 25. C.f. also Glenn Mitchell, *The Laurel & Hardy Encyclopedia* (London: Batsford Books, 1995), 27.

41. Published by Amalgamated Press Ltd., without year, presumably at the end of 1952, the retelling of *Robinson Crusoeland* appears on pages 98–107. In all, twelve movies were retold for this issue. Eleven of the movies had been completed in 1951 or 1952, and all of them were released in 1952. The only exception is the 1949 western movie *Range Justice* (Ray Taylor). The yearbooks of the British movie magazine *Picturegoer* do not mention *Robinson Crusoeland* for the periods 1951–1952 and 1952–1953. The magazine was designed for an adult readership.

42. *Robinson Crusoeland* was noted in the *Film Review* yearbook *1951–52,* London 1952, and announced in a short review of *Monthly Film Bulletin* 19 no. 217 (February 1952), 25. However, neither *Robinson Crusoeland* nor *Atoll K* are mentioned in the *Film Review* yearbooks *1952–53* to *1954–55,* covering the period from October 1951 to March 1954. The British release date is also missing from the yearbooks.

43. National Film Theatre's program September–November 1964, 24. Alongside *Robinson Crusoeland,* the line-up of feature films included: *Bonnie Scotland* (1935), *The Bohemian Girl* (1936), *Our Relations* (1936), *Block-Heads* (1938), *The Flying Deuces* (1939) and *Saps at Sea* (1940). C.f. also *Films and Filming* 11 no. 2 (November 1964), 33. Minchinton's commentary contains a slight error. Stan does not smear ketchup on Ollie's hand, but marmalade.

Chapter 12

1. It is unknown whether Bookbinder's decision was the result of his concentration on earlier Laurel-and-Hardy movies as well as films of other artists throughout Europe.

2. Requests as well as License for Duplicate Prints and Application for Duplicate License, all dated December 14, 1954; in the authority's files no. A 68,391.

3. C.f. Everson's screening notes dated February 7, 1967: http://www.nyu.edu/projects/wke/notes/titles/atollk.

htm. Rather than showing *Utopia*, Everson screened the original, full-length English-language *Atoll K* to the Theodore Huff Memorial Film Society.

4. In earlier days such reactions were Ollie's domain, not that of secondary characters like Antoine and Giovanni.

5. "Company History," Welch Foods Inc., http://www.welchs.com/company/company_history.html.

6. *Alfred Hitchcock Presents*, the first series, debuted in the United States on October 2, 1955.

7. Quoted according to MacGillivray, 146.

8. MacGillivray, 147.

9. Laurel's letter to Betty Healy, in The Stan Laurel Correspondence Archive Project, http://www.lettersfromstan.com. *The Independent Record* (Helena, Montana), January 2, 1952, 4 (column "In Hollywood").

10. *New York Times*, December 15, 1954, 41.

11. *Variety*, December 22, 1954.

12. It is not known how many copies were distributed in the United States. In June 1955, Waldman was granted an approval to distribute another print of *Utopia* in New York; in August of that year he requested another substitute seal. C.f. License for Duplicate Prints and Application for Duplicate License, both dated June 20, 1955, as well as the New York authority's substitute seal license dated August 8, 1957; in the authority's files no. A 68,391. From 1957 onward, Waldman no longer acted under his own name, but for Waldman Films, Inc.

13. MacGillivray, 147.

14. Distributor's letter dated September 3, 1957, to the Motion Picture Division of the New York Education Departments, as well as All Star's letter dated September 16, 1957, referring to *Utopia*'s exclusive distribution by Exploitation Productions, in the authority's files no. A 68,391.

15. MacGillivray, 147. It is uncertain whether *Utopia* was employed as part of the double bill.

16. Realart Film Exchange's letters dated September 23, 1957, November 26 and December 1, 1958 to the Motion Picture Division, in the authority's files no. A 68,391.

17. First claimed by Everson, 210. Seized by Jay Robert Nash and Stanley Ralph Ross, *The Motion Picture Guide TV 1927–1983* (Chicago: Cinebooks, 1987), 3,652, 3,653.

18. A search of the period from 1950 to 1985 shows no record of the film in either the *Catalogue of Copyright Entries — Motion Pictures* of the Library of Congress or in the U.S. Copyright Office database (http:// www.copyright.gov).

19. Macek, 49.

20. Order no. 686. It is not known whether the reel, which was not available for viewing, includes Suzy Delair's first song as well as the German radio announcer, both of which are missing from *Atoll K*'s 98-minute English-language version.

21. MacGillivray, 147.

22. U.S. Copyright Office, file no. PA-891–351.

23. *What A Wonderful Utopia* was removed on request of the Liechtenstein-based Cinematographische Commerz Anstalt, which has held the KirchGroup's rights to the Hal Roach Library since 1971 (c.f. Aping, 513).

Chapter 13

1. The rediscovery of an Australian *Robinson Crusoeland* 16mm print on 1952 Kodak safety film bearing the distributor's label "International" attests to the likelihood that the British distributor released the movie in Australia the same year, when *Robinson Crusoeland* was released in Canada. As late as 1986 Great Britain asserted its rights in Australia. According to the information of the Australian National Film and Sound Archive, no specific files have been compiled referring to *Atoll K*, *Robinson Crusoeland* or *Utopia*.

There is also a Belgian poster titled *Atoll K*; details on the Belgian version are unknown. This was probably the French version of the same title, which could have been marketed successfully in this bilingual country. The Dutch-subtitled English-language version *Robinson Crusoeland* could also possibly have been released in Belgium.

2. *C.I.C.E.* ["Centro Informativo Cinematográfico Español," Madrid] *bulletin* no. 62

3. José Luis Portolés and Luis Carlos, *Estrenos cinematográficos en Zaragoza (1913–2002)* (Saragossa 2003).

4. Ministerio de Cultura; http://www.mcu.es/jsp/plantillaAncho_wai.jsp?id=13&area=cine (site discontinued).

5. Reverses of the Spanish poster and a Spanish flyer. The movie was shown at Santoña on September 10, 1952.

6. File nos. 40,902 and 40,969, May 20 and 27, 1952: 2,535 metres; file no. 44,388, March 20, 1953: 2,495 metres. Probably the distributor submitted the English-language version to the Danish movie authority, the version that had been licensed in November 1951 in London at a length of 94 minutes and 27 seconds.

7. According to Bjørn Rasmussen's and Janus Barfoed's filmography in Lindberg, 76. The filmography lists a running time of 100 minutes, while the reviews correctly refer to a length of 93 minutes.

8. "Clout" describes a strike, à la Bud Spencer, with the fist on another one's head.

9. The three reviews from the collection of the Danske Filmmuseum are neither dated nor do they disclose the papers in which they were published. The second and third review report on the Carlton premiere. According to the second review, the movie had started at the Carlton "yesterday"; most likely this review was published by a Copenhagen newspaper on August 2, 1952.

10. *Toronto Star*, October 20, 1952.

11. License dated July 14, 1952. Ontario Film Review Board, http://www.ofrb.gov.on.ca/ofrb/OfrbWelcomeAction.do, referring to *Robinson Crusoeland*. The Web site database entry for the movie lists an incorrect running time of 100 minutes. This information does not derive from the authority's files which have since been scrapped, but has been culled from promotional material. The same applies to the information from the Manitoba Film Classification Board (http://www.gov.mb.ca/chc/mfcb), according to which the movie was licensed on an unknown date at a length of 82 minutes and was distributed by Interglobal. There is no information available on the marketing of *Robinson Crusoeland/Atoll K/Utopia* at the Film Classification Boards of Alberta, British Columbia, Nova Scotia and Saskatchewan or at the La Régie du Cinéma du Québec. The 16mm version which reportedly ran 80 minutes was licensed by the Ontario Film Review Board on January 19, 1955.

12. "Atoll K," Québec City Tourism, http://regiondequebec.com/s/quebecscope.asp?Id=5990. Screenings from August 5 and 8, 2003. Although he does not know details, Yves Laberge is convinced that there were screenings of the French version in the 1950s; this seems likely due to the country's bilingual nature.

13. *Jahrbuch der Schweizer Filmindustrie 1952* and *1953* (Geneva: La Tribune de Genève, 1952 and 1953), pages 148 and 150, respectively.

14. C.f. Thomas Leeflang, *Laurel & Hardy Encyclopedie* (Zutphen: Walburg Pers, 2001), 26 (left column); Nieuwe Blotto no. 1 (November 2005), Hilversum, 33.

15. María Luisa Amador and Jorge Ayala Blanco, *Cartel-*

era Cinematográfica 1950–1959 (México D.F.: Universidad Nacional Autónoma de México, México, 1985), 39. Entry # 418 reads: "*Había una vez dos héroes/ Los dos Robinsones (Atoll K/ Atollo 'K').* Franco–italiana. Dir. Léo Joannon. Int. Stan Laurel, Oliver Hardy, Suzy Delair. Prod. Franco London Films-Fortezza Film. 1950. Cine Nacional, diciembre 20 de 1950." The running time of *Había una vez dou héroes* is stated as 75 minutes which applies to *Bonnie Scotland,* but not to *Atoll K.*

16. It is not known when the movie passed the Mexican board of censors. The Mexican files are not available. The newspaper ad mat printed by the Mexico City daily newspaper *Excelsior* from November 28, 1956, bears the numbers "22,859" along with the addendum "A," possibly meaning a file number.

17. *Excelsior* (Mexico City), November 28, 1956: "Dos horas y media de sana diversion para chicos y grandes" ("Two and a half hours of clean entertainment for young people and adults"). The four cartoons each ran between seven or eight minutes. It can be safely assumed that publicity and trailers for upcoming movies, a newsreel or even a short documentary helped to make up the impressive running time. Of course, it is also possible that the total running time of the program was generously rounded up to promise moviegoers more bang for their buck.

18. According to the lobby cards, Mario J. Dada presented the movie for the Mexico City–based Oficinas Jorge M. Dada.

19. *Excelsior* (Mexico City), December 19, 1956.

20. *Filmowy Serwis Prasowy* no. 4 (June 15, 1961), 18–20. *Atoll K* censorship files could not be found at the Warsaw Archiwum Akt Nowych. This is not surprising since the 1989 turnabout of the Polish political system resulted in many documents of the previous ruling regime being destroyed or hidden in places still unknown today.

21. *Film* no. 26 (June 25, 1961), 15, column "Idziemy do kina," and Jacek Fuksiewicz's article in no. 33 (August 13, 1961), 4: "Laurel i Hardy po latach."

22. The Prague Národní Filmovy Archiv has neither further information nor a copy of the movie itself.

Chapter 14

1. This chapter is basically an expanded version of Aping, 232–242 (chapter 8, part II). An abbreviated English version (translation: Dr. Ulrich Rüdel) was published under the title *The German Fate of Atoll K* in *Nieuwe Blotto* no. 1, Hilversum, November 2005, 34–39.

2. It is not mentioned in the 1952 and 1953 *Jahrbücher der Schweizer Filmindustrie.* During these two years no version of *Atoll K* was reviewed by Swiss *Film-Berater.*

3. *Licht-Bild-Bühne* no. 87 (April 15, 1937), 3.

4. *Abendpost* (Frankfurt am Main), April 14, 1950; *Die Verleiher melden* ("Distributor's Report"), supplement to: *Der Neue Film* no. 18 (May 1, 1950).

5. *Film-Echo* no. 17 (May 27, 1950), 402, and *Illustrierte Filmwoche* no. 23 (June 3, 1950), 382. *Kassenschlager für Ihr Haus* ("Blockbusters for Your Theater"), in: *Filmblätter* no. 33 (August 18, 1950), 670.

6. *Saarländische Volkszeitung* (Saarbrücken), August 25, 1950.

7. *Saarländische Volkszeitung* (Saarbrücken), October 8, 1950.

8. Helmut Müller in *Abendpost* (Frankfurt am Main), October 15, 1950.

9. *Film-Echo* no. 30 (August 26, 1950), 704, and no. 47/48 (December 23, 1950), 1,158.

10. *Film-Echo* no. 18 (May 5, 1951), 394.

11. *Fach-Informationen für die Filmwirtschaft* no. 19 (November 27, 1948), 87; *Berliner Filmblätter,* October 26, 1948, 3, and advertisement on the last page of the November 23, 1948 issue; *Filmpost Archiv* no. 19 (November 10, 1948), category A10, 17: premiere on October 15, 1948, at the Berlin Marmorhaus on the occasion of the opening of the free Berlin movie business. The movie screened for four weeks, receiving the "cordial sympathy" of the "remaining Berlin prominence." In the Kurfürstendamm area it was shown under the title *Jenny Lamour,* but screened elsewhere under its German title.

12. For example, cover of *Illustrierte Filmwoche* no. 25 (June 25, 1949).

13. Premiere at the Titania-Palast: *Die Filmwoche* no. 22 (June 2, 1951), 277, and no. 24 (June 19, 1951), 309; *Film-Echo* no. 23 (June 9, 1951), 470, and no. 25 (June 23, 1951), 511. The *Filmwoche* review praised "capriciously dancing and singing" Suzy Delair.

14. Approval of the movie contract between distributor Prisma and Franco London dated May 12, 1951 by the Bundesminister für Wirtschaft ("Federal Ministry of Economical Affairs") July 26, 1951, in FSK file no. 3,243.

15. *Film-Echo* no. 34 (August 25, 1951), 710.

16. Alsatian Colin-Reval spoke fluent German without an accent. Prior to World War II he was an editorial journalist for the French trade paper *La Cinématographie Française,* for which he continued to work as a consultant after the war. He founded the trade paper *Die Filmwoche* as well as the movie magazine *Film und Mode Revue* in the French area of postwar Germany. Furthermore, for many years he produced the newsreel *Blick in die Welt* in the Federal Republic of Germany. Together with publisher Hubert Burda he launched the popular media award Bambi in 1948, which has been awarded every year since. (Originally it was a porcelain figurine of a deer, since 1958 it has been cast in gold.) The first laureate was dancer/actress Marika Rökk.

17. Contract September 10, 1951, in IFU file *Atoll K.*

18. Card of approval, September 26, 1951, in FSK file no. 3,243.

19. Correspondence in IFU file *Atoll K.*

20. IFU memorandum October 3, 1951, in IFU file *Atoll K.*

21. Ibid.

22. Prisma's letter dated October 10, 1951 to IFU, in IFU file *Atoll K.*

23. C.f. Aping, pp. 116, 117, 156, 188, 189, 462, 463, 490, 491.

24. He was replaced by actor Arno Paulsen. Paulsen set a new standard, to no small extent due to the unique artistic chemistry between him and Bluhm.

25. Advertisement in *Film-Echo* no. 1 (January 5, 1952), 11.

26. Biermann's letter dated November 24, 1951 to IFU for an appointed day, in IFU file *Atoll K.*

27. *Paimann's Filmlisten* no. 1,898 (January 2, 1952; published December 27, 1951), 3.

28. *Filmschau,* no. 51/52 (December 18, 1951), review no. 391.

29. According to the movie overview of the Austrian magazine *Die Jugend,* quoted by *Evangelischer Film-Beobachter* no. 13 (April 1, 1961), 168. C.f. also *Paimann's Filmlisten* 1960, 80. The four-part version was not available for inspection.

30. Die *Filmwoche* no. 9 (February 9, 1952), 109, 112. The large cinema offered 2,300 seats, while the Gabriel-Lichtspiele was a 330-seat theater.

31. *Film-Dienst* no. 46 (December 9, 1949), review no. 515: *Abenteuer auf hoher See* (*Saps at Sea,* 1940).

32. *Film-Dienst* no. 2 (January 14, 1952), review no. 1.530.

33. *Evangelischer Film-Beobachter* no. 4 (January 27, 1957), 44, 45: review no. 59: *Dick und Doof als Studenten* (*A Chump at Oxford*, 1940).

34. *Evangelischer Film-Beobachter* (January 24, 1952), 29, 30: review no. 42.

35. *Der Neue Film* no. 13 (February 14, 1952), 4.

36. *Wiesbadener Kurier*, May 3, 1952.

37. *Die Welt*, January 12, 1952.

38. *Frankfurter Rundschau*, February 25, 1952.

39. *Hamburger Morgenpost*, January 12, 1952.

40. *Rheinische Zeitung* (Köln), January 2, 1952; *Kölner Stadtanzeiger*, January 3, 1952.

41. *Kölnische Rundschau*, January 3, 1952.

42. *Uelzener Allgemeine Zeitung*, January 12, 1952.

43. *Film-Echo* no. 2 (January 12, 1952), 40.

44. *Westdeutsches Tageblatt* (Dortmund) and *Düsseldorfer Nachrichten*, quoted in *Film-Sonderdienst Ott* no. 1 (January 3, 1952), and no. 5 (January 17, 1952).

45. *Echo der Filme* in *Film-Echo* no. 10 (March 8, 1952), 244. The reports were based on the notes of the theater owners. This category was published for the first time in *Film-Echo* no. 8 (February 23, 1952), 196. *Atoll K* was not mentioned at that time.

46. *Echo der Filme* in *Film-Echo* no. 19 (May 10, 1952), 446; no. 31 (August 2, 1952), 676; and no. 41 (October 11, 1952), 928. *Film-Sonderdienst Ott* no. 8 (January 28, 1952), no. 10 (February 4, 1952), and no. 45 (June 9, 1952).

47. *Münchner Merkur*, February 10, 1954.

48. C.f. Aping, 253ff, 271ff, 281ff, 309.

49. *Rheinische Post* (Düsseldorf), August 15, 1964.

50. This eleven-minute version was screened along with *Hilfe-Beinahe wären wir ertrunken!*, the 1950 German version of Laurel and Hardy's *Sons of the Desert* (1933), formerly titled *Hilfe, wir sind ertrunken!*

51. The German titles of the other two Laurel-and-Hardy feature films are *Dick und Doof-Rache ist süss* and *Dick und Doof in der Fremdenlegion*. They had been released in the Federal Republic of Germany in 1961 and 1951, respectively.

52. IFU invoice October 15, 1965, to Pietrek, in IFU file *Superschau des Lachens*. C.f.: Aping, 395, 396.

53. C.f. Aping, 309.

54. *Westfalen-Blatt*, June 11, 1966; *Freie Presse*, June 11, 1966; *Bergedorfer Zeitung* (Hamburg), August 17, 1966.

55. *Film-Dienst* no. 15 (April 13, 1966), review no. 13,963. From the beginning of 1964, the writing of the title *Film-Dienst* was changed to the use of lower case letters.

56. *Film-Sonderdienst Ott*, Film-Register no. 92/93, October 13, 1966.

57. *Kassameter*-results, in *Filmblätter* no. 29 (July 16, 1966), 652; no. 30 (August 13, 1966), 678, no. 32/33 (August 27, 1966), 714; no. 34 (September 3, 1966), 742; no. 35 (September 10, 1966), 758 [last entry].

58. *Erlanger Tageblatt*, July 5, 1967; *Film-Sonderdienst Ott* no. 54 (July 6, 1966). Pietrek's bookkeeping documents no longer exist.

59. *Filmschau* no. 44 (November 5, 1966), 7, review no. 7,380.

60. Without differentiating the versions, Pietrek indicated 2,481 meters, which corresponds to the length of the German version.

61. C.f. Aping, 455ff, 459, 493, 520, 535, 536, 541.

62. MacGillivray, 116.

References

Primary Sources

Sylvette Baudrot (employment contract, Atoll K; trilingual shooting script with supplements and annotations, photos from the set)

Bibliothéque du Film, Paris; documents referring to *Atoll K* (outline, first and second treatment, scripts, information about the funding)

Centre National de la Cinématographie, Paris (*Atoll K* file)

Deutsches Filminstitut, Frankfurt/Main (judgments of the Ober-Filmprüfstelle, Berlin)

Education Department, Motion Picture Division, New York (*Atoll K* files, including English dialogue book)

Estate documents (Heinz Caloué)

Freiwillige Selbstkontrolle der Filmwirtschaft [FSK], Wiesbaden (*Atoll K* files)

George Eastman House, Rochester, New York (movie poster collection)

Harry Hoppe (French dialogue book, *Atoll K*)

Internationale Film-Union AG, Studio Remagen [IFU] (German *Atoll K* dubbing files)

KirchMedia, KirchMediaTechnik [formerly: Beta Technik] (production files of the German TV series *Dick und Doof* [Zweites Deutsches Fernsehen])

A. J. Marriot (transcription of Stan Laurel letters)

Newsreels: Movietone (Great Britain) no. 56,695; Welt im Film (Germany) no. 131 (November 1947)

Promotional material (international promotional advice, posters and lobby cards)

Randy Skretvedt (notes from Lucille Hardy Price's scrapbook from April–September 1950)

Ufficio centrale per la cinematografia, Rome (*Atollo K files*, including the Italian dialogue book)

Interviews and Correspondence

Sylvette Baudrot (June 11, November 10–11, 2005, February 2005–April 2006)

Carlo Croccolo (December 4, 2002 and March 2007; interviews by Bendetto Gemma)

Suzy Delair (November 10, 2005)

Pierre Nivollet (May 2006)

Official Papers, Federal Republic of Germany

Information of the Bank Deutscher Länder and Deutsche Bundesbank on various exchange rates, Statistisches Bundesamt Wiesbaden: Cost of Living Index Since 1948 basis May 2006

Internet Resources

ANICA (Italian board of movie censors): www.anica. it

British Board of Film Classification (formerly British Board of Film Censors; British Board of Movie Approval): www.bbfc.org.uk

Internet Movie DataBase: www.imdb.com

Kodak Edge Codes: www.filmforever.org/Edgecodes. pdf

Lexikon des Internationalen Films ("Encyclopedia of International Movies"): www.filmevona-z.de

Manitoba Film Classification Board: www.gov.mb.ca/ chc/mfcb

Labournet.de Germany (includes Bernhard Schmidt, "Der französische Mindestlohn SMIC" ["The French minimum wage SMIC"]): www.labournet. de

Stan Laurel Correspondence Archive Project: www. lettersfromstan.com

Ministerio des Cultura (Spain): www.mcu.es

New York University, William K. Everson Collection (including screening notes): www.nyu.edu/projects/wke

Ontario Film Review Board: www.ofrb.gov.on.ca

Québec City Tourism: www.regiondequebec.com

U.S. Copyright Office: www.copyright.gov

Welch Food Inc.: www.welchs.com

Contemporary Periodicals

Movie trade papers and magazines

Austria

Filmschau
Mein Film
Paimann's Filmlisten

Belgium

Ciné Revue

France

Cahiers du Cinéma
Cinéclub
Ciné France Afric
La Cinématographie Française
Cinémonde
L'Écran Français
L'Exploitation Cinématographique
Filmafric
Le Film Français
France Film Export
Positif
Revue du Cinéma
La Voix du Cinéma

Germany

Berliner Filmblätter
Deutsche Film Illustrierte
Evangelischer Film-Beobachter
Fach-Informationen für die Filmwirtschaft (loose supplement of the trade paper *Filmwoche*)
Filmblätter
Film-Dienst
Film-Echo
Filmpost Archiv
Film-Sonderdienst Ott
Film und Mode Revue
Die Filmwoche (postwar)
Illustrierte Filmwoche
Licht-Bild-Bühne
Der Neue Film

Great Britain

Daily Film Renter
Films and Filming
Kinematograph Weekly
Monthly Film Bulletin
National Film Theatre Program
Picturegoer
Sight and Sound
To-Day's Cinema

Italy

Bianco e nero
Cinema
Cinematografìa
L'èco del cìne e dello spettacolo
Filmcritica
Hollywood
Intermezzo
Novellefilm
Rivista del cinematografo
Sipario
Unitalia

Poland

Film
Filmowy Serwis Prasowy

Spain

Bulletin Centro Informativo Cinematográfico Español (C.I.C.E.), Madrid

Switzerland

Film-Berater

United States

Variety

Other Periodicals

Canada

Toronto Star

France

Aux Écoutes
Le Canard Enchainé
C'est la Vie
Education Nationale
Le Face A Main
Le Figaro
Franc Tireur
Journal du Dimanche
Libération
Nice Matin
Nouvelles Littéraires
Le Parisien Libéré
La Patrie
Paris-Match
Le Provençal
Radio Cinéma Télévison
Semaine de Paris
Le Soir Illustré
Sud-Ouest
Var Matin

Germany

Abendpost (Frankfurt/Main)
Allgemeine Zeitung (Uelzen)

Bergedorfer Zeitung (Hamburg)
Düsseldorfer Nachrichten
Erlanger Tageblatt
Frankfurter Rundschau
Freie Presse (Bielefeld)
Hamburger Morgenpost
Kölner Stadtanzeiger
Kölnische Rundschau
Münchner Merkur
Rheinische Post (Düsseldorf)
Rheinische Zeitung (Köln)
Saarländische Volkszeitung (Saarbrücken)
Der Spiegel
Die Welt
Westdeutsches Tageblatt (Dortmund)
Westfalenblatt (Bielefeld)
Wiesbadener Kurier

Italy

Il Tempo
Il Secolo XIX
La Settimana Incom
La Stampa

Mexico

Excelsior

United States

Independent Record (Helena, Montana)
Los Angeles Times
Lowell Sun
New York Times

Laurel and Hardy Magazines

Blotto (Netherlands)
Bowler Dessert (Scotland)
Nieuwe Blotto (Netherlands)

Books

Books on Laurel and Hardy

Aping, Norbert. *Das Dick-und-Doof-Buch*. Marburg: Schüren-Verlag, 2004, 2nd edition 2007.
Everson, William K. *The Films of Laurel and Hardy*. Secaucus, NJ: Citadel Press, 1967.
Gehring, Wes D. *Laurel & Hardy: A Bio-Bibliography*. New York: Greenwood Press, 1990.
Giusti, Marco. *Stan Laurel, Oliver Hardy*. Florence: Il Castoro Cinema, 1978.
Governi, Giancarlo. *Laurel & Hardy. Due Teste Senza Cervello*. Turin: Edizioni Rai Radiotelevisione Italiana, 1985.

Guiles, Fred Lawrence. *Stan*. New York: Stein and Day, 1980.
Haydock, Ron, ed. *The History of Laurel & Hardy*. E-GO Collector's Series 2. Sherman Oaks, CA: E-GO Enterprises Inc., 1976.
Lacourbe, Roland. *Laurel et Hardy ou l'enfance de l'art*. Paris: Editions Seghers, 1975.
Leeflang, Thomas. *Laurel & Hardy Encyclopedie*. Zutphen, Netherlands: Walburg Pers, 1993; new edition 2001.
Lindberg, Ib. *Laurel & Hardy*. Copenhagen: Det Danske Filmmuseum, 1970.
Lorcey, Jacques, and Basile Courtel. *Laurel et Hardy*. Paris: Editions PAC, 1984.
MacGillivray, Scott. *Laurel and Hardy: From the Forties Forward*. Lanham, MD: Vestal Press, 1998.
Malmkjaer, Poul. *Hr. Gøg og Hr. Gokke*. Copenhagen: Nyt Nordisk Forlag Arnold Busck, 1986.
Maltin, Leonard, and Richard W. Bann. *The Laurel & Hardy Book*. New York: Curtis Books, 1973.
Marriot, A. J. *Laurel & Hardy: The British Tours*. Blackpool: A. J. Marriot, 1993.
McCabe, John. *Babe: The Life of Oliver Hardy*. London: Robson Books, 1989.
_____. *The Comedy World of Stan Laurel*. New York: Doubleday, 1974; expanded Centennial Edition, Beverly Hills, CA: Moonstone Press, 1990.
_____. *Mr. Laurel and Mr. Hardy*. New York: Doubleday, 1961.
McCabe, John, Al Kilgore, and Richard W. Bann. *Laurel & Hardy*. New York: E. P. Dutton, 1975.
McIntyre, Willie. *The Laurel and Hardy Digest: A Cocktail of Lore, Love and Hisses*. Largs: W. McIntyre, 1998.
Mitchell, Glenn. *The Laurel & Hardy Encyclopedia*. London: Batsford Books, 1995.
Moscati, Camillo. *Stanlio e Ollio*. Genoa: La Coppa della Risita/Lo Vecchio, 1989.
Nollen, Scott Allen. *The Boys: The Cinematic World of Laurel and Hardy*. Jefferson, NC: McFarland, 1989.
Pantieri, José. *I magnifici Laurel & Hardy*. Forli: Centro Studi Cinetelevisivi, 1986.
Potts, Mark, and David Shephard. *What Was the Film When...? The Films of Laurel and Hardy*. Nantwich: Wonderbooks Design, 2001.
Skretvedt, Randy. *Laurel and Hardy: The Magic Behind the Movies*. Beverly Hills, CA: Moonstone Press, 1987.

Other Books

Amador, María Luisa, and Jorge Ayala Blanco. *Cartelera Cinematográfica 1950–1959*. Mexico City: Universidad Nacional Autónoma de México, 1985.
Angelicchio, Francesco, ed. *Segnalazioni cinematografiche del centro cattolico Vol. XXX, 1951*. Rome: Centro Cattolico Cinematografico, 1951.
Barr, Charles. *Ealing Studios*. Berkeley: University of California Press, 1998.
Kohner, Frederick, and C. N. Anderson, eds. *The*

Magician of Sunset Boulevard: The Improbable Life of Paul Kohner. Palo Verde, CA: Morgan Press, 1977; German edition (translated by Karl Otto von Czernicki): *Der Zauberer vom Sunset Boulevard: Ein Leben zwischen Film und Wirklichkeit*. Munich: Droemer Knaur, 1974.

Lonero, Emilio, and Aldo Anziano. *La storia della Orbis-Universalia: Cattolici e neorealismo*. Turin: Effatà Editrice, 2004.

Nash, Jay Robert, and Stanley Ralph Ross. *The Motion Picture Guide TV 1927–1983*. Chicago: Cinebooks, 1987.

Portolés, José Luis, and Luis Carlos. *Estrenos cinematográficos en Zaragoza (1913–2002)*. Saragossa, 2003.

Sammlung Paul Kohner Agency: Inventarverzeichnis. Berlin: Stiftung Deutsche Kinemathek, 1995.

Speed, F. Maurice. *Film Review*. London: Macdonald & Co., 1951–52, 1952–53, 1953–54, 1954–55.

Super Cinema Annual 1953. London: Amalgamated Press Ltd.

Tavernier, Bertrand. *Amis Américains: Entretiens avec les grands auteurs d'Hollywood*. Institut Lumière/Actes Sud, no date.

Traven, B. *Das Totenschiff: Die Geschichte eines amerikanischen Seemanns*. Berlin: Büchergilde Gutenberg, 1926.

Treverton, Edward N. *B. Traven: A Bibliography*. Lanham, MD: Scarecrow Press, 1999.

Wranovics, John. *Chaplin and Agee: The Untold Story of the Tramp, the Writer and the Lost Screenplay*. New York: Palgrave Macmillan, 2005.

Film Industry–Related Books

Annuaire du Cinéma 1951. Paris: Èditions Bellefaye, 1951.

Annuaire du Cinéma 1952. Paris: Èditions Bellefaye, 1952.

Annuario del Cinema Italiano 1963–64.

Index de la Cinématographie Française 1951. Paris: La Cinématographie Française, Paris 1952.

Index de la Cinématographie Française 1961. Paris: La Cinématographie Française, Paris 1961.

Index de la Cinématographie Française 1962. Paris: La Cinématographie Française, Paris 1962.

Jahrbuch der Schweizer Filmindustrie 1952. Geneva: La Tribune de Genève, 1952.

Jahrbuch der Schweizer Filmindustrie 1953. Geneva: La Tribune de Genève, 1953.

Library of Congress. Catalogue of Copyright Entries. Cumulative Series. Motion Pictures 1912–1939, 1940–1949, 1950–1959, 1960–1969, 1970, 1975. Washington: Library of Congress.

Noble, Peter, ed. *The British Film Year Book*. 4th annual ed. London: G. White, 1952.

Répértoire Général des Films 1959. Paris.

La Saison Cinématographique 1948/49. Paris: Marchand, 1984.

La Saison Cinématographique 1959. Paris: Marchand, 1960.

La Saison Cinématographique 1960. Paris: Marchand, 1961.

La Saison Cinématographique 1961. Paris: Marchand, 1962.

Index

Numbers in **bold italics** indicate pages with illustrations.